I0819365

ARCHITECT OF WINGS

A Biography of Roy Chadwick –
Designer of the Lancaster Bomber

ARCHITECT OF WINGS

A Biography of Roy Chadwick – Designer of the Lancaster Bomber

HARALD PENROSE

THE CROWOOD PRESS

First published in 1985 by Airlife Publishing

This edition published in 2025 by
The Crowood Press Ltd
Ramsbury, Marlborough
Wiltshire SN8 2HR

enquiries@crowood.com
www.crowood.com

British Library Cataloguing-in-Publication Data
A catalogue record for this book is available from the British Library.

For product safety-related questions, contact:
productsafety@crowood.com

ISBN 978 0 7198 4599 4

The publishers would like to thank Ian Penrose (the author's son) and Delphine Stephens (Roy Chadwick's granddaughter) for their invaluable help in the production of the 2025 edition.

Cover design by Keith Wootton

Printed and bound in India by Nutech Print Services

Contents

An important work monopolizes a man and, besides many other sacrifices, claims the whole personality. The glory of a great discovery or an invention which is to benefit humanity, appears to him the more dazzling the closer he approaches it; he perceives not the thorns in that crown, he heeds not its weight, but his whole life is shaped to attain it.

Otto Lilenthal, 1891

Author's Alibi

Biography has been defined as a composition based on too few facts, many half-truths, and a great deal of imagination. Nevertheless it also requires considerable research to establish probabilities and sequencing because half-truths are often contradictory. At best, much depends on deductions from one's own experience. Thus although Roy Chadwick was eleven years my senior and had such extensive pioneering aviation experience, we both lived through the same contemporary events, and from 1922 onward encountered much the same succession of political administrators, Air Ministry officials, aeronautical researchers, designers, industrialists, and Service personnel.

Certainly the top executives, designers and pilots of the dozen major firms comprising the British aircraft industry all knew each other at least by repute; but this more detailed picture of the great Avro designer and his colleagues has been augmented by his relatives, business associates, staff of each decade, and the recollections and extensive investigations of his daughter Mrs Margaret Dove, who established a maze of contacts and references.

In earlier years I also had occasion to meet Chadwick's great mentor and original employer, sprightly Sir Alliott Verdon-Roe whose brief powered flights of aeroplanes of his own design and construction were the prelude to Chadwick's career.

Roe's other renowned protegé, Roy Dobson, long familiar to me as 'Dobbie', was the dynamic chairman of the Hawker-Siddeley Group in 1963 when we last met at the twelfth 'Avro 504K Club' dinner, where, in his speech of welcome, he gleefully told how he used to race his Avian against my Westland Widgeon at some of the early northern air-meetings, though tactfully avoided saying that we were beaten by other pilots!

Avro's test pilot, Sam Brown, was another whom I came to know fairly well from 1929 onward; but I also met Raynham and Hinkler on several occasions as well as others who variously flew for that famous firm.

On the design side, John Ratcliffe, for many years chief draughtsman of A. V. Roe & Co, joined Westland when I was manager of our civil aircraft department before appointment as chief test-pilot, and Herbert Mettam was a former colleague with whom I had collaborated on development of the swept wing, tail-less Pterodactyls. From both these technicians I gleaned a little of the atmosphere of working with Roy Chadwick.

To some degree A. V. Roe & Co. Ltd. has seemed part of my life, for my first flight was in 1919 as passenger with the then impecunious Alan Cobham (later famous for his long distance flights and duly knighted) flying an Avro 504K — and in the course of the years I flew the 504L seaplane, 548 variant of the 504K, Cirrus-powered Avro Baby, Avians of several vintages, the Avro Five, a Tutor, the Commodore, an Anson, the Manchester, the York, and an Avro 671 (Cierva C.30A) Autogiro. As the home of my youthful days was near Martlesham Heath, I also saw the range of Avro prototypes from Aldershot to Antelope, thus affording fascinating evidence of Roy Chadwick's earlier versatility, substantiated by later professional visits to the A & AEE there and at Boscombe Down.

All these associations, coupled with personal experience of design, construction, flight testing, and the politics and problems of selling military and civil aircraft, have afforded a parallel with Avro activities which I hope have at least been interpreted in chronological sequence, though not necessarily with detailed exactitude, but it is the essence of acquaintance with man and aeroplane which I have tried to infuse into this biography.

Chapter 1
Path of Destiny

A great Vulcan delta-winged bomber thundered through the dark night sky at 400 knots, 10,000 ft above Port Stanley in the Falkland Isles. It was 4.38 am local time on 1 May 1982. Came the crashing, detonating impact of a stick of twenty-one 1,000 lb. high explosive bombs diagonally straddling the runway as a first step towards preventing its use by Argentine aircraft. That made stirring headlines next day, for the world at large had been astounded that Argentina had made a successful coup in occupying the Islands with military forces at the beginning of April. The Vulcan attack, succeeded by five others during the month, was the beginning of retribution.

Despite the remoteness of a target 8,000 miles from Britain, it was typical of the RAF's adaptability to undertake the operation, for it required a highly complex organization of air-to-air re-fuelling contacts using a fleet of Handley Page Victor tankers both for the initial 4100 miles non-stop flight of two specially adapted Vulcans from England to the mid-South Atlantic base of Wideawake Airfield, Ascension Island, on 29 April, and even more crucially on the following night to the Falklands and back, 3,900 miles further south.

For the vital bombing journey the Vulcans would have to flight-refuel five times, and the Victor tankers themselves would need flight refuelling leap-frog fashion to enable the final one to reach the Vulcan's last pre-attack re-fuel point. The combined aircraft fleet took-off from Wideawake in two waves, the two Vulcans leading, but the primary Vulcan had to return because of a pressurization fault, leaving the other to carry out a solo operation. Nearly sixteen hours later this Vulcan, piloted by Flt Lt Withers, landed back at Ascension having completed the

The trail-blazing transonic Avro Vulcan.

Marsh Hall Farm in the days before cars.

mission in the course of an intricately navigated hazardous flight.

During the 25 years' use of Vulcans by the RAF, first as Polaris carrier, then atomic bomber, and eventually for coastal reconnaissance, many people must have seen the ominous triangular shape of this big machine speeding across the skies — yet few would remember the name of the man who had devised the original design of what then seemed so futuristic a machine, as well as the legendary Lancaster bomber of World War II and many another famous aeroplane in a sequence harking back to before the First World War.

He was Roy Chadwick, born on the last day of April 1893 at Marsh Hall Farm, the residence of his mother's parents in the pleasant Lancashire countryside of Farnworth. His father, Charles Henry Chadwick, was a 20-year-old steam plant assistant at the United Alkaline Co. of Widnes, who had married 21-year-old Agnes Bradshaw in 1892. Young Roy grew up in a Victorian decade where steam had triumphed everywhere. Coal mines were flourishing. Power was there in plenty to feed the great engines of industry and transport. The key to Britain's prosperity was the cotton industry of Lancashire and its hundreds of humming looms. Even at three years old Roy knew all about steam engines. When he and his father encountered the local Vicar as they crossed the railway bridge he corrected the cleric's exclamation of: 'Look, little boy! There's a puff-puff coming,' with a mature: 'That's a locomotive!'

But soon a recession began. The days became anxious. There were factory closures. When Roy was five his father was forced to find other employment and was lucky to secure a post as supervisor of Steam Laundry installations made by Thomas Bradford and Co, some 20 miles distant at Salford on the outskirts of Manchester. It was while living there that Roy Chadwick, at nine years old, had the thrilling experience of discovering that mankind could fly — for a great multi-striped balloon bearing the legend *Lifeboat Saturday* drifted from nearby Trafford Park high across their house on 20 September 1902.

After six years at Salford the family moved

Urmston on King Edward's Coronation day, 26 June 1902.

to Urmston on the outskirts of this great Industrial Park Estate where Charles Chadwick had secured an administrative position at the newly established British Westinghouse Electrical & Manufacturing Co. By that time Roy had two sisters and a brother, and the two elder children attended schools nearby. Though he showed no great aptitude at lessons, Roy was a brightly imaginative youngster already learning to play the violin, and like his father, was recruited as a chorister at adjacent Flixton in company with Harold Rogerson, a lad of the same age who became a lifelong friend.

Kites became a new experience when he was 10. He watched enthralled when an older boy flew one from the school playground. Up there was the great dome of sky — a vast empty space in which the kite on the end of its long string moved gently to and fro, steadied by a waving tail. That must have been the awakening of aeronautical consciousness: the feel of the wind and the tug of the tethered kite — but in December 1903 none knew that two brothers named Wright had managed the impossible by flying an engined biplane of their own design in the USA. Not until three years later, when it was reported that an aeronaut named Santos Dumont had flown 70 yards in France, did people begin to accept that man could fly with wings. The *Daily Mail* gained instant publicity with an offer of a £10,000 prize for the first man to fly from London to Manchester. Preposterous, said everyone!

Cresting the wave of publicity, the newspaper next announced that an Aeronautical Show would be held in April 1907 at the Agricultural Hall, Islington, London, and offered prizes totalling £250 for model aeroplanes capable of flying not less than 100 yards during trials at Alexander Palace. The winner was a 30-year-old Manchester-born engineer named Alliott Roe, but because the judges considered that none of the entries was of sufficient merit, he was awarded only £75. Though that was a bitter disappointment to Roe, he began to think that the money would at least enable him to start constructing a man-carrying, scaled up version of his tail-first winning model.

Precarious hop by Santos Dumont.

Two of Roe's models. Winner at top.

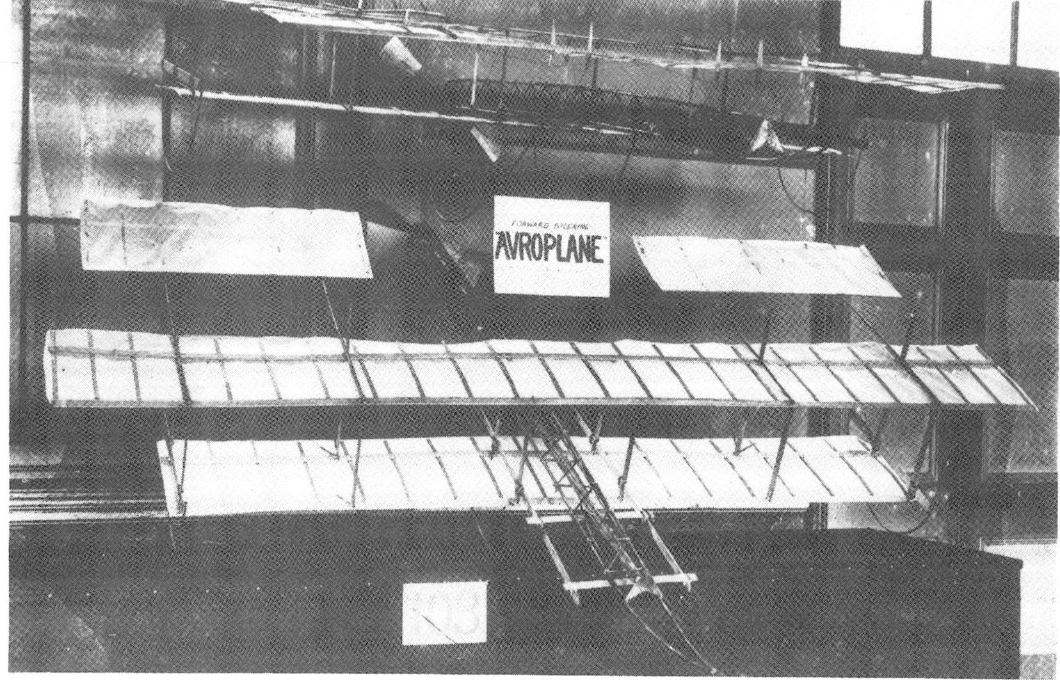

Newspaper pictures of that prize-winning model revealed to young Chadwick not only the secret of elastic propulsion and necessary twist of propeller, but also the complexities of construction. While sitting with him in the choir stalls the following Sunday, Harold Rogerson noticed that Roy's attention was apt to wander from the sermon while he pondered how to emulate Roe's flying model using simpler materials such as piano wire for wing profile and ribs, and a bare stick for the fuselage. Presently his preoccupation led to gentle reprimand from the choirmaster: but in any case the envisaged model was doomed from lack of finance.

But now that Roy was 14 came change. The affluent Harold was sent to Manchester Grammar School to achieve matriculation standard, whereas he himself turned to the practical course of an engineering apprenticeship. Here he had the advantage that his father had recently been appointed supervisor of a new premium apprentice scheme at British Westinghouse and could secure privileged entry for his son by virtue of his own service there. The rest of the lads at Westinghouse were trade apprentices, limited to a particular skill, such as welding, or machine operating, picking up what knowledge they could for future employment as skilled artisans at 18. Roy was more fortunate because his father was able to arrange a three-year course similar to that of the premium apprentices, whereby his son started as a learner office boy in the drawing office, where George Bayley was the uprising but sympathetic chief draughtsman — destined in time to be knighted and venerated by all who had been youngsters in his day.

Young Roy, feeling very grown-up after initial apprehension of working among matured men, daily accompained his father on the short train journey to and from the Westinghouse works at a cost of 2d a head each way. Like everything at Westinghouse the drawing office was vast, occupying the entire central third floor of the main office block, which was a replica of the Pittsburgh

The Chadwick Family: L. R. Charles Chadwick; standing: Doris. Front row: May, Roy, Agnes Chadwick, Alan. (Elsie born 1913).

The big British Westinghouse factory in Charles Chadwick's time.

headquarters in the U.S.A. Soon young Chadwick felt well established and presently was transferred to the factory for successive spells in each department, learning to operate machine tools and assemble mechanical and electrical equipment or structural components. The din in the triple-eaved, enormously long main machine shop was like the roar of Niagara Falls.

Steadily he progressed. The days sped past. With the dawn of 1908 he felt he was an old hand. From time to time that year came reports of flights in France, capped in August by Wilbur Wright demonstrating his catapult-launched biplane at the Military manoeuvering ground of Auvours with a series of flights which amazed everyone by his skill in executing gracefully banked turns, culminating on 31 December with a solo flight of two hours. By then he had made over 100 ascents at Auvours, totalling some 25 hours and had taken up more than 60 passengers.

Inspired by the stories of flight, Roy Chadwick began to spend much of his spare time making flying models. Recollecting those efforts many years later he recorded: 'For a long time these models would not fly and friends used to sympathize with my mother about her strange offspring, but she still helped me to make them and eventually I got quite good results, and finally a model which could make long flights. This led to my first "spot of bother" in aviation. Being rather shy about the neighbours' comments I often flew my models on moonlit nights in a large field behind our house. On the other side was a road with a gas light at the end. One night I flew a model in that direction without noticing that an elderly couple were taking an after-dinner stroll along the road. Unexpectedly the model made a record flight and to my joy I saw it circle the light. Next instant my blood was frozen by a piercing scream, and I saw the lady vanishing down the road followed by her escort. Presently I summoned courage to go and search for the model, and while thus engaged was hailed by

Young Chadwick with Wright-type model.

31-year-old Alliott Verdon Roe.

him and told fiercely and to the point that I had frightened his wife into hysterics.'

Roy's middle sister, May, said: 'Mother used to sew the covering on the wings, and I remember him saying to her: "It must be *real* silk, Mother," so the backs of old silk blouses were kept for this purpose. Our friends would keep asking when Roy was going to fly a model, and we would pester him continually until finally the great evening would arrive and we would spread the good news, resulting in quite a big turnout of children and fathers. I think Roy used to try and fox us to avoid this audience in case the model, to his discomforture, took a sweeping nose-dive into the ground or shot vertically into the air — but I only remember the times when the plane sailed through the skies until the elastic motor gave out, and we were rapturously enchanted.'

There was the almost incredible news in mid-Summer 1909 of Blériot successfully flying the Channel, and that Autumn aviation drew nearer with an International Air Meeting at Blackpool, organised by the newly formed Lancashire Aero Club, but the railway journey from Manchester was too costly for Roy Chadwick to attend, though he read with interest that Alliott Roe, the Manchester man, whom he remembered had won the model aeroplane competition at Alexander Palace, was there with a little yellow triplane of his own creation. Early next year Roy discovered that the firm of A. V. Roe & Co had been established in the Brownsfield Mill factory of Everards in Manchester's Great Ancoats Street. That was delightfully confirmed early in March when he visited an aircraft exhibition organized by the recently formed Manchester Aero Club at the local White City. Not only were 50 scale replicas and rubber driven models displayed on a long bench from end to end of the room, but staged behind them were three locally built full-sized aircraft, comprising a monoplane, a biplane on Farman lines and most attractive of all, the new and beautifully structured *Mercury* triplane produced by Roe's small team at Brownsfield Mill. Roy Chadwick spent a long Saturday afternoon gazing up at this enchanting first sight of real aeroplanes.

For most people there was keen interest in April when Claud Grahame-White and Louis Paulhan contended with Farman-built biplanes for the almost forgotten £10,000 prize which the *Daily Mail* had offered far back in 1906. News that both men had taken off raised public excitement to fever pitch. Bets were laid. Special editions of the newspapers were printed with almost hour-by-hour reports. The winning post was a large

Bullseye Triplane briefly airborne.

Grahame-White en-route.

field in Manchester's southern suburb of Didsbury, where thousands collected to witness the finish, among them Roy Chadwick, who had risen at dawn and cycled from Urmston five miles away. The *Daily Mail* Manchester office had set up telephones and loudspeakers to keep the crowd informed, so it was soon known that Grahame-White had started in darkness on the final lap, followed by Paulhan at 4.09 am. Excitement grew. Everyone wanted the Englishman to win.

At five in the morning on that cold field at Didsbury all eyes were fixed on the southern skies. Half-an-hour later a flying machine came distantly in sight. Nobody was sure whether this was Paulhan's or Grahame-White's until the long top wing of the former was recognized. 'Paulhan, Paulhan!' yelled the crowd — international rivalry forgotten. In delight at the accomplishment of this great two-day journey of 183 miles. *Flight*, price 1d, gave Roy Chadwick the full story with insular bias as a 'British triumph', saying: 'To the plucky winner Paulhan we offer hearty congratulation, but Mr Grahame-White's wonderful flight has literally set all England talking about nothing else but British aviation and its possibilities.'

Of more immediate concern to Chadwick was a decision of the Manchester Aero Club to form a model section at a subscription of 7s 6d per annum for those over 18 and 5s for those under. As Roy now received 7s 6d a week, he was rich enough to join! On 9 July the members visited Brownsfield Mill to discuss the syllabus for their Autumn and Winter lectures and Roy was fascinated to glimpse Roe's next aeroplane under construction. This was destined for Blackpool's second International Aviation Meeting which opened on 28 July, and this time Roy Chadwick at 17 felt authoritative enough to tell his father that he proposed attending at his own expense as the excursion fare was only 2/6d. There he found that the two triplanes Roe had entered had been destroyed by fire during the railway journey from Manchester, yet in three days a replacement triplane had been built at Brownsfield Mills and arrived a day later at Blackpool. For Alliott Roe the rest of the Blackpool Meeting became his usual story of trial and error, but at least he was awarded a compensationary prize of £50. When Roy Chadwick heard the full story, the image of Roe subconsciously began to displace George Bayley of Westinghouse as the kind of man for whom he would like to work. Was there a career in aviation, he wondered as he made the 90-minute rail journey home, lost in a dream of flying?

The year 1911 opened with dawning promise for Roy, when he was appointed an improver-draughtsman at 15s at week, with prospect of becoming a junior-draughtsman at 18 in April. Most evenings he would study in the relative privacy of the sittingroom while his brother and sisters did their homework in the kitchen. Once a week he would go direct from Westinghouse to the Manchester College of Technology, where one of his fellow-students was John Cockroft, destined long years ahead to become head of Britain's Nuclear Physics Adminstration. But it was not all work and no play for Roy. He still practised the violin and sang, despite much time spent on model aeroplanes, and was also devoted to books of adventure. *Flight* kept him informed of the progress of the rising British aircraft industry, and among the reports of new types of aeroplanes he learned that Alliott Roe had abandoned triplanes in favour of biplanes.

However, September became a significant month for Roy Chadwick. Things had gone very well for this handsome young man at Westinghouse, but now he was caught fighting a cheeky fellow ex-apprentice and was suspended for a week. 'To see him at home in his decent clothes, eating his meals, impressed itself in my mind,' his sister May recollected. 'It was absolutely unheard of for the average conscientious workman to be away from his job unless he was incapacitated. I remember going to the kitchen and hearing mother and Roy talking. "Oh Mother! I just do not want to go back to Westinghouse," he insisted.

' "Well, what *do* you want?" she asked, and he told her that he wanted to work with the aviator Mr Roe and help to build his aeroplanes.

' "If that's really your ambition why don't you go and see him? You'll never get a better opportunity," '

Next day Roy Chadwick took the train to Manchester and walked down Great Ancoats Street to the big ex-cotton factory of Brownsfield Mills — but Alliott Roe was

A. V. Roe stalls his Green-engined Triplane III at Blackpool.

Where it all started. Brownsfield Mills presents the same unwelcoming appearance today.

away and instead he was interviewed by Roe's elder brother Humphrey

'Good morning, Sir,' said Roy diffidently. 'Excuse my intrusion, but I am a junior draughtsman trained at British Westinghouse, and wonder if you could give me a job building aeroplanes?'

Humphrey eyed this neatly dressed young man, and by his manner assessed him as good material, but said: 'I am afraid only my brother can decide about that. I run the business side and am primarily concerned with our webbing production. . . . Let me see — my brother is visiting here next Wednesday. Perhaps you would like to call that afternoon?'

A week later he was there zealously early, but had to wait because the brothers were in conference. By the time he was called upstairs his pulse was fast with anticipation, though he looked as calm as ever. Alliott Roe was in his brother's chair, and Chadwick was struck by the likeness to Humphrey, but Alliott was slighter.

'Sit down,' the far-famed aviator invited. 'Now tell me about it. I gather you would like to join us?'

Roy felt in complete accord with this eager 34-year-old for whom he already had such high regard. They talked of aeroplanes. They talked of models. Presently Roe said: 'Good enough. I think perhaps I could find you a job as my personal assistant. What pay do you expect?'

'25s a week.'

'Too much. I had 15s in mind.'

'Well, you see, sir, I had 20s a week at Westinghouse, but I shall have to pay more for the train fare to get here and must also buy lunch.'

'20s,' said Roe firmly, primed by his pioneering struggles to build aeroplanes with insufficient capital.

Chadwick realised that his opportunity of joining the company was slipping . . . 'All right, sir,' he said, and they shook hands in traditional Lancashire manner.

Next day he reported for work. Alliott Roe introduced him to his keenly intelligent 24-year-old engineering assistant Reginald Parrott, and he was allocated a table in the latter's small office on the ground floor, adjacent to the main erecting hall. His mentor was a man of cool detachment who had given practical reality to the many sketches made by Alliott on the back of envelopes amid oft reiterated injuctions of 'streamline'; 'lightweight'; 'simplicity'; 'low cost'. By now, the elegance of detailed design compared with rival aircraft was becoming a hallmark of Avro construction.

What held Chadwick's eye were the two aeroplanes under construction in the assembly bay, of which a 40 hp Alveston-powered biplane was almost complete. 'This Avro E development for Mr John Duigan

Reginald Parrott.

represents a considerable advance on type D,' Parrott told him. 'Every detail has been carefully thought out, and every line smoothed down. Head resistance is less than any previous biplane. The radiators each side of the front cockpit cut resistance to a mere nothing. The undercarriage is of much less resistance than a twin skid arrangement of the Avro D, and the two wheels have a cross-laminated axle spring from which the load is taken by steel-struts with apex carrying a centre skid hinged to give a certain amount of movement by compressing a spring fitted to the strut under the engine. The framework of tailplane and rudder is steel tube, and all control wires are inside the fuselage. The drum-like fabric covering is produced by treating it with a dope called *Emaillite*.'

Parrott turned to the adjacent machine erected in skeleton. 'This is the one on which the Company's hopes are pinned. It is a two-seater, slightly bigger than the other, has a 36 feet span, and is powered with a 60 hp ENV water-cooled engine. We call it the 'Military Biplane' because it has been built to interest the army as a rival to the de Havilland designed 60 hp tractor BE-1 biplane under construction at Farnborough's Government-supported Army Aircraft Factory. I want you particularly to note the type of metal fittings we have standardised. Drawings must show how they are cut and folded from flat steel plate or made from machined aluminium forgings.'

Chadwick found many other aspects to attend to in the course of the ensuing weeks and months, such as reports from Barrow where Cdr Oliver Schwann, who was

The Avro D establishes tractor biplane construction. Test pilot Raynham on left.

The Brownsfield Mills aircraft factory and the new Avro Type E.

unqualified as a pilot, had piled up his Avro D when the machine skimmed so effectively on 8 November that it suddenly left the water and shot 20 ft up, stalled, dropped back with a splash and capsized. However the experiment of maritime use of aeroplanes was too important to abandon. The machine was salvaged and reconstruction began.

At the end of the month it became clear that plans were afoot for new designs. C. G. Grey, editor of the newly established journal *The Aeroplane*, had been visited by Roe and shown drawings of a fully enclosed monoplane. Cautiously he reported; 'Resistance has been reduced to an absolute minimum, and altogether the machine is of more than usual interest. A biplane on similar lines will probably be built at the same time.' That indicated anticipation of a long expected War Office aircraft competition to be held on Salisbury Plain in 1912. The total prize money was £11,000, but no competitor would be permitted to have more than £5,000 aggregate and the War Office reserved the right to withhold any prize. Aircraft had to be transportable by rail in a packing case not exceeding 32 ft x 9 ft x 9 ft. They must carry a load of 350 lbs in addition to equipment, fuel, and oil for 4½ hours, and in that condition be capable of flight for 3 hours including one hour at 4,500 ft, achieving the first 1,000 ft at not less than 200 ft a minute, and attain a horizontal speed of not less than 55 mph in a calm. There was insistence on dual control and easy communication between pilot and observer.

At that, Alliott Roe took a new look at the suitability of the Type E military aeroplane and decided that full cabin enclosure for the crew might prove a winner — but initially he would build the already publicised small, single seat, Type F cabin monoplane in order to study the pros and cons.

* * *

By the New Year 1912, Roy Chadwick felt well established. The unbounded enthusiasm and unsparing energy of this artistic, neat young man had quickly won the unstinted approval of the two Roes and Parrott. But it was not all serious work. Roy had a great sense of fun, and at Christmas enjoyed the annual family visit to Manchester for the pantomime. However, model aeroplane making was abandoned, though he sometimes attended the Manchester Model Aero Club meetings on Saturdays at the Trafford Park Aerodrome. He still sang in the Urmston Church Choir; his interest in music was expanding, and a visit the the D'Oyley Carte Opera Company at Manchester opened new vistas.

Work soon started on the Type F monoplane, but Duigan's biplane was proving a disappointment. Straight hops were made early in February, but either his inexperience or the low power of the engine led to lack of climb, and tests with several different propellers gave no improvement. He therefore decided to send the machine to the Avro flight-testing HQ at Brooklands for replacement of the Alveston engine by an ENV of 35 nominal hp, but probably giving 40. Forewarned of problems, Alliott Roe decided to fit a 60 hp ENV to the 'Military Aeroplane'. Both aircraft were independently freighted to Brooklands, arriving before the end of February and were quickly assembled. A week later, Duigan was making straights from end to end of the aerodrome with his prototype, but still there was insufficient power for climb, so he took out the engine for re-tuning, made a propeller of his own design, and subsequently gained his aviator's certificate.

As Alliott Roe's oncoming pilot, Freddy Raynham was busily transferring the Avro

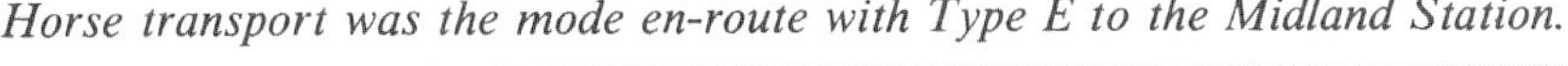

Horse transport was the mode en-route with Type E to the Midland Station.

Flying School as a limited company from Brooklands to Shoreham, the brilliant former Avro pupil Lieut Wilfred Parke RN was enlisted to make the first flight of the Type E Military Machine on 3 March. So excellent was the performance and handling that Roe decided to enter it for the Mortimer-Singer competition open to military and naval pilots, and as a publicity gimmick had the name AVRO painted full depth each side of the fuselage. To that end Parke made a spectacular climb to 2,000 ft in 13 minutes with a heavy passenger aboard — but the sequence of testing was beset with engine problems, and on 20 April, when he was about to attempt a duration flight for the Mortimer-Singer prize, the engine cut while taking off at Hendon, resulting in a stall when at 20 ft and on hitting the ground the undercarriage and one side of the main planes were ripped off and the machine rolled over.

The task of re-building was undertaken in almost optimistic vein because a *White Paper* published on 12 April, announcing the establishment of a Royal Flying Corps with Military and Naval Wings gave hope of sales. It was also stated that the Army Aircraft Factory would be re-named the Royal Aircraft Factory.

The Avro contingents, both at Brownsfield Mills and Brooklands, were now busier than ever. A modified Type E biplane, with fuselage widened to take a 50 hp Gnome, had been built since Christmas and was being assembled at the Brooklands hangar. Chadwick had been given sole responsibility for altering the fuselage with longer horizontal spacer struts and making a full-scale drawing of the transverse metal mounting devised by Roe for the rotary engine, and under Roe's guidance had set out the structure of the enclosed Type F monoplane. These were proud responsibilities for a young man who had not reached his nineteenth birthday until the day of Duigan's final flight.

The first flight of the Type F monoplane followed on 2 May. Everyone at Brooklands gathered to see this striking new machine which seemed the epitomy of low-drag design and ingenious detail. Some expected instant disaster and avered that Parke would not be able to see ahead because of oil thrown back on the flat Cellon windscreen forming the top of the nose, though the extensive side windows in fact gave adequate diagonal view for landing. More serious was the risk of trapping the pilot if the machine turned over, for the only access was through an aluminium trap-door in the roof.

The wing area was barely half that of the Avro D school biplane from which the 35 hp

Type F Cabin monoplane.

Chadwick's modification of Type E with Gnome which becomes the Avro 500.

Viale engine had been taken to power the monoplane, yet despite the heavy power loading of 23 lbs per horsepower and a wing loading three times as great as the biplane, a sequence of 'straights' seemed promising and were the first flights in the world with a cabin aeroplane. Here was the shape of the future — but the cheers were largely relief that this novel machine survived without crashing!

Two days later, circuits were tried, and on 12 May Parke managed to ease the machine up to 1,000 ft and also achieved 65 mph. Pleased that his monoplane performed reasonably well, Roe decided to show it to rival Hendon where demonstrations and racing around pylons attracted great crowds every Sunday — but within minutes of taking off on 25 May the engine failed, and in attempting to land in the nearest field, the machine ran into a fence and turned over. Roe sighed at another repair bill, so it was dumped at the back of the Brooklands shed where it languished for the next three months. However, Parke's enthusiastic report of the relatively unhampered vision through windscreen and windows, coupled with the comfort of being shielded from the slipstream, encouraged Roe to continue with his proposed fully enclosed biplane for the Military Trials Competition, but design was somewhat delayed by the great success of the new 'Military' Avro E powered with the 50 hp Gnome. The engine had been taken from the tatty Avro school Farman, so had plenty of use, but nothing could beat it in lightness, for it weighed only 2.2 lbs per horsepower compared with the 300 lbs weight of the 35 hp Viale.

On 8 May this biplane was flown for the first time, and climbed to 2,000 ft in what was considered the remarkable time of 5 minutes. So enthusiastic was Parke's report that the machine was sent to Farnborough next day for official demonstration to the Factory Superintendent and Army representatives. Parke flew the 17 miles in 20 minutes and by the end of the afternoon had completed all tests demanded. One of the interested spectators was Geoffrey de Havilland who in the early days had visited Roe at Leigh Marshes, and now was very interested to see how the new Avro compared with his BE1 which he had been flying since the end of January, and recently was granted the first official 'Certificate of Airworthiness'. In fact, the Avro at 61 mph was 2 mph faster and climbed twice as fast.

Delighted with those results, Roe lost no time in visiting the War Office and, after much haggling, not only sold the machine but received an order for two more similarly fitted with dual control — the first of its kind.

The Avro E, Alliott Roe decided, marked a turning point; so he re-designated it more impressively *Type 500* 'as a piece of office swank', he said. After such success there seemed all the more reason to strike out with the tentative enclosed Type G biplane for the Military Trials Competition rather than enter an already accepted machine, so Chadwick had been kept hard-pressed at the drawing board with numerous design changes by Roe who could always imagine a better way of doing things. The major problem was lack of a powerful radial engine to mount in the nose like the monoplane in order to obtain unobstructed view between the cylinders; but on Parke's assurances that he could see well enough through the side windows, it was decided to use a 60 hp four-cylinder vertical Green affording a nose width of only 15 ins. to the 2 ft. 3 ins. wide cabin which accommodated two crew in tandem.

Because of War Office priority, construction could not be commenced until completion of the next two Gnome-engined 500s — yet zealous overtime by the Manchester factory hands, ensured delivery of the first to Brooklands at the beginning of June, and on the 5th Parke flew that crucial RFC aeroplane. Those days, tests were scanty. It was only necessary to show that a machine could fly, so there was no hesitation in delivering it next day to Farnborough. Fast on its heels came the third 500, but to save time the components were transported eight miles to Eccles cricket ground on the west side of Manchester and quickly assembled for testing by Parke.

Eagerly Roy Chadwick asked Humphrey Roe if he could go as passenger 'just to see what it is like'. Humphrey smiled at the enthusiasm. 'Don't know what my brother will say if I give you time off at this busy stage . . . However, fix it with Lieut Parke.'

As customary with aircraft projects, the start was later than intended but presently the mechanics finished fussing with the waiting Avro. Roy followed Parke aboard and lowered himself into the front cockpit, boxed-in by the gleaming rows of varnished struts and glittering wires. The propeller was swung; the engine buzzed: behind him Parke waved a hand, and the men holding the aeroplane back let go. Lightly the Avro swayed across the turf, smoothed its passage as the wings took the load, and to Roy's surprise they were 50 ft high with a gale of wind pressing his

Finishing touches to Avro G at Larkhill.

Urgent repairs required after turning over.

head. All too soon the circuit was completed and they came slanting down with blipping engine, but Parke misjudged the landing. The machine bounced, swung round and hit a wing, then tipped on its nose with a scrunch. Hours late, it was a sorry tale that Roy had for Humphrey Roe. The damage was considerable, and nearly three weeks passed before the repaired aeroplane could be flown to Brooklands; but on 20 July Raynham delivered it to the Central Flying School at Upavon in Wiltshire, where it joined the other two Gnome Avros. *Flight* commented: 'One cannot praise the Avro Military biplane more highly than by bracketing it with the Cody, BE2 tractor, and new Bristol. The planes are noteworthy in having been designed with the care usually devoted only to monoplanes.'

Throughout July the Avro G Cabin biplane was taking form in company with a second fuselage intended for a spare machine with alternative 60 hp ABC engine — but both airframes were behind schedule and the ABC was having development problems, yet despite hold ups and snags, the team won through just in time and dispatched the prototype in packing cases by rail and truck direct to Larkhill on the Downs north-west of Amesbury. There had been no possibility of flight-testing, nevertheless the Avro made a splendid start by beating every competitor with an assembly time of only 14½ minutes, and Parke, who by now had flown more types of aeroplane than anyone, made an immediate brief preliminary flight — but disaster followed on 7 August when he attempted the mandatory three hour endurance test. Half-an-hour of struggling in the gusting wind prompted him to land. The machine touched down, turned to taxi to the hangars, the wind caught it under a wing and over it went in full view of Alliott and Humphrey Roe. Damage was too great for repair on the spot, so back went the machine to Manchester — but in that purposeful decade there was no delay on the railways, a day sufficing for the journey. The team at Brownsfield Mills were swift and sure, and the semi-completed second machine was there to rob of components. A week later the prototype was back at Larkhill in what had become a contest between eighteen machines comprising the Avro biplane as the only one with a British engine, eight British aeroplanes with foreign engines, and nine foreign aircraft. The weather was discouraging — with torrential rain and gales at times. Mostly the gum-booted teams of mechanics tramped around in an ocean of mud, but on sunny days were attacked by hordes of midges which

The winning Cody biplane of anachronistic design.

invaded the massed tents where the crews were uncomfortably housed; but officials, pilots, and company directors found better accommodation in the Amesbury and Salisbury hotels.

The calm of early morning and evening was aimed at for most of the trials. At 6 am on Sunday 25 August the Avro, with Parke as pilot and Lieut Le Breton as observer, took off for an endurance trial, but after 2½ hours the monotony was too much for Parke and he enlivened the time by demonstrating to his passenger a succession of increasingly steep dives and pull-outs, but stalled on the last and the machine went into a spin. Hitherto that wild whirl had always ended in a crash — usually fatal. For 2,000 ft Parke's machine inexorably spun down, while he tried different control settings to stop the turn, and eventually made a lucky combination of opposite rudder and control column central or slightly forward, for the whirl suddenly changed to a dive from which he easily recovered. The incident, later known as 'Parke's dive', caused widespread discussion, for it established a fundamental step towards aerial safety. Despite that near crash, Humphrey Roe was so convinced of Parke's mastery that later in the day he flew with him to Upavon, and typically secured maximum publicity for his novel cabin aeroplane by typing a letter on the way.

Final assessment of the complicated marking was open to criticism. Indisputably the Avro was best in terms of efficiency and low fuel consumption, let alone its advanced design, but it was Cody, the affectionately-regarded hero of earlier flying days, who won with his big, old-fashioned biplane in which the pilot was fully exposed to the rushing air and thus anachronistically gained top marks for view! Astonishingly, nobody begrudged his victory, though it was only made possible because his 120 hp Austro-Daimler was more powerful than any other entrant's engine — but the Avro gained a consolation prize of £100 in company with the French-built Hanriot and Blériot monoplanes.

Said Charles Turner, Air Correspondent to *The Observer*: 'In the biplane class, the Avro had little to fear by comparison with any other. The tangle of results is unfair to the Avro in a major respect. Its climb is given as 9½ minutes for the first 1,000 ft. Apparently it must have struck a bad patch for the second 1,000 was climbed in less than 3 minutes. The glide of this machine was remarkably good, being of 1 in 6.5. Its range or radius of action was second only to that of Cody, and it carried petrol for six hours' flying.'

Chapter 2
The Widening Prospect

Recent success of the Type D floatplane at Barrow had encouraged the Admiralty to consider seaplanes realistically, so a contract was placed with A. V. Roe & Co for a big 'Hydro-aeroplane' powered with the recently introduced 100 hp Gnome. Roe instructed his henchmen Parrott and Chadwick: 'We'll virtually scale up the 500 to give, say, an additional 150 sq ft, and we'll get Oscar Gnosspelius to design a central float like the one for the Duigan-Avro which Stanley-Adams has just flown at Lake Windermere.

Currently Lieut R. Burga, the Peruvian Naval Attaché had visited Brownsfield Mills to discuss construction of an experimental shoulder-wing monoplane which unconventionally had vertical rudders operating differentially above and below the fuselage at the c.g. to give lateral control. Roy Chadwick's task was to adapt an Avro 500 fuselage for that purpose. As a budding designer he was keeping meticulous records of such things as ratio of tail volume to wing area, estimates of resistance, and detailed weights of every part of each new aeroplane. When design of the Burga had sufficiently

Fred Raynham, who emigrated from Australia with Harry Hawker and both became famous test pilots.

advanced, assembly of components built in Manchester was undertaken by the team at Shoreham where this somewhat dangerous monoplane was hopped in late Autumn by R. H. Simms and later flown by H. Sweetnam-Powell, both of whom had gained their pilot's certificates a mere few months earlier.

Meanwhile Fred Raynham had been appointed Avro chief pilot, and shortly afterwards the Military Trials biplane achieved a last triumph. He had been flying it since the beginning of October, but because of the poor fabric condition after long parking in the open at Shoreham, he flew the machine back to Brooklands for overhaul preparatory to an attempt at the British Michelin Endurance Prize, and on 24 October was successful in achieving a record for a British-built machine and engine of 7 hrs 31 mins — but an hour later his friend Harry Hawker won the £500 prize with a flight of 8 hrs 23 mins on Sopwith's modified Wright biplane! Bad weather prevented a further attempt by Raynham, so the Avro G was flown back to Shoreham and stored.

That Autumn of 1912 gave Humphrey Roe the opportunity of extended practical experience with aeroplanes. Following delivery of the third Avro 500, he had received the firm's first export order in the form of a contract from the aeronautically enlightened Portuguese government for an identical machine, and it was despatched to Lisbon with Humphrey in charge of an expedition comprising Copeland Perry as pilot and W. H. Sayers as engineer. On arrival at Lisbon they had the illuminating experience of conveying the crates by bullock cart to the flying ground at Bellem for assembly and test flight. National papers blazed the story of its arrival, eagerly read by a public which had been coerced into subscribing its costs, and the name *Republica* was painted in scarlet letters on the fuselage and in green under the transparent wings. On 16 October it was officially handed over to the Minister of War attended by a crowd of 20,000 — but next day the temperamental Gnome engine lost power, and Perry had to alight in the shallows of the Tagus. However, Humphrey and his men, assisted by much vociferous help, salvaged the machine without damage and saw it safely stored for the winter and better flying days.

While Humphrey Roe was away, Alliott received a letter from his enthusiastic aviation and motoring friend the Hon. Maurice Egerton recommending 22-year-old Harry Broadsmith for a job. Educated at Manchester Grammar School, he had been apprenticed to the Lancashire and Yorkshire Railway Locomotive Workshops at Horwich, and like Roe had served several voyages as a marine engineer with a famous shipping line. That in itself was high recommendation, but so was his obvious keenness for aviation, and equally his personality had appeal. Roe engaged him.

'Though he's three years older than you,' Roy Chadwick was told, 'I'm not taking him on as your senior because he hasn't your aeronautical knowledge, but I shall expect you and he to work as a pair under Mr Parrott's direction.'

The new team-mate fitted in well, though sometimes Roy felt a little out of things when Roe and Broadsmith exchanged yarns of interesting events associated with their maritime travels to distant and romantic countries.

Increased orders were necessitating more floor-space. The tenancy of bigger premises 1½ miles away at Clifton Street, Miles Platting on the edge of Newton Heath, was being negotiated, and the brothers decided that Humphrey would concentrate specifically on the A. V. Roe business as managing director. Brownsfield Mills would revert solely to webbing manufacture, so he elevated his doughty assistant, John Lord to partnership in Everards with complete freedom to run it his own way. Everyone loved this stocky little Lancashire man who had an irrepressible fund of funny stories made distinctive by his droll native accent, and whether workman or high-placed official, he treated all as equals.

With expansion as the target, more capital was required for the aeroplane business. It had always been a case of money going out and little coming in until the current year with

One of the developed production Avro 500s.

its Military and Naval contracts, but as Alliott Roe recorded: 'It so happened that towards the end of 1912 my brother invited members of the Manchester Aero Club to visit our Works. Among them was a young man, Piers Groves, who told his father, a wealthy brewer, that our new business was worth looking into. As a result, Mr Groves senior came along and after going into matters, agreed to join us as chairman when our firm was registered as a limited company, and also to put up the extra cash to develop the business properly.'

That created a general air of optimism, but on 16 December every member of Avros was saddened by news that their friend, the ubiquitous Lieut Wilfred Parke and his passengers had been killed the previous day shortly after taking off from Hendon Aerodrome for Oxford, flying the latest crescent-winged Handley Page monoplane. As so often with Gnome engines, the power was down and the machine staggered off towards Wembley in a cloud of blue smoke, and it became apparent that height was being lost. With engine failure facing him and only 400 feet in hand, Parke attempted to turn into wind for a forced landing, but stalled and dived vertically to the ground.

* * *

The year 1913 dawned amid great activity. In the opening week the big single 'Hydro-biplane', Type 501, was crated and delivered to the Lakes Flying Company for testing by H. Stanley-Adams in view of his experience with float-planes — but the first test showed insufficient lateral buoyancy, so stabilising wing-tip floats were added. Even that proved unsatisfactory, so eventually Gnosspelius fitted conventional twin floats which proved acceptable to the Admiralty, and the machine was delivered to the Isle of Grain.

Meanwhile 11 January became a red letter day for the Roe brothers' aeroplane business with registration as A. V. Roe & Co Ltd and capital of £30,000. Within days, as though sealing the deed, came an Admiralty order for five single-seat versions of the Gnome-powered Type 500 designated Type 502, together with an enlarged Type 503 version of the seaplane with three bays instead of two and the top wing spanning 50 ft.

By now Chadwick had become a typical 'city' man, invariably neatly clad, wearing Homberg hat and occasionally sporting a rolled umbrella. Pay had been increased to 30s, from which he made a weekly contribution to the family budget, kept himself in clothes, and after paying £4 7s for his 12 month 'contract' train ticket still had money in hand for an occasional concert by the Hallé Orchestra or the pleasures of Manchester theatres displaying such attractions as Miss Horniman's Repertory Company — but more often than not, Saturday evenings were devoted to musical gatherings with Urmston friends. Though Harold Rogerson had become a university student, he remained Roy's closest friend, so there were frequent visits to the Rogersons' big house in nearby Church Road at Urmston, where an added attraction was a billiard table in the cellars converted to a large recreation room.

As a special mark of approval, Alliott Roe decided that his very presentable young protegé Roy, whom he regarded with almost paternal interest, should attend the Avro Stand at the great Aero Show held at Olympia in February. A beautifully slicked-up version of the Avro 500 had been prepared, and the neatly arranged but unpretentious Stand gained considerable attention because it placarded this aeroplane 'as supplied in numbers to the RFC'. On the opening day, Roe was particularly gratified to be presented to H.M. King George V and discuss with him not only the outstanding features of this machine but also the favourable reports from the Central Flying School and the interest in Avro seaplanes shown by the Royal Navy.

Walking around the Show, noting details of every aeroplane, Alliott Roe perceived yet again that it was not novelty, but well-proved practical design in which easy maintenance, robustness, and good flying qualities coupled with outstanding performance, were essential to maintain a leading place in the swiftly growing aviation industry. 'Always make things simple enough to build with your own hands,' he told Roy Chadwick. 'Lightness for climb; cleanness for speed; unit construction for manufacturing ease.'

To the end of his days Roy kept to these precepts and many another instilled by this great pioneer, who was described by R. H. Bound of later fame as having 'the happy knack of being able to work with his staff as one of them, and keep them as happy as himself'.

Returning to Manchester by train, Roe began sketching an improved version of the Avro 500 which he proposed to power with an 80 hp Gnome as the lightest engine to ensure best possible performance despite its high oil consumption. 'When I designed this machine as Type 504 I thought we would be fortunate if we received an order for half-a-dozen,' he said. 'I was very particular about the detailed design, and while travelling in trains, most of the time was spent scheming the detail features. Every item was given most careful thought before being entrusted to the draughtsmen.'

Throughout March, Roe and his brother were busy organising the transfer from Brownsfield Mills to the Clifton Street premises. In April the new factory was ready. At that time, A. V. Roe & Co Ltd employed a total of 78, including office staff and the teams at Shoreham and Brooklands. Harry Goodyear, a new recruit from the rival Yorkshire business of Blackburn Aircraft Ltd, recorded: 'The number actually employed making the aeroplanes at the new factory was between 30 and 40.'

Chadwick gained a new assistant in Cliff Horax, who told me: 'My first few months were spent in the shops until I was offered a vacancy in the D.O. where most of my early work was on the 504, which was under construction throughout the early summer. By then our offices were in a building the equivalent of a fair-sized house, with a drawing office in the two best bedrooms made into one open space. Drawing boards were on benches around the room, where Roy Chadwick sat at one end. Near him was Frank Vernon, who had recently been engaged to do the stress work on the wings. Alliott Roe had the title of chief engineer and used the small office near the drawing office. Downstairs his brother Humphrey, as managing director, had a more generously appointed room.' These days the staff discreetly spoke of the brothers by their initials 'AV' and 'HV', but always addressed them as 'sir'.

Though both Parrott and Chadwick had proved competent to perform structural strength calculations based on somewhat arbitrary assumptions of loads and use of

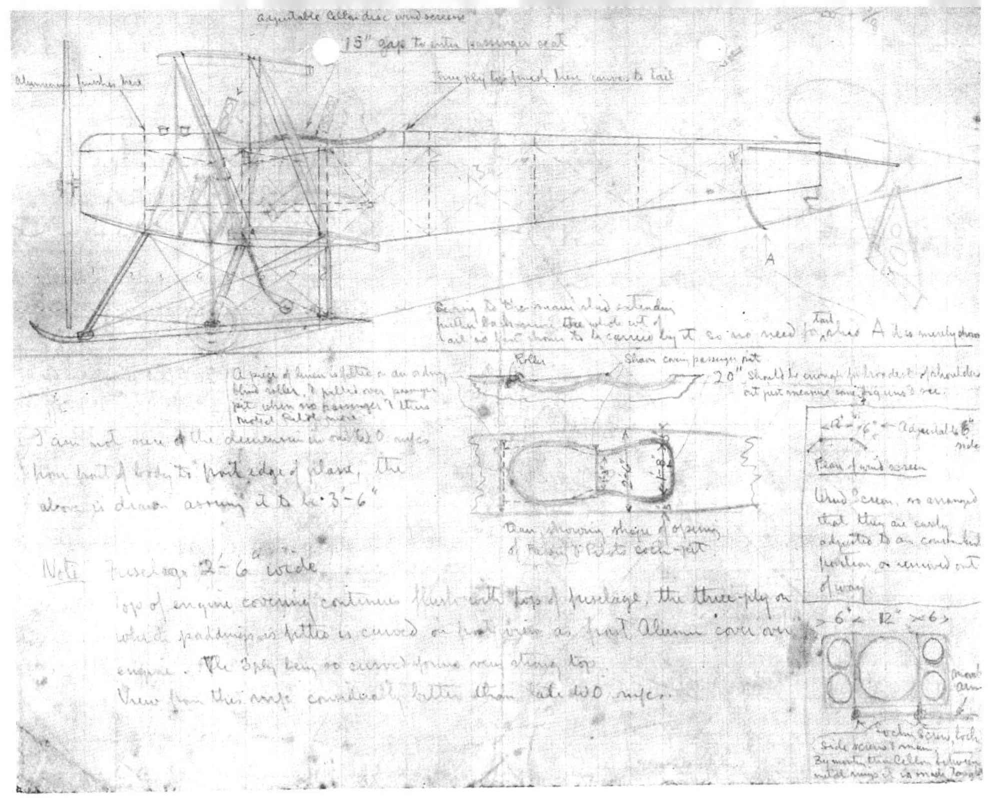

Roe's sketches of Type 504 development of 500.

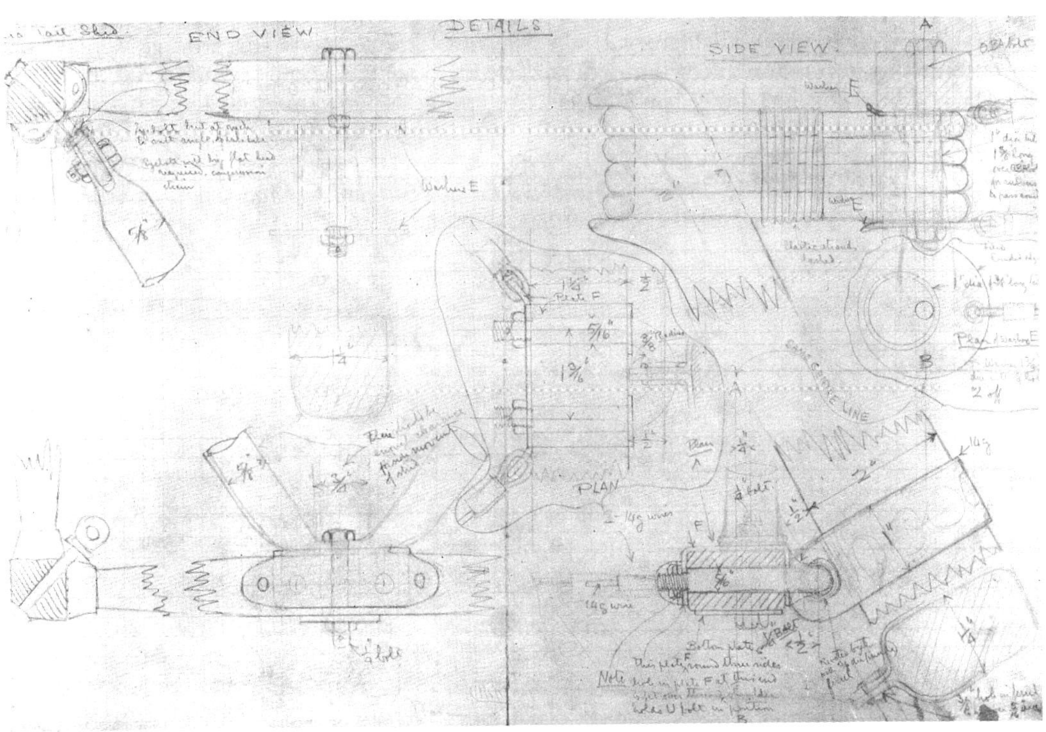

simple formulae for ascertaining the stresses, this was no longer acceptable. So many foreign and British aircraft had suffered fatal structural crashes that margins of safety for new designs had become a matter of uneasy speculation.

Instability was a further problem. The Royal Aircraft Factory and National Physics Laboratory had therefore been studying these matters as a priority in order to formulate mandatory requirements. In the Spring R & M No 77 became the first complete explanation of stability correlated with mathematical investigation. That was followed by the even more important R & M No. 83 as 'a preliminary note of Methods of Calculation which may be employed in the determination of the stresses in the Spars of Aeroplane Wings'. Here at last was an authoritative, practical system which took into account the offset loads of attachment points, additional stresses due to deflection between points of attachment, and those from deformation of the spar. In these calculations it was necessary to include adequate margins of safety to cover contingencies, and a factor of 5 was currently thought satisfactory. It was because of this new requirement that Frank Vernon had been engaged, for he was familiar with the 'Theorem of three moments' as a necessary part of the calculations.

April marked the beginning of construction of the new Avro 504 at the Clifton Street factory which seemed crowded with 500s and single-seat 501s, and prominent among them was the impressive new twin-float Avro 503 seaplane, soon to be dismantled and packed for despatch to Shoreham. Because of inadequate facilities assembly took longer than expected, but on the misty morning of 28 May it was launched on the River Adur, and Fred Raynham took off in a very short run, carrying John Alcock as passenger. Alcock was a Manchester mechanic who had gained his pilot's certificate in November 1912, but now was an instructor at the A. V. Roe Shoreham Flying School. That he would be the future conqueror of the Atlantic was beyond wildest dream.

Flight tests of the 503 Seaplane proved most encouraging, even though Raynham had to acquire the marine techniques by trial and error, occasionally resulting in damage to the wooden floats; but on 12 June he accomplished an hour's flying on official tests carrying Lieut J. W. Seddon, RN, the Inspector of Naval Aircraft, and showed that the machine could climb 1,300 ft in five minutes — regarded as very satisfactory. In due course the Admiralty placed contracts for

The 503 seaplane was slightly larger than the similar 501 but had less top wing overhang and was designed for rapid assembly and dismantling. (G. Quick).

three production machines, and the German Navy purchased the prototype.

Meanwhile, the new Avro 504 two-seater had been taking form. Chadwick and his assistant C. R. Taylor were responsible for design of the fuselage and new type of undercarriage, and Harry Broadsmith for the wings. As leader of the section, Chadwick's pay had been increased to £2 10s on reaching his 20th birthday.

Describing the new design to reporters, Reg Parrott said: 'The principal differences from the previous Type 500 are heavy wing stagger to increase efficiency and improve downward and forward view; increased span and wing chord; a better wing section; improvement in streamlining the fuselage; fitting a unique undercarriage.' Although the latter was reminiscent of Type 500, the cantilever leaf-spring axle was replaced by a steel tube sprung by ingeniously 'bungee'-mounted telescopic struts from each lower longeron, but the central skid and its fore and aft V-struts were retained. As the fuselage width was less than the diameter of the 80 hp Gnome, the aluminium cowling of the square section nose was outwardly dished at top and sides to give clearance to the cylinders, and the type of front bearing plate for rotaries recommended by the Monoplane Accident Committee was adopted. Like its predecessors, the machine was finless, but the long, slender fuselage ensured sufficiently long lever arm for the distinctive semi-circular, balanced rudder and rectangular tailplane to give adequate stability. 'Lateral control is achieved by warping ailerons,' Parrott explained, 'the inner ends of which are fixed and the outer ends, which have increased chord, are coupled by a strut and warped by a system of wires.'

Transported to Brooklands in July, this translucent-winged, attractive looking biplane with glittering yellow struts and the name AVRO boldy painted on the linen-covered fuselage, was immediately the cynosure of all eyes. Raynham, usually so impassive, landed from the first flight wreathed in smiles. 'Absolutely delightful!' he said.

Roe had hoped to enter a seaplane in August for the *Daily Mail's* £5,000 prize Circuit of Britain Race, flying stage by stage eastward from Southampton and round, but the next 503 seaplane was not ready, and perhaps his enthusiasm was damped because the Sopwith entry, powered with the reliable 100 hp Green, was 10 mph faster. In the event, the Sopwith piloted by Harry Hawker with H. Kauper as mechanic was the sole participant, but it proved a long, long battle, and the third day brought disaster, for within sight of Dublin the engine began to lose power, and in attempting to alight a wing-tip struck the sea and broke under the impact. Hawker was picked up unhurt, but little Kauper was injured. Recognising this flight of 1,043 miles as the greatest feat of air pilotage yet achieved, the *Daily Mail* awarded Hawker £1,000 and declared that the £5,000 prize would be re-offered for identical competition next year.

Observing that Sopwith had received enormous publicity, Alliott Roe decided to display the prowess of the new Avro 504 prototype by entering it for the Aerial Derby around a 94-mile circuit, starting and finishing at Hendon on 20 September, but Raynham was pipped at the post for third place by the 3-seater Sopwith flown by Hawker, who beat him by 37 seconds. The performance of these two biplanes came as a great surprise, for nobody imagined they were fast enough to exceed the speed of the several monoplanes. That made the future of both Avro and Sopwith companies look very promising.

Elated by this relative success, Roe agreed to a race between the Avro 504 representing Lancashire, and Robert Blackburn's latest monoplane on behalf of Yorkshire — and the *Yorkshire Evening News* offered a trophy for the winner. A circuit of almost 100 miles was chosen, with Leeds as start and finish. A large bipartisan crowd watched the machines take off side by side on the early afternoon of 2 October. Humphrey Roe was navigator for Raynham, and the Blackburn was flown by Harold Blackburn, who was unrelated to the builder, and the monoplane's owner, Dr.

Christie, was passenger. Visibility was bad. That gave Blackburn the advantage, for he knew Yorkshire well, whereas Raynham was flying over foreign territory. However, the Avro proved the faster until Raynham lost the way and eventually landed at Dewsbury, where he abandoned the race and flew back to Leeds.

However, his cross-country flights had confirmed that warping the unconventional inversely tapered ailerons gave too heavy a control, so they were replaced with normally hinged rectangular ailerons interconnected by two vertical wires instead of the single strut. That gave opportunity to stiffen the interplane bracing system by fitting slightly stouter streamline struts secured to the spars with metal sockets instead of the original flexible pin joints necessary for warping. As the engine was difficult of access for the constant maintenance required, Roe devised an ingenious 'spider' of steel tubes converging centrally to form the front mounting, and enclosed the nose with detachable neatly rounded cowling tapering conically to the flat fuselage sides for better streamlining than the original bulges.

Three weeks later the prototype 504 was re-delivered to Brooklands, and after its first flight Raynhjam declared that the control was 'just perfect'. Thus assured he flew the machine in a handicap race from Hendon to Brighton and back for which the Sussex Motor Yacht Club offered a Trophy and £100 for the winner, but of the nine starters, five made forced landings, including Raynham who managed to get into a very small field near Horley when the wire to the air mixture control of his carburettor broke, but at least he did not turn over like another competitor who landed at Beachy Head. Of the remaining four, Hamel with his racing Morane-Saulnier monoplane was the easy winner.

Raynham flew the 504 to Farnborough for official government tests on 24 November. With passenger and fuel for three hours, the Avro climbed to 1,000 ft in 1 min 45 secs, and clocked a remarkable 80.9 mph over the speed course and thus was faster than the much-vaunted BE2. Stall was 43 mph, giving a speed range of 37 mph, but was eclipsed by Sopwith's newest creation, a side-by-side two-seat 'Tabloid' biplane of only 25 ft 6 in span which arrived at Farnborough on the 29th and with similar 80 hp Gnome achieved 90 mph and a speed range of 55 mph. That same afternoon this little machine caused a sensation when displayed before a crowd of 50,000 at Hendon's usual Saturday aviation meeting. This led Alliott Roe cause to envisage a little swept-wing racing biplane which his staff at Manchester would tackle on completing design of a two-seater, 44 ft span, tail-boom pusher biplane. Designated Type 508, construction began in December with intention of displaying at the next Olympia Aero Show at the beginning of March 1914. No sooner were initial drawings completed than Roe tentatively schemed a big twin-float

Dusk flight by Raynham with modified 504.

seaplane, Type 510. 'Roy,' said Alliott Roe. 'We've got to beat those Short Brothers. They've built a new factory on the banks of the Medway at Rochester, but Cdr Schwann tells me that their folding-wing seaplane is not the last word, so they're revising it. We therefore want you to re-draw the 503 with longer fuselage, bigger top-wing overhang and smaller lower wing to keep the same area but stressed for 1 lb per square foot more — and we'll use a 160 hp Gnome, like the Short.'

With all this work in hand Chadwick was able to obtain the post of assistant mathematician for his great friend Harold Rogerson who had recently completed his University course in mechanical engineering. Though Reggie Parrott, as chief engineer, was nominally in charge of design, responsibility for structural integrity was now Frank Vernon's in conjunction with Roy Chadwick, who as supervisor of the seven or eight draughtsmen now had the prestigious salary of £3 5s a week, characteristically handled his draughtsmen in much the same manner throughout his life: usually authoritative politeness but momentary anger when irritated, then calm consideration of whatever was at fault. Certainly the girls at the family Christmas party that year were very much aware of this tall, good-looking, young man. Even 50 years later one of them recollected: 'Oh! He was so very nice. Easy to talk to and so pleasant to be with.

* * *

The new pusher biplane proved somewhat simpler to build than the Type 504 tractor, so the bare airframe was even available for exhibition at Manchester's Belle Vue Gardens from 1 — 3 January, 1914, together with a production Avro 504 demonstrated by Raynham at the sports ground.

Despite being a pusher, the ancestry of Type 508 was obvious, for the complete undercarriage was a standard 504 unit, the nacelle was the fore-part of a 504 reversed, bringing the Gnome astern, and the front was formed with a vertically curved sheet of aluminium. The wings used production 504 ribs, spars, and struts in conjunction with an 8 ft centre-section carrying the steel tube tail outriggers and spacers conventionally wire-braced, and terminating in a vertical knife-edge mounting a deep rudder and extended span tailplane.

Roe now proceeded with design of the arrow-winged biplane referenced Type 511. 'Swept-back wings must be right for speed,' he told Parrott and Chadwick. 'Take a gliding peregrine falcon, for instance. Under gravity

The officially sponsored BE2A.

alone it can do 100 mph. So I want you to draught the outline of a single-seater about the size of the Sopwith Tabloid. In effect, take the rear half of the 504 fuselage and join it direct to the engine bay, then project the centre section leading edge vertically above the engine bulkhead and sweep back the wings at, say, 30 degrees. Juggle the pilot's position until the c.g. comes at about one-third of the mean chord at half span.'

By the beginning of February, construction had started in hope that this machine also could be exhibited at the forthcoming Aero Show. For more immediate publicity Humphrey proposed that the 504 prototype should attempt to beat the solo British altitude record of 13,140 ft which Capt J. M. Salmond had set up on the 13 December at Upavon, flying the new BE2A. To test the possibility, Rayhnam took off with the 504 from Brooklands on 4 February, his Gnome engine tuned to perfection. Up and up he went in the cold winter sky, presently passed Salmond's record, and reached an indicated 15,000ft. Switching off, he came gliding down, steering for Hendon 20 miles away, and reached it with 5,000 ft in hand, so he continued his silent spiral and landed there 10 minutes later without using the engine again, thus adding to his laurels the longest glide anyone had made.

However, the attempt was not officially observed by the Royal Aero Club, so six days later he made a formal attack on the two-seater record, taking off from Brooklands with passenger and barograph, beat Hawker's record of 12,900 ft with similar load, and established a new British record of 14,420 ft. Consequently when the Olympia Aero Show, the fifth of its kind, opened on 16 March, considerable attention focused on the Stand of A. V. Roe Ltd, for the Avro team had worked miracles. There between a beautifully finished Avro 504 Seaplane and the impressive new pusher Type 508 reminiscent of an FE2, was the sensational Avro Scout 511 with unique I-strutted, swept single-bay wings, and the 80 hp Gnome daringly completely cowled in a bulbous nose. Rectangular flaps on the lower wings inboard of the ailerons were ingeniously pivotted to present an aerodynamically balanced vertical surface as a drag brake, but though typical of Roe's pioneering, was not patented. A minor but important feature of all Avro aeroplanes on which he insisted, was fitment of safety belts. Few manufacturers followed suit, for there was extraordinary prejudice among pilots against being tied to their machines, yet there had been many fatalities through crews being flung from their aircraft, either through atmospheric turbulence in crashes.

The neatly signposted, large Avro Stand was managed by Humphrey Roe, assisted by some of the technical staff, with Alliott Roe himself in frequent attendance. However, Roy Chadwick could only visit for a limited time because of involvement with the Type 510 Seaplane, of which five had been ordered by the Admiralty straight from the drawing board, but with the nose revised to exchange the speculative 160 hp rotary Gnome for 150 hp Sunbeam water-cooled engine of proven reliability during flight trials in a Farman piloted by John Alcock.

Certainly the Aero Show was a great educational opportunity for Chadwick and every other aeronautical technician. Of the 25 British and foreign aircraft displayed, 16 were land aeroplanes comprising 10 biplanes equally divided between pushers and tractors, and six were monoplanes. Hydro-aeroplanes formed the balance of which three were flying boats, with the Sopwith 'Bat-boat' as the most practical. The others were twin-float seaplanes, though surprisingly Short Bros Ltd were not represented. Of them all, the Avro 504 was easily the most imposing and workmanlike. Before the Show ended, the *Daily Mail* purchased it for a summer publicity tour of coastal resorts, for which purpose the newspaper's name was emblazoned in big letters under the main plane and along the fuselage, but Alliott Roe at least got away with 'Avro Biplane' inscribed across the rudder. The first flight as a seaplane was made by Raynham at Paignton in time for the Easter holiday, and the subsequent tour was shared with George Lusted, backed by Harry Broadsmith as

Avro stand showing production 504 seaplane and swept-wing Arrowscout.

technician and manager during visits to Falmouth, Southport, and eventually Ireland.

Soon after the Show Roe interviewed several draughtsmen applicants and selected a brightly confident 22-year-old Yorkshireman named Roy Hardy Dobson who had a very practical outlook though was somewhat vague on scholastic attainments.

'Have you done considerable drawing?' asked Roe.

'Yes,' said the smart young man, failing to reveal he knew nothing of *mechanical* drawing.

'Right. I'll send you to Mr Parrott for further discussion.'

Fifty years later Sir Roy Dobson told me: 'I initially went under Chadwick as one of his draughtsmen, but did not stay long — six months in fact — and then was sent to the Test House on material evaluation. Though Roe was the inspirer, Chadwick was a very outstanding personality. I don't think "Chad" ever learnt much in the purely technical sense from A. V. He got the basis of this from his early training at British Westinghouse, followed by his own studies at Manchester School of Technology, and became quite a good mathematician. Parrott and Chadwick certainly led the whole team on the 500 series.

'The 504 was never the hit and miss affair that a lot of people make out, and I know this from the personal experience of being very

Waiting on the waste ground outside the Clifton Street factory prior to handing over to the Daily Mail.

closely mixed up with it. I think the actual drawings were done by Roy Chadwick, C. R. Taylor, Cliff Horrax, Norwood, and Pemberton. The "state of the art" in the DO was much more mathematical than aerodynamic, but Chadwick and Harry Rogerson had rapidly gathered much aerodynamic knowledge, and Rogerson became quite an authority on airscrews.' April held more excitements. There was the Schneider Trophy Contest at Monaco, with entries from France, Germany, Switzerland, the USA, and Great Britain — and it was Tommy Sopwith's special single-seat 100 hp Tabloid biplane seaplane flown by Roe's early pupil Howard Pixton which won at an average 87 mph.

The end of April also marked Roy Chadwick's 21st birthday, celebrated by a splendid party for friends and cousins at his parents' house during which his distinguished-looking 44-year-old father presented him with the key to the house, amid the applause of mother and sisters and a scowl of jealousy from 12-year-old brother Alan.

Sopwith Tabloid rival.

However, Roy was currently beset by the engine cooling problems of the arrow-winged Avro 511 which on its very first flight Raynham had to force-land on Southport Sands after taking off from Trafford Park. Matters improved after removing the bottom quadrant of the tight-fitting cowling, and the

Avro 511 Arrowscout. (G. Quick).

machine was then flown to Brooklands — but it was already clear that the swept-back wings had not given the great increase in speed which Roe had expected. Nevertheless it was as fast as the prototype Tabloid with similar engine, so Roe decided to enter it for the Aerial Derby scheduled for Saturday, 23 May. The event was regarded with great expectation because the Avro 'Arrowscout', victorious Tabloid, equivalent Martinsyde, and even smaller Bristol Scout would be racing against each other for the first time. However, wind and rain caused postponement, but Raynham made several demonstration runs to entertain the despondent spectators. Later that afternoon came appalling news that England's outstanding airman, Gustav Hamel, was missing, probably drowned, for he had last been seen just after mid-day taking off for Hendon from Hardelot in France, flying the new racing Morane-Saulnier which he had entered for the Aerial Derby. No trace of him was ever found.

As the Derby had been postponed for a fortnight Roe decided there was time to overcome the defects of his racer. What these were was not disclosed. Photographs show the machine flying past the Hendon hangars in what seems perfect trim, with elevators in neutral position; but if angled wings are slewed by yaw, what was later known as 'Dutch roll' undoubtedly would follow due to the unequal spans presented to the airflow. The contemporary state of aerodynamics could not explain such phenomena, so Roe's practical solution was to make direct comparison by replacing the sweep-back with conventional wings at right-angles to the fuselage. He also fitted a V-undercarriage of lower resistance, hoping to increase the speed. That all this could be accomplished in a mere ten days shows the devotion of draughtsmen and workmen, for the modified aeroplane was ready for tests on the evening before the race — and yet after all that effort came disaster. The undercarriage collapsed as Raynham began to taxi, and in nosing over, the propeller was smashed and the wings sufficiently damaged to make it impossible for the machine to be ready for the race next day. Nor did the Bristol or Martinsyde compete that 6th of June because visibility was so bad at Brooklands that they were not allowed to leave. Nevertheless, eleven of the 21 entrants were at the Hendon starting line, but thick mist turned the race into a grim farce, though the American W. L. Brock flew a brilliant course to win with his Morane-Saulnier.

*   *   *

June also revealed a flare-up of trouble in the uneasy Balkan countries when the Archduke Francis Ferdinand of Austria, nephew and heir of the Emperor Francis Joseph, was assassinated while visiting the Serbian town of Sarajevo. Reading the news next day, the British shrugged their shoulders. This was just another deplorable little affair in a remote country. Official sympathy over the royal bereavement was duly expressed by the British Government to the Austrian Court and then forgotten. The threat of civil war in Ireland seemed much more serious — though most people had no real anxiety about this or any other political problem. They were quite content with the daily round of work, weekend cricket, and the oncoming holidays — whilst for aviation enthusiasts there were thrilling exhibitions of looping-the-loop, and on 11 July the punters were betting on a great air race from London to Paris and back in which Brock again proved the winner.

But behind the carefree scene of quiet middle-class content there was increasing political and industrial concern over Germany. In the markets of the world she had become a challenge to British supremacy. There was her great armament factory of Krupps, the steel production, her powerful fleet, and her expanding ambition and national pride — yet there was nothing factual to justify alarmist talk. Certainly Alliott Roe had taken pride in selling to the Gota Wagonfabric a licence to construct Avro 503 seaplanes and he hoped this publicity would lead to more naval sales. To that end he and Humphrey proposed to enter a special big span Type 510 in the forthcoming Circuit of Britain seaplane race, scheduled for September.

Meanwhile at the end of June the naval wing of the RFC had become the autonomous Royal Naval Air Service, with Capt Murray Sueter as head of the Admiralty Air Department. Orders for seven 504s followed, and five for the incipient 510 were promised. The RFC, commanded by Col Frederick Sykes, was directly responsible to the War Office, and the last of its current batch of 504s had been tested on 2 June, during which Raynham 'looped-the-loop' for the first time.

Although a 70 ft span, twin-float design revision of the pusher Type 508 had recently been completed, it failed to interest the Navy, but ambitious plans followed for an aeroplane bigger than any hitherto built in Britain. Designated Type 509, it was a strikingly advanced, gun-carrying, twin-float fuselage seaplane of 80 ft span with wing-mounted twin 120 hp pusher engines. Not content with that, there was a design for a twin-engined bomber version of the 510 seaplane which was far ahead of its time. Roe's naval and military contacts had only to hint at a possible requirement and he would get Chadwick to prepare a design study of great practicality.

But now the spark of Sarajevo flickered into flame. On 23 July Austria presented an ultimatum to Serbia, accusing her of the murder of the Archduke and demanding satisfaction. Two days later Sir Edward Grey gravely reported Austria's rejection of Serbia's conciliatory reply. On the 28th Austria declared war on the Serbians. That meant Russia would be drawn into the conflict and involve France as her ally — whereupon Germany took immediate preventitive steps by aggressively marching its grey-clad troops into Luxembourg. Next day the traditionally expected flanking movement through Belgium began, despite a long-standing Treaty signed by the great European powers guaranteeing the neutrality of that country.

There were extra Sunday editions on August Holiday weekend, telling ominously of hordes of German troops pressing relentlessly on. The air of unease spread. Churchill, on vacation with his children at Cromer, instructed the Fleet not to disperse as

Another step forward. The prototype naval Avro 510 spanning 63 feet and powered by a 150 hp Sunbeam Nubian.

(J. M. Bruce).

they were still moored in position following July's Naval Review by the King.

On 3 August, Germany declared war on France. Next day the Prime Minister told the tense Commons that the British Government had telegraphed to the German Government for a categorical undertaking to respect Belgian neutrality, demanding an answer by mid-night that day. There was no reply. We were at war.

On that same Tuesday the 63 ft span Avro 510 seaplane was being erected at Calshot — but now there would be no race of that kind: instead a very different one ensued.

Chapter 3
Trial and Error

At the RNAS station on Calshot Spit, at the entrance of Southampton Water, there was teeming activity when Alliott Roe arrived on 5 August for the first flight of the new Avro seaplane, but after speculative discussion with Raynham on the impact of war he became completely absorbed with superintending the launching, and watching with eagle eye as his pilot taxied out, turned, and skimmed away airborne across the waters. Soon the Avro reappeared, flew exultantly past several times, and alighted with a skittering smoothness which indicated that the new design of floats, tapering abaft the step, was a great improvement on the pontoon type of the *Daily Mail* 504 waiting on the slipway.

That afternoon both machines were commandeered by the Admiralty. Two days later Raynham took off in the 504 seaplane for delivery to the RNAS, but when over land the touchy Monosoupapé Gnome cut, and with insufficient height to turn back to the water, he put down in a field, and the floats were torn off, and the machine damaged beyond repair.

On completion of the 510 seaplane tests Roe hurried to Manchester for a meeting with his anxious key staff. 'This war imposed on us by the Germans will bring tremendous demand for aeroplanes,' he told them with a faintly detectable satisfaction. 'Fortunately, these new premises of ours have been organised just in time, but undoubtedly we shall have to expand. To that end we are appointing Mr Parrott as Work's manager, Harry Broadsmith as his assistant, and Mr Chadwick will have entire charge of design procedures and engagement of staff — though I shall continue to direct design policy for whatever eventuates as War Office and Admiralty requirements.'

Chadwick's newly extended authority brought further salary increase to £250 a year, and as the £ sterling of those days had enormously greater purchasing power than today he felt a millionaire. Nevertheless throughout the next few weeks he deeply debated whether his real duty as a 21-year-old was to join the RFC, and his anxieties increased on learning that Humphrey Roe, as a Reserve officer, had been instructed by the War Office to report to his old Regiment at Wool, Dorset — though a few days later the order was cancelled.

Widespread public opinion held that 'the war would be over by Christmas' — but Field Marshal Lord Kitchener, the country's great soldier hero, had a very different conception, and on appointment as Minister of War immediately appealed for 100,000 men 'for four years, or duration of war'. Soon every hoarding depicted his resolute face and pointing finger arresting attention with the declaration: 'Your country needs YOU'. He expected his target to be achieved in six months: instead, 500,000 volunteered in the first month, and thousand upon thousand followed, among them Roy Chadwick's great friend and colleague Harold Rogerson.

'Though technical men are in short supply, I can't stop him if he wants to go,' said Alliott Roe in fatherly fashion to his disconsolate young head draughtsman, 'but I know that men like you on work of national importance are to be officially classed in a special category exempt from military service.'

The urgent task was to modify the Type 504 drawings in the light of production experience to ensure swiftest possible construction so that this aeroplane could be built in substantial numbers. Such things as the seating unit, comprising seat bearers, dual control shaft, rudder bars, heel rests and mounting beams were redesigned for

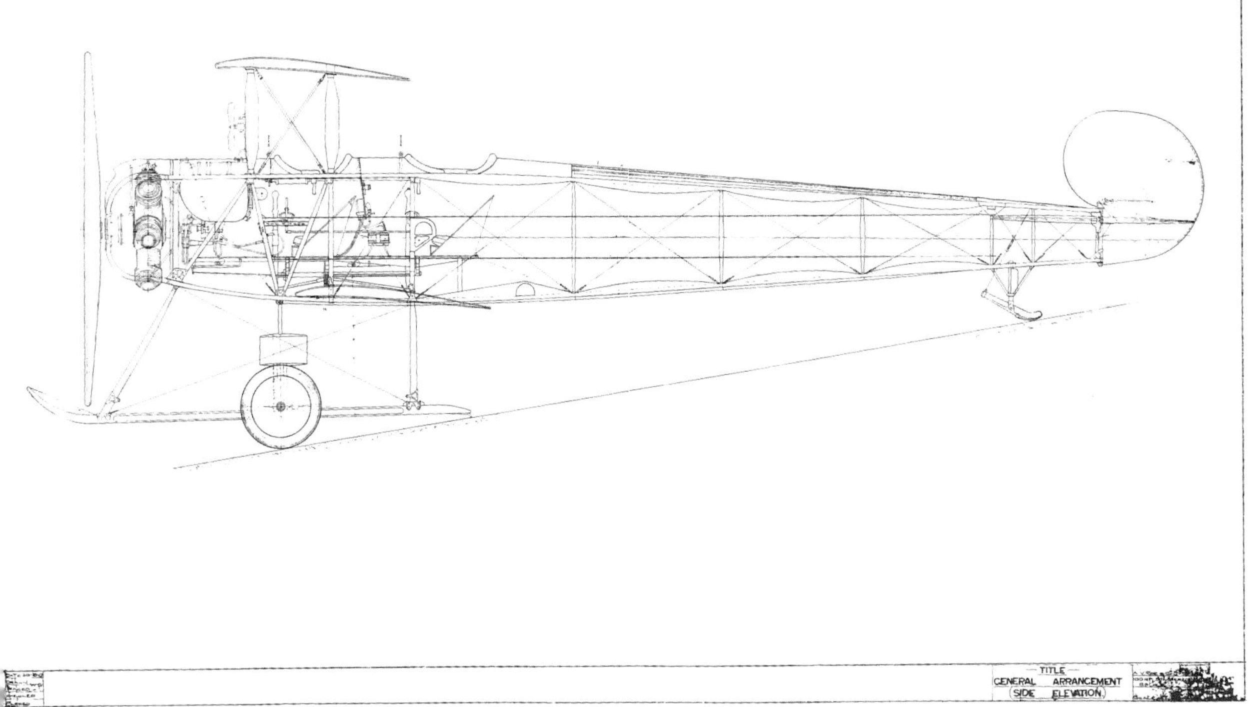

GA of 504 fuselage.

installation in the fuselage skeleton as a complete assembled unit, and of even greater benefit was standardisation of a single type of metal fitting for all the thirty-six fuselage spacer strut junctions and their multi bracing-wire lugs. The original individual composite sockets of aluminium and steel lugs had first been replaced by square section strut sockets of steel welded onto a steel baseplate which had angled projecting lugs; but now at Parrott's behest, Chadwick devised an ingenious steel plate strut connection located on the wiring lug plate by small integral lugs secured to the longerons with a slim diagonal bolt.

Said Parrott: 'Despite lack of provision for change of angle between the struts and longerons, the fitting proved highly satisfactory. Objections were completely outweighed by the advantage of using the same fitting throughout, thus avoiding a multiplicity of small components, all practically alike, and because it did not completely embrace the longeron, this fitting could be used on a tapered longeron and also enabled a longeron to be bodily removed without pulling the whole fuselage skeleton to pieces. As there was great difficulty in obtaining adequate deliveries of A.G.S. turnbuckles we adopted Mr Roe's simple wire tightening device of a tightening nut and pressed-steel yoke piece as used on his first aeroplane. There were 288 in each machine, including the wing bracing. Each wing utilised only five formed ribs which were also the drag struts. Stringers were threaded through these ribs parallel to the spars, and the remaining ribs formed in position merely by fastening strips of wood on the leading edge, spars, stringers, and trailing edge. This enabled swift production by relatively inexperienced men.'

Unfortunately, there was an immediate counter-problem to standardisation because the Military Aeronautic's Directorate and the Air Department of the Admiralty had their own independent technical sections and each made differing structural assessments of the 504's strength. Although the Farnborough scientists on behalf of the RFC accepted the 504 structure in its designed and proven form, the Admiralty mathematicians insisted on spars of greater cross-section. Despite Parrott's arguments for a standard wing to avoid complication of production and spares, neither Service would give way, so to avoid dangerous confusion the 504 was designated

A for the military version and B for the stiffened naval machines.

However, there was no immediate contract for more 504s. Instead, BE 2c construction was offered and indignantly rejected by Alliott Roe, who firmly believed that the 504 was superior and should have been adopted as the standard two-seater. He therefore initiated an anticipatory further batch but was sternly told by the War Office that production could only continue until definite instructions were issued for construction of BEs — though in fact they were never received. Two days after the arrival of the British Expeditionary Force in France on 16 August only a single BE 2c was available to fly there, though preceeded on 13 August by No. 5 Squadron which had several gunless 504s, one of which was the first aeroplane to be shot down by the Germans. All that could be mustered as first-line strength at the beginning of the war were 63 aeroplanes for the RFC and a mixed bag of 50 landplanes and seaplanes for the Royal Navy.

Certainly 2nd Lieut Louis Strange, a wealthy young pre-war pilot, saw possibilities of the aeroplane as a fighting machine, and in mid October induced his C. O. Capt L. de C. Penn-Gaskel, to let him mount a Lewis gun on an Avro 504K. 'The mounting consisted of a metal tube, which I carefully selected from the tail boom of a wrecked Henri Farman,' he recorded. 'The gun lay on the fuselage deck, and a piece of rope, lashed around its c.g., went from the cross-member forming the front seat petrol tank bearer to the metal tube, and a pulley enabled the observer to sling the gun to mid-air, with the stock on his shoulder, and fire all round as well as back over the pilot's head.'

A week later, Strange and Penn-Gaskel when flying this machine, spotted a train and enemy troops in Perenchies siding. Diving down, they made the first ground straffing attack of the war, and on 22 November, Strange, with Lieut F. G. Small as gunner, forced down an Albatross two-seater near Neuve-Église.

Concurrently four top-secret special Avro 504s under assembly at Manchester were being fitted with tanks of more than doubled capacity to give an operational duration of 4½ hours, and racks under the fuselage were devised by Roe to carry four individually releasable 20lb incendiary or high explosive bombs for a surprise attack on the Zeppelin sheds at Friedrichshaven on Lake Constance, 1300 ft high on the northern foothills of the Alps between Switzerland and Austria. The aircraft would be crated for shipment to Le Havre, then freighted by train across France to save wear and tear on the new engines. Roy Chadwick was delegated to go with them to ensure that the untried bomb mechanisms operated correctly. The thought of seeing France and participating more directly in the war thrilled him.

He arrived with the dismantled aircraft at Belfort, 40 miles from Basle on the Swiss border by train on 13 November

Naval 504E showing fin, heavier struts, bigger elevators, longer ailerons, and reduced stagger.

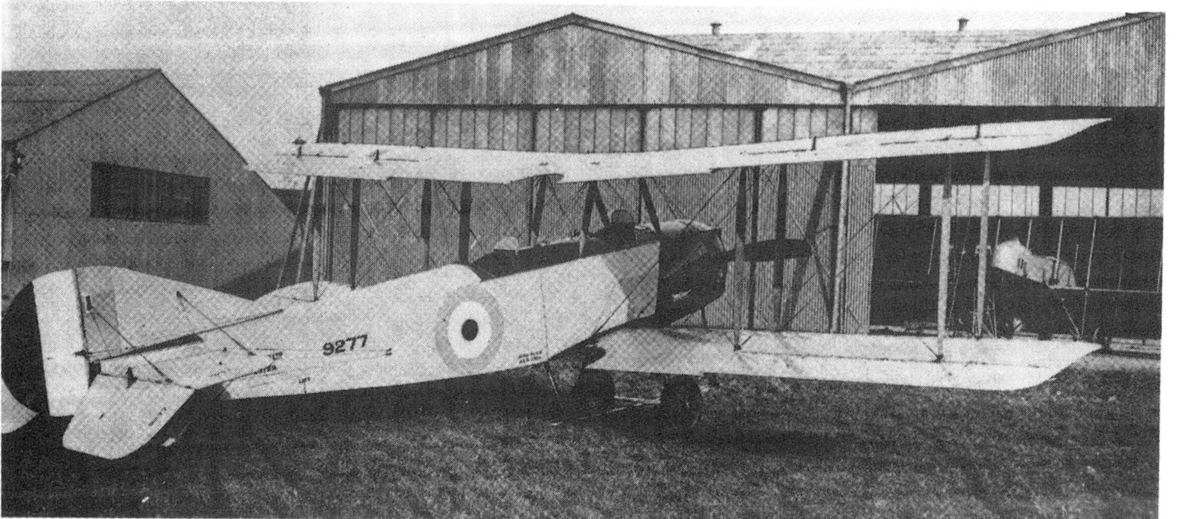

Friedrichshaven line-up. (J. M. Bruce).

accompanied by Sq Cdr Shepherd as C.O., Sqn Cdr Briggs, Flt. Cdr. Babington, Flt. Lieut. Sippe .who had been one of Roe's pupils, Flt. Sub-Lieut Cannon, and a contingent of mechanics who swiftly erected the aeroplanes. Weather proved bad, but on Saturday morning, 21 November, improved sufficiently for the attempt to be made, and Chadwick anxiously watched the four pilots take off at five minute intervals for the 100 mile flight to the Zeppelin base and back — though Cannon's machine failed to get airborne because the tail-skid broke.

'It was a very rough ride, but the Avros were splendid,' Air Marshal Sir John Tremayne, KCB, DSO (formerly Babington) told me in later years. 'Briggs was shot down, crashed, and became prisoner but later escaped. I made the next run, followed by Sippe, and between us we managed to hit one of the sheds, damaging a Zepp inside, and also destroyed their hydrogen plant. It was all very exciting while it lasted, and the Germans were greatly astonished that we could reach such a faraway object — but you can't do much with a 20lb bomb.'

Major Sydney Sippe, OBE, DSO, FRAEs was equally modest when we corresponded in 1960. 'Yes — I remember that the last of my four bombs failed to go off . . . Dear, gentle little A. V. Roe,' he meditatively said.

* * *

In France matters were going badly for the Allies. The Germans had crossed the River Marne on 5 September, and their eastern flank was within 40 miles of Paris. The French Government fled to Bordeaux. In mid-October the Germans moved towards Ypres to outflank the French, and the British army was shattered on encountering the enemy guns. Everyone began to realize that the war was likely to be long, for the front line extended from the North Sea to Switzerland, and both sides were 'digging in' with an intricate system of trenches.

At all aircraft factories the process of employee recruitment and training was steadily progressing. As foster parent the Government-sponsored Aircraft Inspection Department (AID) was similarly extended to ensure that the highest standards of materials and workmanship would be maintained. But the engine position was crucial. In the first two months of war only 27 engines were produced. However, A. V. Roe & Co Ltd had obtained sufficient 80 hp Gnome engines to deliver eight 504Bs to No. 1 Squadron of the RNAS by mid-December. On the assumption that more would soon be available the War Office issued a contract for fifty 504As.

Meanwhile Roy Chadwick had returned elated by his experiences, and was busy not only with 504 modifications but re-organising his extended drawing office and doodling preliminary design studies to discuss with Alliott Roe. The streets of Manchester these days often echoed to the thud of the hobnailed boots of khaki-clad volunteers on training marches; but there were fewer waggons and carts because so many great horses had been commandeered. News continued to be disheartening, and on 16 December, despite ceaseless vigil by the British Grand Fleet in the North Sea, the German Navy bombarded Hartlepool, Scarborough, and Whitby. On Christmas Eve few gave thought to the sound of an aeroplane flying low over the sullen English Channel. A few moments later it flew over Dover, and there came an echoing explosion. It had happened. A bomb had been dropped for the first time on England.

A subdued Christmas followed. On New Year's Day 1915 the *Daily Mail* editorial solemnly predicted: 'A year opens today that will decide, or go a long way to deciding, the destiny of Europe for many decades to come.'

Five months of tremendous endeavour and recruitment in the aircraft industry had resulted in less than 200 landplanes and 50 seaplanes — but 60 were merely experimental. The need for more aircraft had become obvious. Supplementing production of the fifty Avro 504s for the RFC came a similar Admiralty contract for 504Bs. Concurrently, Roe and Chadwick were scheming an 80 hp Gnome-powered monoplane which probably incorporated the Vickers-Challenger mechanical 'propeller bullet deflector', for Alliott Roe was a keen scrutineer of patent specifications and this had been issued on 11 December. However, the resulting Avro 516 design was never built, possibly because the deflector gear had not yet proved reliable. Instead, they turned to a biplane equivalent that may have been a resurrection of the arrow-winged Avro 511.

By now production facilities had enormously improved because the Government had commandeered for Avro use the unoccupied large south-eastern extension of the Mather and Platt factory at Newton Heath which had been the subject of Humphrey Roe's negotiations for some months and was now renamed Park Works. Roy Chadwick's major concentration was on the naval 504s because the Admiralty now required them with a fixed fin which eliminated the original distinctive balance portion of the rudder, and to give improved piloting view the top longeron each side of the rear cockpit was daringly sawn through and a reinforced open segment inserted to lower the opening. Each lower wing-root trailing edge was cut away in an arc to improve the downward visual angle, and a large

Avro staff and workmen with Alliott Roe 6th from left, front A. V. Roe, with Humphrey Roe, his secretary, Roy Chadwick, Reg Parrott.

cylindrical fuel tank giving an endurance of six hours was installed in the covered-in front cockpit. Designated 504C it became an anti-Zeppelin single-seat fighter armed with incendiary bombs and an upward angled Lewis gun firing over the centre-section. As both the Avro factories were now at full scope, the Brush Electric Co undertook initial production.

Six of the assembly line for the RFC were converted to single-seaters with bomb racks, and in the cold pre-dawn of 3.30 am on 17 May, Sub-Lieut Mulock, flying one of these aircraft from Westgate RNAS station, managed to intercept Zeppelin LZ 38, but it climbed away so rapidly that he was unable to attack with his two hand grenades and two incendiary bombs. However, that same night Flt Cdr Biggsworth, piloting a similar Avro, spotted the Zeppelin's sister ship LZ 39 and pursued it on a long, slanting climb, managing to surmount it at 10,000 ft above Ostend and attacked with four 20 lb bombs; yet though smoke streamed from the airship's stern, it was not destroyed but in crippled condition made a rough landing at Evére in Belgium.

That same month destiny opened a new chapter for Roy Chadwick. One by one over the past few years a succession of adoring young girls had been introduced to the Chadwick household. Roy preferred blondes, particularly if well-educated and shapely, but by no means was dedicated. However when visiting the Rogerson's house to enquire if there was news of Harold in the army, he met a fair-haired 17-year-old girl, Mary Gomersall, who was quietly thrilled to meet this tall and handsome, polite young man.

'I'm told that you are an aeroplane designer,' she said with awe.

'What a wonderful thing to do. You must be very clever.'

Roy smiled deprecatingly. 'Well it's not exactly that. You see Mr Roe, the pioneer aircraft inventor, is in charge and several of us combine to design the type of aeroplane he wants. My job is to co-ordinate everyone's work and ensure that the drawings are correct for issue in the right sequence to Mr Parrott who is in charge of construction.'

'Do you fly them too? she asked.

'Well, not exactly — but sometimes I go up with our Mr Raynham when he tests them, and he lets me try the controls.'

'How wonderful,' she said.

Roy was quite overcome by her charm and submissive manner, but never discovered that among the earnest precepts of truth and kindliness which Mrs Gomersall had instilled in her young daughter was the advice: 'Listen to everything that people have to say, and then do exactly what *you* want.'

In the background there was the inescapable sense of war rumbling beyond the English Channel. On 2 May there had been horrifying news that the great liner *Lusitania* had been torpedoed and sunk by a German U-boat off south Ireland — and that led to agitation in the USA for America, in the cause of humanity, to enter the war. In France, continuous bombardment had made the battle-front a sea of mud and there had been desperate fighting over the Ypres salient with enormous losses on both sides. In the new war zone of Gallipoli there had been initial success by British and ANZAC troops, but on 26 May HMS *Goliath* was torpedoed in the Dardanelles and a fortnight later HMS *Triumph* suffered the same fate. However the

22-year-old Roy Chadwick.

sombre national mood lifted a little on 7 June when a Zeppelin at 6,000 ft above Belgium was destroyed by Sub-Lieut Warneford flying a BE 2c.

Of this period 21-year-old J. W. 'Jock' Ratcliffe later recorded: 'Because of their increased design requirements, A. V. Roe & Co Ltd were advertising in the *Manchester Guardian* for draughtsmen. As I had just left the Municipal School of Technology in Manchester, where I had a Bolton Scholarship, I applied, and was engaged by Mr Roy Chadwick at a salary of 45s per week, starting work on 14 June at their Clifton Street works in a back street of Newton Heath, Manchester. My letter of engagement, dated 1st June 1915, was signed by the managing director, Mr H. V. Roe, who was responsible for the clerical and financial side of the business. Mr John Lord, who had operated the 'Bullseye bracer' business for him, became his assistant. Mr A. V. Roe, as chief engineer, had a small office near the D.O. There were 10 or 12 draughtsmen in the drawing office, each responsible for his own detailed stress work. Chadwick virtually carried out the functions of chief draughtsman, chief stressman and chief aerodynamisist, but he had a very capable assistant in Mr F. W. Vernon, a Whitworth Scholar, who carried out the main stress work on wings, and I think was the first at A. V. Roe's to base these on the Theorem of Three Moments with adjustment for bracing wire offsets. Production was controlled by Mr. R. J. Parrott, the works manager, who was a good all-round engineer, and had been chief draughtsman at the original works at Brownsfield Mills where Chadwick was originally his assistant, though H. E. Broadsmith now occupied that position and was building up facilities for extended production.'

The Avro technicians were continuing the theme of the big Avro 510 Circuit seaplane, leading to design in September 1914 of Type 515 with 150 hp water-cooled Sunbeam, and now revised as a single-seat, folding wing, landplane bomber, Type 519. Typical of Alliott Roe's inventiveness was the jacking system of the adjustable tailplane which added Patent 100,875 to his many other inventions.

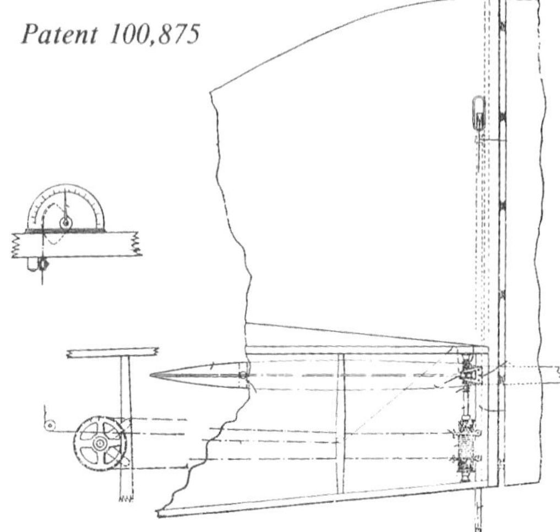
Patent 100,875

Two of these big biplanes were ordered by the Navy in August after a number of visits to London by Roy Chadwick for technical and operational discussions with the Admiralty Air Department headed by that erratic genius Harrie Booth — whose technical assistant Clifford Tinson had been Barnwell's stressman at Bristol and would later come more prominently to Chadwick's notice.

The RFC followed with a contract for two 519A, two-seater versions which had a Vee undercarriage eliminating the 504 type central skid of the naval prototype. A month later the RFC technicians decided to change the power plant to the 225 hp Sunbeam.

By now the Fokker monoplane was making its mark on the Western Front because of vicious ability to attack nose-on, using a mechanical gear to fire through the propeller disc without hitting the blades. The BEs were easy victims, so it became essential for the RFC to have two-seaters with synchronised forward-firing guns as well as a rotatable rear cockpit gun. Roe had seen Harry Hawker flying an experimental Sopwith single-seater and discovered that it was being re-designed as a 33 ft span, two-seater fighter powered with the newly introduced 110 hp Clerget rotary engine. Could a modified 504 be used for the same purpose? Drawings were speedily prepared for a Clerget variant having long tail fin, Vee undercarriage, pilot in front cockpit, and Scarff gun-ring for the rear. In turn that was developed by Chadwick into an aerodynamically cleaner single-bay Type 521 version of 30 ft span, for which the RFC placed orders for 26 as a safeguard in case the similar new Sopwith 1½ strutter proved unsatisfactory.

* * *

In Great Britain the reality of war was being emphasised by increasing Zeppelin raids. To Alliott Roe, Manchester seemed particularly vulnerable because of its many factory targets, such as British Westinghouse — now independent of American capital and vital to the war effort as employment in the area. There were the docks and the crowded shipping to which the airships could be guided on moonlight nights by the glitter of the Manchester Ship Canal — and, who knows, a bomb might fall in the vicinity of Newton Heath and destroy the Avro factory!

In describing those days, Roe wrote: 'I did not like the position of having our Works in Manchester, so I conceived the idea of establishing a modern new works and a Garden City of our own for our employees somewhere on the south coast of England where we could build aeroplanes or flying boats, or both, according to demand, and our employees could breathe God's fresh air. My wife and I motored round the Southampton district, and on finding a very large field at Hamble on the banks of Southampton Water, I said "This is our spot." I wired for Humphrey to come down and see it. Within a fortnight we had bought the field and a mile of foreshore, well over 100 acres in all, and subsequently aquired a further 200 acres.'

Construction of a large and distinguished factory building was immediately put in hand on a site between the Southampton Water foreshore and Hamble Village. Meanwhile Manchester production continued to expand, so a building in Heath Street at Newton Heath and the Empire Works at Failsworth were taken over. J. B. Scott-Wilson recorded that: 'In both factories a major part of the work-force were female metal workers, called lady fitters. Completed aircraft at the main Newton Heath factory were assembled and engine tested, then the wings and tail were removed and with a man sitting inside the cockpit the plane was towed to London Road Station and transported by rail to the appropriate Aircraft Reception Park. Few Avro Aircraft were flown in the Manchester area, though limited use was made of a shed at Trafford Park airfield and occasionally some were flown from a small playing field alongside the Works at Newton Heath.'

By now it was very clear that Roy Chadwick, though regarded by Service and government officials as a mere stripling, had a genius for aircraft design. Roe would decide the type of aeroplane on which they would gamble as the result of advice from his contacts with Murray Sueter and Farnborough, and would chair technical discussions with Parrott as general manager and Chadwick backed by his team comprising C. R. Taylor as chief technician and Frank Vernon the chief stressman; but it was Chadwick who was primarily responsible for the design details. He and his score or so of technicians and draughtsmen were extremely busy because an Admiralty contract had been confirmed in September for a big twin-engined anti-Zeppelin fighter for which Roe schemed a 1½ lb shell-firing Coventry-Ordnance gun installation, rotatably mounted in the nose-cockpit.

Jock Ratcliffe recorded in later years: 'I still possess some of my early stress work dated December 1915, fixing the sizes of the tailplane spars and other parts of the empennage of this first Avro twin-engined three-seater fighter Type 523 which was named 'Pike' typifying its bite.'

Construction became an urgent priority and proceeded with remarkable rapidity despite competing demands requiring the second RFC Avro 519 single-engined bomber, redesignated Type 522, to be built with equal span wings and the cubical radiator on top of the nose replaced by side radiators. Chadwick was also dealing with a sequence of 504 variants requiring considerable design work, of which the 504E powered with a 100 hp Monosoupapé Gnome was the latest, characterised by a tail fin and reduced stagger to compensate for further aft pilot location; but there was also a 504 powered with a 150 hp Sunbeam under test at Farnborough and sufficently different to be designated Type 527.

Meanwhile the neat two-seater, single-bay Avro 521 had been erected under Broadsmith's supervision in the Avro hangar at Trafford Park and towards the end of the year was flown by Raynham. To Roy Chadwick's chagrin he reported that it lacked the pleasant flying characteristics of the 504 from which it was derived yet it was geometrically similar to the successful Sopwith 1½ strutter. The deterioration seemed inexplicable, but was undoubtedly due to greater wing loading than the 504 coupled with a very wide, blunt cutaway at wing roots and centre section as the price of good upward-firing angle from the rear cockpit and rearward upper view for the pilot now seated forward under the centre-section.

In hope of improvement, Chadwick immediately began design of alternative wings of 36 ft and 46 ft span, but first the machine would have to go to Farnborough's famous 'two black sheds' of the Testing Flight for RFC handling, performance, and gunnery trials.

* * *

The opening prospects of 1916 were not encouraging. Military affairs in France had gone so badly that Sir John French had resigned the British command and Sir Douglas Haig succeeded him. On 5 January Mr Asquith, the Prime Minister, introduced a Bill for compulsory military service to sustain a war costing £5 million a day which had resulted not only in stalemate but evacuation of all troops from Gallipoli. The need for more munitions, more ships, more aircraft had vastly increased.

Early in January the Avro offices, including the drawing office, were transferred

Avro 521 single bay fighter.

Rival Sopwith $1\frac{1}{2}$ strutter.

from Clifton Street to the new Park Works, and recruitment of draughtsmen intensified — all of whom had to be tutored in the exacting demands of aircraft design by Chadwick and his key men. Structures had not basically changed since the days of Roe's triplanes and the value of practical experience remained paramount, but science was now playing a much greater part. A wealth of information was pouring from the researchers at the Royal Aircraft Factory presided over by the forceful, scintillating Mervyn O'Gorman. Their reports, known as R & Ms, required much study by Chadwick to keep up-dated and led to long hours of work on returning home each evening. No wonder there were occasional outbursts of anger when interrupted, yet despite worries, his sense of humour still sparkled.

On 20 January the Avro 521 two-seater fighter was 'booked in' at Farnborough as 'Avro Scout 1811', and in due course flown to the recently established test section of the Central Flying School (CFS) at Upavon, Wiltshire, with the warning that 'this machine plunges its nose viciously towards the ground in a right hand turn'. That was typical of testing in those early days. A machine was either good or bad.

Roe's early Brookland's pupil, the now notorious Capt Gordon Bell, was one of the pilots. 'V-v-vicious is it?' he exclaimed to the reporting civilian technician. 'J-j-just h-h-hop in and we'll soon see.'

There were also looming problems with the four 'big Avros', of which the first naval single-seater Type 519 was under test at Eastchurch, but its 150 hp Sunbeam was proving too low-powered to give reasonable climb despite the long-span wings. The prototype RFC two-seater, which had seventy-five more horse-power, was only marginally better and still inadequate for a long-range bomber — so Roe and Chadwick were pinning their faith on the derivative Avro 522 which was being assembled at Hamble with equal span wings.

Concurrently the second naval machine was flying, differing from the first in having a similar cubical radiator to that of the RFC's prototype 519. However the naval pilots were showing preference for the rival Short Bomber, which initially had the familiar Short 184 fuselage fitted with two-bay wings having long overhangs like the Avro — but these similarly had proved deficient in lift, so an additional bay had been added giving an enormous span of 85 ft which enabled a substantial load to be carried, and resulted in a production contract.

Not to be outdone, the Avro team in July initiated a major design revision of their Admiralty bomber as Type 528 with long overhangs extending the three-bay wings to 68 ft span; but though construction started immediately at Manchester, the possibility of series production was minimal because the Newton Heath factories were fully engaged in building increasing numbers of 504s.

By now there was sufficient hangarage at Hamble to establish all flight trials at this new aerodrome, so the components of the twin-engined COW-gun Pike had been sent there in May for assembly. Although famed as a delightful yachting centre, Hamble in those days already had an aeronautical content, for Charles Fairey, who was keen on sailing, had recently expanded his small Works on the banks of the River Hamble at the other side of the narrow peninsula. There, Sydney Pickles, a well known Hendon pre-war pilot, was testing the Fairey Campainia seaplane of almost identical size and arrangement as the Avro 510 of which six were established at nearby Calshot. A boat builder's shed and slipway at Hamble used for Short seaplanes built by Westland at Yeovil was also adding to the activity.

All this led to heavy pressure on local accommodation and although Alliott Roe had built 24 houses for approved employees, most of the men had to find accommodation at the near-by villages of Hound or Bursledon two miles away, or across the Hamble Ferry to Great Brook or Warsash. Early every morning a great stream of cloth-capped cyclists converged on the Fairey Works on one side and Avro on the other.

'The Hamble organisation was under the control of Mr R. J. Parrott, who had moved south before the general transfer for experimental work, leaving Mr H. E. Broadsmith in charge of the Manchester Works,' recollected Chadwick's leading draughtsman, Jock Ratcliffe. 'Mr F. G. Clifton was aerodrome superintendent, responsible for aircraft undergoing trials, and as the factory expanded, Mr Chick became Works superintendent and Mr H. Denny was in charge of the inspection department (AID). Later Mr Roe's brother the Revd Everard Verdon Roe joined as assistant manager.

'It was at Hamble that I first met Mr Roy Dobson, who was the flight mechanic looking after the new types undergoing flight trials at various aerodromes, and latterly those based at Hamble including the prototype pusher-engined Pike which, on its first flight with Raynham piloting from the mid-cockpit, necessitated Roy Dobson crawling from rear cockpit to front, along the decking between the rotating propellers — a very daring operation. That was necessary to correct the c.g., which was too far aft, so Raynham had been forced to hold the control column fully forward, but now was just able to turn the aircraft and land safely. Roy Dobson thus saved a disaster.

'Soon after this, Dobson was caught and chastised by Parrott for assembling, in his spare time, a Ford car in one of the sheds left behind by the builders of the new Hamble works. Consequently, he left Hamble and persuaded Mr John Lord to give him a job at the Manchester factory. It was not long before

The peaceful wartime Hamble scene opposite Warsash, with Short seaplane on slip.

The new Hamble Factory.

he became assistant manager, and eventually Works manager, and with his great ability and untiring energy, eventually rose to a great position in the aircraft industry.'

These had been busy days at Hamble. The new main building was now complete and included a handsome watch-tower, giving views of Southampton Water and a glimpse of the Isle of Wight looming on the horizon. Raynham had finished extensive testing of the 519 and 522 versions of the big single-engined 'Class 4 Bomb Carrying Aeroplane' and they were now at Farnborough. Meanwhile the trend-setting Pike was his first experience of multi-engines, which he dryly described as 'giving twice the chance of engine failure'.

Flight testing at Hamble necessitated increasingly numerous visits by Roy Chadwick to discuss problems of engine and aircraft with Raynham, and whenever possible, instead of using time-consuming trains, the journey was made in a 504 flying dual with one or other of the Service pilots attached to the Manchester Works. These were pleasant escapes, for the pressure of work in the DO was unrelenting. Since commencing design of the Avro 519 bomber in September, 1914, there had been 10 major projects as well as six versions of the ubiquitous Avro 504 which he was currently proposing as a two-seat fighter trainer with synchronised forward-firing Vickers gun and Scarff gun-ring on the rear cockpit; but his imagination also led to many doodles of possible fighters, seaplanes, or bombers, which he might sometimes show to Alliott Roe, who would scrutinise them with interest, then affectionately pat Roy's shoulder and say: 'That's the way. Keep thinking up the bright ideas — but I'm afraid we've got enough on our plate at the moment.'

In fact work was so time-consuming that young Chadwick had all too rare an opportunity to visit Mary Gomersall; but from time to time at weekends they whirled away on his noisy motor-bike for an hour or two in the quiet countryside, her fair hair streaming while riding pillion — a daring activity for a young lady in those days. They were now secretly engaged, but neither the uncertainties of war nor Roy's financial circumstance promised a sufficiently assured future for her father to give consent for the marriage of his teenage daughter.

Always the echo of war resounded. At the end of May there had been a great naval battle off Jutland, which ended in both sides claiming victory. The Germans were said to have lost 18 vessels, including two battleships and two battle cruisers, but the British fleet

Interior with 504s under construction. (P. J. Capon).

had received an equally tremendous blow by losing six cruisers and eight destroyers. However the German fleet did not venture out again.

Adding to British problems was Ireland, where the Sinn Fein had risen in revolt — but on 6 June angry contention over Irish loyalty and dismaying rumours about Jutland vanished before the appalling news that Lord Kitchener, on whom most people believed the destiny of Britain rested, had been drowned when his ship, the *Hampshire*, was torpedoed off the Orkneys at the beginning of a voyage to Russia to stiffen resistance against the Germans.

In France, a great new offensive on the Somme was beginning, and would rage for the next six months, during which 420,000 British soldiers died, and as many again were wounded or incapacitated by German use of chlorine gas — among them Harold Rogerson's brother, Charles, who was permanently blinded.

Roy Chadwick's current task was completion of the extensively redesigned single-engined Avro 522 bomber as Type 528, with the same basic fuselage and the new three-bay wings fitted with a nacelle-like bomb container on each lower wing between inboard struts and fuselage. Assembled with the usual Avro speed, this prototype was ready for testing in September — after which it vanished from the pages of recorded history.

No less urgent was revision of the twin-engined Type 523 Pike 'Fighting Biplane', the second of which, designated 523A with twin 150 hp Green engines installed more efficiently as tractors, was flown in August and had similar speed and climb to the equivalent DH 3A. However, the RFC saw no immediate operational use for twin-engined machines and abandoned a potential contract for the De Havilland, but the Admiralty continued their interest in the Avro as a possible back-up to the 100 ft span, twin-engined Handley Page 0/100 bombers. Chadwick was therefore engrossed with a derivative Avro 529 which had wings of longer span and wider chord, though the same aspect-ratio as the 523. A 150 gallon fuel tank in the fuselage gave greater range, yet despite the resistance the two tractor 190 hp Rolls-Royce Falcons were again mounted like the Pike's engines midway up the inboard wing-gap, completely uncowled for easy maintenance. To improve directional problems with one engine cut, a smaller triangular tail fin had been substituted and to reduce asymmetric footload the rudder was given an Avro 504 type unshielded forward balance. However this new machine would not be ready until Spring of the following year.

Concurrently, all hope of putting the small Avro 521 into production disappeared when it crashed on 21 September at the Central Flying School, killing its pilot, Lt Garnett — and at that, the batch of 25 under construction were converted to Avro 504Es. Maybe this defeat triggered Roe's decision to make a further attempt at a two-seater fighter, and on learning that a new and more powerful French engine, the 200 hp water-cooled Hispano Suiza, would soon be available, he sanctioned Chadwick to begin design of a two-seat, 36 ft span reconnaissance aeroplane, designated Type 530, intended to surpass the Bristol Fighter which had been built in a bare three months, and powered by a 290 hp Rolls-Royce Falcon had flown in September. Not surprisingly his initial design study had superficial likeness to this machine but instead of a relatively slim fuselage in mid-gap position, the Avro Type 530 had a very deep body resting on the lower wings and from the high cockpit there was eye-level view over the centre section.

That Alliott Roe was still closely concerned with design is indicated by his Patent 126,350, which was validated on 2 January, 1917 and described the ingenious cable control mechanism which he applied to this fighter, whereby 'the whole of the trailing edge of the main planes are adapted to be tilted up or down to vary the camber of the planes, the outer portions of the trailing edges being also adapted to be moved in opposite directions to preserve the lateral balance of the aircraft.' In the following week, Patent 126,365 by Roe appeared with a drawing showing the front portion of the Type 530, and stated 'the space between the top of the body and the plane of an aeroplane is filled in by a turret-like

Line up of Pike 523, Green-engined 523A and enlarged Type 529 with Rolls-Royce Falcon.

structure of steamline form to which the wings are secured. The pilot's cockpit is arranged at the rear of the turret, which is cut away to provide new openings and provides housing for one or more guns firing through the propeller disc. The height of the body enables the rear gun, operated from the gunpit behing the pilot, to be raised clear of the top plane.'

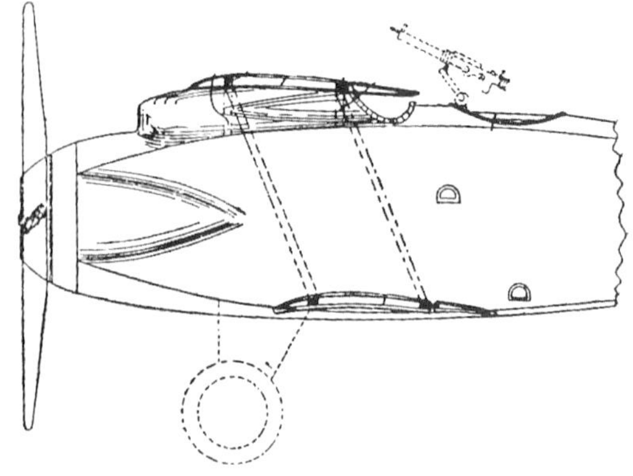

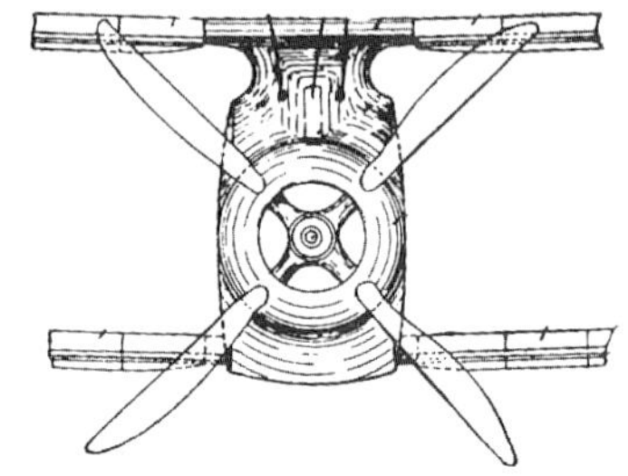

Patent 126,365

Cliff Horrax commented: 'I am not sure if A. V. sketched out the Pike and 530 fighter, but along with Parrott and Chadwick he certainly had influence on the designs, and as soon as a project was under weigh he made changes and detailed modifications. A. V. had a very active mind, so when looking at a drawing that one was making, his interest would waver if it had no bearing on his thoughts at that particular moment, and one realised he was thinking of something quite different, oblivious of his surroundings.'

Patent 126,350

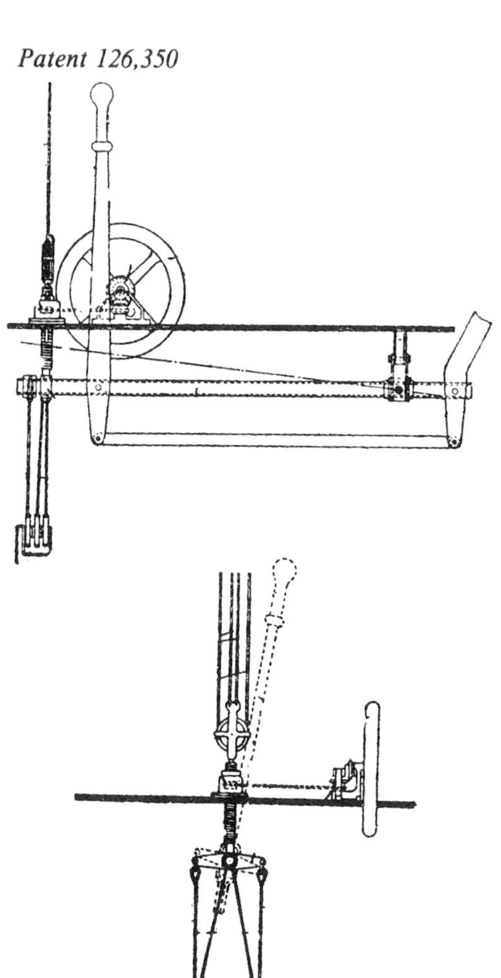

In effect, the conception of every new type was a joint affair in which Roe and Parrott, and occasionally Broadsmith, participated, and the actual execution of the design was the responsibility of Roy Chadwick and his early chief draughtsman Ratcliffe who affirmed: 'Chadwick was the master-mind behind most, if not all, design work during World War I, particularly the latter half, and as Frank Vernon had left to join the Admiralty Torpedo Establishment at Portsmouth, he and I did all the stress calculations and performance work, including flight testing evaluation.' Meantime Chadwick's 'mods' section was busy with a cleaned-up variant of the ubiquitous 504 as a Naval machine with strengthened pick-up points for catapult launching and an arrester hook. Designated 504H, it was sent towards the end of the year for trials on a dummy deck supervised by that famous pre-war Bristol pilot Harry Busteed, currently Sqn Cdr RNAS.

Chapter 4
Turn of the Tide

On 9 January 1917 the Coalition Government instituted a new and expanded Air Board for the express purpose of supervising design, construction and production of aeroplanes, engines, armament, and material, and would co-ordinate output to avoid competition between the Navy and the RFC.

'In the following month', wrote Jock Ratcliffe,' the drawing office staff, by this time increased to about 40, was moved from Manchester to the new Works at Hamble, where the experimental aircraft were being tested.' Here a splendid well-lit drawing office had been added to the management quarters on the northern side of the main building, and Chadwick — who had taken lodgings at the village of Brooklands near Bursledon — was coping not only with the disruption of moving, but with the design of the Type 530 two-seater and revising the basic 504A as the dual control 504J. Affectionately known as the 'Mono Avro', it became the delight of every pilot because of its pleasant handling characteristics and notably improved performance.

The rival BEs were long obsolete, but the Avro 504J opened new vistas of still greater production, for it was soon to become the country's universal *ab initio* training machine — and that was revolutionary because until now pupils had been trained on easy-going, crudely responsive, Farman-type biplanes before graduating to Service aircraft.

Behind the new technique was Major Robert Smith-Barry, a brilliant character who had joined the RFC in 1912 and was severely injured when he crashed in France at the beginning of the war, but with grim determination, despite a crippled leg, insisted on continuing in active service as commander of a 'Scout' Squadron.

The Drawing Office at Hamble.

Avro J trainer.

Appalled by extensive casualties among half-trained pilots sent to the Western Front, he wrote flagrantly to Major-General Trenchard, the G.O.C. of the RFC in France; 'No attention whatever has been paid to the fundamental importance of instruction in the mere manual part of flying. The writer has been surprised to find how little interest in flying is taken by many young pilots who come out to the Front. They have to be ordered to go up from the very first; they never ask permission to fly even for a practice flight. Before the war young fliers were begging to be allowed up. This is largely due to the mental supineness of instructors in England whose attitude towards flying is reflected in all the pilots they turn out.

'It is submitted that a good way to remedy this would be a School of Training for instructors, where they could (a) have their flying brought to the very high standards necessary before they can teach with confidence and ease; (b) be combed out if they do not speedily reach this standard; (c) be given definite lines upon which to instruct. The institution of such a school would produce an *esprit de corps* among the instructors and improve the atmosphere surrounding the whole business of instruction.'

Largely as a result of this letter Major-General John Salmond was posted from France to England to organise a pilot training Scheme. Coincidentally he had been Smith-Barry's instructor at CFS before the war and, knowing his pupil's reputation, appointed him to command No. 1 Reserve Squadron at Gosport on the South Coast. The new CO's first move was to get rid of all obsolete aircraft and standardise the Avro 504J from the start. Hundred upon hundred were ordered. As described by John Taylor in *C.F.S.*: 'Smith-Barry knew what he was doing. He wanted a trainer that would teach pupils to fly combat aeroplanes, and the 504J had every qualification. Its controls were light and powerful, it could perform all known aerobatics, and its engine taught pupils from the start to watch out for the torque effect inevitable with a comparatively large, rapidly turning rotary. They learned to correct any tendency to swing or drop a wing during take-off, and forced landings could be taught realistically because the engine continued spinning when switched off and re-started easily. What is more, they learned in safety, because there was always an instructor in the front cockpit ready to take over in any emergency, and instead of communicating only by stick-wagging and hand-waving, an elementary but effective speaking-tube "telephone" system enabled the instructor to explain exactly what was happening or about to happen and ensure that the pupil understood the precise action of the controls in everything from first circuit and bumps to spinning and aerobatics.'

In that Spring of 1917 the devastation imposed on Allied and neutral shipping by U-boats forced the USA on 6 April to declare war on Germany, but though that decision brought vast resources to aid the Allies, millions of men would have to be trained before America could effectively participate in the fighting. A few days later, the British Forces, after terrible months of Flanders mud, clambered from their battered and crowded trenches to attack the Germans at what became the third battle of Arras, but though Vimy Ridge was captured by the Canadians, the British casualties were 150,000, and the French were massacred to such an extent that 100,000 deserted. By now the prototype Avro 529, No. 3694, was ready for Fred Raynham, but half-an-hour's flying revealed problems. Though the new fin and rudder disposition had improved single-engine handling there was turbulence from the bulky 12-cylinder uncowled Rolls-Royce engine at mid-gap, causing elevator buffeting at certain speeds; and the long, unbalanced ailerons gave heavy lateral control, though possibly acceptable in matching the inertia of this relatively big aeroplane. Accordingly it was flown to Martlesham at the end of May for brief trials duly reported in June, leading to urgent re-design of the second prototype as the 529A to meet the Air Board's new Specification A3b for a night-bomber.

To overcome buffeting, two of the newly designed 230 hp vertical 6-cylinder BHP engines were substituted because they were narrower and could be neatly cowled to a vertical rest knife edge. In expectation of less drag interference they were mounted directly on the lower wing — a bold step in design. the main fuselage fuel tank was eliminated, and a 50 gallon tank behind each engine, with fuel pumped by windmill to a 10 gallon gravity wing tank directly above, gave individual supply. Where the main fuselage tank had been, a special bomb rack was devised by Roe and Chadwick, which held twenty 60 lb bombs housed vertically.

Contemporaneously with the 529A was the Avro 530 two-seater fighter on which Chadwick had been working virtually night and day. Construction at Manchester had top priority, with each item put in hand as quickly as the DO could produce the drawings. On 3 May the components were sent to Hamble for assembly. As the machine grew, the slight resemblance to the Bristol Fighter became more obvious — but as Roy Dobson said: 'All designers were influenced by other designers' aeroplanes.' In fact details of the Avro and Bristol were very different, for the latter had no landing flap to reduce touch-down speed, and the eye-catching feature of the 530 was the patented streamlined central structure housing twin Vickers forward-firing guns whereas the Bristol Fighter had one. Testing commenced in July, but though originally designed for a 300 hp Hispano-Suiza, all had been allocated to urgent SE 5A single-seat production; so to Chadwick's dismay an Hispano of only 200 hp had to be substituted. Even so the Avro was 4 mph faster than the Bristol. As always with prototypes there were problems. When Sq Cdr Harry Busteed tried the 530 at the Isle of Grain's Marine Experimental Depot he described it as: 'A brute of a machine to fly and very dangerous'.

There were directional problems which were only imperfectly understood. Had a wind tunnel been available these defects would have been spotted before completion of design by using models suspended in the airstream. Instead Chadwick, like most designers, was forced to rely on his

530 two-seater fighter in original form being assembled at Hamble. (G. Quick).

considerable collection of data on earlier aeroplanes. However he managed to make improvements by increasing the rudder height and area and adding a triangular forward balance, and the streamlined gun-box supporting the centre-section was replaced by conventional centre-section struts to improve airflow and view, utilising a narrow central fairing to house an Aldis sight for twin guns beneath conventional decking. The Vees of the under-carriage were faired across with sheet aluminium to reduce drag, and an open-fronted spinner for the propeller gave a smoothly contoured nose. But the latest Bristol Fighters proved to be slightly faster, and were already in extensive production because pilots were delighted with the easy-to-fly characteristics — so the Avro faded from the contemporary picture like its Vickers and Martinsyde rivals, and Chadwick began to concentrate on draught lay-outs of possible single-seater fighters for Roe's consideration.

* * *

Though discreetly veiled from public gaze there were signs of strain behind the scene at Avro, indicated by the sudden decision of Humphrey Roe to resign and re-join the Army. Jock Ratcliffe had always meticulously kept a Drawing Office Time Book which recorded, in diary form, the flow of design decisions, such as the many changes which A. V. requested him to make to the drawings for the Type 529 interplane strut wing fittings which Roe had devised and patented (Nos. 126,000 and 127,658). Recollecting that difficult period, Ratcliffe recorded: 'This Time book, I remember, provided evidence at a Board Meeting which, I think, started the rift between A. V. Roe and his brother, H. V., who suddenly left the Company at the end of July.'

John Lord, his stocky, cheery partner at Brownsfield Mills, succeeded him as Avro managing director, and in acknowledgement of the help that Lord had been giving on aircraft contractural matters, Humphrey made him sole owner of Everards. Lord's rich sense of humour had always delighted Roy

Bristol Fighter rival.

Chadwick, and now he became indebted to his advocacy resulting in an appointment as 'head designer'.

In later years Ratcliffe told me: 'Subsequently Mr Roe did not join in much of the aeroplane design work but was more interested in the mechanical development of items like bomb gears and gun mountings, and he also invented a host of things that were not connected with aviation.'

Having fulfilled the qualifying requirement of five years' extensive design experience, and additionally achieving a leading position in A. V. Roe & Co Ltd, Roy Chadwick was currently elected an Associate Fellow of the cautiously selective Royal Aeronautical Society, so he bought a Swift car in celebration.

Roy Chadwick acquires his first car – a 10 hp Swift.

By now there were some 300 employees at the Hamble factory, few of whom could find accommodation nearer than the Itchen aera some four miles distant; so five London General omnibuses were purchased to transport them from the floating bridge at Wolston each day — but people seemed to be losing heart over the outcome of the war. Bitter battles had been fought in the Ypres salient and the town was in ruins. Far as the eye could see were acres of mud endlessly pitted with shell holes. In the distance was all that remained of Passchendaele Ridge, and it was there that Roy's friend Lieut Harold Rogerson had been hit as he scrambled to the attack, resulting in the amputation of his right arm. Anxious to get him back on the staff at Hamble, Chadwick induced Alliott Roe to apply for Rogerson's release from the Army. Presently that led to a great reunion, and six months later, despite his grave disability, Rogerson was able to rejoin the technical section of the Hamble DO, working on performance calculations and propeller design.

Assembly of the BHP twin-engined Avro 529A derivative of the 529 had just been completed, and after the usual engine adjustments and taxying, had its maiden flight on 23 October in the hands of Raynham, zealously accompanied by Chadwick. Speed was 10 mph faster than

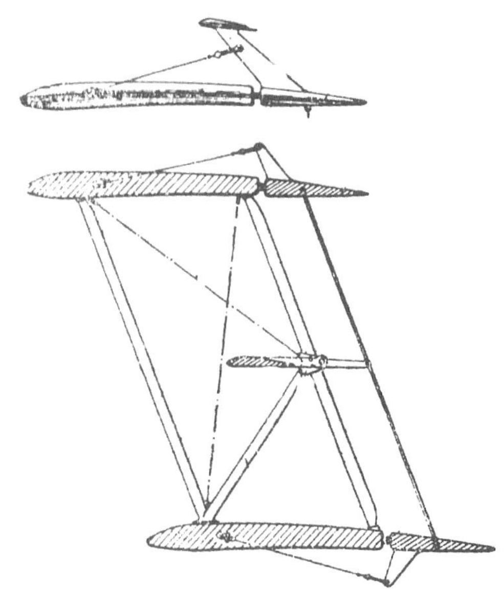

Patent 129,696

Piloted by Raynham (left) and Air Ministry observer Dr. Peter Thurston and designer Roy Chadwick about to fly the enlarged Pike derivative, the BHP engined 529A

estimated, but although now readily manoeuverable with one engine out of action and the elevators no longer subject to buffeting, lateral control was too heavy. Reg Parrott as general manager still had a big say in technical matters, so he proposed that rather than make a major spar modification to accommodate a horn balance it would easier to mount a small pivotted auxiliary aerofoil at mid-gap in front of the rear outboard struts so that it added its pull to the cable interconnecting top and bottom ailerons. That led to a better idea whereby the aerofoil was fitted directly to the top aileron using little sloping struts that brought it forward of the hinge. Flight tests revealed immediate improvement, so the 529A was flown to Martlesham for trials early in November — and on 28 November, 1917, Patent 129,696 was granted to Parrott for his type of control balancing, jocularly referred to by Chadwick as 'Parrott's Park Bench'.

* * *

By Order in Council of 2 January, 1918, an Air Council was established with Lord Rothermere as Secretary of State and President of the Council, and in the following month Alliott Roe was awarded the OBE for his devoted services to aviation.

By now the Gosport training system was in full swing. A. V. Roe & Co Ltd had been instructed to build up Manchester's already enormous production of the 504s in their several versions to a fantastic 500 a month — but there was a problem with engine supply. The flow of 100 hp Monosoupapé was tapering off because it was no longer used for front-line aircraft so production emphasis was on engines of greater power. Even the 130 hp Clergets were obsolete and being surplanted by newer designs such as the more powerful Bentley rotary for the new Sopwith Snipe fighter.

To keep the trainer Avro 504s in production was vital. 'The man to help us is Capt Verney in charge of the Base Engine Repair Shop at Pont de l'Arches near Rouen,' Chadwick told A. V. 'If you can obtain permission I could make a quick visit to France and get him to send every available rotary to us.'

Within a week he was there, and though the place was originally a boot factory it was now 'a veritable cathedral dedicated to aero engines.' There was willing co-operation, and Avro gained a mixed bag of Clergets, Le Rhônes and Monosoupapés. The larger engines would not fit into the current 504s, but the ever-practical Harry Broadsmith solved the problem by eliminating the front 'spider' mounting, comprising a bearer ball-race supported on four tubular arms to each longeron, and replaced it with two rear bearer plates so that the engine could be mounted cantilever fashion and enclosed in an open-fronted circular cowling like that of the Sopwith Pup and Camel but of sufficient diameter to take the biggest engines. Chadwick then added formers and stringers to give a curve to the fuselage sides, smoothly tapering from nose cowling to abaft the pilot's cockpit. Designated the 504K, all future production was to this pattern and the 504Js under construction were similarly converted.

Avro 504 production was also absorbing almost one-third of the total supply of imported spruce. Urgent effort ensued at tackling the unfamiliar problem of designing and constructing wing frames of strip metal, so specialist firms were enlisted. Using a spar design proposed by Major Green, former chief designer of the Royal Aircraft Establishment but now leading the technical team of the Siddeley-Deasy engine and aircraft business, Humbers succeeded in record time with a flanged and corrugated box section of 25 gauge 31 ton steel exactly interchangeable with the standard wooden spar and using the same fittings and wire-

The Avro 504K of improved streamline.

Avro 531 Spider of 28½′ span proved delightful to handle.

bracing. Standard Avro wooden ribs and built-up metal interplane struts fabricated by Messrs Sankey completed the design and were eventually assembled on a standard 504 wood-structured fuselage for flight trials, though Chadwick proposed to replace it with one of steel-tube construction in due course.

However, schemes for eventual metal construction of 504s were overtaken by the march of war when the Germans launched their biggest offensive to-date on 21 March, resulting in the Fourth Battle of Aras during the next fortnight, and then again on 9 April until the 25th, forcing the British to retreat. News of the defeat added to Roy Chadwick's anxieties as he watched the new little Avro Spider 531 single-seat, rotary-engined fighter being wheeled out for its first flight that month.

The first drawings had been issued to the shops in January but though built with great speed, this private venture was too late for selection by the RAF. Nevertheless it had the production advantage of incorporating many 504 fittings and modified components ingeniously introduced by Chadwick, but the distinctive feature was a Nieuport-type 'one-and-a-half' wing system, comprising what was virtually a shoulder wing monoplane of 28 ft span, braced Warren-girder fashion with steel Vee struts from a small lower wing of very narrow chord. In case there were problems with this bracing, Chadwick had schemed an alternative conventional 2-bay set of small span wings. Access to the pilot's cockpit was through a large hole in the centre section which also gave exceptional upward view but had the aerodynamic defect of increasing the induced drag. Powered with a 130 hp Clerget instead of the original 110 hp Le Rhône, the top speed of 120 mph was as fast as the production Snipe of greater horsepower, and their rates of climb were almost identical — yet despite enthusiastic reports by RAF pilots this delightful little Avro fighter was doomed to solitary existence and presently was stowed away in the back of a hangar.

Meanwhile it was design of a new derivative of the twin-engined Pike and 529A which was occupying Chadwick's thoughts. Maximum power for greatest performance was the target. Sir William Weir, as Director-General of Aircraft Production, had staked everything on the ABC light-weight 350 hp radial Dragonfly engine as the future standard power plant, whether for fighter or bomber. Accordingly Chadwick designed his new machine with two of these still unproved engines. Originally designated Type 529B, the new bomber became Type 553 and subsequently was named the 'Manchester'. This time construction from start to finish would be at the Hamble Works so that design

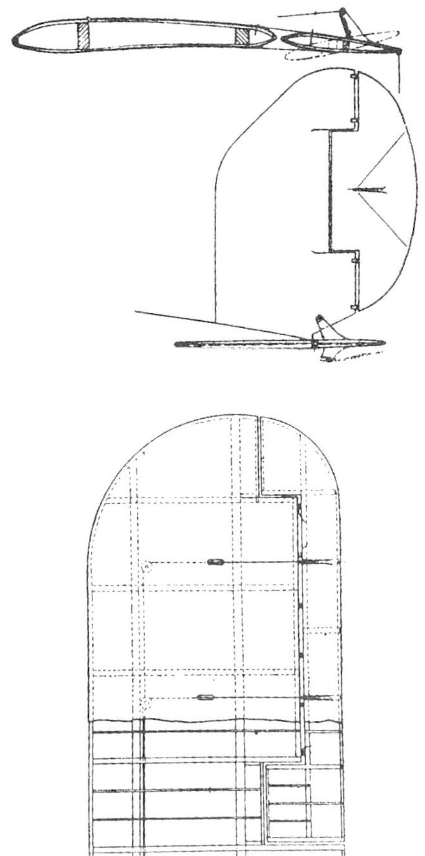

Patent 131,975

snags could be evaluated at any stage of construction.

Concurrently he was able to establish paternal Charles Chadwick there as the Works plant engineer. Roy also managed to arrange a job for his young brother Alan as an 'improver' at the Southampton Works of Thornycroft Ltd, cutting short his apprenticeship at Westinghouse and in July, Agnes Chadwick, accompanied by her three daughters, Doris, May, and Elsie, set up house at Cobbett Road in Bittern Park.

Summer passed into early Autumn. The 60 ft span Manchester was nearing completion, but there was a hold-up through continuing unavailability of the up-rated 320 hp ABC Dragonfly engines. William Weir, now elevated to the peerage as Baron Weir of Eastwood, had blundered in believing that this engine alone could give assured success to all the new aeroplanes designated for operational use in 1919. Reports told of prototype engines catching fire in the air; power 40 to 50 hp down; the rocker-arm box loosening and vibrating when hot, giving erratic operation; and engine 'life' was only 2½ hours compared with 50 for Rolls-Royce engines — yet 11,000 Dragonflies had been ordered from 30 contractors. Disaster loomed.

Chadwick's desperation was to get the Manchester into the air to explore aerodynamic behaviour, for it had such imponderables as Park Bench aileron balances, large horn balance for the rudder but none for the elevator. In July he had been granted his first-ever Patent (No 131,975), describing 'hinged aerofoils with symmetrically placed balancing extensions which project into recesses in the fixed aerofoil', and wanted to apply them to elevators and rudders in one form, and ailerons in another for comparison with the existing controls.

Major re-design was rushed through to substitute the only immediately available 300 hp power plant comprising two experimental vertical high-compression Siddeley Pumas. That necessitated changing from two single interplane struts in the engine bay to an inverted V-strut system in order to accommodate the long 6-cylinder crankcase and maintain the correct c.g. but on hearing that de Havilland had secured a contract for 450 DH 10s powered with Rolls-Royce Eagles Chadwick grasped at a straw by proposing American-built 400hp Liberty engines — only to find they were ear-marked for the new DH 9A devised by Westland in conjunction with de Havilland.

Early in October the Puma-engined Manchester was ready for flight, and with a top speed of 119 mph was slightly faster than the new DH 10; but the Avro had directional anomalies, and the elevator was too heavy. Of these defects Chadwick, for the time being, knew nothing because he had fallen victim to the wave of influenza that was spreading across Britain like a plague. People were dying like flies, and in London alone deaths were over 750 a week. Was this Armageddon?

Yet on the Western Front matters were hopeful. On 26 September the Allies had commenced their final assault on the Germans. At last the British sector had armament superiority with a concentration of over 4,000 guns. The Canal du Nord was crossed, and the troops went clean through the Hindenburg line. On 3 October all the German Secretaries of State resigned and the German troops were fast retreating. On the 9th, Cambrai was taken by the British and Canadians. A fortnight later the British occupied Ostend. On 30 October, Turkey surrendered, and on 3 November, Austria followed suit. Five days later a revolutionary movement began in Germany, and on 9 November the Kaiser abdicated and fled to Holland. Next day the town of Mons was re-taken by Canadian troops, and at 5 am on the 11th, the German plenipotentiaries met Marshal Foch in a railway carriage in the Forest of Compaiégne to sign a 36-day Armistice with effect from 11 am that morning. The firing of maroons in London heralded suspension of hostilities and brought wild jubilation which spread to every town and village when the joyous news came through.

Still convalescent and somewhat shaken by the turn of events, Chadwick took up the reins again, and on 20 December despatched the Manchester bomber to No. 186 Development Squadron at Gosport in full knowledge that it would never go into production. Equally evident was the fact that the entire aircraft industry would have to be largely disbanded because there were enough military aeroplanes of every kind to last the RAF for many years. Of the 55,093 airframes manufactured in Britain between 1914 and 1918, 8340 were Avro 504s, built at an average contract price of just under £900. A 100 hp Gnome Monosoupapé cost £696, and the equivalent Le Rhône was £770. Meanwhile, the combined production of Avro 504s from the Manchester factory and several contracting firms continued at 80 a week, but soon would cease.

A. V. Roe.

There was anxious discussion between Roe, John Lord, Parrott and Chadwick over possible plans for the future. Meanwhile, one section of the DO was kept busy with minor re-design of the Manchester to incorporate a taller fin and rudder and balanced elevators for the anticipated Dragonfly version; another group was designing a conversion of the 504K to 504L as a Training seaplane fitted with timber-built, single-step mainfloats; but new structural techniques for metal wings and fuselages were also under investigation as a follow-up of the wartime experiments.

Meanwhile Chadwick himself, in the intervals between supervision, was wondering how the uncertain future would affect his long-planned marriage with Mary, but was also hopefully drawing layouts of possible small single and two-seat aeroplanes which might find a peacetime market among keen ex-RAF pilots. Roe retained his gentle optimism and put a framed notice in his office for all to see: 'Work 8 hours a day and do not worry and eventually you will become a boss and work 11 hours a day and have all the worry.'

Chapter 5
Peacetime Initiative

With the advent of 1919 demobilisation of Britain's soldiers, sailors and airmen was being controlled at 50,000 a day. Few had jobs to go to. A Ministry of Reconstruction had been formed, but was of little avail when all the wartime factories were shedding employees as fast as possible. Finance quickly became a major problem for the aircraft manufacturers because profits had been rigorously controlled, leaving little capital for reserves. Caution was the rule, but having discovered that Fred May of the Green Engine Co Ltd still had the original 35 hp engine of the 1911 Avro Type D biplane, Roe agreed to let Roy Chadwick proceed with design of an attractive little single-seat biplane powered with this engine. Low cost was the target, so production 504 fittings were used wherever possible. Even the wing stagger was the same, and the machine had that

Drawing of 534 Baby fuselage.

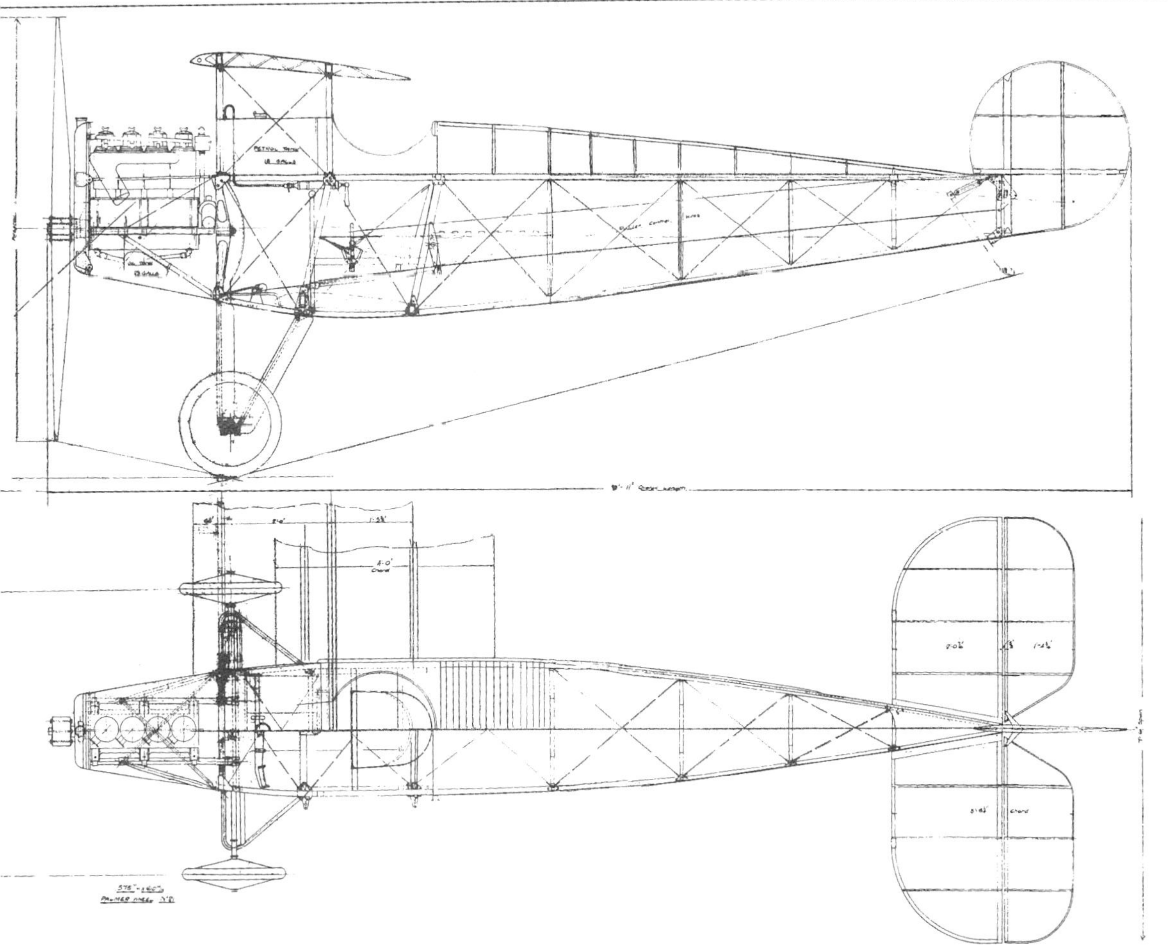

indefinable Avro look typified by the comma-shaped rudder. Construction was well established in February.

That same month the 504L twin-float seaplane was launched from the slipway on the Southampton Water foreshore fringing the grassy aerodrome. Fred Raynham was closely involved with Martinsyde these days, so the new seaplane was flown by Sqn Leader H. A. Hamersley, a tall, hook-nosed, forceful ex-RAF pilot who had instructed on Avro 504Ks. Handling was as delightful as ever, but performance proved inadequate with the 110 hp Le Rhône, and even with a 130 hp Clerget the maximum speed was barely 87 mph, and 75 mph cruising. When tried in rougher sea conditions the undercarriage cross-bracing slackened under the racking loads, so stronger cables were substituted. Unfortunately the RAF had lost interest in light trainer seaplanes, so Chadwick revised the design as a three-seater powered with a 150 hp Bentley. Roe was confident that there would be civil sales for the 504L as well as the 504K and therefore made an offer to the Air Ministry for all the 504 airframes in the factory — only to have it rejected because a Salvage Board had been set up by the Department of Aircraft Production to take over all disposable airframes, engines, and equipment of every type of ex-war aircraft. Those needing repair were dismantled and all serviceable parts saved and stored. Thousand upon thousand steel fittings were sold as scrap, and non-ferous materials melted down for sale in ingot form. The end result was some 5,000 serviceable aeroplanes and 10,000 engines for sale.

Shrewdly John Lord advised Roe to buy only when requisite and thus avoid capital outlay on bulk purchase. Much depended on the outcome of the anxiously awaited Air Navigation Bill, which would control civil flying. Meanwhile interest was focussing on the renewed offer by the *Daily Mail* of a £10,000 prize for the first non-stop flight across the Atlantic. As a possible contender, Chadwick schemed an unstaggered 45 ft span cabin biplane designated Avro 535, powered with a 275 hp R-R Falcon for maximum economy and range, but was worried at the moral responsibility of risking a pilot's life on so vast a distance where rescue would be impossible if the engine failed.

'I'd rather drop the project,' he told Alliott Roe.

The 42-year-old pioneer looked at him in silence, perhaps remembering his early voyages across the empty oceans, then said: 'Yes Roy, I agree . . . We can use the money to better effect. See if you can make the 504L carry four passengers.'

At Easter civil flying was sanctioned by special dispensation and at Hamble was initiated by A. V. Roe & Co Ltd with a well advertised programme of flying at 2s 6d for admission, and flights at £1 for a circuit. Using three 504Ks still in their wartime khaki but with AVRO boldly displayed on the fuselage, some 360 passengers were carried on the first day, piloted by Lieut-Col Henderson, Capt Hamersley, and Capt Warren Merriam, each of whom additionally gave aerobatic displays. John Lord had also engaged a number of ex-RAF pilots for joy-riding with three-seater Avros from the beaches of Southport, Blackpool, Weston-super-Mare, and fields at Scarborough, Harrogate, and Manchester.

Three weeks later, Lord set up the Avro Transport Company at Alexandra Park aerodrome to run a daily return service via Manchester and Southport to Blackpool Sands, using four 3-seater 504Ks which Roe

A famous joy-riding 504K.

expected to replace with the Avro 536 that Chadwick was devising with fuselage 9 ins wider to accommodate two pairs of passengers in a longer cockpit, and their weight balanced by the heavier 150 hp Bentley BR1 engine that was necessary for adequate take-off and climb. He was also engrossed with every detail of the little single-seat Avro 534 'Popular', to which he even devoted his evenings to help with construction, and in March was additionally involved in draughting an airline version of the twin-engined Manchester 533 with widened fuselage and deep ten-seater cabin extending to the centre section. Designated Avro 537, it would have two 330 hp Puma engines. However, four other major manufacturers were considering passenger-carrying conversions of their own wartime designs, so Lord and Roe dropped the scheme as too great a gamble.

The Hamble Works that Spring was very busy. Yet another conversion of the 504K was being built as the 504M for the Avro Transport business, featuring a neat coupé cabin for pilot and two passengers; but surprisingly the engine was only a 100 hp Gnome Monosoupapé. Additionally on the drawing board was a Bentley-powered Type 546 version with open cockpit for the pilot and 3-seater cabin with rectangular windows below the top longeron.

Early in April the black-nosed five-seater 536 prototype, with AVRO emblazoned in white on the khaki fuselage, was given its maiden flight by Hamersley, who found that it took off like a rocket on flying solo, and even fully loaded it handled remarkably well after fitment of an offset fin to maintain directional trim in the heavier slipstream of the relatively powerful Bentley, nor was more area needed for subsequent trials as a twin-float seaplane. Eight more 536s were being built at Hamble as landplanes with standard skid undercarriages for the forthcoming summer season, and twelve were put in hand at Manchester.

On 25 April the Hamble Works was virtually on parade for a visit by the Lord Chancellor, Lord Birkenhead, who inspected

The 504M with two staggered passenger seats to give leg-room under hinged roof.

the various Avro types with interest amid enthusiastic sales chatter by Alliott Roe, and was given a ride in the 536 to experience the joys of seaplane flying. However, 30 April proved a day of disaster. The pretty single-seat Type 534 which Roy Chadwick had so cherished was now ready for flight test, renamed 'Avro Baby' painted in white on its khaki sides and the typical 504-type rudder flaunting red-white-and-blue stripes as though intended for the RAF. Youthful-looking Roy Chadwick was duly photographed with hand possesively on the walnut propeller. After a little more instruction on a 504K he hoped to fly the 'Baby' himself. But today it was Hamersley's task.

The wheels were chocked. Hamersley took his seat. The propeller was spun and the little four-cylinder engine fired, presently roaring out its minute 35 hp at maximum throttle. Hamersley waved chocks away and taxied off. Reaching the far end of the airfield, he turned into wind. The purr of the engine increased. Lightly the small biplane ran forward and was airborne in 100 yards, climbing gently away. At 300 ft, to Roy's horror, the engine suddenly cut. The machine dropped a wing and spun into the Hamble river foreshore with a distant crump. Everyone ran in dismay to the crash, but found Hamersley unhurt. Later it was rumoured that he had accidentally knocked off the ignition switch, but more probably there was an airlock in the

Chadwick with Avro 534 Baby prototype, 30th April 1919.

petrol system and Hamersley was caught out by the slow speed at which he was flying immediately after take-off. The crash was kept dark lest it affected future sales, and a second machine was urgently put in hand and henceforth regarded as the first prototype on the score that at least it had the same engine and some of the components!

Tests of the solid-looking 504M cabin prototype followed, revealing higher top speed than the more powerful 504K because of the better streamlining due to closure of cockpit apertures and efficiency of the Rogerson-designed propeller; but not until 25 July was it certificated after mandatory airworthiness tests by RAF pilots at Martlesham where there was much argument as to whether it was disadvantageous to be completely enclosed. Pilots ever were conservative, and for many more years would prefer open cockpits.

Meanwhile the Avro 531 Spider fighter had been resuscitated by Harry Broadsmith at Manchester, and as Type 538 had two-bay, wire-braced wings of considerable stagger using adapted 504K struts and fittings. Powered with a 150 hp Bentley BR1, this re-vamped single-seater was intended as a racer when it emerged from the flight shed at Alexandra Park in May and was flown by J. C. C. 'Joe' Taylor, an early Avro apprentice who had joined the RFC in 1916 as an observer, later becoming an RAF pilot, and recently had re-joined A. V. Roe & Co as chief

Harry Hawker, with his racing car.

service engineer. Possibly because Chadwick's experts had not initially been responsible for stressing the new wings a cockpit notice warned that flying was restricted to 'straight and level'; but that was no barrier to Joe, who was delighted to use it as a commuter between the factory and Avro Transport joyriding sites.

Concurrently reports of the first attempts at flying the Atlantic were enthralling the public. The Short contender had already been wrecked when the engine failed 12 miles off shore after taking off from Anglesey. On 16 May came unexpected news that three American naval 4-engined 'giant' Curtiss flying boats began a stage-by-stage attempt. Determined not to be defeated by the Americans, Harry Hawker, with Lieut Cdr Grieve as navigator, left Newfoundland on 18 May. Then silence until a small Danish steamer, the *Mary,* hove-to off the Butt of Lewis on 25 May, signalled with flags to Lloyds station on the cliffs above: 'Saved hands — Sop — aer — opl — ane.'

It was a story which thrilled the world. The *Daily Mail* presented £5,000 to the two aviators in recognition of their daring attempt in such bad weather conditions; but there was no consolation prize for ex-Avro pilot Raynham, who an hour after Hawker's departure decided to try with the heavily laden Martinsyde, but before it could attain flying speed the undercarriage collapsed bringing the machine to a jarring halt, though luckily without any great harm to the crew. However success now came to the USA when the NC4, as the only serviceable survivor of the Curtiss flying boats, reached Plymouth Sound on the afternoon of 31 May, alighting within sight of the steps from which the *Mayflower* had set sail 300 years earlier, but was not eligible for the *Daily Mail* prize because this had not been a non-stop flight.

A fortnight later the Vickers Vimy contender made the prize winning crossing in 16½ hours, piloted by Manchester-born Capt 'Jack' Alcock — that ex-Brooklands mechanic and later pilot of pre-war days whom Roe had engaged to assist Raynham in testing the 1913 Avro 503 seaplane — and on 20 June at a great lunch at the Savoy, Winston Churchill, as Secretary of State for Air, presented Alcock and his navigator Lieut Whitten Brown with the £10,000 prize and £3,000 in subsidiary awards, and with typically Churchillian peroration announced that each had been awarded the KBE. Next day they received the accolade from the King at Windsor.

That same day the revived Aerial Derby was flown at Hendon. Among the contestants was the re-born Avro Baby, with entry number 14 on the rudder and temporary registration K 131 on the tag-end of the fuselage. The Avro team was there in force. A big crowd filled the public enclosures and the peace-time aura made an Ascot-like scene. Most of the aircraft were adaptations of Service types, such as the Avro 504K. A much-modified DH4 with small lower wing and 450 hp Napier Lion was the winner, and Hamersley averaging 70.3 mph with the Baby won the handicap. That seemed a good augury for the six production machines at Hamble which would be fitted with new 35 hp Green engines built by Peter Brotherhood Ltd of Peterborough, the descendent of Brotherhood-Crockers Ltd where Roe had been draughtsman from 1902 to 1906, the original drawings having been found in the archives of the Green Engine Co and duly updated.

Delighted at Hamersley's win, A. V. turned to Roy Chadwick: 'What about having a crack at the Schneider Contest with a machine based on the Baby powered, say, with one of the Disposal 475 hp R-R Falcon engines? I think Mr Lord might be induced to fund it. He's been doing pretty well with his overseas 504K sales, so there should be some cash in the kitty.'

That pleased Chadwick immensely. Ever since the pre-war Avro Scout he had wanted to try his hand at a high-speed machine. 'We have only two months, but I am sure I could do it,' he agreed.

The time-honoured way to advance an existing design was to pencil the original lines with appropriate modifications, such as lengthening the fuselage or altering the wing position to maintain correct c.g. with a heavier engine. For the Avro 539 Racer, that resulted in a stubbier fuselage than the Baby, with unstaggered wings of similar span and slightly greater chord, but the Rolls engine could not be obtained in time, so a 240 hp Siddeley Puma was substituted to the detriment of performance. By working all hours the enthusiastic Avro workers managed to complete this compact little twin-float seaplane with a few days in hand and it was launched at Hamble on 29 August. She seemed remarkably fast, but Hamersley reported directional instability and inadequate rudder power for steering on the water. A bigger rudder and fin was immediately draughted by Chadwick, but they were not ready by the time Hamersley had to fly the machine to Cowes for eliminating trials on 3 September between the four British entrants of which only three would be permitted to compete. The Stubby Sopwith with Cosmos 450 hp Jupiter radial was the fastest, but the equivalent Lion-powered Fairey was regarded as best bet if the weather was rough. Choice between the Avro and Supermarine Sea Lion flying boat (designed by Chadwick's equally young contemporary Reggie Mitchell) remained in doubt because Hamersley's mount damaged a float on 3 September through hitting drifting debris. Further trial was deferred to 8 September, giving time to fit the larger fin and balanced taller rudder and paint the new registration G-EALG on the fuselage and AVRO on the fin. Speed runs had shown the Avro and Supermarine to be much the same, but on the day of the race, 10 September, a new propeller for the Supermarine gained 5 knots, and the Avro was relegated to reserve.

The contest at Bournemouth became a fiasco. Both the slick French Nieuports sank before the start and their speedy Spad damaged its floats when being beached. Nicholl with the Fairey retired because of the thick mist. The Sopwith on alighting close to the shore began to heel over, so Hawker shot onto the sand, ruining his floats. Sq Cdr Hobbs with the Supermarine, holed the hull on alighting at Swanage — and that left only the Italian Savoia flying boat; but it vanished in the mist, and because the Swanage mark boat did not see it at all, the Royal Aero Club declared the race null and void, but agreed to recommend the Fedération Aéronautique Internationale (FAI) to award the Trophy to Italy on the premise that the pilot flew the full distance. But at least Avro won considerable publicity because by taking off from Hamble the Racer was able to encircle Bournemouth Pier time after time during the contest.

* * *

Avro 539 Schneider seaplane. (Flight).

Though the Avro Transport Company had been having tremendous success with its country-wide joy-riding teams, the Manchester factory, like all other aircraft companies, was finding that sales of aircraft and engines at give-away prices by the new Disposal Board was affecting the overseas market potential. However, there was encouragement in Maj-Gen Seely's statement on 14 August that the Department of Civil Aviation proposed to offer prizes aggregating £64,000 for three categories of commercial aeroplane, representing single-engined aircraft, twin-engined passenger carriers, and amphibious seaplanes or flying boats. Trials would commence in the summer of 1920 at Martlesham. Conditions were not onerous. Small types must achieve 100 mph, the large 90 mph, and seaplanes 80 knots. Climb must not be less than 500 ft/min for small types and 350 ft/min for large aircraft and seaplanes. Take-off and landing distances over a 50 ft obstacle in still air at full load were particularly important, and there would be reliability duration tests of 3½ hours for small types and 7 hours for large, though not applicable to seaplanes as marine interest primarily centred on safe low-speed behaviour and a 24-hour mooring test. Design features would be marked for 'soundness and quality of construction, such as fire protection using self-sealing tanks, reliability of systems and durability of the machine, particularly if there was any advantage due to metal construction'.

'We must tackle this, ' said A. V. to Roy Chadwick 'We could do it at quite low cost if we used standard Avro 504 parts and go back to the triplane. They did very well on minimum power. Supposing you took three pairs of standard 504 wings, you could fit them onto a cabin fuselage like the one we did for the 1912 Military Trials and use a disposals 160 hp Beardmore.'

Roy gave a sigh. Why go backwards instead of forwards? At the moment he was busy with a twin float reconnaissance seaplane project in the form of a folding wing Sesquiplane powered with as 450 hp Napier Lion.

'Wouldn't it be better if we went for the highest possible performance, using the Lion for, say, an eight-seater?'

'Economy is the watch-word these days,' replied Roe with a smile, and certainly there was good reason for his caution. By this time the early production batches of 504Ks for the RAF had been completed, and the Manchester factory was now trying to subsist on overhauls, rebuilds of crashed Service aircraft, and a trickle of overseas sales. Orders for general engineering projects were sought, and even a contract for milk churns was eagerly accepted. More finance was necessary, and because Crossley Motors Ltd had been outstanding in managing the wartime No. 2 National Aircraft Factory at Heaton Chapel, as well as a monopoly in Staff cars for the Army, John Lord made tentative approaches on the possibility of fabricating coachwork for their peacetime cars. He also decided to close down the Avro Transport Company at the end of the year. It had been difficult to keep tabs on so widespread a business, and expenses proved very high — worsened by a mid-August gale which wrecked half-a-dozen 504s, reducing those operational to seventeen. However, by the end of the season, Avro Transport had carried over 30,000 passengers and flown the equivalent of 12 times round the earth.

Meanwhile design of the triplane as Type 547 went ahead, though a long postponed contraction of Hamble Works personnel was also taking place. Among them was Charles Chadwick — but he and Roy had already prepared for the eventually by forming 'The Window Service Co Ltd.' with intention of employing demobilized soldiers who had no particular training for a civilian occupation. With the many large glass-fronted shops of Southampton so near, there seemed every prospect of profitable employment. As a cautious start Charles Chadwick decided to operate from his house.

But now it was November and Sunday the 11th instituted Armistice Day memorial services all over the country. Next morning an Australian pilot Capt Ross Smith, with his brother Keith as navigator, accompanied by two sergeant crewmen, took off from

Hounslow with a Vickers Vimy in an attempt to win yet another £100,000 prize offered by the *Daily Mail* — this time for a flight to Australia, but few believed the skies could become a far flung Empire link across the world.

Coincidentally, Harry Broadsmith left by ship that month to take up residence in Australia as Avro representative, and took with him several 504ks and a quantity of 'knock-down' parts for local assembly. With Australian associates, he formed the Australian Aircraft & Engineering Co Ltd. and leased an area of tufty ground at Mascot, near Sydney, as base for the company's activities little dreaming that the field would eventually become Australia's International Airport.

The Vimy flyers managed to beat him to Australia, but took 29 days to cover the 11,500 miles in 124 hours flying. In tribute, the brothers were knighted and the two sergeants awarded the Air Force Cross.

A few weeks before this epic flight, Roy Chadwick had been relieved to learn that at last two Dragonfly engines would be made available for his Avro 533 Manchester on which such hopes had earlier been pinned. In December installation began in the waiting second airframe confusingly designated Mk 1 because the original design was based on those engines but by now RAF interest centred on the more recent twin-Dragonfly engined, all-metal Boulton & Paul Bourges, which he had seen putting up a breathtaking show of looping, rolling and spinning at the RAF Pageant that summer.

Meanwhile, John Lord was steadily discharging the factory workers from the Avro works at Manchester where the prospect of a production line for the Avro Baby and cabin version of the 504 was now so small that it could be entirely handled by the Hamble factory where A. V. was determined to continue experimental work at all costs. Concurrently he was delighting in construction of the triplane.

* * *

Only a fluke of fortune prevented January 1920 terminating Roy Chadwick's career. Further instruction by Hamersley in the firm's hack 504K had recently resulted in a private pilot's licence, so he proceeded to fly the much more sensitive Avro Baby when there was suitable weather on free weekends. Here was fulfilment! The countryside spread Liliputian beneath his wings, with the green Sussex heights away to the east and the russet New Forest spreading westward, and holding his eye to the south were the waters of Solent and Spithead embracing the Isle of Wight.

So having a spare moment on the bright afternoon of 13 January he had the Baby brought out and climbed aboard. Away he went — but after a few circuits the bitter winter cold caused him to return. Those watching saw him gliding down, his wings rocking in the gusty atmosphere. Low and slow he flew across the Hamble village, heading for the aerodrome. Suddenly the machine dropped steeply at though stalled and crashed through the trees into the garden of Roe's brother Everard who, at the end of hostilities, had become Vicar of Hamble.

Hearing the crash, people ran to Roy's aid from every direction, and cars streamed across from the Works. They released him

The wrecked Baby dumped behind the Manchester Mk.II K3492 which was awaiting proposed fitment of Lion engines.

from the wreck and rushed him to the Royal South Hants Hospital where the surgeons immediately operated on finding a broken pelvis, shattered left leg and right arm, and broken kneecap. For a month he was in serious straits — but in March, though still in pain, he was attempting a few steps with the aid of crutches. At that, the family's recently retired physician, Dr Quayle, invited him to recouperate at his house in Bournemouth, but was dissatisfied with Roy's progress. Mary Gomersall's father thereupon suggested that the world-famous wartime pioneer of bone-grafting, Sir Arbuthnot Lane, should be consulted, so the invalid was moved to Sir Arbuthnot's London nursing home in Manchester Square, and within a few days underwent a massive 4½ hour operation in which the great surgeon had to break down all the newly-formed adhesions, reset the arm and leg, and bond the kneecap together.

For Roy it was touch and go, necessitating blood transfusions; but presently he began to recover, thanks to the devotion of the staff of mainly elderly Irish nurses whom he thought marvellously kind and humourous, matching his own sense of the ridiculous. Like Mary Gomersall, Alliott Roe was regular visitor, and Roy had beseiged him with questions on learning that the Avro 547 Triplane, registered G-EAQX, had been flown early in March by Hamersley.

'He said handling and performance was much the same as the 504K,' enthused the gratified pioneer, 'so Mr Lord has agreed we can go to the expense of building a second version with 50 per cent more power for the Air Ministry Competition.' Roy Chadwick nodded as though in approval, but was dreaming of vastly better aeroplanes if given a free hand.

Harold Rogerson also lost no time in seeing his friend, and light-heartedly quizzed him on the technicalities of the operation.

'So how did they tackle the arm?'

'Ulna and radius repaired with rivets and silverplate just like joining a longeron.'

'Femur?'

'Fastened with three-inch woodscrews.'

'What about the knee-cap which was in four pieces when I saw you in Southampton!'

'They used wire as though repairing household pottery.'

'When will you get your new Certificate of Airworthiness?'

'Soon I hope — but I've had to promise Mary that I'll give up solo piloting.' He nodded confidentially, then added with a grin: 'But I didn't say I'd give up flying!'

Aware of how greatly Roy was fretting over design matters, Rogerson kept him informed with an erratic flow of letters. Using paper headed *The Office, Sat. Morn.* he typically wrote:-

'Dear old Roy . . . Just a line during working hours to accompany the copy of our last climb test on the "Tripe". We sent 10 copies to the Board meeting. I bet some of them were enlightened!

'As perhaps you know, I went the Hendon last week to change that dud Beardmore prop, and as we have two other Beardmore props which are satisfactory I decided to wangle a "Puma" prop and managed to get a low pitch one loaded on the Ford van!

'I believe you wrote London about testing Green engines on a Froude Dynamometer instead of with a prop. Priest mentioned this to Fred May who said that it was better to use the prop owing to the thrust it gives. As the letter came to me, I thought I would stick up for our side; so pointed out to Mr Priest that our test prop certainly gave thrust, but being a pusher it was in the wrong direction, and as the machine is a tractor the wrong thrust race is being used. However Peter Brotherhood's are testing on both prop and dynamometer so your point is being carried.

'Hoping to have a long pow-pow with you soon

Yours *ad inf* to the Nth power, Harold'

The Spring issue of the AVRO *Joy-stick* paid tribute to Roy Chadwick: 'Quiet, unassuming, he has a charm of personality which inspires a feeling of confidence. Joining the company early in 1912 (sic) he has assisted in the design of practically all the company's aircraft that have made the name AVRO a household name throughout the world. He is a firm believer in getting first-hand information and practical flying experience to help him in designing, and in consequence has spent many hours in the air with all types of machines. It was whilst carrying out one of these flights that he met with his unfortunate accident, but we are able to report his excellent progress, and take this opportunity on behalf of every member of the company to wish him a sure and speedy recovery and an early revival of his valuable efforts in the development of aviation.'

By now he was with his parents at Gwello Lodge, Bitterne Park, where the drawing-room was his bed-sitter. His sister Elsie, then seven, remembers: 'I spent a lot of time there with him. He supplied me with paper and pencils and rubber and taught me to use a ruler. When he was working at his drawing-board I sat nearby drawing too. His tease was that when he got back to his office he'd find a rubber big enough to rub out my funny little face and draw me a pretty one. I asked him several times why he couldn't draw my pretty face, and he solemnly said they hadn't yet made a rubber big enough to rub out my first face.'

Rogerson was now daily in touch because the Dragon-engined Manchester F3493 was being tested at Hamble so Chadwick was avid for news. He had expected it to be much faster than the Puma-powered prototype referenced as MkII, but despite an additional 40 hp it was 7 mph slower, though climbed slightly faster — but that was a matter of compromise in propeller design. Stability was also marginal, and it became essential to increase the tail surface areas. When that was done the machine became a pleasure to fly, and proved fully aerobatic like the rival B & P Bourges — yet the prospect of production was negligible.

Behind the scenes John Lord on behalf of A. V. Roe & Co Ltd had brought negotiations for sale to Crossley Motors Ltd to a successful conclusion. At the time of purchase, Crossley Motors owned 34,283 of the 50,000 shares, and of the balance Alliott Roe had 6,118 and John Lord 1,604, but though Reggie Parrott held 40, Chadwick had none.

Sir Kenneth Crossley stated: 'Mainly with the object of manufacturing our own car bodywork we have acquired a controlling interest in A. V. Roe & Co Ltd who have excellent factories in Manchester and at Hamble. Nevertheless we are anxious not to hamper development of aeroplane manufacture, but we cannot afford to run the aeroplane business as a philanthropic institution, so until the Government makes up its mind how to act, the provision of profitable bodywork for the Roe company will enable it to retain the best of its labour and improve still further its staff and organisation.'

He placed his tall and breezy general manager, John Hubble, in charge of Avro. Charles Fielding, who at this juncture had just joined as a 24-year-old and ultimately became works director, recollected with amusement: 'There was a widely quoted a saying in the Company at that time: "Never trouble Hubble, lest Hubble trouble you". However Roy Dobson had long proved his worth as works manager and was more than a match for Hubble, especially when it came to aircraft.'

Roe and Chadwick with RAF crew on dispatch of the Dragonfly Manchester Mk. I to Martlesham.

A. V. Roe & Co Ltd continued under its original name, but though Alliott Roe and dynamic John Lord remained key members of that business, Crossley appointed Henry Fieldes MP as Chairman, with W. M. Letts, OBE, as Managing Director, and H. E. Shuttleworth as third director, thus securing a voting majority. To consolidate the Avro position, John Lord obtained an interim injunction restraining the Handley Page-inspired Aircraft Disposal Co Ltd from selling any aeroplanes or goods as Avro products unless of Avro manufacture because various other companies had produced the patented 504K components during the war, but there was no objection to these machines being sold as 'Avro type'.

In later years Roy Dobson (by then managing director and a KBE), told me: 'Poor old Alliott! He seemed rather in the dumps over this take-over and building bodies for Crossley Cars — but he cheered up a bit when little Bert Hinkler, an Australian who had done some flying for us after leaving the RNAS, took off from Croydon in the Avro Baby on 31 May heading for Turin, which he reached in 9½ hours, having covered 650 miles on 20 gallons of petrol. Those were the days!'

Hinkler had acquired the Chadwick-crashed Baby early in April when Lord and Roe realised the potential publicity of his proposal to make a long distance flight. The gamble paid off. Hinkler's arrival at Turin was greeted with headlines in all the world's newspapers; but in no way did that affect the natural modesty of that great little man who presently was awarded the Britannia Trophy for the most outstanding flight performance of the year.

By then Roy Chadwick, though still a cripple and using sticks, had ventured back to his Hamble drawing office and once more took command. His immediate task was to revise the single-seat Baby design as a two-seater Type 543 by cramming the pilot slightly forward and extending the cockpit a little aft to seat a passenger with just sufficient room for movement of the dual-control joystick and a rudder bar under the pilot's seat. The engine was moved fractionally forward to achieve proper balance, and the overall length was 2½ ft greater; yet Chadwick managed to ensure a tare weight only 14 lbs more than the prototype and achieved design clearance for 100 lbs more than the original all-up weight. Possibly by now the little Green engine was giving 40 hp, for top speed was 2 mph faster though climb was unchanged.

Completion of the two-seater was just too late for the Olympia Aero Show when it opened on Friday 12 July, but as Hinkler had arrived back at Hamble two days earlier, his machine was eagerly substituted and drew admiring crowds. Every major manufacturer had a Stand in that big glass-roofed hall, but by comparison with other exhibits Roe's Mk II Triplane (547A) was archaic despite improved cabin accommodation which now had a trap-door in the aft bulkhead for passing messages to the pilot as required by the Air Ministry Competition rules. Even fitment of a 240 hp Puma had given no increase in speed, but climb and range had improved. Roy Chadwick hobbled round the Show to study the techniques of his rivals. Of outstanding interest was the revolutionary Short Silver-Streak biplane with beautiful circular section duralumin monocoque fuselage and aluminium-covered wings. Clearly this was by far the greatest advance of any British aeroplane to date, but he cautiously decided that until this costly

Re-build of two-seater mono-cockpit Baby with Cirrus 1 engine.

technique was thoroughly tested and approved by the Air Ministry it was wiser to stick to the system of metal structures initiated for the Avro 504.

* * *

After the Show concluded on 20 July several days went in dismantling the Avro Triplane, returning it to Hamble, and preparing for dispatch to Suffolk's Martlesham Heath for the Air Ministry competition. In the interim the Aerial Derby was held on 24 July. Among the interesting new racers, such as the Sopwith Rainbow, Martinsyde Semiquaver, and Nieuport Goshawk, was the landplane version of Chadwick's Avro 539 fitted with smaller fin and larger horn-balanced rudder — but all to no purpose, for its pilot, Capt Westgarth-Heslam, was forced to land on the very first lap at Abridge, Essex, saturated with petrol from a leak. The winner was Capt Frank Courtney with the scarlet Semiquaver, but he bounced badly on landing and the machine cartwheeled onto its back, though without hurt to the pilot. However there was still a triumph for the Avro team because Hinkler had entered his now famous Baby G-EACQ, and the next production Baby, G-EAUG, which Chadwick had revised as Type 534B with millimetre plywood-covered fuselage and slightly shortened lower wing, was flown by Hamersley who won the Royal Aero Club Handicap, with Bert Hinkler hot on his tail in second place.

A few days later the two-seater Type 543 Baby was test flown by Hinkler with the undefeatable Chadwick as passenger, and subsequently climbed to an astonishingly high ceiling of 11,000 ft for so low-powered an engine. Undoubtedly this pioneering formula of the two-seater light aeroplane was a triumph — and yet there was no rush of sales. New aeroplanes were too expensive for the small civilian market.

The prospect for the Triplanes was even worse. On 3 August Hamersley flew the 547A to the broad heather-covered expanse of Martlesham Heath for the Competition Trials. Entries had become drastically reduced. Difficulties soon became evident. The Avro flew so wide of the *camera obscura* on slow speed tests that it could not be plotted. The Bristol Seely coupé made unacceptable left-hand spirals in the uncontrolled test, and the Vickers Vimy Commercial, known as the 'Leaping Egg' because of her bounding take-off, pushed into the 50 ft high balloon-suspended tape barrier instead of clearing it when demonstrating initial climb. The Avro was nearly as bad but cleared it fractionally, then on landing ran well outside the 175 yard limit, and on a second attempt Hamersley touched down so heavily that the undercarriage struts were badly bent. When repairs were completed Westgarth-Heslam came from Hamble to test it, using the new Avro Baby 534B as transport, but crashed *en route* when attempting a forced landing with failing engine and was badly injured.

Further tests with the Triplane revealed instability, and maximum speed proved 4.3 mph below the minimum requirement — accordingly the Avro was eliminated. However, trouble continued with all other entrants; but in the end the big Westland Limousine proved winner in the small class, Handley Page won the principal prize in the large, and the Vickers amphibian beat the Fairey.

Hinkler's triumphant Baby at Olympia Air Show.

The Puma-powered 547A triple built for the 1920 Air Ministry Competition. A. V. Roe far right.

Despite A. V.'s enthusiasm for the Triplane, there were no purchasers. Among the embryonic airlines only S. Instone & Co Ltd had considered the possibility, but when Bert Hinkler ferried the prototype G-EAQX to Croydon the Instone Chief pilot, Frank Barnard, turned it down as too antiquated. It was freighted as a demonstrator to Harry Broadsmith in Australia who later described it as: 'A rather bloody kite, extremely sensitive fore and aft, and difficult to keep on the ground when landing even in a moderate wind.'

Though the second Avro Triplane was demonstrated several times in the following months, there was still no sale and eventually it was dismantled and stored at Hamble, together with an unfinished fuselage. In fact the aircraft market was going from bad to worse. At an auction of the bankrupt Cambridge School of Flying an Avro 504K in perfect condition fetched only £50, and three DH 6 trainers were sold for £1 5s, £3 10s and £6 10s respectively. A 50 hp Gnome went for 35s and two propellers for 7s 6d each. The industry's only hope was the RAF, for though the Government deemed there would be no war for the next 10 years, it was fully realised that design staffs must be retained as an effective nucleus so that Squadrons could be re-equipped from time to time with aircraft incorporating the latest developments in science, technology, and weaponry, and this led to limited contracts on a time/cost basis for experimental machines.

New Specifications were being dealt with by AV-M Sir Edward Ellington the Director-General of Supply and Research (DGSR), whose technical staff of RAF officers and Air Ministry civilians established the specific terms of performance and equipment and issued an invitation to tender to appropriate firms, depending on their previous experience. Consequently Roy Chadwick was delighted to be entrusted with Specification 2/20 (D of R Type 4B). In fact this was a considerable honour for a young designer, but was attributable to the ambitious competancy displayed in all his earlier designs, backed by his versatility in adapting the Avro 504K to wide-ranging requirements. The new Specification defined a big day and night bomber powered with what seemed the enormous 650 hp of a single Rolls-Royce Condor 12-cylinder Vee engine of recent development. Calculation showed that to carry the stipulated disposable load and achieve the requisite range and landing speed at a wing loading of some 10 lbs per sq ft required an aeroplane which would be the biggest of its type in the world, spanning nearly 70 ft with wing area of over 1,000 sq ft. That seemed a tremendous project demanding great skill to keep the structural weight to a minimum; but Chadwick was confident and tackled the project as the forty-ninth of the 500 series, later known as the 'Aldershot'

His design team had considerably diminished from the war-time 40, so more designer-draughtsmen were engaged including Clifford Tinson, whom Chadwick had first encountered in 1916 at the Admiralty but subsequently became chief designer at Sage's of Peterborough until recent closure of their aeronautical department. Because of his extensive experience he was put in charge of the design section dealing with the Avro bomber's wings.

In establishing a new creation widely differing from any previous design, Chadwick would outline the general disposition base on his accumulated lore of structures and aerodynamics, and a preliminary drawing would be made by Rogerson. The drag of wings, fuselage, tail, and undercarriage was then calculated from available data to determine total resistance and assess performance based on the engine manufacturer's power tests. An initial stress investigation determined spar sizes and bracing loads, Chadwick having decided on wings of conventional timber construction with fuselage framework of steel tubes and tie-rods as devised for the metal Avro 504. Calculated weights could then be checked against first estimates; performance re-assessed and adjustments made, or the entire conception changed. Like everything else in aviation, it was a game of trial and error requiring a discriminating, very knowledgeable brain.

When satisfied that the design study was effective, Chadwick would indicate to Jock Ratcliffe and the several section leaders how detailed design should proceed. The issue of drawings would then be programmed to ensure the best sequence for the shops, and the specialist section leaders would suitably brief their draughtsmen. Every day Roy Chadwick, Jock Ratcliffe, and Harold Rogerson would go round the boards inspecting the drawing detail and often amending or even scrapping an entire scheme.

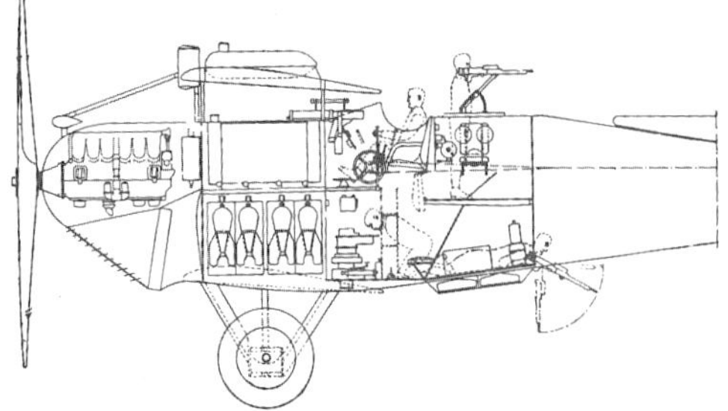

Patent Drawing 206,537 of Aldershot.

The Tender was duly accepted, and on 2 December a Contract was issued for the construction of two prototypes. The delighted Avro Board sent a letter of congratulation to Roy Chadwick with felicitous wishes for Christmas and the New Year.

* * *

January 1921 opened hopefully for A. V. Roe & Co Ltd with a 14 per cent dividend for Ordinary Shares and a further $3\frac{1}{2}$ per cent on Preference. Because of the Ministry's confidence in allocating the 'Aldershot' contract, the newly knighted Sir William Letts as Avro chairman soon realized that their most important asset was the chief designer; so despite the ominous post-war recession he considerably increased Roy Chadwick's salary — though by equivalent modern standards it was relatively low. With the future thus apparently assured, marriage to Mary was at last in sight.

The bulky Annual Report of the Advisory Committee for Aeronautics (reconstituted as the Aeronautical Research Committee) issued in February, confirmed that the current aim of technical development was to establish the parameters of successful, though stereotyped biplane design, and included seventy R & M Reports dealing with longitudinal stability, lateral stability, airflow behaviour, dynamic control, and a profusion of research on propellers, instruments, and engines, among which were experiments with a Wasp-powered Avro 504 on the worrying question of fireproof installation, resulting in pioneering proposals for mandatory asbestos bulkheads, metallic petrol pipe joints, and other precautions.

Regular contact with the Air Ministry in London was maintained by Chadwick for technical discussions with the civilian scientists and administrators, as well as officers of DSR and DOR, and from the Naval experts there was similarly the fullest co-operation. As a consequence A. V. Roe & Co was invited in May to tender for a deck-landing biplane to Specification 3/21 (D of R Type 7a) for Fleet gunnery spotting and reconnaissance.

There were also visits by A. V. himself and Chadwick to the seaplane stations at nearby Lee-on-Solent and Calshot Spit for discussion of piloting requirements and Naval maintenance practice — followed by a brief day's cruise aboard a Carrier from Portsmouth to study the operations of take-off and landing and the strict drill of wing folding for lift stowage to the hangar deck. The result of Roy Chadwick's deductions was the 450 hp Lion-powered Bison 555 — a 46 ft span unstaggered biplane with full gap depth of fuselage reminiscent of the 1912 Type G, but with the pilot uniquely in front of the wings to give the commanding field of vision demanded by the Specification.

Though the wings were structured in wood the fuselage frame was steel tube with ply-covered central cabin of adequate headroom for the crew to stand upright with freedom of movement to operate at the navigation table or move to the Scarff gun-ring on the flat top of the fuselage, permitting a good field of fire because of its high position relative to the top wing. A special valve was devised so that the

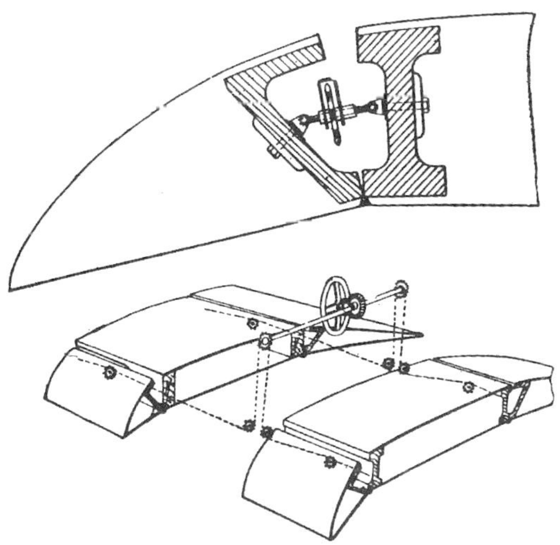

fuel in the 93-gallon main tank could be jettisoned in emergency to give sufficient buoyancy in conjunction with and aided by air bags in the rear fuselage for the machine to float if forced to alight at sea.

Chadwick's initial intention was to give the nearly full-span ailerons dual role as landing flaps combined with a deflectable leading edge forming a variable camber wing operated by self-contained mechanism for which he had been granted Patent 179,358 but presently abandoned the idea in the interests of simplicity.

Because of design priority of the Aldershot bomber he established a separate DO Section specializing on Naval requirements. This led to further recruitment and among the new entrants was 19-year-old George Dowty. As a fatherless war-time youngster, he had been apprenticed to the famous engineering firm of Heenan & Froude, working on aero engines at 6s a week, but gaining knowledge of hydraulics. As with Chadwick, he had to learn the rudiments of engineering the hard way, and on his own initiative attended evening classes at the Worcester Polytechnic Institute. That led to promotion to the drawing office; thence at the Armistice to the short-lived British Aerial Transport Co. A sequence of temporary jobs ensued giving experience of range-finders, lifts and conveyors, and even the Portland Cement business, followed by a research job at the Dunlop Rubber Co on compression rubber pads for aircraft shock-absorbers.

As Dowty at least was acquainted with simple hydraulics and the manufacture of compression rubbers, Chadwick allocated him to the undercarriage section with proposals for a pump-like, telescopic shock-absorbing compression leg in which initial travel was taken by an oil dashpot with taper needle aperture giving contant energy absorption before impacting on a sequence of small rubber compression discs. That was to safeguard the Bison against the hard knocks of deck landing, though standard rubber cord 'bungee' springing had been adopted for the prototype 549 Aldershot. Presently Dowty was joined by Roland Bound, a 26-year-old draughtsman who one day would become his closest associate.

There was also young Alan Chadwick who was now transferred from bench to the DO, where he had to mind his 'ps and qs' under the eagle eye of his brother. Certainly Roy Chadwick was a very busy man, for in addition to the two widely-different prototypes, work continued on a variety of modifications to the basic 504, and the Avro 539 Racer was being re-built to take a Napier Lion, necessitating strengthening the fuselage with plywood sheeting and fitting a more robust undercarriage — but nothing would deter Chadwick from considering other specifications and sketching possible designs.

However the end of March heralded a miners' national strike with all the grave consequences attendant on coal as our major export. Closure of manufacturing plants was threatened through lack of fuel. Talks between Government and Trade Unions ended in deadlock on 7 April. Lorry drivers and railwaymen answered with strikes in support of the miners. Foreseeing the close-down of the Hamble powerhouse, Parrott got hold of an old, two-decker bus, jacked it up, breached a hole in the factory wall, and by using a broad leather belt drive from a back wheel, fed power to the wood-mill and lathes. There was a cheer from the men and work proceeded, but not until 1 July did the coal strike end.

During that time, re-design of the Avro Baby as a seaplane powered with an 80 hp Le Rhône engine added to the diversity of Roy Chadwick's tasks. Designated Type 554, this was a special project for Sir Ernest Shackleton, the Polar explorer, who was organising a further Antarctic Expedition and had decided to carry a two-seat reconnaissance aeroplane aboard his auxiliary-sail steamship *Quest.* Space was limited. Folding wings were essential, necessitating major revision of the wing structure using steel N-interplane struts and diagonal lift struts with ends secured by single over-size bolts to facilitate assembly with gloved hands, and the tailplane incidence could be re-set on deck for correct trim if a passenger was carried. The many modifications, including the floats, increased the laden weight by over 50 per cent so take-off was relatively long and climb a mere 350 ft/min. However, altitude was of no great importance for Arctic exploration because even 500 ft would give sufficient vista to aid navigation.

But there was yet another Avro Baby having Roy Chadwick's attention: referenced

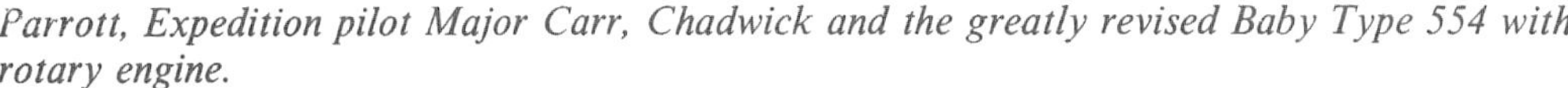

Parrott, Expedition pilot Major Carr, Chadwick and the greatly revised Baby Type 554 with rotary engine.

Type 534C, the top wing was reduced to 20 ft and the lower to 18 ft. as Hinkler's mount for the Aerial Derby on 16 July. Capt Tully with the two-seater Baby was entered by Sir William Letts, and there was also an Avro 552 version of the 504 with Vee undercarriage and 180 hp water-cooled Wolseley Viper, piloted by Leslie Tait-Cox; however prime concentration was on the third Avro entry, the newly Lion-powered Avro 539B Racer, piloted by Westgarth-Heslam, but in fashion all too common with crucial events, it was only ready at Hamble after much engine

The re-built Racer in ill-fated new guise powered by a Napier Lion.

tuning on the eve of the race. Anxiously Chadwick watched the take-off. All seemed well. Presently, Westgarth-Heslam came swooping round and sped past at what was obviously great speed, and circuited the

The Napier-powered Gloster.

aerodrome. Now for the landing. The wing loading was the highest Chadwick had tried and would indicate the equivalent landing run

The Viper-powered company 'hack' Avro 552 ready for trials as a seaplane.

of the almost completed Aldershot. Fast and flat came the approach. Surely the pilot was overshooting? Westgarth-Heslam touched down too far up the aerodrome, and the machine continued at speed, for like all contemporaries it was brakeless. A breathless moment later it crashed into the railway cutting beyond the perimeter — and when the desparate Avro team raced to the spot, they found that the aeroplane was completely wrecked and the pilot seriously injured.

That was bad enough, but there had been an even greater tragedy. Four days before the race, Harry Hawker, hero of the Atlantic attempt, was flying the fast Nieuport Goshawk after taking off from Hendon, the venue of the race. Those watching saw the aeroplane suddenly come slanting down and explode into the ground. Inevitably his death made the Aerial Derby a subdued affair. Accidents already had reduced the field to twelve. Tully was first away, followed by Hinkler. A Sopwith Pup was next, then a Bristol Tourer, Tait-Cox with the Avro Viper, a Sopwith Camel, two SE 5s, a Nighthawk and a Martinsyde with the clipped-wing Bristol Bullet close behind and finally the beautifully streamlined Gloucester Bamel, rival of the deceased Avro Racer. Meanwhile, Hinkler and Tully forced-landed at Brooklands, the Pup gave up and tipped on its nose during touch down, one of the SE 5s was

The prototype 'giant' Aldershot 549 with 650 hp Rolls-Royce Condor.

disqualified, and the Bullet came back with engine trouble. As predicted, it was the Bamel which won. To Roe and Chadwick there seemed no point in re-building the Avro Racer because the Bamel outclassed it. Nor was there much consolation in Tait-Cox coming fifth with the Viper 552 despite achieving 102.5 mph; but on return to Hamble it was fitted with floats, and this pleasantly powerful machine, after launching that August, provided several refreshing flights for Chadwick with Bert Hinkler as pilot on the score that its dual control gave opportunity to experience the lightened lateral response due to fitment of tapered ailerons. More commercially important was a substantial order for this mark of seaplane following a September demonstration at Hamble to the Naval Air Division of the Argentine Ministry of Marine, and assembly of these machines began in October.

By then the Aldershot bomber was nearing completion, dominating the Hamble erection shop with its massive bulk. The centre-section was very wide so that the foldable outer wing assembly was as compact as possible, and the fuselage comprised three portions of unit construction with longeron abutments connected by machined cupped fittings and circumferential lock. Chadwick had been granted Patent 206,537 embracing disposition of crew, armament above and below a midship deck, fuselage stowage of vertically stacked bombs, fuel tanks, navigational facilities — all uniquely illustrated by a detailed drawing of the Aldershot and backed by Patents 206,85 and 206,86 for the fuselage framework and fittings. However rigging the wings proved tricky because each steel-tube interplane strut was only located by a spar-mounted vertical pin. That caused heated comment from Parrott, but he solved the problem by assembling top and bottom outer wings edgeways on the floor and fitting a special box cradle for hoisting into position.

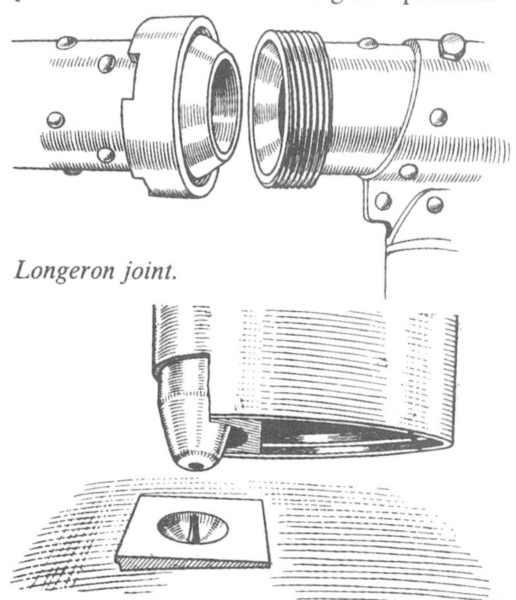

Longeron joint.

Attachment of interplane strut to lower plane.

Roy Chadwick and Mary.

Early in October the majestic Aldershot was wheeled out for its first flight after several days of engine tuning and testing. Bert Hinkler was now the official test pilot and though normally a quietly determined little man, was very outspoken in his criticisms, as the draughtsmen had soon discovered when designing the cockpit layout and controls, for he himself was ingenious at design and a very skilled mechanic. One of his devices was a special engine mounting which could be used as an integrated workstand on removing the entire power unit for maintenance.

Warmly clad and hatted, all the senior Avro staff were on the aerodrome for this great occasion, and it was with difficulty that Chadwick had been restrained by the fatherly Alliott Roe from accompanying Hinkler as passenger. The leather-coated pilot seemed a diminutive figure as he scaled the 7 ft portable side-ladder which gave access to his cockpit. Workmen were peering through gaps between the huge sliding doors of the factory frontage, intent on seeing the mighty biplane fly. The engine thundered. The machine taxied out, and after a few ponderous ground runs a stately take-off followed. Presently Hinkler returned and in the gentlest of landings ran what seemed a remarkably small distance, then taxied to the hard standing in front of the impressive factory building.

With a grin, he gave thumps up. 'Pretty good,' he said on descending. 'Rudder feels rather heavy. More on next flight when I'll go faster.'

Turning to the famous Rolls-Royce mechanic, jovial Vic Halliwell, he said:

Bison prototype N153 showing temporarily unfaired Dowty springing.

'Engine OK. Ran splendidly. Temperatures OK.' Then with Roe on one side and Chadwick and Parrott on the other, this great little airman headed towards the offices for more detailed discussion.

* * *

But it was not only the achievement of the Aldershot's first flight that made October the most important of Roy Chadwick's mature life, for on the 21st he married 22-year-old Mary Gomersall at St. Clement's Church, Urmston and the devoted Harold Rogerson was best man. After the honeymoon in London, the Chadwicks began married life in a comfortably spacious furnished flat at Peartree Green, rented from the brother of Supermarine's dynamic managing owner, Hubert Scott-Paine — but during their brief absence Hinkler had flown the Aldershot again and experienced anomalies of directional control; so on returning to the Works, Chadwick had a long and narrow dorsal fin fitted to the bomber.

One of his traits was the ability to diagnose a pilot's comments in terms of aerodynamics and then devise methods of reducing the handling problem, aided by his own piloting experience. Sitting side by side with Hinkler on the next flight he found on displacing the machine directionally that it returned to its course but the 'feel' was unsatisfactory and footload excessive. This led him to decide on a major operation of extending the leverage arm by making the fuselage six feet longer and reverting to the original fin and rudder.

Meanwhile the keen team building the Bison 555 had managed to pull ahead, and a few days before Christmas this deck-lander was ready for flight. There was the usual bout of engine running by the Napier mechanic, then Hinkler clambered to his high cockpit, taxied out, and made preliminary runs into wind to get an impression of the 'feel'. All seemed well. Turning by the leeward hedge he opened up, and within 200 yards was off. Chadwick heaved a sigh of relief. Twenty minutes later Hinkler landed as smoothly as though he had flown this machine for years.

The new oleo type of undercarriage springing was outstanding, he reported; but the cockpit was very draughty because of the suction of the centre section. Directional stability was touchy, and the elevators and full-span ailerons were somewhat heavy.

Chadwick's look of expectation changed to slight concern, but what he said was: 'I expect we can improve things, Bert.'

Chapter 6
Diversity of Wings

On 5 January 1922 news was picked up by 'wireless' that Sir Ernest Shackleton had died that day aboard the *Quest*. The ship had left its Thameside berth at Tower Bridge four months ago with the two-seat Avro Baby seaplane aboard, but though the *Quest* continued to the Antarctic to fulfil at least part of its scientific programme, the aeroplane was never used, allegedly because the ship had sailed direct to Rio de Janiero instead of via Cape Town where vital spares were waiting.

Meanwhile weeks became months busy with modifications and trials of the Aldershot and Bison. The lengthened bomber proved satisfactory, and in the Spring was flown to Martlesham for official testing during which the Avro Baby G-EAUM became a familiar sight bringing Roy Chadwick flying dual with Hinkler from Hamble for discussions with the pilots and CTO — but the Bison was making slower progress largely because the novel position of the low-drag radiator on top of the centre-section gave inadequate cooling, so climbs could not be attempted until a conventional radiator was angled under the engine behind a ventral nose duct with shutters which could be opened wide for maximum airflow.

As occasional test-observer, Hinkler had Chadwick's 20-year-old brother Alan, who delighted in flying as an escape from his somewhat undistinguished job as junior draughtman under strict surveillance.

'On one of these flights with the Bison,' he told me, 'Bert Hinkler made a climb to ceiling, and I was in the cabin taking readings. Suddenly I felt the machine wobble, and instantly was flung sideways but managed to grab a metal column that went from floor to roof. A second later, still grimly holding on I was head down on the cabin wall, and then we seemed to somersault and I collapsed on the floor under enormous pressure, unable to move.

'When we landed I said to Bert: "What happened?" He grabbed my arm and led me to his office. "Not a word!" he said. "Don't tell your brother or he'll be furious. We got into a spin."

'As you know, Bert was a little man, and we had no parachutes in those days, so he used two cushions at his back to ensure he could reach the rudder bar. Apparently they slipped onto the floor and he was not strapped in. Falling sideways he must have pushed hard on the rudder bar and it took many turns before he could pull himself back into the seat.'

'Was your brother difficult to deal with?' I asked.

'He was very strict, and even Bert was rather careful with him. So was Parrott, whom I disliked intensely. I think he was jealous of Roy.'

Early in April, Hinkler tested the Viper-powered Avro 552A, re-modelled with twin fuel tanks under the top wing and a skidless N-type oleo undercarriage designed by George Dowty. Several flights later, to Chadwick's alarm, Hinkler demonstrated the machine's indestructibility by making stalled landings from 20 ft. On the 12th he won the Wadden Handicap Race with it, and was again victorious at the Croydon Air Races on 3 June. By then the lengthened Aldershot had been cleared by the A & AEE bomber pilots, whereas the equivalent DH 27 Derby was still being built. Martlesham also was testing the Bison's rival, the bull-nose Blackburn, but there were similar complaints of draughty cockpit. Consequently the Avro and

Blackburn designers were proposing to raise the top wing of their aeroplanes a foot or so above the pilot's head level.

There followed cheering news from Russia that the Soviet pilot Gwaiter, flying the Avro Baby G-EBDA recently purchased by that country, had completed the first ever flight from London to Moscow.

The great popular event of the year was the RAF Pageant at Hendon on 24 June, though it rained so heavily that the enclosures became a sea of umbrellas. Nevertheless the display attained its established spectacular pattern, and innovated a 'New Type Aircraft Park', with the Avro Aldershot towering above the Blackburn Dart and Handley Page torpedo droppers, Parnall Puffin and Supermarine Seagull amphibians, together with a Westland Weasel representing the latest in two-seat fighters yet showing no great advance on Chadwick's war-time Avro 530. Later, the mighty Aldershot flown by Martlesham's smallest pilot, crusty F/O 'Tiny' Horrex, won the RAF Handicap Race, but though that was a proud moment it was the race for eighteen Avro 504Ks which enchanted Alliott Roe when they took off like a flock of startled birds.

A few days later the company received an Air Ministry contract for conversion of the prototype Aldershot to take the new 1,000 hp Napier Cub 16-cylinder engine — the most powerful in the world. Though Roy Chadwick and his team became engrossed with this re-design, including fitment of a twin unit, 4-wheeled oleo undercarriage, these were light-hearted summer days despite a few disappointments. On 7 August there was the Aerial Derby of 200 miles around London, starting from Wadden, but Hinkler's Avro 552 could only achieve fifth place in the handicap. A month later, while flying at Hamble with the clipped wing Baby Racer entered by Sir William Letts for the newly established and much publicised King's Cup Race, the engine failed and Hinkler received a ducking when he ditched in Southampton Water and the machine was wrecked.

Meanwhile the Bison had arrived at Martlesham, where handling was assessed as good enough for it to go to Gosport on 19 August in company with the Blackburn for sea trials on HMS *Argus* which had longitudinal deck-wires to keep aircraft directionally straight by engaging a swivelling snap hook at each end of the undercarriage axle to obtain a brake effect. As both aircraft were built to the same specification, they were somewhat similar in appearance and performance, though the bull-nosed Blackburn was even uglier than the functional appearance of the Avro. When it came to deck landing, it was the Avro which the maritime pilots preferred because of its better shock-absorbing undercarriage. Pending further attempts by the Blackburn with a new undercarriage and modified fuel system, an initial contract for 12 Bisons was awarded to Avros that Autumn. A similar order was promised to Blackburns on the assumption that defects in their machine would be overcome, but a bad set-back followed in October when the second prototype was destroyed in a hangar fire at Martlesham.

Both firms continued as rivals with a new Specification 16/22 (DOR Type 9) for a long-range coastal defence aircraft carrying a 21 inch torpedo or equivalent bomb load, which preliminary Avro calculations indicated as feasible in the form of an enlarged Aldershot of 50 per cent greater tare weight, rising to 20,000 lbs at full load, though Chadwick had alternative solutions in mind — but amid the whirl of work, he and Mary were moving to a neat, self-contained villa named 'Farnworth' in Chessel Avenue at Bitterne. Alliott and Mildred Roe also had moved, and with their three sons and five daughters now lived in a large house named 'High Firs' at the pleasant yachting centre of Bursledon at the head of the Hamble estuary.

Scarcely had Roe and Chadwick returned from the Paris Aero Show that Autumn that *The Aeroplane* published a photo of the still 'secret' Blackburn prototype after a forced-landing at Lowestoft where it was snapped by a local photographer. Not to be outdone, Chadwick discreetly ensured that a photo of his identically listed machine was published in *Flight*, and the editor commented: 'Since the

The Cub Aldershot II with four-wheeled double undercarriage.

war, Mr Roy Chadwick, who has been with Mr Roe since the early days and is now a chief designer, has designed several types and among the latest is the Aldershot Bomber, the Aldershot Cub, and Bison Fleet Spotter.'

In the next issue that journal reported: 'Last Friday afternoon, the Napier-engined Avro Cub carried out the first official test under flying conditions — marking another eventful day in the history of the world's progress in aviation. The big bomber bore aloft the Cub, roaring "gently as a sucking dove", watched by Air Vice-Marshal Sir Geoffrey Salmond, the DOR. Hinkler said he could not realise he had 1,000 hp in front of him, and told us that the machine was very nice on controls and easy to manage. Later in the afternoon, we saw him loop a Bison.'

* * *

The 26th of January 1923 brought new rewards with a contract for fifteen R-R Condor Aldershots with strutted half-axle oleo undercarriage and internal stowage for a 2,000 lb bomb load. What with steady demand for 504s of various types, the Manchester Works would be very busy for the next two or three years. In appreciation, the directors up-graded Chadwick's salary, but it was the birth of his daughter Margaret in February that caused overwhelming jubilation.

Business pressures remained unrelenting. When Sir William Letts invited the Press for a visit on 15 February to his Manchester Crossley car factories including A. V. Roe & Co Ltd which had a large section building motor car bodies, Roy Chadwick sped there with photographs and models to ensure maximum publicity for the Hamble factory and the new line of magnificent Avro aeroplanes because little could be gauged from the preliminary stages of Aldershot and Bison production at Manchester — though in future only experimental aircraft would be built at Hamble.

As always, his team of technicians was working full-out. The Cub-engined Aldershot had been flown to Farnborough on 10 January for engine reliability trials, but now a troop-carrying version was contemplated, and the design study for the big torpedo

Production Aldershot with longer fuselage and strengthened multi-strut undercarriage.

Bison line-up with Westland Walrus predecessor far left, and on right Bison 1 A with deeper gap.

bomber to Specification 16/22 was evolving from an enlarged Aldershot to a twin-engined 97 ft span biplane Type 556 with metal-framed fuselage deep as the gap between the wood structured wings. Chadwick was also revising the Bison as Mk 1A to production Specification 16/23, based on the second prototype which had the raised centre section and a large dorsal fin, and under his direction Dowty was designing a single float amphibious undercarriage for the Mk 1 Bison.

What particularly pleased both Alliott Roe and Roy Chadwick was a throw-back to the romantic pre-war days through the offer of a £500 prize by the Duke of Sutherland (the new Under-Secretary of State for Air) for an International competition between light single-seat aeroplanes with engines not exceeding 750 cc capacity. Eagerly Roe and Chadwick debated the challenge. The possibilities had already been demonstrated by a fascinating light-weight, high-aspect ratio shoulder-wing monoplane powered with a tiny two-cylinder, 400 cc ABC motorcycle engine, developing a maximum 7 hp. Designed by W. O. Manning of the English Electric Co and known as the Wren, it displayed alarming wing twist when first flown by Sqn Ldr Maurice Wright, but after adding torsional stiffening it performed remarkably well despite the enormous power loading of 51.5 lb/hp — though the climb was hardly spectacular! Describing his experiences in a lecture to the newly formed Institution of Aeronautical Engineers, he concluded: 'It would pay to adopt higher wing-loading at the expense of slight increase in power. With careful development it may be possible to build a single seater of 12 hp with payload of 230 lb, a top speed of 80 mph, and land at 28 mph.'

The prize-winning English Electric Wren.

In the ensuing discussion, Roy Chadwick agreed that power should not be less than 12 hp if the machine was to be robustly constructed. 'I have gone into the subject rather carefully,' he said, 'and reached the conclusion that the light biplane offers possibilities. You reduce overall size, and the narrower wing should give better elevator control.'

His spare-time homework led to an unmistakably Avro-looking biplane design of 30 ft span and 3 ft chord; but A. V. himself, after brief enthusiasm for a compact little triplane, turned to the opposite extreme with ideas for a clean monoplane with tapered 36 ft wing like the Wren, but required a 700 cc engine compared with the 500 cc for the biplane. In any case, design of both machines would be Chadwick's responsibility so he was amused to think that he was competing against himself.

Though too busy to attend the general run of aeronautical meetings that Spring, the fourth annual RAF Pageant at the end of June was too great an occasion to be missed, so Roy and his young wife Mary drove to Hendon and joined the SBAC enclosure near the Royal Box — and to Mary's delight she saw King George and his regal Queen arrive, accompanied by Queen Alexandra and the newly-married Duke and Duchess of York with other members of the European royalty. Like Ascot, the seal of social approbation had been conferred.

In the New Type aircraft Park the massive Cub-powered Avro Aldershot dominated ten smaller biplanes, including the Bison, and on closer inspection the dainty little Wren was revealed. Though the bright sky of morning turned overcast, it was a monumental day of flying, the low cloud ceiling adding to the thrill of the aerobatic displays; but it was an Avro 504K flown by Flt Lt Walter Longton that tensed everyone into awed expectation of a crash because of his crazily skidding turns and sideways flight of what became known as 'crazy-flying'.

The King's Cup Circuit of Great Britain

The King and Queen, with the Dowager Queen Alexandra.

The Avro 558 was given heavy stagger primarily for easy access to the cockpit.

followed on 13 and 14 July, but though a Viper-powered Avro 552 had been entered, Chadwick was too busy to witness the race because the Cub Aldershot had arrived back at Hamble to be overhauled for the great Gothenburg International Aeronautical Exhibition which would open early in August with full British representation. Keen to inspect the latest aircraft displayed there by France, Holland, Italy, and resurrected Germany he eventually accompanied Hinkler on the delivery flight of the Aldershot and managed a day at Gothenburg. That necessitated return to England by night ferry to get on with the job of finishing the two light aeroplanes and finalising the design concept of the huge twin-engined Avro 557, soon to be named Ava, which now had a conventional centre section above a slightly shallower fuselage and would be powered with two 650 hp R-R Condor III engines giving a 300 hp superiority over the single Cub-engined Blackburn rival known as the Cubaroo.

Meanwhile the *Daily Mail* had seen the ultra-light aeroplane competition as a source of publicity and virtually took over by offering a prize of £1,000. At that, Sunderland added a further £500 for British competitors flying all-British machines.

Chadwick's Avro 560 re-design of Roe's initiating Type 559 shoulder-wing cantilever monoplane seemed much more practical than the two heavily staggered I-strutted Avro 558 biplanes because the wheels were mounted on 20 ins cantilever wooden struts projecting below the fuselage whereas the biplanes had wheels through the fuselage bottom giving negligible ground angles. Simplicity was the keynote. For quick detachability and reassembly, the deep box spars of the monoplane's biconvex wings protruded beyond the inboard rib and slid into rectangular openings in the fuselage and were bolted together to form a continuous girder. A typical inspiration was altimeter location just within the port wing root to avoid disconnecting pipelines to the pitot head — but even Chadwick was astonished when the tare weight of the monoplane proved 10 lbs less than the 294 lbs of the biplane.

The opening morning at Lympne on 8 October dawned calm and misty with low cloud, but with £1,500 beckoning as prize for the principal test of low fuel consumption, 15 of the 23 British competitors were ready to fly the 12½ miles triangular test course, and first away was Longton with Wren No. 4 which completed seven laps on a gallon of petrol in 2 hrs 40 mins at 80.3 mpg. Several followed, among whom Jimmy James flying the ANEC No. 17 achieved 87.5 mpg — but a freshening

Alliott Roe anxiously supervises tuning the B. & H. engine.

The 580 monoplane with 698cc Vee engine had biconvex-section wings for low drag but gave poor stall characteristics.

breeze caused postponement, so competitors concentrated on additional prizes offered by Abdula & Co of £500 for highest speed over two laps: £150 each from the Society of Motor Manufacturers and Society of British Motorcycle Manufactures for the greatest number of circuits *in toto* by British machine and pilot; Sir Charles Wakefield's £200 for greatest altitude; and £200 which the Duke of Sutherland and the RAeC jointly subscribed for a landing competition. When the weather became sufficiently calm, Longton matched James with 87.5 mpg, so they eventually shared the Sutherland and *Daily Mail* prizes.

Meanwhile Hinkler excelled with the Avro monoplane. Day in and day out, whenever weather permitted, he made circuit after circuit, and by the end of the contest had worn out all opposition with 1,000 trouble-free miles in the course of 80 laps and by sheer physical endurance won the £300 reliability prize. Unfortunately, the B & H powered Avro biplane remained too handicapped by its unreliable engine and on the last day of the competition on 13 October had a minor crash when forced-landed by Lieut Barrett in turbulent wind conditions. Nevertheless Hamersley with the Douglas-engined biplane did remarkably well in competing for the altitude prize, though poor weather prevented an attempt on the ultimate ceiling until the last day.

But that Saturday produced tragedy. There were clear skies and tremendous visibility, though the wind was rather rough for lightly laden little aeroplanes. One of the altitude competitors was the Frenchman Alexis Maneyrol who climbed away with his Peyret high-winged monoplane and reached a barograph height of 10,000 ft, which corrected to 9,400 ft. Shortly afterwards, Hamersley with the Avro biplane and little Piercey with the ANEC monoplane made their attempts, but Piercey just managed to beat the Avro by reaching 13,600 ft, so Hamersley decided to defer a second climb until the wind decreased. On discovering how high they had gone, Maneyrol took off again in an effort to beat them, and soon he was lost to sight. An hour later the Peyret was discerned gliding down. Chadwick watched its swaying approach in the gusty breeze. Suddenly and horrifically at 100 ft the wings collapsed downward and the machine dived into the ground with a crumpling crash that spelled the end of Maneyrol.

Presently the competition continued, and the De Havilland pilot, Hubert Broad, flying the little DH53 Humming Bird tried to distract the crowd from the tragedy with a brilliant display of aerobatics, and Longton with the Wren gave an exciting performance of his crazy-flying speciality. Later, Hamersley and Piercy again mutually competed for the altitude prize, and the ANEC won with 14,400 ft beating the Avro by a mere 590 ft, so the £100 prize of the abandoned landing competition was given to Hamersley as consolation. But at least that restored Chadwick's spirits a little, though he remained appalled by the Maneyrol crash.

A fortnight after the Lympne competition, a special meeting for the ultra-lights was held at Hendon, organised for the sheer love of the thing by their buoyant group of ex-war pilots. As the B & H engine of Barrett's machine was too unreliable, Chadwick had the repaired fuselage adapted to take the more powerful Blackburn Tomtit, and to overcome the lack of ground incidence a simple conventional vee undercarriage was fitted. The same effect was gained with the second biplane by adopting a similar cantilever plank undercarriage to that of the monoplane, now fitted with a shorter wing originally intended for high-speed events in the Lympne competition.

Despite a brisk and gusty wind, nine of the Lympne ultra-lights arrived and the meeting opened with aerobatics by Broad flying the Humming Bird, followed by individual demonstrations of the other ultra-lights. The major event was a Handicap race for a £50 prize given by Sir Charles Wakefield, but in the first round Hinkler had engine trouble with the monoplane and withdrew. Broad won the final heat and Hamersley was a gallant last with the Avro biplane — but Chadwick was relieved to see him land safely, for his wings had been flexing alarmingly in the turbulent air.

The concensus of opinion was that development of motorcycle-engined single-seaters had been fascinating but efforts should be directed towards a light two-seater design. To that end the Duke of Sutherland offered a prize for a two-seater contest next year — and even more encouragingly Sir Samuel Hoare, as Secretary as State for Air, intimated the probability of an Air Ministry prize for such machines with engine limited to 1,500 cc.

* * *

January, 1924 introduced the first-ever Labour Government, with Ramsay Macdonald at its head. Overshadowing everything was massive unemployment of one million, but Roy Chadwick, now nearly 31, had a new hurdle to surmount. Despite his aura of authority he shunned publicity, but now had to overcome his qualms and on 8 February present a paper on *Aeroplane Performance Estimates* before the Institution of Aeronautical Engineers at the Engineers' Club, Coventry Street, London.

In fact he had written a most educative treatise of empiric calculations rather than higher mathematics, based on statistical and graphical data of great practical value to budding aeronautical designers and students. But surprisingly neither Alliott Roe nor Reg Parrott were present, though Roe sent a telegram regretting inability to attend.

Certainly they were all very busy at Hamble. In addition to the complexities of the twin-engined Ava, Chadwick was supervising re-design of the Aldershot fuselage to take 12 passengers or 6 stretcher cases, for which he had devised a 22-ft-long, commodious, well lit cabin portion of ply-skinned wooden monocoque. Pilot and navigator had an open cockpit beneath the top wing leading edge, with access to the cabin through a door in the bulkhead behind them. As the space requirement eliminated fuselage fuel tanks, two large cambered gravity tanks were carried each side of the top centre sections. In all other respects this Avro 561 used Aldershot components to ensure substantial saving in cost. Designated Andover, four had been ordered in January to replace the wartime DH 10s used for the Cairo-Baghdad desert air-route.

The Andover, unlike the Aldershot, had pilot and navigator in an open cockpit below the leading edge of the centre-section.

Low cost was always of paramount importance. That the aircraft industry was still the Cinderella of the Defence system was re-emphasised by the Air Estimates published on 7 March allocating a mere £14½ million compared with £45 million for the Army and £55½ million for the Navy. The Secretary of State for Air said: 'Re-conditioning of existing machines and engines is being continued so far as is judged economical and compatible with efficiency; but it is of utmost importance there should be no relaxation in experiment and research, and increased provision has been made for this purpose.' To that end the Directorship of Research (DOR) was abolished in April and the responsibilities divided between a civilian Director of Scientific Research (DSR) and an RAF Director of Technical Development (DTD).

As a sideline to priority work on the Ava, Bisons, Aldershots and Andovers, Chadwick was considering a two-seater development of the previous year's ultra-light biplane for the new Light Aeroplane Competition just announced by the Air Council with prizes totalling £3,000. Both he and Roe regarded this as a purely sporting venture, and even Sir William Letts took that view despite his profit-making orientation. For Roy the concept initially became one of the evening exercises after returning from work. Even with a small aeroplane there was much to ponder. There was the problem of light structural weight coupled with simplicity to ensure low cost. Wing-folding was essential and led to visualisation of hinges and geometry of cabâne struts for easy access to the cockpits. When all details of this imagined Avro 562 were clear, Chadwick would have a layout made for stressing, then Ratcliffe must ensure that drawing the details design did not interfere with work on military aircraft, and therefore allocated closely supervised junior draughtsmen, such as Alan Chadwick, for the job. The eventual result would be a pretty little biplane named Avis of almost the same size as the single-seat Avro 558 of the previous year.

Adding to the load of design activity, John Lord had agreed to co-operate with the Oxford University Arctic Expedition whose leader, George Binney, required a spotter

The Arctic Avro 504Q launched onto Southampton Water for test by Bert Hinkler.

seaplane carrying a 3-man crew. Chadwick therefore revised the 504N design by widening the fuselage into much the same form as the Avro 546 with small cabin abaft the pilot, replaced the 150 hp Bentley BR1 with a 160 hp Armstrong Siddeley Lynx, and mounted the machine on a twin-float chassis similar to the Type 536 seaplane. Designated 504Q and registered G-EBJD, it was launched from the Hamble slipway in May for test by Bert Hinkler. After brief trials by the Expedition's pilots, A. G. V. Ellis and J. C. C. Taylor (the pilot-engineer who used to fly the one-time Spider fighter derivative) the machine was crated and despatched to Newcastle for shipment aboard S.S. *Polarbjorn* to Spitsbergen, where it was re-erected in a record four days and nights at the one-time whaling base of Green Harbour within the Arctic Circle.

On the eve of departure Binney (later knighted) presented Roy Chadwick with an inscribed silver ashtray, and wrote to John Lord; 'I shall always remember your enthusiasm for our cause — splendid enthusiasm which barged its way with a laugh through every conceivable obstacle. If other businessmen were of your generous calibre it would be pure joy to run an Arctic Expedition. All I can say on behalf of the expedition is this: "Here's to John Lord — the best friend that any Arctic Expedition ever had".'

Reg Parrott and Roy Chadwick are invited to inspect the 'S.S. Polarbjorn' at Newcastle.

By then it was June, the completed Andover 'ambulance' fuselage was being rigged with Aldershot wings, undercarriage and tail units, and ten days later was flown by Bert Hinkler, who confirmed similar performance to that of the Aldershot and much improved pilot's view due to his forward location with seating offset to port. At that the Air Ministry decided to exhibit it at the 5th RAF Pageant which followed on 28 June in perfect weather.

As always, the prototypes in the flypast were an index of progress. In a reversal of dignity and impudence they were led by the diminutive Humming Bird and Parnell Pixie ultra-lights made even more toy-like by a three-engined Handley Page lumbering behind them, followed by the big Avro Andover whose glittering windows gave the impression of an airliner. Close on its heels

The Bison Trainer, known as the Bull, with side-by-side pilots' cockpit.

growled the rest of the procession of fighters, bombers and reconnaissance aircraft, but to Chadwick's hidden relief the impressive Blackburn Cubaroo rival of his Avro was missing — so was the latest Bison, he more anxiously reflected! However the inevitable bevy of Avro 504s went racing, and Longton gave his usual marvellous display of crazy-flying. For the rest, it was formation after formation of what the Press described as 'heart-stopping evolutions'.

Bison anxieties were eliminated a fortnight later by a contract for eighteen Mk 2s with top wing raised above the fuselage. Nevertheless there was no room for complacency because the Blackburn Mk 2 had been similarly modified and was likely to be ordered. Later that month the Blackburn factory stole a reciprocal march on Avro by completing the Cubaroo before Chadwick's twin-engined Ava torpedo bomber, and it was tested by Flt Lieut 'George' Bulman who had the advantage of having flown the similar though somewhat smaller Cub-powered Avro Aldershot during the many months it had been stationed at the RAE Engine Research Flight at Farnborough in 1923.

* * *

Big Press publicity ensued for the Cubaroo when demonstrated on 21 August by Bulman to VIPs at Brough, where in a gentle 8-knot wind 'he floated into the air in half the available distance'. Chadwick's reaction was to put the Ava design section on overtime, but there was a long way to go before that aeroplane could be completed. Concurrently George Dowty, feeling that his valuable experience on undercarriage design was worthy of more pay, moved to the Gloucester Aircraft Company to engage on similar work and lost no time in patenting an arresting gear he had devised, comprising a hydraulically-braked aircraft cable with grapnel engaging a series of transverse cables on a ship's deck.

That August the Air Ministry encouragingly announced that the Air Council would financially assist the establishment of ten Light Aeroplane Clubs of approved constitution, and each would have an additional grant to purchase approved light aeroplanes. That gave added zest to the two-seater competition which opened at Lympne on 28 September. C. C. Grey had dryly prophesied that whenever there was a competition, work on the entrants only started a fortnight before the event, so the Lympne machines would have their finishing touches while the pilot was on his first lap — and he was nearly right because many contestants had been awaiting their engines. Among them was Chadwick's Avis, which was delivered to Lympne by road on the opening day because the intended geared Bristol Cherub had only just arrived, though the machine had been tested at Hamble with a

The Cherub-powered Avis reveals ingenious centre section strutting to give access to the front cockpit.

three-cylinder 35 hp Blackburn Thrush. Working day and night, the Avro crew managed to instal the Cherub in the next two days, but when Hinkler attempted to fly the Avis, the engine appeared to be giving only half-power and he barely managed to get airborne, so dared not attempt the qualifying course and was eliminated from the competition.

Flight reported: 'Started in gloom, figuratively speaking, the Air Ministry Competition for two-seater light planes may be said to have finished in sunshine. The eliminating trials, which everybody had regarded as child's play, proved far more difficult to pass than expected during the Saturday and Sunday reserved for that purpose. Of the nineteen machines entered, only eight were admitted to the competitions when they started on Monday morning. Even this small number was reduced to six by Tuesday evening. What was the cause of all these failures? The answer is that the capabilities of the 1,100 cc engines were over-estimated by those who drew up the rules. It takes very much longer to develop an aero engine than a new type of aeroplane, so it is not surprising that most engines failed to stand up to the strain of the competition.'

However, the Bristol mechanics were able to tune up the Avro's engine, and on 2 October, Hinkler managed to climb to 2,000 ft. That was well below calculated performance, so a direct drive Cherub 1 was substituted and proved so reliable that he even gave flights to Sir Sefton Brancker and AV-M Sir Geoffrey Salmond. Next day, with eight other competitors, he tore round the eight-lap, 12½-mile course of the Grosvenor Challenge £100 Trophy Race and won at an average of 65.87 mph.

Over-all winner of the Air Ministry Competition was the Beardmore *Wee Bee* 38 ft span monoplane derived from the previous year's successful ANEC single-seater of similar plan. 'It might be thought,' reflected *Flight's* editor. 'that the net result is that the Air Ministry has caused the aircraft industry to spend something like £30,000 to win £3,000. Much of the value of the competition was lost because so many machines were prevented from showing what they could do. However, the Air Ministry proposes to try out the various competing aircraft at Martlesham.'

A few days later the Air Ministry stated that none of the types could receive official recommendation, and Clubs were warned that delay was inevitable. Nevertheless, the widely varying Lympne designs were of considerable technical value. Thus Alliott Roe himself had designed a neat worm gear which enabled the full span ailerons of the Avis to be depressed as lift flaps.

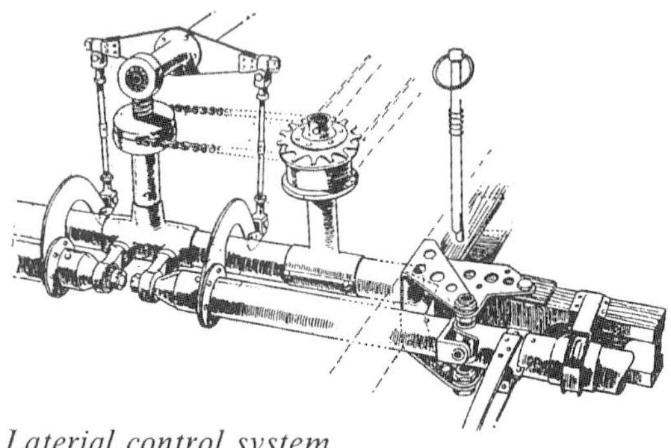

Laterial control system.

During discussion at the Royal Aeronautical Society on lessons of the competition, Fred Sigrist of Hawker Aircraft, who had entered the pretty little Cygnet biplane, said: 'We have been trying to produce too efficient a machine. Light construction means expensive construction. What is wanted is a larger engine, enabling heavier and cheaper construction. A larger engine could be produced as cheaply as a small engine, and the question of fuel consumption is immaterial as the petrol would be so small a percentage of total expenditure that it is not worth bothering about.'

That had been Chadwick's philosophy in devising the two-seat Avro Baby, and was now echoed by de Havilland with design of a light plane powered with a four-cylinder engine he had induced Frank Halford of ADC Ltd to devise from components of a wartime 8-cylinder RAF 1A air-cooled engine. But for the moment other ideas for ultra-light aeroplanes lapsed into the background. Far more important was the election of a new Conservative Government on 7 November with Baldwin as Prime Minister and confirmation that 'a force of 52 Home Defence squadrons will gradually be created'.

A month later, senior officials and designers of the aircraft industry were flocking to the Grande Palais in Paris for the opening of the 9th International Aero Exhibition, where it became very apparent that no aeroplane in Britain could match the cleanness of the Bernard Racer or the Nieuport-Delage Sesquiplan, nor the advanced design of the I-strutted Breguet XIX Sesquiplan, which was entirely metal except for fabric covering of wings and rear fuselage. The sole British representative was an Armstrong Siddeley Siskin V, shown in skeleton, with steel tube fuselage frame and wooden wings. Britain could have done better than that had not designers been hampered in extending their ideas to monoplanes because Air Ministry officials and the RAF still held to their belief that only biplanes were structurally sound. Nevertheless, Roy Chadwick had recently submitted a hopeful design study for a two-seat fighter monoplane with thick-section eliptical wings — powered by a 650 hp Condor like the production Aldershots and Andovers and his twin-engined Ava which now was having its wings fitted and dominated the Hamble floor space. For Roy, the year ended on a confident note with a further contract for twelve Mk 2 Bisons.

Last phase of the amiable 504 design – the 504N with long-travel undercarriage which made every landing seem perfect!

* * *

With no intention of closing down the Hamble works as the experimental section dominated by the effervescent A. V., the Crossley management, guided by John Lord, had recently purchased 153 acres at

Bison II, of which 41 were built in addition to 12 Mk. Is, had no dihedral in raised top wing and cruised at 90 mph.

The Ava prototype after incorporation of square fins. A 37 mm gun firing $1\frac{1}{2}$ lb. shells at 100 per minute was mounted in the nose, and 2000 lbs of bombs could be carried internally or a big 21 ins Whitehead torpedo externally.

Woodford, Cheshire, for a new aerodrome outside the Manchester smoke ring, and the three hangars of over 100 ft span at Alexandra Park were removed and reassembled at Woodford as erecting shops for Manchester-built production aircraft. That had been a wise move because Martlesham trials of the Armstrong Siddeley Lynx-powered Avro 504N prototype during 1924 now resulted in its adoption as the RAF's new standard trainer to Specification 6/30 — and a long vista of production opened, establishing a close connection between John Siddeley's engine interests and A. V. Roe & Co Ltd. As for Alliott himself, it was a quiet and happy triumph that his 1913 design had been resuscitated for another splendid lease of life.

When some years later I flew a 504N it had an intangible charm: it felt right — which meant no more than its stability, inertia, control weight, and response to stick and rudder bar movement had satisfactory inter-relation. This subtle question of *feel* made or marred an aeroplane of those days, and the controls of the Avro seemed ideally suited to its purpose and performance as a trainer. Taxying in a gentle breeze, it was docile enough if one used full rudder and a burst of engine for turns, though a wing dropped markedly owing to the soft, long travel, narrow under-carriage; but when the wind was more than 15 mph, assistance was required at each wingtip to prevent bowling away down-wind, as well as help to turn into position for take-off — otherwise there was risk of blowing over until a wingtip skid touched, though a complete turn-over was rare.

Take-off was simplicity itself. A little aileron was momentarily necessary to correct for torque reaction during initial acceleration with tail lifted; but in an amazingly short distance the Avro became airborne without further action, and climbing at 65 mph could get out of quite small fields with a feeling of complete security. In level flight if flew with docile steadiness, displaying a gentle, quickly damped 'hands free' phugoid if any disturbance was imposed longitudinally. In retrospect, its behaviour seemed perfect.

That was what Chadwick hoped for early in 1925 when the impressive twin-engined Ava made its first flight in the hands of Bert Hinkler. Whether a lightly-handling Avro Baby or the ponderous Ava, he was equally at home even though this was the first time he had flown a twin. From the high cockpit in the steeply sloping nose there was a superlative view of the world, but inevitably there were the usual adjustments and modifications to ensure conventionally acceptable control and stability, particularly under asymmetric pull with one engine out of action. That presently resulted in changes to the three typically Avro 'comma'-type rudders, and ultimately the central one was eliminated and each outboard rudder acquired a square fin between top and bottom tailplanes. The machine was then flown to Martlesham for extended trials which covered torpedo dropping, day and night bombing, and gunnery from the ventral position under the rear cockpit where an integrated gun and seat could be lowered to reclining position to give unrestricted rearward field of fire.

Whether the Ava would be produced in quantity largely depended on the Air Estimates issued on 19 February, which showed a net increase of £763,000, but *The Times* warned: 'Only two regular units are to be added to the small force of eighteen regular squadrons,' and that certainly lessened chances of more orders for the Aldershot, though fifteen had been operating very successfully these last ten months with 99 Squadron at Bircham Newton, Norfolk, and the excellent stability made them particularly suitable for night bombing. However, Chadwick had high hopes that the newly formed Imperial Airways might adopt the Air Ministry's civil version of the Andover furnished with six single seats each side of the central gangway, and toilet and luggage compartments aft. Registered G-EBKW, this Avro 563 was about to be flight tested.

Concurrently de Havilland's 60 hp two-seater biplane emerged as the dainty DH 60 Moth for its maiden flight at Stag Lane aerodrome on the Sunday afternoon of 22 February. Despite the distinctive DH hallmark, its conception might well have been influenced by Chadwick's pioneering, slightly smaller, two-seat Baby, G-EAUM which had been flying for almost five years. Had he lost out because of Avro's concentration on profitable military contracts?

On 2 March, the Moth was exhibited to an enthusiastic Press. *The Aeroplane* reported: 'She obviously handles extremely easily, performs all the usual stunts in exemplary manner, and lands very slowly. She is undoubtedly a thorough, practical training machine and should certainly meet the needs of the Light Aeroplane Clubs and that of the private owner.'

Chadwick took note and the inevitable doodles ensued of ideas for a rival two-seat biplane in anticipation of a further Light Aeroplane competition for which the Royal Aero Club decided in April that restrictions of engine capacity of horsepower would be abandoned in favour of a 170 lbs limit on engine weight. That certainly ruled out the 60 hp Cirrus, and as no lighter engine could be established in the currrent season the RAeC decided to postpone the next competition until the summer of 1926. Prizes totalling £5,000 were announced by the *Daily Mail* in June stipulating dual-controlled two-seaters capable of 20 flights aggregating 2,000 miles for assessment on a ton-mpg basis carrying a load of not less than 340 lbs. But for the moment Chadwick had a more important task than to design little aeroplanes, for he and his technicians were busily engaged on studies for another deck-landing, torpedo-carrying and bombing aeroplane to Specification 21/23, intended as a replacement for the Fleet Air Arm's Blackburn Dart, and presently evolved as the Avro 571, later named Buffalo.

* * *

Whatever their preoccupations the entire aircraft industry seemed to migrate *en masse* to Hendon on 27 June for the summer's great pageantry of the RAF Display. This time, Air Chief Marshal Sir Hugh Trenchard had ruled that it must be a demonstration of typical Service work rather than an exhibition of picked stars performing individual evolution — but the formation flying by out-moded DH 9As, Flycatchers, Grebes, and Virginias was no less spectacular then before, and the public was spellbound by three parachutists making live drops with the newly standardised Irvin parachutes to show that the RAF at last had been equipped with them. But as always, it was the demonstration of the latest prototypes which overwhelmingly interested Chadwick and his fellow designers. Regretably the outstanding Hawker Heron fighter had split a propeller-tip so the procession was led by the rival Gloster Gamecock, followed by the Short Springbok, which foreshadowed future all-metal techniques. Then to Chadwick's chagrin came the huge and stately Cub-powered Blackburn Cubaroo without the equivalent twin-engined Avro Ava, which was still on the secret list and locked away at Martlesham with others of latest design. Somewhat disconsolately he eyed the next machines — the Bristol Brandon equivalent of his Aldershot and the de Havilland DH 54 Highclere, rival of his absent civil Andover which was being tried out by Imperial Airways on the Croydon to Paris run. However, there was compensation when a squadron of Aldershots flew past in ponderous formation, filling the skies with thunder, yet destined to be their last public appearance because the RAF had decided that risk of the single engine failing made them potentially dangerous for night flying.

The RAF Display was barely forgotten when the classic King's Cup Race was flown in two circuits of 800 miles on 9 and 10 July, but so many aeroplanes forced-landed that only a quartet was left at the end of the first day, of which Bert Hinkler with an Avro 504N was last by nearly three hours, so he scratched from the next day's lap and Barnard, flying John Siddeley's Siskin, proved an easy winner.

Don Juan de la Cierva y Codomiu, on the right with the most famous pilot of that time, Captain Frank Courtney.

The C.6A Autogiro taxies out to accelerate the windmilling rotor which had been initially spun by rope like a top.

The long serving ex-wartime DH9A.

That 'What Lancashire thinks today, England thinks tomorrow' was re-established on 21 July when the Lancashire Aero Club opened as the first of its kind to be selected by the Air Ministry for financial support — soon to be followed by London, Newcastle, Midlands and Yorkshire. Clever publicity by de Havillands had resulted in establishing the outstanding Moth as the approved machine for them all. However, it had been touch and go for Lancashire's great day because engine trouble prevented despatch of their blue-painted Moth and the situation was only saved by Cobham flying in with the well-tried prototype G-EBKT to give joy-rides.

That same Moth was flown by Hubert Broad to the August Bank Holiday meeting in Lympne, where a wide range of aircraft had gathered. Most of the ultra-lights came by road, but Hinkler flew direct from Hamble with the Avro Avis, the wings visibly flexing in the bumps, confirming that something as sturdy as the Moth was essential for next year's Air Ministry Competition. Nevertheless the Avis created much interest and on Bank Holiday Sunday it was slyly reported that 'Mr Hinkler was busy all afternoon picking up passengers, nearly all feminine, and drew a certain amount of chaff by disappearing behind clouds with them!'

Later that month he was quietly delighted that Roe and Chadwick agreed to loan him as reserve pilot for the oncoming Schneider Trophy Contest in the USA, yet so marginal was time before shipping aircraft, crews and officials on 26 September that Hinkler only had one opportunity of flying the Gloster III reserve machine at Felixstowe. But the British were out of luck and the Americans won.

During his absence a novel breakthrough in aircraft development was demonstrated on 15 October to a gathering of British aircraft designers at Farnborough, when the Spaniard Juan de la Cierva displayed his helicopter-like Autogiro, comprising an Avro 504 fuselage with a pylon-mounted freely windmilling horizontal rotor that featured the novelty of hinged blades with freedom of movement to give equality of lift between up-wind and down-wind sweeping rotation. Here at last was a machine which could be flown safely at very low speed, though hovering in still air or rising vertically from the ground was not possible — nor was starting the rotor by pulling a rope like string round a top and taxying the machine round the aerodrome to speed the blades aerodynamically really practical. Nevertheless in the hands of tall, bespectacled Frank Courtney the demonstration was most impressive. 'Here is the first step towards helicopters,' thought Chadwick.

The following week, with Roe's approval, he visited the Air Ministry for discussion with the Director of Research, Major H. E. Wimperis, and within a few weeks that resulted in a contract for A. V. Roe & Co to build two similar machines based on the 504 fuselage and standard Avro skid undercarriage, but with a 110 hp Clerget rotary instead of Le Rhône, and using rotor-head and blades of Cierva design.

Sourly, C. G. Gray commented: 'Meantime one does not recommend members of the SBAC to shut down all work on ordinary aeroplanes. Considering that the Air Ministry has just placed an order for 100 of the dear old DH 9As of 1917 design with ex-war engines, one may safely assume that even if the Autogiro fulfills its inventor's expectation, we shall still be ordering the present obsolete bombers and fighters in 1933, and machines on the present secret list will still be going strong in 1940.'

Of the latter, Chadwick's technicians were completing drawings of a remarkable private venture competitor to the latest Gloster Gamecock and Hawker Hornbill single-seat fighters. Designated Avro 566, and in humorous vein dubbed 'Avenger', this aerodynamically clean biplane had a superbly streamlined, smooth-surfaced, semi-monocoque fuselage constructed in similar fashion to locally-built racing yachts of diagonally double-planked mahogany on elm frames and spruce longitudinals. A 450 hp 'broad arrow' Napier Lion was skilfully streamlined into a pointed nose of aluminium cowling and cooled by French-derived Lamblin radiators recessed into the underside of the top wing.

At this juncture Chadwick's earlier colleague Harry Broadsmith returned from Australia to re-join A. V. Roe & Co at Hamble as assistant designer. His firm had been forced by the prevailing financial stringency to close down after four successful years during which he built numerous Avro 504Ks and a prototype 6-seater of his own design. Subsequently he became Consulting Engineer to the Commonwealth Government but felt frustrated by the limited design prospects and consequently decided to return to Avro. That relieved some of the load on Roy Chadwick imposed by Sir William Letts' decision to proceed with construction of the projected Avro 571 Buffalo as a private venture challenging the Air Ministry's acceptance of the Blackburn and Handley Page tenders to Specification 21/23 but not the Avro.

Though the Avro Bison was in effective use by the Fleet Air Arm and further orders expected, one Naval officer had sourly commented: 'The Admiralty, of course, chose the Bison because of its lovely cabin for the Admiral, although a very bad aeroplane with a gliding angle of a brick!' The new design was dimensionally the same span and almost the same length as the Bison, but the crew this time were abaft the centre-section, necessitating a 10 degrees sweep back for correct relation between c.g. and c.p., yet Chadwick was able to incorporate many Bison fittings to facilitate quick production.

Chapter 7
Time and Change

The Diamond Jubilee of the Royal Aeronautical Society was celebrated on 12 January 1926 with a *conversazione* in the Aeronautical Section of the Science Museum, attended by noteable pre-war pioneers amid a galaxy of leading personalities from the aircraft industry. Under the spreading wings of the Vickers Vimy of trans-Atlantic fame, Cody's ancient biplane, and Roe's fragile-looking 1909 triplane, there was reminiscent talk of early times and hopeful discussion of the future. Roy Chadwick was in optimistic mood because he had just received an Air Ministry contract for a lightweight, single-seater Autogiro of his own *ab initio* design, for which it seemed feasible to use the same plywood fuselage as his envisaged Avro 581 biplane for that year's Lympne trials fitted with simple tripod for the rotor, and specially sprung undercarriage attached to the same strong points as the lower wing anchorage of the biplane. The latter, soon to be named Avian, had a span of 32 feet with big wing area of 294 sq ft to achieve maximum possible disposal load, and would have the newly developed 70 hp Armstrong Siddeley Genet as this was the most powerful engine available within the competition allowance of 170 lb.

As always, his volatile imagination was concurrently picturing other designs of various purpose. Since the Aldershot he had schemed some 30 aircraft ranging from fighters to torpedo-bombers, and was preparing to submit proposals to Specification 26/24 for a 3-engined commercial biplane of 100 ft span resembling an enlarged Andover with a Hercules in the nose and one each side like the Ava. Though he offered an all-metal structure similar to the second prototype Ava currently under construction, the contract was eventually scooped by his perpetual rival Geoffrey de Havilland with the DH 66 Hercules which had a metal-framed fuselage but wooden wings. Chadwick was also considering a projected general-purpose biplane, Type 577, and a 4-engined heavy bomber, Type 580, having draughted four other types in the meantime, for it was always essential to examine every Air Ministry Specification and tender for those suiting the company's facilities; but throughout the industry 'though many be called, few are chosen'.

Each year's Air Estimates dictated the prospect. The *Daily Telegraph* commented on those of the current year: 'The outcome is of exceptional concern because of the need of balancing production and expenditure with national security. Our impression is that we are to mark time for two or three years in the air programme of 52 Squadrons that was adopted in 1923 as the minimum for Home Defence. Successive governments of opposing politics have endorsed and confirmed both policy and principle. Are there now adequate reasons for throwing it overboard?'

The Air Ministry policy of placing competitive orders with two or more firms for aircraft of identical specification had become firmly established, but as the Avro Buffalo had been denied that benefit it was registered as G-EBNW and in March was given its first flight by Hinkler, but there was trouble getting fin and rudder areas right and adjusting the control balances. Its rival, the Blackburn T5 Ripon, was flown on 17 April by George Bulman; however, longitudinal stability proved deficient, so increased sweep-back was necessary to bring the c.g. forward, and the cowling was re-shaped to fair the exposed cylinder blocks of the Lion engine. Meanwhile the Bison's fin and rudder was being replaced by a large rectangular unit, and the second Ava, which had square-tipped

The private-venture Avro 571 Buffalo prior to first flight. Pilots preferred the cockpit position abaft the centre-section as somewhat less hazardous in a splashdown, and the landing view was no worse than the Bison's.

wings structured in steel, was flown on 22 April, Hinkler reporting that no major change was required.

Yet another miners' strike, which began on 3 May, was threatening Britain's commerce. 'Not a penny off the pay, not a minute on the day,' was their slogan. Railwaymen, transport workers, and printers followed suit next day. The Government refused to negotiate. Emergency plans were put into operation, and an army of volunteers ranging from students to top-hatted businessmen drove buses and tube trains or guarded dumps of supplies.

The Aeroplane reported: 'Judging by the aircraft factories in the London district, about 50 per cent of the men were out at the end of last week. Allowing for the difficulty of getting to work, this is satisfactory from the viewpoint of law, order, and decency, but eminently unsatisfactory to the TUC, though even the pickets were quite polite to the staff and to the men who remained at work. Whatever their personal grievances, there is no doubt that the general feeling among aircraft workers is that the coal trade might well be left to settle its own affairs without interfering with others managing to make a living.'

At Hamble, the 'national stoppage' made little impact because of the daily bus service long instituted by A. V. Roe & Co. Nine days later the TUC called off the strike as a complete failure, though the miners obstinately remained out, adding a million to the workless.

Elsewhere industrial affairs proceeded smoothly — but there was certainly friction which had long been fermenting between Roy Chadwick and Reg Parrott. In all innocence Walter Fenton, the company secretary at Manchester, had written to Parrott stating: 'It has been decided to apply for a secret patent in respect of the gunner's seat beneath the fuselage of the Ava machine. Would you therefore be good enough to give me a very short description of this device?'

Parrott, unsuspectingly, replied: 'For the purpose of your application, I think the following would suffice: "A retractable seat below the fuselage of an aeroplane, arranged in such manner that the gunner faces aft, the

Retractable ventral gun position on the Avro Ava.

framework carrying the seat being provided with a mounting for a Lewis gun arranged so that the gun may be trained to a field of fire from horizontal to vertically downwards, directly aft, and on either beam." The suggestion for this type of seat was made by Major Scott in the course of conversation in my office. In these circumstances, I think that if any patent is applied for it could be taken out in the name of the firm and no particular individual's name need be associated with it.'

Heatedly Chadwick wrote to Parrott on 8 May, addressing him not as 'Dear Reggie', but 'Mr Parrott':

'It has come to my knowledge that you have taken upon yourself to advise the company secretary as to how a patent relating to a device of my design should be taken out. You have done this without reference to me or Major Scott. This in itself is bad enough, but more serious is the fact that you have actually advised that the patent should be in the company name only. I consider that is absolutely indefensible from every point of view. As the company's designer, all matters relating to the design of our aircraft should be submitted to me before any decision is arrived at, especially in regard to designs for which I am personally responsible. You have no responsibility to take the action which you have done. As to the design of the lower gun position as fitted to the Ava, there can be no doubt as to whether or not I am the person to whom it should be credited. Substantially the arrangement as now fitted is shown on drawing A.678, dated 15 October 1922, and as you are perfectly aware, the device is only a rational development of the arrangement I devised for the Aldershot aircraft. The details as fitted to the Ava were developed in the ordinary way in the drawing office under my supervision.'

This was formally signed with the designation 'Designer', not 'Chief Designer', for he considered the adjective superfluous as he alone was responsible for all the technical drawing office work.

A more temperate letter went to Fenton stating: 'What surprises me is that you should have taken the matter so far without seeking my advice or opinion. It appears to me, as the company's designer, that you, as the company's secretary, should naturally deal with me on all questions relating to the design of our aircraft and I should be very much obliged if in future you would do so.'

Ten days later, Fenton wrote a concilliatory letter explaining that:-

'I had no knowledge whatever of the existence of the invention until I saw it on the day of the last executive meeting. It was my intention to raise the point at that meeting but I had to leave before it concluded business. I did, however, take the first opportunity afterwards of speaking to Mr Lord and Mr Hubble and they both agreed that it was a feature which could desirably by protected. I therefore wrote to Mr Parrott as the manager of the Hamble Branch asking who should be joint applicant with the Company. I trust the foregoing will clear your mind of any idea that your participation in the creation of this device was being deliberately over-looked by me.

'As regards your letter to Mr Parrott, I feel this is better left without comment, but I am sending a copy of this letter to him and am sure that if his original letter contained any suggestion which would lead to an injustice

Rivalling the Moth for the two-seater Light Aeroplane trials was the functional Genet-powered Avian 581, which initially had the characteristic 504 comma-type rudder.

being done to you, he will not withold the necessary action to rectify it.

'There is one other point, and that is the circumstance that a device now generally recognised to be of novel character should have been conceived, designed, constructed and made ready for delivery without any steps being instituted to protect it by patent application, so I recommend you to bring to my notice any novel device you may introduce in your designs in future and that would not only serve to protect the Company's interests, but would infallibly prevent any possibility of the recurrence of the misgivings you have entertained.'

To that, Chadwick replied:-

'Of course, what upset me was that Mr Parrott wrote to you on the subject without referring to me. I consider that he is in the same position as, say, Mr Hubble at Manchester, but the responsibility for design of our aircraft is mine and they should consult me in all matters relating to it. The reason that I had not referred the question of the patent of the gunner's seat to you was that I did not think of the matter from that view at all, as the device is still in the elementary stage, subject to modification and improvement. However, I will bear in mind this point and whenever I think a novel feature has been introduced into our design, either by myself or other people, I will ask you for you opinion as to the advisability of patenting it.'

This time, the letter was signed 'Yours sincerely', but inevitably the cross-fire did nothing to improve relations with Parrott, despite the necessity of working in close co-operation at Hamble under Alliott Roe's surveillance but operating as an almost autonomous unit independently of Manchester.

* * *

May was a busy month. With typical Hamble speed the Avian prototype had been completed, and registered G-EBOV was flown by Bert Hinkler at the beginning of the month. There were no snags, except that the ply covering of the fuselage was so thin that there were small skin indentations, known as 'cockles', which slightly spoilt the neat and distinctively Avro appearance. As always, Roy Chadwick was the first passenger and

Unique among British aircraft because of its elegant double planked mahogany fuselage constructed by Hamble boatbuilders, the Avenger was Chadwick's reply to the Air Ministry's exclusion of Avro from single-seater fighter tenders.

delightedly tried the dual controls. A few days later, Hinkler flew the Avian to Martlesham Heath for C of A trials and suitability as a Club aircraft.

Soon after its return there was concentration on the pioneering rotary wing activities — resulting in everyone at the Hamble Works turning out to watch the initial flight on 19 June of the first Avro 574 Autogiro C.6C, based on the familiar 504K fuselage with skid undercarriage. Frank Courtney, as the sole expert, flew it. Rotor starting was still by rope, followed by fast taxying to speed it — then Courtney applied full power and it was immediately obvious to Chadwick that take-off was even shorter than that of the original C.6A prototype and the climb steeper. Elevators and outrigger ailerons were bigger than before giving more effective control. All seemed well enough for presentation at the forthcoming RAF Display on 3 July.

More importantly to the Avro rank and file, the elegantly aerodynamic Avro 566 Avenger in civilian guise with registration G-EBND painted on its beautifully streamlined white fuselage, was given its maiden flight by Hinkler on 26 June. To Chadwick's gratification, he achieved the designed top speed of 180 mph, marginally beating the new Fairey Firefly, which though appearing very slick, had a fabric covered rear fuselage. But victory is often brief. A few days later, Bulman flew Camm's rugged-looking V-strutted Hawker Hornbill, which had an R-R Condor of 170 hp more than the Avenger's Napier Lion, and it proved 7 mph faster than Chadwick's fighter. Both had their snags.

The prototype Aldershot in final guise powered with the experimental six-cylinder in-line, inverted semi-diesel 850hp Beardmore Typhoon.

Though the Avro had ailerons only on the top wing like the Hawker, control was heavier and slow in roll; but the Hornbill had cooling problems with the big engine, as well as undamped directional oscillations if power was suddenly changed, and the rudder was too small. Compared with the roomy Avenger, its cockpit drastically restricted the pilot's movements. However, the odds were against acceptance of either of the three fighters.

The Cub-powered prototype Aldershot, J6852, now came into the picture again. For months it had been standing idle in the big main assembly building at Farnborough, the engine trials long completed. However, fuel consumption economy was a major interest of the RAF in order to obtain the longest possible bombing range. To that end, the Beardmore Engine Co had been developing a very large inverted six-cylinder, water-cooled diesel engine of 850 hp named the Typhoon, and of all aircraft the Aldershot seemed the most suitable for trial installation, so A. V. Roe & Co were awarded a contract to fit this power plant and replace the four-wheeled undercarriage with the standard two-wheel version.

The all-metal Ava concurrently was being performance tested by the RAF pilots at Martlesham Heath, and as an illustration of Britain's might in the air, the Air Ministry directed that it should appear at the next Display. At that, Alliott Roe secured permission for the civil registered Avenger to be there as well.

On that hot and brilliant day at Hendon a great crowd of 120,000 attended. Though there were fewer events than usual they were none-the-less spectacular, but where the Display differed from its forebears was the proponderance of aircraft designed and built since the Armistice. Sixteen silver-doped aircraft took part in the great fly-past, led by the novel tail-less Pterodactyl. After the fighters came the bombers, and the big Avro Ava piloted by Flt Lieut Webster from Martlesham thundered into the air with a cloud of steam streaming from the port engine. 'Webby' immediately turned down-wind using starboard engine only, banked into a steep side-slip followed by a spectacular swish-tail landing. Roy Chadwick heaved a sigh of relief. Concluding the procession with a touch of comedy came the Avro-built Autogiro flown by Frank Courtney, who formated with the Pterodactyl in an entertaining *pas de deux,* causing C. G. Grey of *The Aeroplane* to comment: 'If one of them is right, the other must be wrong!'

There were no Avro entries for the succeeding King's Cup Race on 9 July. Of the 13 starters, five were 60 hp Cirrus-powered DH Moths, three of which completed the race, Broad winning with the white-painted Moth demonstrator.

Three weeks later, the second 574 Autogiro, the C.6D, was flown by Courtney at Hamble. This was a two-seater, so next day de la Cierva flew as a passenger — the first ever to fly in a rotating-winged aircraft. Chadwick was next, enjoying the experience of being suspended in space at very low speed, and noting with interest the rise and fall of the blades and the periodic vibration. His own design of Avro 576 Autogiro, based on the Avian fuselage, was far from ready because the recently formed Cierva Autogiro

The Ava thunders past.

The seaplane Buffalo II with metal-framed wings nearing completion among 504s and an Autogiro under construction at Hamble. (P. T. Capon).

Company had not completed design of the rotor blades and special rotor-head, whereas the two big Autogiros had the same mechanism and blades as the C.6A prototype.

More urgent to the Avro team was completion of flight-testing the directionally modified Buffalo. Early in August it was flown to Martlesham for comparative trials with the Blackburn Ripon which had just arrived. A few days later, Chadwick drove there to renew aquaintance with Grp Cpt Rees the CO, and N.E. 'Nero' Rowe — but chiefly to learn what the pilots had to say about these machines. That also gave discrete opportunity to inspect the latest aircraft in their hangar, where he was surprised to find an extraordinary lozenge-winged parasol monoplane which Blackburns had built in hope of displacing the Bison.

On returning to Hamble he received an Air Ministry invitation to tender for a single-seat fighter to Specification 17/25, but the requirement could not be met by the Avenger because all-metal construction was stipulated. Though that led to initial thought of substituting a duralumin skin for the wooden monocoque, full investigation of this Avro 584 could not be completed until after the Lympne Competition which opened on 10 September.

Of the sixteen light aircraft entries, thirteen arrived on time, but the ANEC Mistle-Thrush was an immediate casualty when it nosed over on touch-down, and the side-by-side Blackburn Bluebird after making a heavy landing had to be withdrawn when the stewards refused to accept a temporary repair. They also turned down the Halton Aero Club's Mayfly biplane after the undercarriage was damaged, and proved equally adamant with the Westland Woodpigeon and Short Satellite. So strong was feeling against these decisions that a strike by the pilots was proposed, but abandoned as undignified in view of the recent general strike of transport workers and miners. Yet it was not the end of contention. Soon there was dispute over slight damage to the Hawker Cygnet after breaking a shock absorber, and even the Avro team became involved over an independently mounted hand-starting magneto which the stewards ruled was part of the engine and brought the Avian's Genet over the 170 lb limit.

Bad weather resulted in elminations following thick and fast, so only four aircraft were left in the end, and the winner was the superlight but impractical Hawker Cygnet flown by George Bulman. Nevertheless, the Society of Motor Manufacturers Handicap

The first Avro Avian at Lympne, 1926, with Bert Hinkler walking towards the propeller.

Race was won by Hinkler with the Avian, though the Genet-engined Moth flown by Broad was 4½ mph faster.

Certainly the long-winged Avian's load-carrying ability seemed unprecedented because the weight of pilot, passenger and fuel represented 130 per cent of the empty weight — a factor far better than Moth or Bluebird; and her figure of merit (representing load multiplied by distance flown, divided by pounds of fuel used) was 2,092 compared with 2,203 for the winning Cygnet, whereas all others were also-rans. But though that was triumphant tribute to Chadwick's genius, the Avian lost its chance of achieving second place because initially the welded aluminium petrol tank had leaked and could not be cured either with chewing gum or the efforts of a local welder, so continued only partially filled; then the duralumin magneto shaft of the Genet engine broke and could not be rectified in time to complete the requisite total circuits — with the obvious lesson that had it been steel, with penalty of fractionally greater weight, its reliability would have been assured, as Chadwick pointedly told the makers!

Meanwhile, the Cierva C.6D two-seater had been flown to Germany; and on 5 September, Capt Ernst Udet of war-time fighter fame, flew it at Berlin's Templehoff aerodrome. When back at Hamble it had a new rotor fitted featuring tapered, paddle-shaped blades on arms that were unfaired inboard, and in this form was re-designated C.8R (Avro 587). It was also decided by the Avro-Crossley board that the company's hack, the Viper-powered 552 derivative of the 504 G-EAPR, should be converted to an Autogiro using similar rotors and head.

Suprisingly there were no Autogiros at the annual Paris Aero Show, but study of the latest French and Dutch aircraft was certainly rewarding for the many British technicians attending the Grande Palais. Metal construction was widespread, and most of the French machines were aerodynamically cleaner than British designs. Thus the latest Breguet was a reconnaissance two-seater with I-strutted wings and semi-monocoque fuselage, resulting in so clean a machine that it had gained the world's long distance record of 3,350 miles in 32 hours non-stop. However, it was the Fokker three-engined commercial airliner which held Roy Chadwick's major attention because its welded steel tube fuselage and plywood covered wing were the essence of simplicity and thus of relatively low cost construction. Versed as he was in the use of pin-jointed steel tube structures, he believed that it might well be worth obtaining a licence for Fokker construction at Manchester.

With Christmas came the family party at which the junior Chadwicks joined the seniors in celebration — but this time not only was his married sister Doris far away in South Africa, but Alan had sailed for Kenya to join her at the sisal ranch operated by her husband at Thika, near Nairobi. Reviewing the past year in the quiet of the night, Roy Chadwick had to face the fact that there had been several big disappointments. The fighter competition between the Avenger, Gorcock, and Hornbill, had resulted in none being accepted, and trials of the Buffalo, Ripon, and Harrow had been won by the Ripon. What were the chances of his Avro 584 design for the 17/25 Specification shipboard fighter, he wondered?

* * *

In later years, P. T. Capon wrote reflectively in *Aeroplane Monthly* that after leaving the de Havilland Co because design work had declined, he was offered a job with Avro at Hamble. 'So on Sunday, 2 January 1927, my faithful old Rudge motorbike was pointed south and the following morning I reported to Jock Ratcliffe, Avro's chief draughtsman.

'At Stag Lane, design had been very much of an "upstairs-downstairs" pattern, with a sequence of descending seniorities. Avro's Hamble set-up was completely different: there were four times as many draughtsmen, all slaving away on such machines as the Aldershot, Bison, and Ava modifications, the Avian biplanes, a naval fighter named Avocet. Cierva Autogiros, and subsequent

Antelope. And of course there was a section devoted (as there had since time began) to development of the Avro 504, which in 1927 had now run the alphabetical scale to 504R. All the aircraft, being more-or-less hand built, were of the highest standard of British workmanship.

'Design activities were the responsibility of Roy Chadwick and his assistant H. E. Broadsmith, and one could safely assume that practically every day "Chaddie", "Broadie", or Mr Rogerson (in charge of the Stress Office) would be around, together with the particular aircraft's section leader, to look at each draughtsman's work. I think everyone liked "Chaddie". Although he occasionally blew up he was usually helpful, appreciative, and had a nice sense of humour. And of course, there was the great man himself, "A.V.". He had a small office just outside the DO. As it was opposite the "loo" I often encountered this friendly and fatherly figure who had been in on the ground-floor when aviation really began in this country.'

Derek Carter, who joined Avro at the same time as Capon and eventually became head of the Projects' Department, similarly wrote: 'Although as a young man (in common with most of my colleagues) I viewed Roy Chadwick's office presence with a certain apprehension, I always appreciated his genius as a great designer — a view which has become even stronger in retrospect. Away from the main drawing office in our small department, the aura of "great white chief" would be relaxed, and one could see just how dedicated Roy was in providing the very best aircraft to do a specific task. He had an instinctive ability to see what was required without the usual trial and error thought process and this, coupled with his considerable ability to co-ordinate and harness the talents of what eventually amounted to more than 200 designers, resulted in some of the most practicable and formidable aircraft of his era. I shall always look back on my time in his service with a great deal of pride, for I believe that I was privileged to work for a very great man.'

Both these young men had the experience of seeing the first flight of the Typhoon-powered Aldershot Mk 4 on 10 January, and mightily impressive she seemed in the hands of Bert Hinkler. A fortnight later, this big aeroplane was demonstrated at Hamble to a distinguished gathering of VIPs and eager Pressmen. A few days later, Bert flew the Aldershot to the Engine Research Flight at Farnborough for extended trials.

As the centre of every kind of aeronautical research, the RAE was paramount. Every aircraft designer made frequent visits to discuss particular problems, such as metallurgy, high lift devices, or advanced methods of stressing aircraft structures. One of the outstanding pundits was the aerodynamicist H. Glauert, who on 20 January lectured to the Royal Aeronautical Society at the Society of Arts on *The Theory of the Autogiro* which reached the not unreasonable conclusion: 'All that can be said is that neither the full-scale tests, nor the wind tunnel observations at the National Physical Laboratory, give any indication of a lift-drag ratio superior to that suggested by theory, and I believe that the giroplane will always be slightly inferior to the aeroplane at top speed. On the other hand, it has very important advantages of a slower landing speed and of the absence of a sudden and violent stall.'

Roy Chadwick diplomatically did not participate in the discussion though he knew more about the practical side than anyone present. However Cierva, who had not been present, wrote fiercely from his headquarters at Bush House in Aldwich: 'I must record my protest against the manner in which Mr Glauert has made assertions in almost axiomatic form from which the evident conclusion must be drawn that the Autogiro is, in effect, useless. Such assertions are based on incomplete and uncertain calculations which are not in agreement with experimental results . . . He is trying to treat in too simple and theoretical a manner a most complicated and novel aerodynamic problem, and has considered his conclusions as proven when he might well have waited for the shortly forthcoming tests to tell us the truths.'

With that, Chadwick fully agreed. By now

Though straightforward, the experimental metal skinned fuselage test section of the Avocet was a pioneering project.

The Avocet fuselage ready for skinning had strongly built-up stiffening frames taking flying and landing loads.

he had met Cierva on a number of ocasions, was delighted with his charm and optimism, and admired his engineering skill. Cierva told him: 'Invention is merely a product of logical thinking, and practically any engineer with a mathematical background can be trained as an inventor.'

Certainly that defined Roy Chadwick. His explorative mind was for ever encompassing new aeroplanes. Not only was he directing his team on design of the Avro 584 Avocet single-seat Fleet fighter with pioneering monocoque stressed skin fuselage, but also projecting possible variants of a two-seater reconnaissance fighter to Specification 22/26, including a three-seat bomber version. He had also heard from his Air Ministry contacts that there would shortly be a requirement for an Army Co-operation machine, for which Specification 26/27 would soon be issued for open competition.

However there was renewed trouble with his right arm as a result of that piloting accident seven years ago. He consulted Sir Arbuthnot Lane, and X-rays disclosed that the ulna was infected. The great surgeon performed one of his delicate grafting operations, taking a sliver of bone from Roy's thigh to replace the damaged portion. A few weeks later, X-rays showed that the operation was successful, but golf was permanently banned, and violin playing out of the question.

* * *

The New Year had brought the Autogiro into prominence in unfortunate manner. At Worthy Down on 1 January, Courtney had tested the single-seat C.6C Autogiro fitted with paddle-type rotor blades, but on 7 February a blade broke away during a flight at Hamble and Courtney crashed from 100 ft, 'the machine fluttering down instead of falling direct and the pilot escaping with a severe shaking and a broken rib or two. He was taken to Hamble Hospital, and is progressing satisfactorily.'

Forty years later, Courtney wrote: 'I quit my association with Cierva after this. I had discovered that the rotor blade roots bent in the drag direction, so had proposed a vertical hinge, but he considered that his funny, weighted cables between the blades were sufficient safeguard. When the blade eventually broke through fatigue induced by drag reversals he tried to blame me and everyone else, but thereafter included the vertical hinges. By then I'd had enough of his indignation at suggestions coming from anybody else, and we parted.'

Chadwick's two-seater C.8L derivation of the C.6C Autogiro.

That did not affect the work at Hamble, for Bert Hinkler had proved adept at rotary wing flight. Such was the Air Ministry's confidence in the Hamble design and constructional ability that a contract was issued for a further prototype designated Avro 611 (C.8L), based on the Lynx-powered Avro 504N with augmented undercarriage shock absorption capacity characterised by long oleo legs attached to the top longerons instead of the bottom.

Chadwick's major concentration was on the Avocet and the mechanical testing of built-up portions of its stressed-skin fuselage for which Parrott was developing techniques of pneumatically rivetting the progressive sequence of circular sections. Only Short Bros Ltd had previous experience of this kind of work. The wing bracing also was a radical departure, but unknown to Chadwick his old friend and rival, Frank Barnwell at Bristol, had adopted the same idea for a fighter currently under construction. Both these biplanes featured N-interplane struts enabling lift loads to be taken by a single plane of bracing — but whereas Barnwell used conventional Raf-wires, Chadwick employed a single downward-sloping lift strut each side, taking either tension or compression loads. By further coincidence, both designers raised the fuselages a little above the lower wing in expectation of reducing flow interference. However, the Avocet had an Armstrong Siddeley Lynx IV of only 180 hp, compared with the 450 hp Jupiter VI radial of the Bristol.

In the background the original Avian was being largely developed by Hinkler, who had bought the prototype at a special discount. He reduced the wing-span by 4 ft, re-located the interplane struts after stiffening the spars, and the rudder was enlarged and fitted to a fin. An 85 hp ADC Cirrus II vertical four-cylinder was installed and neatly cowled to give a pointed nose. Concurrently two similar but considerably strengthened Chadwick versions were being built as prototypes to rival the well-established DH Moths, which recently had been reduced to £730. Hopefully, A. V. Roe & Co advertised this new Avian at '£675 with Cirrus, or £750 with Genet', and a batch of six was laid down at Manchester.

Hinkler's machine and the two new prototypes, G-EBQN and QL were duly certified in time for the Bournemouth Easter meeting, 15 — 18 April. Such occasions gave opportunity for the industry to encourage the goodwill of RAF pilots by loaning demonstration aircraft for sporting events, Wing Cdr Sholto Douglas (eventually Marshal of the RAF, Baron Douglas of Kirtleside) flew Avian QN, and Flt Lt Grey (later Air Vice-Marshal) from Martlesham flew QL, with Hinkler and his G-EBOV as their rival. Chadwick and his wife were there

Chadwick, Hinkler, and Parrott with the revised Avian.

The box-like forward section of the fuselage and simple tail construction of the new Avro 604 later named 'Antelope'.

to join in the fun, having left 4-year-old Margaret with Grandmother Chadwick, and it became a celebratory vindication of the Avian when Hinkler swept the board by winning the 'Killjoy Stakes' at 89 mph, and the Holiday Handicap at 93 mph, with Flt Lt Grey second. There was, however, an emotional moment when the latter's engine failed but he pulled off an impeccable forced landing.

A month later, the whole world was startled by news that an unknown, boyish-looking, lanky American, Charles Lindbergh had flown the Atlantic all alone in a single-engined Ryan monoplane, and had landed at Paris at 10.22 p.m. on 21 May after a flight of 33 hours — the world's first solo crossing by air.

By now Avro design had reached 100 since the original Type 500, and three more followed that Spring, the last being a 3-engined 8-seater monoplane for Austrian Airways Ltd but was never built because of that country's financial problems — so Chadwick was now considering the design study of another all-metal machine for selective competition to Specification 12/26, powered with a 480 hp Rolls-Royce. This time, for easier construction, he decided on a flat metal skin for the fuselage.

'It was remarkable how he could adapt from one requirement to the next,' one of his draughtsmen told me. 'Multi-engined or single, bomber, fighter, light plane, seaplane, or autogiro were all within his scope, and he had an instinctive appreciation of the actual size and gauge required for any fitting or structural member, suggesting, say, a three inch tube of 20 gauge to special specification, and when the stressman calculated the loads it would carry, the strength would be exactly right.'

While Chadwick was busy with the preliminary stages of the new design, Bert Hinkler was devoting his engineering skill to his own Avian by ingeniously fitting a wide track, split-axle undercarriage, so that on folding the wings the wheels were drawn rearward by the radius rod attached outward of the rear hinge on a diagonally cut stub-winglet which mounted the shock absorber leg. Lifting the tail with wings folded was always a problem with any aeroplane because of the weight, but with this simple re-arrangement of undercarriage geometry, the wheels eased the load by moving rearward to the new c.g. This proved so successful that the system was incorporated in subsequent production Avians which were referenced MkII, the first of which was sold to wealthy Dudley Watt, known as 'Dangerous Dan', who flew it at the opening flying meeting of the newly-formed Hampshire Aero Club at Hamble in mid May.

Though the clouds were low and the wind gusty, there were aerobatics by a Gamecock and an Avro Gosport, and a great fly-past ranging from a diminutive DH 53 to the splendid Avro Ava, while three impressive Southampton flying boats from Calshot circled low around the aerodrome. There were glimpses of famous pilots, close inspection of their aeroplanes, and the fascination of discovering that almost mythical pioneer Mr A. V. Roe with his famous designer Roy Chadwick among a group of men and their ladies having tea in a marquee.

The subsequent Whitsun Meeting at Bournemouth was less fortunate. There were forced landings and smashes, and when Major Hemming, of the Aircraft Operating Co stalled the DH 37 *Lois* at 60 ft and hit a steel-framed number board, his passenger was so injured that he died in hospital. But Racing continued. Hinkler won the Private Owners' Handicap, and the Bournemouth Hotel Sweepstake was won by Dudley Watt with his Avian.

There was further tragedy on Monday. Twelve started in the Handicap Race, but Flt Lieut Grey's Avian dropped out. The remaining eleven rounded the aerodrome turning point in a bunch, and as they straightened, the Widgeon flown by Major Openshaw and a Bluebird piloted by Longton collided and fell. Black smoke coiled up. Longton, the great aerobatic pilot, was instantly killed and Westland test pilot Openshaw died after an hour-long agony of burns.

But the peak of all aeronautical events was always the annual RAF Display in midsummer. Although the current occasion on 2 July proved a day of drizzling rain and gusting north-east winds, the British public turned up in their thousands and the huge new grandstand was packed. At 3 pm precisely, while bombing Squadrons were taking off for group evolutions, the King and Queen arrived, accompanied by the King of Spain and the exiled King and Queen of Greece. Then, one by one, the new type aircraft took to the air in striking contrast — but Mary Chadwick only had eyes for her husband's elegant twin-engined Ava. His Avocet was still under construction, and the Avro 572 Buffalo II had just returned to Hamble from Martlesham for fitment of a new set of metal-structured wings which not only had Frise-balanced ailerons to give lighter lateral control but also inter-linked Handley Page slots for greater rolling power at low speeds.

Episode after episode followed, and as though in remembrance of Longton, crazy flying was re-introduced after an absence of three years. This time, it was a duet by two of the recently-introduced Avro 504N trainers, flown by Flt Lts Lydford and Fogarty, who thrilled the crowd with a hair-raising display of what was programmed as 'simultaneous flying at each end of the aerodrome', comprising skidding turns, near collisions, straights and serpentines with wheels or wingtips actually touching the ground, varied with hide-and-seek among three squadrons of day-bombers waiting on the aerodrome with engines running.

Autogiros had not featured at this Display, largely because they were more often grounded than airborne during experimental research at Farnborough and Hamble. Thus

The crazy-flying Avros.

the Viper-powered C.8V, G-EBTX after early trials with the original undercarriage, had been flying since January with a tricycle-like chassis employing twin forward wheels, but now would revert to the original because it was lighter and equally effective.

However, it was the Avian which was now attracting attention as a potential rival of the Moth. When Lady Bailey, accompanied by Mrs. de Havilland, secured a world height record for women by climbing to 17,283 ft with a DH 60X Moth on 5 July, Avro countered the publicity by sponsoring Lady Heath (better known as the sportswoman Mrs Elliott-Lynn) to land her Avian Mk II G-EBRS at 80 aerodromes and 'touch-and-go' fields during a circuit of England on 19 July, followed by a sensational 3,000 mile stage by stage tour to Poland and back, spectacularly ending in a forced landing at Bromley, Kent, after running out of fuel. That meant she had to borrow a Moth for the King's Cup Race at Hucknall on 30 July, but engine trouble prevented her starting. Engine failure also befell Bert Hinkler, who was flying an Avian powered with a hand-made 100 hp Avro Alpha radial which Alliott Roe was hoping to standardize, and to the chagrin of the Avro team, the ever-smiling Wally Hope, flying the scarlet two-year old Moth G-EBME of Air Taxis Ltd, was the winner.

Hinkler had his own idea of publicising the Avian and had fitted a long-range tank in the front cockpit. In the dawn of 27 August he took off from Croydon and in an elapsed time of 10¾ hours flew the 1,200 miles to Riga in Latvia — the world's longest non-stop flight by a light aeroplane. Seizing the opportunity he demonstrated the machine to the Latvian Air Force, and that ultimately led to an order for Avian trainers: then by easy stages he flew back to Hamble, convinced that he could similarly make the long run to Australia.

Lady Heath and her Avian.

Though flying was often headline news, it was becoming an accepted mode of travel whether by light aeroplane or struggling airline. The long distance flights of Hinkler and Lady Heath were soon emulated by many others. Even attempts at flying the Atlantic became almost a matter of indifference to the public, but there was re-awakened national interest in the current British attempt at challenging the Italians for the forthcoming Schneider Trophy Contest at Venice in September, and Bert Hinkler was enlisted to test the privately entered Short Crusader seaplane at Felixstowe. However when flown by F/O Schofield after assembly at the Porto di Lido it half rolled on taking-off and dived upside down into the sea due to a control rigging error which reversed the aileron movement. That foreshadowed a tragic Avro event of many years later.

On the day of the Contest, the shores of the long island separating the lagoon from the Adriatic were crowded with spectators. At five minute intervals each of the three Italian and three British pilots took off. But the Italians were unlucky. Their Macchi seaplanes were forced to alight with engine failure. The field was left open and Flt Lt Webster, flying the beautiful Supermarine S5 won with an average of 281.65 mph, breaking the world speed record by 3 mph. What jubilation for the British!

Avro victories were slighter. Earlier that month Dudley Watt flying his Avian G-EBRC, gained the altitude prize at the Copenhagen flying meeting with 12,750 ft in 90 minutes. Unfortunately his intended return to Hamble went sadly wrong. Well off course, he ran out of fuel and ditched just off the Isle of Wight. Lady Heath did somewhat better, and on 8 October, flying the Alpha-engined Avian fitted with special RAF 28 elliptically-tipped wings, managed to reach 19,200 ft after

Trial assembly of the Avocet reveals built-up box-section spars and duralumin ribs.

two hours at full throttle; but like Watt, she became lost under misty conditions and forced landed in a field at Frodsham in Cheshire.

A month later the next Avocet Type 584 single-seat Fleet fighter was ready for structural assessment by Farnborough pundits. Like the Supermarine S5 racer, the metal-skinned fuselage had been flush-rivetted to secure an absolutely smooth surface — but aerodynamic perfection was impossible because of the turbulent drag of the projecting cylinders of the radial engine. However, the conception of mid-gap location for the fuselage was complementary to an unusual Naval requirement that the wings must be quickly detachable instead of folding. Clever design made it a simple matter to remove the lower wing complete with N-struts, leaving the top wing rigidly strut-braced, but readily be removeable by unpinning the lower end of the diagonal lift-strut and folding along the wing under-surface for storage. A further unusual feature was the landing flap fitted only to the top wing because the lower wing in any case gained enhanced lift from its close proximity to the ground.

Farnborough spent several weeks conducting structural tests of this novel wing-bracing system — but though Roy Chadwick might fume at the hold-up it was bad weather which further delayed the initial test flight; but presently the low cloud ceiling lifted, and on the first calm day in December Hinkler made a short handling flight which revealed that the tail required resetting for longitudinal trim.

Meanwhile the flailing wings of Autogiros had become a common sight at Hamble. In mid September Hinkler made the first flight of the little Avro 576 (C.9) Autogiro which Roy Chadwick had devised from the original Lympne competition Avian design by using the reserve fuselage. Numbered J.8931, and adorned with RAF roundels and tri-colour rudder, this brisk-looking machine was presently flown to Farnborough for more detailed trials. Hinkler had also been giving Autogiro instruction to Cierva, who had recently learnt to fly the standard Avian biplane acquired by the Hampshire Aeroplane Club. Day after day he turned up for more flying, and now was so proficient that he was intensively conducting development of the C.8L with Hinkler and on 30 September made the delivery flight to Farnborough, incidentally setting up the first

The small single-seater C.9 Autogiro devised by Chadwick to use the reserve prototype Avian fuselage. (C. T. Capon).

UK cross-country record for rotary-winged aircraft. The Viper-powered C.8V had also completed tests and on 20 October Hinkler exceeded Cierva's journey by flying it to Croydon for a demonstration arranged by John Lord, and then back to Hamble that same evening.

* * *

Ever conscious of family responsibilities, which included subsidising his father's business. Roy Chadwick kept a close eye on his financial affairs. He was now the most highly paid employee except Reg Parrott and the chief accountant — but unlike Parrott he also received a bonus for every new design. Perhaps Crossley Motors was feeling the pinch, their shares having dropped from 33s in 1920 to less than 5s, and consequently were slow in paying the bonus. Early in January 1928 he tactfully reminded Walter Fenton, the secretary, that he had not yet received the 'design payment according to my agreement' for the C.8 and C.9 Autogiros constructed for the Air Ministry, the C.8V built for the Autogiro Co, and the Avian land and seaplane prototypes with Cirrus and Genet engines. 'In order for you to be able to identify the Autogiros I enclose photographs showing the different types. I shall be much obliged if you will kindly arrange for Sir William to send a cheque covering the designs. These jobs have been spread over a period of eighteen months or two years.'

Sir William Letts promptly replied:-

'I have asked Mr Baker, our accountant, to send you a cheque for £100 in connection with bonuses, but there is the question of three additional Autogiro machines for which you have put in a claim. Do not think that I wish to evade anything which is right, but I cannot appreciate that there can be five distinct Autogiro types with a design altering to such extent that they can be dealt with as entirely new types. Mr Lord is not here today, otherwise I'd have had the whole matter settled. Please always ring me when you are in Manchester even if we have no real business to discuss, for I always like to shake hands'.

Chadwick stuck to his guns and wrote:-

'I am sorry that I did not have the pleasure of seeing you when I was in Manchester, but it was only a flying visit and most of the day was spent at the aerodrome carrying out tests on the Mark III Avians.

'I am assuming that the £100 is a bonus for the Avian design. I take it that you have no query over the C9, which is the Genet-engined machine I designed for the Air Ministry. The only confusion that could arise would be between the C8 Lynx-engined machine for the Air Ministry and the C8V Viper-engined for the Cierva company. Although of similar general dimensions, they are very different in detail of fuselage, undercarriage, stabilising plane and the ailerons, flying controls, engine installation, fuel and oil systems but to reduce design costs I have kept the rotor blades, pylon bearings and blade articulations, tailplane and rudder. As far as possible in designing a new machine, I endeavour to use as much of our standard detail and components as possible, but this should not prejudice the question of whether the design is a new one.'

To John Lord he was a little forthcoming and in deference to him as his senior in age and position was careful to address him as 'Mr Lord' when thanking him for his kind assistance in resolving the matter of bonuses. Perhaps Roy felt his honour had been impinged, for he reiterated that: 'I want to make it clear that I have not in any way attempted to describe two similar machines as two different ones. Thus in the case of the Avian there have been three different types apart from fitting different engines and arranging the machine as a seaplane, but I took the view that these were developments of each other. Had I wished to make the Autogiros look entirely different this would have been an easy matter, for I could have made the few components which are interchangeable between the types, different from each other — but, in my opinion that would have been most reprehensible.'

By then, it was February 1928. Bert Hinkler had resigned after dispute with Chadwick. C. G. Gray, who knew Hinkler well, said: 'I know Bert is difficult to work with. He has all the self-reliance and convictions of the great pioneers who made the British Empire. Consequently, if he says such-and-such a thing should be done in such-and-such a way, he is not greatly impressed when told it ought to be done in a different way.'

Bert spent the next few weeks in fitting his Avian with the special wings from the Alpha-powered, high-altitude 594C Avian, the undercarriage was replaced by a stronger structure, and he obtained one of the newly introduced twisted metal-blade Fairey propellers for his carefully overhauled Cirrus II engine. The Press had been full of Alan Cobham's stage-by-stage flight to the Cape in a Short Singapore flyingboat, but now it was tough little Hinkler who took the headlines. At 6.48 am on 7 February, he took off from Croydon, heading for Australia. Already an attempt to fly there with an Avian III piloted by Capt Lancaster, with sponsoring Mrs Keith Miller as passenger, had come to grief in the Dutch East Indies on 10 January, and the machine had been shipped to Singapore for repairs. While the couple were there, the

The Avocet seaplane as flown by Luxmoore.

The Avenger ready for first flight in racing guise and fitted with ailerons on both wings. (P. E. L. Luxmoore).

indomitable Hinkler passed on his swift passage to Australia and achieved Darwin in 15½ days, having covered 11,000 miles in 128 hours flying time with overnight stops each day. That was almost half the time taken by Ross and Keith Smith in 1919, so Hinkler became the instant hero of the hour.

Fortunately the Avro businesses at Manchester and Hamble had each secured a new pilot. Thirty-one-year-old Capt H. A. 'Sam' Brown, the calmly self-contained but friendly chief instructor of the Lancashire Aero Club at Woodford, was recruited for the Manchester-built aircraft. He was well-known to Roy Dobson, who often flew the Avian I given to the Club by John Lord as replacement for the unreliable Gnome-powered Avro Gosport which Sir William Letts had presented the previous Spring. Capt Brown, who had been educated in Paris, was an ex-RNAS pilot and held one of the earliest commercial B licenses (No. 17) in 1919 when he originally joined the Avro joy-riding team, but subsequently became chief instructor of the Spanish Naval Air Service from 1921 to 1926.

At Hamble the new pilot was the eager and affluent Flt Lieut Frank Luxmoore DFC who later told me: 'I was on a year's half-pay from the RAF and living at home at Beaulieu when I did my flying at Hamble. I had known Mr Roe personally since I was a boy, hero-worshipping him in his early days at Brooklands, so I looked him up when I heard he was short of a pilot and he promptly engaged me. Chadwick was always appreciative of any comment I might make on any aircraft I flew, and most concerned if anything caused a problem. One of my first flights was with the Avocet, and I bent it on my first landing because the axle broke in spite of a near-perfect touch-down. I remember how profuse were his apologies when he admitted that he had employed an inferior material. Unfortunately the Avocet was underpowered, but after a few more flights, Chadwick put the machine on floats —and that was a real challenge as I had never

The C.17 Avro 612 Autogiro was based on a production Avian IIIA fuselage. (P. T. Capon).

flown off the water before. In the event I found the take-off easy, but once airborne the machine became unacceptably nose-heavy as speed increased, and I had a bit of a job putting it down. I can't remember how he rectified the fault, but again he was lavish with his regrets for having subjected me to such a hazard on my first seaplane flight.

'I couldn't do other than hold him in high regard as a designer after flying the MkII Avenger which had smaller, equal-span mainplanes and streamlined I-type interplane struts, and was powered by a beautifully cowled 550 hp Napier Lion IX fitted with an Avro metal propeller. It was an absolute delight to fly. Chadwick's compatability with pilots was very good, but I did not really have any insight of his relations with Martlesham personnel, though I remember him in hilarious form there on one of the Guest nights.

'He told me a certain amount about Alliott Roe that was new to me, including the fact that the great man had been a racing trick-cyclist, and once was grabbed by the Navy and enlisted for a week as a rating so that they could use him to win some cycling or circus event! Chadwick also showed me some stairs in the factory down which he had seen A. V. ride his bike to demonstrate his trick-cycling skill.'

* * *

Bereft of Hinkler's skills with the Autogiros, Cierva was encountering problems. The mercurial Harold Bolas, chief designer of Parnall's at Yate, had also been designing Autogiros for the Air Ministry, but now Cierva crashed the Cirrus-powered Parnall C.11 equivalent of the Avro 617 (C.8L) on attempting to take-off before the rotor attained sufficient speed, and the machine turned over and was wrecked. Soon afterwards the smaller Parnall C.10 was written off at Farnborough during comparative trials with the Avro 576 (C.9.), and a few days later Cierva attempted to fly the Viper-powered Avro 587 (C.8R) in a high wind to gain experience under bad conditions, but again took off before the rotor was spinning fast enough, and once more turned over. Dismayed, he engaged Flt Lt G. I. Thomson, chief instructor of the Hampshire Aeroplane Club at Hamble, as test pilot for the Autogiro Co.

In high hope of cornering rotary wing business the Avro directors sanctioned a private venture Autogiro designated Type 612 (C.17), for which Chadwick employed the basic fuselage of the Avro Avian IIIA, powered with a 90 hp Cirrus III. The strut-braced auxiliary wing carrying full span ailerons aimed at off-loading the rotor and afforded anchorage for the wide-track undercarriage.

In his mind's eye, Chadwick was also contemplating competitive improvements to the Avian, including a seaplane version and a ski undercarriage for Canadian use. However, news that Lady Heath, who had shipped her Avian III to South Africa in December of the previous year, had started a leisurely flight back to Croydon on 24 February was mingled with apprehension until it was learned that the experienced Dick Bentley was accompanying her with his Moth lest she encountered trouble in the wilds. They reached Cairo on 3 April, but here Bentley learned that Lady Bailey, wife of millionaire Sir Abe Bailey, had had her Moth impounded to prevent her flying unescorted across Southern Sudan, so he gallantly accompanied her southward to Kisumu on Lake Victoria, whence she continued alone but crashed at Abora though was subsequently rescued. Meanwhile, Lady Heath was stranded at Cairo because the RAF refused to let her fly the Mediterranean unaccompanied — such was the concern for adventurous ladies. However, after waiting a fortnight in hope of Bentley's return, she decided to fly via Heliopolis and Benghazi to Tripoli where Mussolini promised that a seaplane would escort her to Italy.

Unfolding the morning paper on 17 May, Mary Chadwick read with secret delight: 'Lady Heath stepped from her tiny aeroplane at Le Bourget this morning, after a long journey from Cape Town as fresh as a daisy.

Second prototype with big rudder for Fleet Air Arm.

"It is so safe," she said, "that a woman can fly across Africa wearing a Parisian frock and keep her nose powdered all the way!" '.

But by now Roy Chadwick was more concerned about the Avocet because tailplane/fuselage interference was affecting the airflow over the rudder, which consequently had to be made taller, and then Luxmoore had to experiment with an added horn-balance to lighten the foot-load, so a proportionately similar balance was introduced in the rudder design of the provisionally named Antelope Avro 604 day bomber.

As always, Chadwick was engaged on concurrent projects. Only recently he had completed design of two triple Jupiter-engined monoplane flying boats of 110 ft span to Air Ministry Specification 4/27, intended for Imperial Airways' use on the Mediterranean section of the new India Air Route; but officialdom remained too hide-bound with traditional techniques and still regarded monoplanes with deep suspicion, so the contract went to Short Bros for biplanes. Undaunted, he had proceeded with three other diverse designs and now was scheming a twin-engined night bomber to meet Air Ministry Specification B.19/27. But he was a worried man. The shares of Crossley Motors Ltd had dropped to an all-time low of 1s 6d. Their annual report revealed a loss of £65,518 attributed to the cost of developing a new 20.9 hp six-cylinder car — though there was comforting assurance that the accumulated reserve profit of the Avro aircraft section exceeded £27,000.

On 25 May the *Financial News* stated: 'As recently foreshadowed, arrangements have been completed whereby Sir William M. Letts, Crossley's manager, has sold to the Armstrong Siddeley Development Co Ltd the whole of its share capital in A. V. Roe & Co Ltd. Sir William Letts has handed over the sum of £270,000 in cash to Crossley Motors, for their shares, which shows a profit of more than £200,000 from their original investment in A. V. Roe & Co Ltd.'

To Chadwick it seemed disaster because the take-over might mean complete design subordination to Major Green, the caustically forceful Armstrong Siddeley chief engineer who had been war-time head of the Royal Establishment's design department both for engines and aircraft. It seemed impossible to serve under him — and in any case

40-year-old John Lloyd, FRAeS.

Armstrongs already had an outstanding chief designer in 40-year-old John Lloyd, a kindly man with considerable mathematical ability, whose Siskin had become the standard RAF fighter, and recently his two-seat Army Co-op Atlas had gone into full production.

However, Alliott Roe, now 51, remained optimistic as ever in his fussy, diffident, charming manner. 'There is no question of dismissing the Avro staff,' he assured Chadwick. 'John Siddeley has decided to run the Avro and Armstrong Whitworth businesses as complementary firms. For the time being, at least, we shall continue with design work and experimental flying at Hamble.'

That somewhat eased his designer's disquiet though well aware that John Siddeley had the reputation of being a most difficult man. Like cheerful 'Billy' Letts when foreman of Crossleys, Siddeley had achieved fame and fortune the hard way. His original Siddeley-Deasy car company had become a huge business as war-time producer of the Puma aero engines, and after the Armistice he had taken over the moribund aircraft division of Armstrong Whitworth at Newcastle, which he transferred to Babington, near Coventry, to continue with aircraft design, and concurrently had modernised his original engine works in that city to establish production of radial engines developed by Major Green. Indeed one of the reasons prompting Siddeley to acquire the Avro business had been likelihood of its intrusion on his engine sales by producing the promising Alpha 5-cylinder radial in quantity and continuing with a range of larger engines.

Always known by his workmen as 'The Gaffer', he gave the impression of great energy and determination, even ruthlessness, and characteristically talked with his head inclined over his left shoulder. He knew all employees by name and often asked about their families, though equally would erupt with fury if he thought there was slackness or that material was being mis-handled or scrapped. With swift Midland-accented tongue, he would say to the foreman: 'Eh, Mr Simmonds — that wants to be on move, that's money in the bank: get them into the shops.' Ever blunt, he said what he thought with strong conviction, and was a formidable adversary yet eminently kindly to his friends.

Cautiously, Chadwick advanced a proposition, backed by a technical study, that a licence should be secured for Fokker welded-tube fuselage construction and ply-covered wooden wings — and Siddeley proved amenable. Accordingly, it was arranged that Dobson, Broadsmith, and Chadwick should visit Amsterdam to study Fokker constructional methods in detail, and negotiate a licence if satisfied. Within weeks that was done, and John Siddeley had ratified the agreement.

Chadwick had already schemed a 3-engined commercial monoplane with strutted shoulder wing, but now abandoned it in favour of a replica Fokker VIIA/3m based on Fokker drawings which his technicians were converting to British Standard sizes of material and manufacturing tolerances. Powered by three 240 hp Armstrong Siddeley Lynx IV radials, it would carry eight passengers and two crew, so was designated Avro Ten, Type 618. Some months would

The Royal Air Force purchased a Fokker VIIA/3m from Holland for research.

pass before construction could begin; meanwhile, a small working party was sent to the Fokker factory to learn the techniques of welding and Parrott was searching for a British source of manganese-carbon steel that required no normalising after heating.

* * *

In its new guise with distinctive I-struts, the Avenger II was demonstrated with a brilliant aerobatic display by Luxmoore at the Hampshire Air Pageant at Hamble on 28 May. Five weeks later it was flown by Flt Lt Webster of Schneider fame at an air meeting at Squires Gate, Blackpool, where he averaged 180.25 mph in the Handicap Race though first place went to an Avro Avian flown by Sam Brown. However, Chadwick was still worried about the future and felt that the sale of Avro shares indicated lack of faith in him by the Crossley directors. In a gesture of goodwill, Sir William Letts had sent him a letter of thanks and a cheque for £250. That, in itself, seemed a belittlement, so he boldy replied:

'You have always treated me well and kindly and I am grateful to you personally for giving me a present, but I think the shareholders might have made more adequate provision for myself and one or two others who have helped very materially in increasing the capital value from the original small sum to the very large sum for which shareholders finally sold the company.

'As you know, I have been with Mr Roe in this business since early in 1912 and my designs have produced large profits. For

The Avro 604 Antelope with 480 hp Rolls- Royce F.XI B engine.

many years I took considerable personal risks in experimental flights and finally sustained severe injuries in a crash whilst carrying out experiments in controllability. These injuries have caused considerable suffering and I am still having a lot of trouble with my arm. The £250 which you have kindly given will about pay the expenses incurred last year over the operation on my arm. I think you will agree that this is not exactly a handsome return for the part I have had in building up the firm of A. V. Roe & Co Ltd from its beginning to the valuable concern it has now become.'

There was no reply, and that did not help matters, but perhaps the Royal Air Force Display three days later helped to mollify his worries because except for the hugely dominating, very advanced, metal-skinned Beadmore Inflexible monoplane of 120 ft span all other aircraft had conventionally fabric-covered wings and fuselages, so he at least had the consolation that the metal-skinned fuselage of his Antelope was way ahead of competitors.

That neat two-seat day bomber was at last ready in August. Pre-occupation with its testing prevented attending the subsequent Paris Aero Show where the only British exhibit was a Bristol Bulldog single-seater fighter shown entirely in construction on the port side but fabric covered on the other and 'considered by visitors of all nations to be the finest example ever seen of all-metal girder construction.'

Even higher praise might have been bestowed on the Antelope, for it was as elegant as the rival fabric-skinned Hawker Hart prototype of the same 12/26 Specification but looked far more workmanlike because of the duralumin skin which the Hamble craftsmen had managed to rivet without dimple or wrinkle to the duralumin framework of spacers and L-section longerons. To prevent elastic buckling at low load and afford reserve strength for heavier equipment, Chadwick used somewhat thicker metal than theory demanded, with consequent penalty of 320 lbs greater tare weight than the Hart, though both had the same laden weight of 4,550 lbs. Test flying the Antelope revealed no abnormal snags, and on 13 September this advanced biplane was flown by Sam Brown to Martlesham Heath for comparative trials against the Hart and a completely redesigned Fairey Fox. Both the latter topped 180 mph, but the Antelope though equal in manoeuverability was some 10 mph slower because it was lower powered — yet extraordinarily enough, it was the metal skin which proved the draw-back because the RAF preferred the easier internal access afforded by conventional laced-on fabric covers.

While these machines were at Martlesham I encountered Roy Chadwick in the fighter hangar. Immaculately garbed in light grey suit and Homburg hat, he was examining the Westland Wizard.

'How do you like her, sir?' I asked with the diffidence of a junior to this renowned designer.

'A very neat effort,' he replied with no trace of a Lancashire accent, and with cautious diplomacy questioned me on matters of design at Westland.

That afternoon the re-fashioned Avro Avenger piloted by helmet-less Frank Luxmoore came sweeping in for F/O 'Mutt' Summers to fly in the 1,000 mile King's Cup Race at Hendon on 20 July but on that day his most formidable opponent, George Bulman with the Hawker Heron, was eliminated by blundering into a car while taxying towards the starting line, and among ten others who

The rival Hawker Hart had a conventional metal-framed fuselage which was lighter than the Antelope's. (G. Quick).

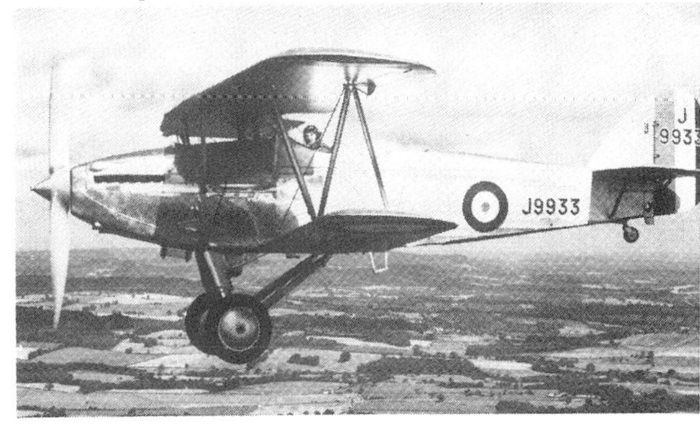

failed to reach Glasgow was Flt Lt Arthur Rawson, the Cierva Co's recently appointed test pilot whose Avro-built C.8L MkII Autogiro ran out of petrol near Nuneaton and windmilled into a small field but could not get out again. Birt with an Avro Baby turned over when landing in a field near Bury St. Edmunds; Boynes with an Avian had a ground collision with a Moth at Nottingham; and Ragg forced-landed his Avian near Atherstone — but over-shadowing everything was uncertainty over the privately-built Mistle-Thrush flown by Warwick, who had not been heard of since leaving Newcastle but in fact had fatally crashed into the Scottish hills near Tweedsmuir in Peebles.

Next afternoon at the Brookland's winning post, a Moth flown by Wally Hope again won the handicap, followed two minutes later by Uwins with his Bristol 101, and then the only lady entrant, Winifred Spooner, flying a Moth. After that it was Moth after Moth, but though the Avenger came 13th it won the £100 prize for the fastest time by averaging 149 mph around the circuit.

The Avenger was next scheduled for demonstration at Bucharest on 6 September, but gained no orders. Inevitably Roy Chadwick was deeply disappointed at lack of sales and even more discouraged by the Air Ministry's announcement that the Hawker Hart had won the two-seater competition. In his own esteem this seemed a bad set-back to future success as an employee of John Siddeley.

In the background he could sense that Alliott Roe and John Lord were behaving oddly, but it was a tremendous shock to learn at the end of October that Siddeley had accepted their resignation from A. V. Roe & Co Ltd.

Behind the scenes Roe had been negotiating with bearded old Sam Saunders, the famous builder of high-speed motor boats who had first established his business at Goring-on-Thames in Victorian days and then in 1901 formed the Saunders Patent Launch-building Syndicate at Cowes, converting it in 1908 to a private limited company named S. E. Saunders Ltd which even before the Great War had secured a footing in the aircraft industry. Alliott Roe, together with John Lord and Harry Broadsmith, now purchased a major holding by investing the £42,500 they had received for their Avro shares, backed by further money subscribed by the Aircraft Investment Corporation, Whitehall Securities Corporation, and Roe's friend Leslie Irvin, the inventor and manufacturer of the parachutes recently adopted by the RAF.

As non-shareholders, neither Dobson nor Chadwick participated. In fact Dobson was too well entrenched as works manager at Manchester and had gained an excellent rapport with John Siddeley despite not infrequent disputes over the *modus operandi,* but for Chadwick it was different. Once again he seemed likely to be faced with competition from another chief designer, tall Henry Knowler of S. E. Saunders — a man of very considerable aircraft experience and great integrity and charm who recently had helped Reggie Mitchell with the latest Supermarine Southampton X by designing for him a flat-sided steel hull similar to that of the Saunders Severn flyingboat, and concurrently had designed a distinctive little biplane fighter which rivalled the new Hawker Hornet and Fairey Firefly single-seaters.

To join in with Alliott Roe and John Lord was therefore impossible for Roy Chadwick — yet with their departure he would become directly responsible to Major Green to whose duties as chief engineer of the Armstrong Siddeley Development Co John Siddeley now added technical supervision of A. V. Roe & Co Ltd. Though Chadwick decided to let matters stand, he was deeply concerned by his invidious position. Nevertheless he retained a loyal sense of gratitude towards his late employers. They had backed him through thick and thin; but now he must take his own line with Siddeley and Green in hope of leading the Avro business to still greater success in partnership with Roy Dobson. That was a tremendous challenge, but he knew he could do it.

Chapter 8
A new Beginning

In the New Year's Honours of 1929 Roe received a knighthood in recognition of his services to aviation. Roy Chadwick sent a heartfelt telegram of congratulation from Manchester where he was busily planning future arrangements with Roy Dobson, but on 31 January was able to visit London for a lecture on *Monoplane or Biplane?* by his friend William Farren. There was the biggest attendance and longest discussion of any lecture so far, for the whole trend of aeronautical development in Europe and the USA was towards the monoplane; but the British were inherently conservative as indicated by the opening remarks: 'I hope to show you that if certain premises are conceded it is probable that for commercial aeroplanes of 15,000 to 40,000 lbs total weight, the biplane arrangement on the whole, has the advantage.'

As professor of aeronautics at Cambridge and distinguished member of the Aeronautical Research Committee, his views were important, but many of those present expressed disagreement with polite urbanity. Most of the others adopted a cautiously neutral attitude, though Capt Barnwell of Bristols and C. C. Walker of de Havilland openly advocated the biplane.

However, Roy Chadwick, who by now had greater knowledge of monoplane parameters than most people because of his Fokker experience, pointed out: 'Apparently Mr Farren has proved that the biplane is superior to the monoplane, but sounds rather sorry about it. The questionable point is that he has taken the structure weight of the monoplane from examples having an aspect ratio of about 8; but in his examples of performance he has adopted an aspect ratio of about 5, which of course is not quite fair because for one thing it increases the induced drag. However, I am glad that the question of load factor has been mentioned as it has recently been brought home to me that compliance with British requirements, as contrasted with foreign requirements, puts us at a disadvantage because it necessitates a very considerable increase in structure weight owing to the nose-diving case.'

That had become apparent when the Air Ministry insisted that the first of the Fokker F.VIIB/3M Avro 'Tens' under construction at Manchester could not have its Dutch C of A validated unless full structural analysis was made covering use of substituted British materials, and comprehensive flight trials were required because 240 hp Armstrong

The 47 ft span Avro 619 'Five' was an 'ab initio' Chadwick design and achieved 118 mph.

The similarly powered Westland Wessex had identical capacity and performance but took off in shorter distance because of the bigger wing.

Siddeley Lynx IVB radial engines had replaced the American engines.

Nevertheless Chadwick obtained John Siddeley's ready agreement to design and construct a smaller version accommodating pilot and four passengers and designated Avro 'Five'; but unknown to the Avro team, Westland also was building a tri-motor of similar capacity, and Harry Broadsmith, as a director of the new Saunders-Roe aircraft business had obtained a structural licence for Fokker wooden cantilever wings as basis for a small, twin-engined flying-boat with metal hull.

Concurrently Martlesham's criticism that the Antelope's metal skin prevented accessibility led Chadwick to design a new fuselage for it of Fokker-type welded-steel tube structure so that removable fabric-covered panels could be substituted. Designated Avro 608 Hawk, its intended engine was a Bristol Jupiter radial, and was registered as G-EBWM on 29 February, but within weeks the project was put aside on completing the fuselage frame because of pressure of work on the big Avro 618 monoplanes and a new version of the Avian with fabric-covered fuselage structured in welded tube and decked with plywood. As the Avro 616, this Avian IVM was tested by Sam Brown towards the end of February. On 23 March, bearing the new sequence registration G-AACV, it was flown to Martlesham for C of A tests and received a favourable report. Though it landed slightly slower than the rival metal Moth which de Havillands had just produced, the top speed was somewhat less because of lower power. Chadwick and Dobson therefore decided to standardise either the 105 hp Hermes I or 100 hp Genet Major for production machines. Soon sales began to mount, particularly from overseas where wood aeroplanes rapidly deteriorated.

Chadwick's visits to Manchester were a reminder that the steady production of the factory's 504N Trainers for the RAF must eventually be superseded, so he began outlining a machine twice the weight of the Avian based on a single-bay revision of the 504N but with deeper fuselage of welded steel tube, and incorporated heavy stagger to enable both cockpits to be located behind the centre section for easy access. Perhaps subconsciously he was remembering the single-bay Avro 521 for which he had been largely responsible in 1915.

As the Armstrong Whitworth design team was engaged on quite a different class of aircraft, Siddeley presently agreed that a prototype designated Avro 621 Trainer (renamed Tutor by the RAF) should be built as a private venture. Concurrently he sold the Canadian constructional rights for the Siskin fighter and the Avro Avian to the Ottawa Car Manufacturing Co. Apart from ensuring that the Avian drawings were fully detailed, the deal was outside Chadwick's province, but he was finding an easy rapport with John Siddeley despite the latter's forceful wilfulness. To cement this new relationship Siddeley insisted that Roy and Mary accompany him on the *Stella Polaris*, a huge 360 ft motor yacht of 650 tons which he had chartered from a Norwegian firm for a cruise to Madeira, and the Canary Islands, calling at Seville on the return journey. That was one of the highlights of their lives, with the thrill of new exploration as well as the relaxation of day after day of sunlit and murmuring sea as they forged onward and onward to new horizons.

On their return in April, Chadwick was involved with Fleet Air Arm trials of the first prototype Avocet N209 at Martlesham. But a shock was in store. Shortly after Ramsay Macdonald's marginal Labour win in the elections on 30 May, Siddeley announced that all design work would be transferred to Manchester. That dismayed most of the Hamble staff, for they had felt happily established in the south with its amenities of seaside and New Forest. Several of the 26 draughtsmen transferred to Saunders-Roe at Cowes and others joined Supermarine at Southampton. Most of the manual workers secured jobs at the local factories of Supermarine and Fairey or the yacht-building establishments. After completing the long process of removing factory machinery to Newton Heath, Reg Parrott had been transferred to take charge of the London office because it was quite unacceptable that he, as the earliest designer-manager, should work under Roy Dobson who had once been one of his juniors. Even the faithful Jock Ratcliffe threw in his hand and accepted the post of chief draughtsman of the Westland civil aircraft department, of which I was manager on the production side, and for the next three years we worked closely and happily together, during which there was often reference to Avro and its people.

By then the new Avro Trainer Type 621 was the main project on which the reduced drawing office staff was principally engaged, and construction of the prototype was initiated by C. E. 'Ted' Fielding, the former chief inspector who was now Dobson's very able assistant works manager. In the background, the Avro Five was nearing completion, but in June Roy Chadwick's attention was largely focused on the Avro Ten which was being flown at Woodford by Sam Brown who found it remarkably trouble-free because it had no rigging to distort, controls had long been proved, and the Lynx engines were of established reliability.

* * *

The skies these days were tuned to the frequent sound of passing light aircraft, and Woodford at weekends was busy with considerable Club flying. Several members flew to Heston Air Park for the King's Cup Race on 5 July, and though it was a rain-threatened morning there were more visitors than ever before. Among those racing was the original two-seat Avro Baby, G-EAUM, which 26-year-old Miles at Shoreham had resuscitated and fitted with a Cirrus I engine. There was the usual array of Moths, Avians, Widgeons, and the more recent Spartan biplane designed by a thrusting young man named Oliver Simmonds who had been a draughtsman at Supermarine. The start had its emotioning moment when F/O Leech failed to take off with the Avro Baby,

The Avro 618 Ten, 'Faith in Australia'.

bouncing and trickling the length of the aerodrome, but after taxying back and working on the engine he managed to get away, though eventually retired because his mount was too under-powered to cope with the gale that was blowing. There were many other retirements, and eventually it was F/O Atcherley masquerading as R. Llewellyn, with Flt Lt Stainforth as navigator, who won with a Gloster Grebe.

A week after the King's Cup came the RAF Display — the tenth — marked by visible signs of social change now that we had a Labour Government. Instead of the regimented bowler hats in the VIP enclosures, almost every man wore a grey trilby and informal clothes matching those of the trend-setting Prince of Wales in the Royal Box.

Because of the imminent Olympia Aero Show there was no parade of prototypes, and the two leap-frogging, crazy-flying 504N's were the only Avro representatives among the squadrons of Siskins, Gamecocks, Fairey Foxes, Wapitis, Atlases, Hyderabads, and Virginas, enlivened by four Supermarine flying boats droning in from Calshot and ponderously skimming across the grass to zoom up in front of the Royal Enclosure in salutation to the Prince of Wales.

But Avro had its meed of publicity a week later when Charles Kingsford-Smith and his crew landed at Croydon in their weather-worn Fokker tri-motor *Southern Cross,* having flown from Australia in a mere 13 days. Smithy merely told journalists that he was 'here to purchase four Avro-built Fokkers of the large type which would be on display at Olympia'.

This great International Exhibition was opened by the Prince of Wales on 16 July, and one of the surprises was the unexpected appearance of the new Avro Five alongside the big Avro Ten on the combined Avro and Armstrong Whitworth Stand, which also featured the slick Antelope, Hermes and Genet Avians, Army Co-operation Atlas, Siskin IIIB fighter, and the hopefully intended AW XIV replacement. C. G. Grey of *The Aeroplane* reported: 'The two Fokker-type machines strike one as among the prettiest and most efficient looking in the Show. One gathers the price is a trifle high, but the superlative workmanship and finish will certainly bring big orders.'

Undoubtedly A. V. Roe & Co Ltd, made the biggest sales in terms of capital value, for Sir Charles Kingsford-Smith on behalf of his currently registered National Airways Ltd, ordered five Avro Tens, but required delivery by December in order to inaugurate a daily 500 mile service between Brisbane and Sydney on 1 January 1930. Two more Tens were ordered by the Queensland Air Navigation Co Ltd, of Brisbane for a twice-weekly service to Townsville opening on 1 April. Such was the simplicity of construction through employing a welded fuselage and plywood wing, these machines could be swiftly and economically constructed on a one-off basis instead of sinking capital on a risky production line.

Even more satisfactory to Roy Chadwick, because it was his own design even though based on Fokker principles, was the sale of the Avro Five to Wilson Airways Ltd of Nairobi. The prototype was required in October, when Tom Campbell Black, their chief pilot, would fly it to Kenya. A further order for an Avro Five soon followed from the Queensland Air Navigation Co. Such keen interest seemed to offer a promising future for Avro Five sales, so John Siddeley agreed that a further machine should be built as a demonstrator.

Though fixed-wing machines dominated the exhibition, the Cierva Autogiro Co Ltd revealed the new Avro 620 (C.19) two-seater designed by Chadwick in collaboration with Juan de la Cierva who had devised a new method of starting the rotor. Three of these stubby little machines had been completed, featuring a remarkable box-tail which could be set at big negative angle to deflect the slipstream onto the rotor blades, spinning to 130 rpm in 45 seconds. At that point the tail was returned to neutral, wheel brakes released, and the final 20 rpm attained in a take-off run of 30 yards. For the first time the Autogiro was on the verge of becoming a practical machine, so Cierva set up a design

The C.19 Mk. IV with conventional tail and mechanical drive to initiate rotor spinning.

office at Hamble comprising several men loaned by Chadwick, and the C.19 was established in production there by Avro; but of the first twelve machines, six eventually crashed. Nevertheless, in its final more powerful form as the C.19 Mk IV, another eighteen were built before Hamble as an Avro possession finally closed down.

Unfortunately the Avocet N 209, which had been returned to Woodford for minor modifications, crashed there through engine failure and Sam Brown was badly injured. The second prototype, N 210, was therefore substituted and flown to Martlesham by Flt Lt 'Bill' Thorn, an ex-instructor who had recently joined Avro as Brown's assistant.

But now came the excitement of the next Schneider Trophy Contest as an outstanding event in home waters off Spithead. Two magnificent blue and white Supermarine S.6s were the British contenders, with the previous S.5 winner as reserve after elimination of the even prettier bronze-coloured Napier-powered Gloster IV through engine trouble. Challenging Britain were the Macchi N 52 and N 67 seaplanes; but the Americans had withdrawn. The second Avro Avocet, fitted with floats, was added to the High Speed Flight as a practise machine and for testing sea and air conditions.

Friday, 6 September was the great day of qualifying trials to prove the seaworthiness of each machine, and then leave it moored for six hours, and if it did not sink was passed cleared as fit for the contest. All succeeded. The British pilots then had a last run round the course with the Avocet seaplane, and D'Arcy Greig ended his flight with masterly loops,

The black fuselaged K1230 was the first 621 Trainer for the RAF.

rolls and spins.

At exactly 2 pm on the following day the starting gun boomed from HMS *Medea*. A tiny dot grew with amazing rapidity into the shape of the S.6 flown by F/O Waghorn, followed at 15 minute intervals by the other British and Italian racers in thundering sequence. Who was winning was never clear to the thousands of spectators each side of the Solent. Seaplane after seaplane flashed into sight on successive circuits, screamed past and vanished into the distance — but eventually the broadcast lap times of each contestant revealed that Waghorn had easily won. On the lawn of the Royal Yacht Squadron at Cowes, where the élite of the aircraft industry were guests, Chadwick smilingly said to his wife: 'At least we've played our part with the Avocet.'

That Autumn the Avro Woodford factory completed assembly of the prototype Mongoose-powered 621 Trainer. The heritage was unmistakable, and the boldly staggered, N-strutted, square-tipped wings had the same aspect ratio as the 504 sequence, but the top wing carried the now mandatory Handley Page slots, referred to by Sam Brown as 'clutching hands', and the Frise-type ailerons were on only the lower wing. Although the rate of roll was slower than Brown thought desirable, Dobson and Chadwick decided that rather than make changes, it was urgent to send the machine for Air Ministry trials at Martlesham to counter the headway made by the rival Hawker Tomtit, so it was flown there early in December in hopeful expectation of adoption.

* * *

For the past six months while seeking a house within easy reach of Manchester, Roy, Mary, and daughter Margaret had been living in a pleasant old country-house hotel on the outskirts of Altrincham, but now he settled for a house named 'Kingsley' in the quiet, rural cul-de-sac of Gilbert Road on the outskirts of Hale in Cheshire.

A new era began for the Chadwicks. Though John Siddeley was some-what restrictive in selecting which military Specifications the Avro and Armstrong designers might individually tackle, Roy was now reasonably satisfied that he was not unduly fettered; but he missed the eager backing of Sir Alliott Roe and his endless, if sometimes frustrating, flow of ideas.

Britain was approaching an economic crisis in 1930 with two million unemployed, yet most people were content with their jobs and happy with entertainment ranging from pubs and football matches to steadily improving 'wireless' and cheaply luxurious cinema. 'Motoring for the millions' was the slogan of Sir Herbert Austin with his £125 miniature 'Seven' hp car — but Chadwick and Dobson now could afford much bigger family cars and furnish their houses more pleasantly then most. For Roy, it was still music that enthralled, although on many an evening he still dreamed aeroplanes and might be seen from time to time sketching some new idea on envelopes or margins of his newspaper.

There was also the constant necessity of keeping up-to-date with new expositions on aerodynamics, development of materials, and structural techniques. Currently he was arguing that strength requirements were too stringent for commercial aeroplanes, and this led the Aeronautical Research Committee (ARC) to re-investigate methods of defining strength, resulting in somewhat less ponderous regulations in which the factor of safety would relate to varying categories of aircraft weight from the smallest to the biggest.

Perhaps it was speculative rivalry with Avro that led Sir Alliott Roe at Saunders-Roe to continue his involvement with rotary wings by accepting an Air Ministry Contract to build a Helicogyre, combining rotor features of the Autogiro with rotor tip propeller drive. Observing the success of the Avro-Fokker venture, he also pressed for a flyingboat rival of the Avro Ten in the form of an enlarged version of the Fokker-winged *Cutty Sark* accommodating two crew and eight passengers. But he went even further by competing against the Avro Avian with construction of a big batch of the new all-metal Bluebird IVs designed by his erstwhile rivals of the Blackburn Aircraft Co. Maybe he chuckled at what John Siddeley might think, but certainly he remained as friendly as ever to Roy Chadwick.

A splendid demonstration of the Fokker-type aeroplane was a pioneering flight in April to India and back by the Duchess of Bedford and her pilot Capt Charles Barnard flying her FVII Spider — but it was of course the Duchess, as a national heroine, who received enormous publicity but not the Fokker, nor its reliable Jupiter engine, nor Barnard as pilot! *The Aeroplane's* Empire concious editor drew invidious distinction between her flight and the absence of any airline service to the Cape by Imperial Airways; but he was unaware that Imperial had recently issued invitations to tender for just such an airliner, and to Roy Chadwick's chagrin it was his rival colleague John Lloyd at Armstrong Whitworth to whom Siddeley allocated design of a new type of 4-engined, cantilever-winged airliner for that purpose.

Fortunately, the Avro 621 Trainer prototype had found favour both at Martlesham and the Central Flying School where F/O Tredrey described it as a gentlemanly little thing from the flying point of view. 'Nicely balanced controls, light and smooth to handle, beautiful for all manoeuvres, no tricks or vices, sweet flying at 70 mph, and as easy to land as buttoning up your coat.' In view of the excellent reports the Air Ministry had ordered two batches of ten renamed Tutor, and the first, K1230, with enlarged Avian-type horn-balanced rudder, was delivered to Martlesham for performance trials in May. Meanwhile, three with rounded rudders were supplied to the Irish Army Air Corps and named Triton.

Concurrently, Chadwick had been making a major re-design of the Avro Five, which appeared that month as the Avro 624 Six of 4 ft greater span and widened cockpit seating two pilots side-by-side with dual controls, increased cabin headroom and separate toilet compartment, but notably different in having the outboard engines experimentally fitted directly to the under surface of the wing. Unfortunately that resulted in less lift and caused turbulence across the tail, so he reverted to the previous under-slung mounting, and in case the flat windscreen was a contributory factor it was replaced by vertically angled panels which also improved visibility by deflecting rain. Nevertheless, the 624 proved 5 mph slower than the five-seater 619, and at full load climbed at only 500 ft/min compared with 650 ft for the smaller machine.

There were also developments of the Avian IVM, including several single-seaters with extended range for carriage of mail in the front cockpit space. For pilots intent on higher performance there was a Hermes-powered Sports version with simplified undercarriage and lower-cut cockpits shielded by wide semi-circular windscreens. As a pure racer there was a wire-braced, low-wing monoplane Type 625 variant with Avian IVM fuselage and tail as a poor man's version of the costly DH 71 racing monoplane of 1927 — but though the Avro had spectacular climb of 1,000 ft/min, it was much slower.

But it was a Moth which was holding breathless attention. On 5 May a rather shy young woman had taken off unpublished from Croydon with her DH60 named *Jason*, intent on flying to Australia. On reaching Vienna she was suddenly headline news, for reporters discovered that this 'unknown little typist', Miss Amy Johnson, had never crossed the Channel before, nor flown more than 200 miles. From that moment her stage by stage flight became an epic page of history, and after tremendous adventure she landed at Port Darwin on her 19th day from England — the world's heroine!

'What a wonderful girl!' exclaimed Mary Chadwick, 'But what a pity she did not use an Avian.'

'What a pity,' her husband agreed. 'But at least we had Bert Hinkler as the solo pioneer with his Avian.'

Four days after Amy Johnson's triumph the eleventh RAF Display provided a new landmark in Avro history because in the New-type Park, amid the latest prototypes, the Avro Tutor was attracting considerable

The Avro 625 monoplane G-AAYD powered with a 115 hp Hermes II.

attention from representatives of Air Forces all round the world. There was also the time-honoured hair-raising crazy flying of two Avro Lynxes, which, said *Flight* 'executed impossible evolutions all around the aerodrome, about 5.999 inches from the ground.' That was the third occasion on which F/O Campbell had been the annual performer, but this time his partner was a rather quiet young man, P/O Frank Whittle, whom his fellow pilots regarded with amused scepticism because of his avid interest in turbo-supercharging and the novel possibility of jet propulsion. Though scientists thought that one day the latter might be feasible, it was far beyond the outlook of the industry's designers who were having difficulty enough even in selecting the right fixed-pitch propeller for the not wholly reliable piston engines of their latest aircraft.

The King's Cup Race followed a week later, with start and finish at Hanworth Air Park on London's outskirts where the recently formed and subsidised National Flying Services (NFS) had headquarters in the splendid Manor House and gardens at the very centre of the area. This time, the race was of particular interest to all at Avro because Sir Philip Sassoon had entered the tri-motor Avro Five, piloted by Sam Brown; Chadwick entered the prototype Tutor flown by Sq Ldr Bennett-Baggs of Armstrong; Dobson sponsored the Genet Avian flown by Don Green the Armstrong assistant chief pilot; Siddeley entered the Genet-engined racing Avian monoplane with Tommy Tomkins as pilot, and the Hermes version was entered by the engine makers and flown by Neville Stack, chief pilot of NFS. Though 39 contenders were Moths and 14 were Bluebirds, there were eight Avians of which one was flown by the renowned hockey player Winifred Brown who had learnt to fly at Woodford in 1927 at the Lancashire Flying Club. Among other contestants Chadwick was intrigued to find two single-seat Southern Martlet biplanes devised by burly Fred Miles from surplus Avro Baby airframes.

Competition was tremendous, for there were 101 entrants comprising 22 types of aeroplane, though not all were starters. The course of 750 miles to Newcastle and back saw many forced landings including the two Sports Avians, flown by Instructor J. C. Cantrill of the Lancashire Aero Club who nosed over, and former Avro apprentice Flt Lt John Oliver, and the two Avian monoplanes were handicapped out of the race. But what did that matter when Winifred Brown proved the winner, and a popular one at that, for not only was she the first woman ever to win the King's Cup, but was regarded with affection by fellow pilots because of her camaradie and sense of humour and fun. Chadwick and Dobson had often seen her at Woodford where she would be the centre of attention at the Club bar, swopping stories with the men.

However, it was Amy Johnson who replaced her as headline news on arriving back at Croydon aboard the Imperial Airways *City of Glasgow* on 4 August. Dusk had fallen, and in the floodlights the Air Minister, Brig-Gen Lord Thompson, and a coterie of the distinguished were waiting to welcome her. Cheer after cheer came from the public enclosure as she stepped from the airliner, and on arrival at Grosvenor House, where the *Daily Mail* had reserved a suite for her, another huge gathering roared a welcome. Next day that paper held a celebratory lunch at the Savoy, where she was handed a cheque for £10,000 and a gold cup, and a week later the King honoured her with a CBE.

But for the Chadwicks all was overwhelmed by the birth of their second daughter, Rosemary, on 31 August. As a distraction for his elder daughter on the following Saturday, Roy took her with him to the Newton Heath factory in his new Armstrong-Siddeley car. 'How well I remember that one and only visit,' she recollected. 'On entering the large workshop there was a pungent "acid drop" odour from the doped wings and fuselages, and in the adjoining woodmill the floor was deep in fresh-smelling woodshavings. While my father held a short conference in his office, I wandered around the erecting shop where there were several aeroplanes in various stages of construction. Everything about the small aeroplanes delighted me and it all made me feel a part of my father's world. Not long after this he began taking me from time to time to Woodford at weekends so that I could watch the aeroplanes while he talked to our test pilot, Capt Brown. There were two large hangars on the airfield in which aeroplanes were ranged either side as though in a giant and lofty garage. Some were small cabin machines, but most were open cockpit biplanes with silver wings, all smelling exotically of cellulose acetate. Some had registration letters, others the British roundels at the tips of the wings. There were smudges of oil on the concrete floor, and huge black steel doors rattled at the end of the hangars. I longed to climb into the cockpit of an aeroplane and fly away — but I had to wait until I was nine for my first thrilling ride.'

These days, Chadwick's designing ability had been forced into a slower tempo because Siddeley regarded his Armstrong Whitworth business as the more important through gaining extensive production of the Atlas for Army Co-operation duties, and because of the high favour with which Imperial Airways regarded the economically viable tri-motor Argosy biplane airliner, resulting in a current contract for design and construction of Lloyd's 4-engined monoplane airliner soon to be known as the Atalanta. As Chadwick's proposal for a big Avro airliner based on Fokker construction had been abandoned he turned to a Mailplane Specification issued by Canadian Airways Ltd., and taking the discarded welded tube fuselage of the Antelope-derived Hawk as basis, reworked the design as an open cockpit single seater, powered by a 525 hp Armstrong Siddeley Panther IIA, and referenced it Type 627.

Fortunately interest in the Avro Tutor had extended, and he was granted Patents 372,100 and 372,101 for a new version as Type 626 adaptable in various forms for instruction in bombing, photography, gunnery, radio communication, navigation, night flying, blind flying, and seaplane training — and with Siddeley's consent, construction of a multi-purpose prototype commenced in October.

Air Marshal Sir John Higgins conducts H.M. King George to the Royal enclosure at the RAF Display.

But that month opened with tragedy. Throughout the year two huge airships had been headline news, and at the RAF Display the Government sponsored R 101 had floated majestically across the aerodrome. A month later, the rival Vickers-built R 100 precariously flew the Atlantic and back but next came disaster. On 4 October the R 101 crashed into a hill near Beauvais, France, and caught fire. Of the 54 occupants, 47 were killed, including the Air Minister and the ever helpful DCA Sir Sefton Brancker. The entire world was shaken by the news.

An important witness at the ensuing Enquiry was dapper, monocled Air Marshal Sir John Higgins, affectionately known as 'Bum-and-eyeglass', who had for the past three years been Air Member for Supply and Research (AMSR) but had just resigned from the RAF to become Chairman of Sir W. G. Armstrong Whitworth Aircraft Ltd and A. V. Roe and Co Ltd, coupled with non-executive directorship of Armstrong Siddeley Motors. Though no technician, he was a forceful administrator; but more important to Siddeley were his close contacts in the Air Ministry and RAF. His replacement was AV-M, Sir Hugh Dowding, known to the RAF at large as 'Stuffy', and the next crucial appointment was that of Lord Amulree in succession to the late Lord Thompson.

Metal structured Avian fuselage reveals long-range tank.

Kingsford-Smith's record-breaking Avian IV Type 616.

Concurrently, Kingsford-Smith had been visiting the Avro factory at Woodford to take delivery of a single-seat Sports Avian IVA, which had special 30 ft wings with gravity tank supplemented by a 91-gallon aluminium tank in the covered front cockpit of a specially strengthened fuselage. Powered with a 120 hp de Havilland Gipsy II, this Avian had a still air range of 1,860 miles, cruising at 92 mph. Australia was the objective. Leaving Heston at dawn on 9 October, he made a meteoric dash to Darwin with this *Southern Cross* Junior in a triumphant 9 days 21 hours. Jubilant advertisements followed from A. V. Roe & Co, linking the new record with Hinkler's earlier Avian flight.

But there were also catastrophes. Almost every week a civilian or RAF fatality occurred and on 30 October, Avro's recent ex-Armstrong pilot, F. B. 'Tommy' Tomkins, was seriously injured and three others killed when the twin-engined Handley Page W8 in which they were passengers, flew into the ground near Neufchâtel.

A few days later, Roy Chadwick, accompanied by the Armstrong Whitworth designer John Lloyd with whom there was now cautious friendship, motored to Calshot where the fantastic 157 ft span Dornier DoX flying-boat, powered with a sextet of tandem engines, was anchored near the Spit for inspection by British designers. All were impressed by the ship-like metal structuring of this giant, though the enormous lateral sponsons seemed quite unsuited for heavy seas, and the absence of servo controls was surprising. But as one technician commented: 'The effort of controlling the DoX should be fifty times that of manoeuvering a light aeroplane, so to have brought each control within practicable limits by using an external balancing vane, in the style originated by A. V. Roe, is triumphant for a machine weighing 50 tons.'

The subsequent Paris Aero Show found Chadwick and Lloyd with increasing sense of mutual participation, and the Armstrong Whitworth Stand displaying the Atlas had large photographs of the Avro Ten and Tutor: but once again the French stole the Show with new structural concepts in their Breguet 270, and there were many other all-metal aeroplanes which seemed strikingly advanced compared with British reliance on fabric covered biplanes, yet Britain's designers had all the skills to make metal skinned aircraft as exemplified by Chadwick's Avocet and Antelope — but there was neither Air Ministry interest nor available money to risk this as a private venture.

* * *

By now the trade depression was so deeply affecting every sector of Britain's manufacturing that employees and government officials alike accepted the necessity of a 10 per cent cut in pay. Strenuous efforts throughout the aircraft industry were being made to secure overseas' sales. To that end, early in January 1931, Armstrong Whitworth Aircraft engaged the Fairey ex-chief pilot, Capt Norman Macmillan, as foreign sales representative. He and I met a few months later at the British-sponsored *Exposician Britannica* in Buenos Aires, respectively endeavouring to secure sales for the Atlas, multi-role Tutor 626, and standard Avian on one hand, and I with a Westland Wapiti demonstrated as landplane and seaplane. Flight practice for the latter had re-introduced me to Hamble, where Siddeley had established Air Service Training Ltd (AST) as an international flying and navigational school initally equipped with Avian IVs as preliminary trainers, and the well-tried hack Avro 504N, so familiar to Chadwick as G-EBKQ, was the seaplane trainer. Launched from the old Avro slipway abutting Southampton Water, I spent several happy hours practising landings and take-offs, fascinated by the glorious sense of skimming from the buoyancy of water into the smoothness of airborne flight with so harmonious a machine as that old Avro.

However, the Atlas was wrecked at El Palomar aerodrome by an Argentine pilot who collided with an Avro 504 school machine at 15 ft above the ground while approaching to land — but luckily nobody was killed. As far as Westland was concerned there were no sales, but the Argentine and other South American Air Forces with limited funds were extremely interested in the rebuilt Avro 626. After demonstrations at El Palomar, Macmillan crossed the Southern Andes to Santiago and Mendosa, but on returning to El Palomar his Tutor was commandeered by the Argentine military authorities to help quell a provincial uprising, and as *La Prensa* reported, 'performed so well that fourteen additional Avro 626s were purchased a few months later'. Undoubtedly Chadwick's design was a winner, and presently orders began to stream in from many other countries.

Meanwhile the RAF acquired the Avro 620 Autogiro (C.19 Mk III) G-ABCM, which after overhaul as K1948, was despatched to Martlesham for evaluation in March, and in the following month an Avro Ten, K2682, was purchased for assessment as a Troop Carrier. However, no further RAF orders were placed for either the Autogiro or the Ten. Economic circumstances were too stringent for more, and the Air Estimates of £6½ million for supply of aeroplanes, seaplanes, engines and spares was even less than the previous year. Only three more Home Defence Squadrons would be added to the 39 currently existing, and the Under Secretary for Air declared that there was no desire to indulge in a race for air armaments as war was only a remote possibility.

Welded-tube fuselage structure of the Genet powered Type 631 Cadet.

That led Roy Chadwick to design a scaled-down version of the Tutor for Club or private use. Aptly named Cadet (Avro 631), it was almost geometrically identical and certainly had John Siddeley's interest because it broadened the market for his 135 hp Genet Major engine. So enthusiastic was Roy Dobson that he grabbed Chadwick's sketches and performance calculations and flew off in his private Avian to Ulster in hope of a sale to the Irish Army Air Corps who had expressed great satisfaction with their three Tutor 'Tritons'. As the ebulient Dobbie, at least out of hours, was on matey terms with everyone, the Irish so took him to their hearts that he came away with an order for six of these putative Cadets.

'Quick carbon-copy drawings of fittings will do for the first machine,' he told Chadwick — and as a result the prototype was designed and built in six weeks, using a modified welded tube Avian rear fuselage and various Avian parts such as ribs. An interesting initial feature was Chadwick's reversion to his 1918 patent for an inset aileron balance, but Sam Brown found this gave too light control, so it was changed to a conventional Frise, making it ideal for *ab initio* instruction, and an initial six were ordered by AST, though the selling price with the relatively expensive Genet engine was too high for most private owners.

However, the background Avro production was still the 504N updated to Specification 6/30, of which the last was scheduled for March 1932. Ever since Alliott Roe had instilled the importance in pre-war days of designing aeroplanes as a number of separate units brought together for major assembly, it had been a fundamental of all designs. The Tutor was typical. Ted Fielding had therefore established a factory mass production system of jig-built components to ensure complete interchangeability instead of hand fitting, and he controlled this with systematic progress procedure using indicator boards at every assembly point 'so that an

Line up of AST's Cadets in front of Avro's original Hamble factory.

Derived from the unfinished private-venture Hawk fighter, the Mailplane had Avro's standard welded-tube fuselage construction and utilized Antelope wings and tail.

executive could see the position immediately without having to resort to special meetings which took staff off the shop floors.' That also permitted individual construction of the limited Avro Tens and Avro Fives amid small batches of Avians.

Roy Chadwick's restless imagination was still brimming with ideas. Since completing the Tutor he had made design studies of ten more aeroplanes, of which the latest was a two-seat Fleet Air Arm torpedo-bomber-reconnaissance biplane to Specification S9/30 which avoided conflict with Armstrong Whitworth projects and would be powered with the big Armstrong Siddeley Tiger radial.

In mid-June his Avro 627 Mailplane, painted gaudy yellow for easy identification if force-landed during the prairie Air Mail Service, had its initial flight by Sam Brown, who found it pleasant to handle, and thanks to the 525 hp Panther fitted with drag reducing Townend ring, it was as fast as its slightly less powerful, 170 mph progenitor, the Antelope 604. Though the Mailplane was inadmissible as a civil aircraft in the New Type Park of the RAF Display on 27 June, the Avro 626 multi-purpose trainer was there, and so was the Panther-powered XVI Fleet fighter from the Armstrong Whitworth stable. As always, other people's latest aeroplanes were of prime interest to the gathering of rival designers, but it was the enthralling background of thrills and thunderous noise that delighted the British public.

Flying meetings, air races, demonstrations, record breaking, filled the calendar of that brilliant summer. The world of aviation seemed flourishing. For young Margaret, it was all a golden dream of never-ending sunshine. 'The Cheshire countryside beckoned,' she recollected. 'On Sundays, Roy, immaculately attired, would take me through nearby Bowdon to Dunham Park, where I might go skipping and rustling along a great drive and we might tip-toe to the deer shelters to see if any were inside.' But behind those idyllic times was the growing uneasiness of possible war, and Baldwin warned: 'Nothing is more urgently wanted than to press for reductions in the Air Forces of the world and attempt parity in Western Europe — for I regard each Air Force as the spearhead of invasion and the most dangerous arm against peace that there is today.'

Certainly the annual Air Defence Exercises, commencing on 20 July, supported his contention, and showed that: 'Twenty-four raids by day bombers penetrated London defences. Twenty raids were intercepted on the way in or out. Sixty-eight raids by single night bombers also penetrated the defences, but 39 were intercepted by opposing fighters. In all, 84 Blueland bombers and 59 Redland fighters were destroyed in enemy combat.'

The excitement of more peaceful competition accompanied the King's Cup Race on 25 July. Winifred Brown and her Avian were favourite, but rain and mist and low cloud caused retirement after retirement and to the disappointment of the Avro team it was P/O Edwards flying a Blackburn Bluebird who won.

After the Bank Holiday the Mailplane, registered G-ABJM, was flown by Sam

Brown to Martlesham for C of A trials. Returning via Heston he displayed it to the new Director of Civil Aviation, Lt-Col Francis Shelmerdine, who previously was DCA in India and had shown great tact in dealing with the Indian Government which, through financial stringency, had refused delivery of four Avro Tens built for the Indian State Airway. Roy Dobson and Roy Chadwick, working in practised collusion, were at Heston to greet him and talk quiet business, with the result that one of the Avro Tens was re-established for use by the Viceroy, Lord Willingdon.

Certainly Shelmerdine comprehended the financial risks of export sales, but neither he nor the two Roys could have expected such problems with the Avro Mailplane when shipped to Canada for operational trials — yet the Canadian Government like the Indian Government was having monetary problems and while this aeroplane was in transit, cut all subsidies for civil aviation; consequently Canadian Airways Ltd, had no money to complete the purchase and the machine was eventually returned to England.

The world-wide financial depression was hitting Britain very hard. Dobson and Chadwick were perturbed by the report of the Committee on National Expenditure declaring: 'At present aircraft in the experimental stage are bought by the Air Ministry either for (a) research on aerodynamic problems, or (b) development into types which can be produced in quantity for the RAF. We have no quarrel with expenditure under (a) but have considerable doubt whether purchase under (b) of what may be called 'prototypes' is a proper liability of the State; we have accordingly examined the possibility of leaving it to the industry to develop such machines at their own expense and risk.'

The Avro Ten for the Viceroy eventuated as the luxuriously furnished seven-seater, four-engined 642/4N "Star of India".

Cockpit 4-engined Avro 10.

There was immediate protest by the SBAC. The Air Ministry well knew that without big production orders the margin of profit was too small to finance experimental types. What was needed was bolder support in developing such futuristic devices as lift flaps, variable-pitch propellers, and retracting undercarriages — but all that the RAF wanted were machines of minimal complexity. Coincidentally, George Dowty, whom Chadwick had introduced to undercarriage design, left Glosters and registered his own Aircraft Components Co, to manufacture improved aircraft landing gear, and internally sprung wheels. He had only two skilled workers, but that was the beginning of a great business of world-wide fame.

More immediately expressive of international endeavour was the Schneider Trophy Contest on 13 September — but it was a foregone conclusion because the French and Italians had withdrawn, leaving only Great Britain to fly the Course. Aboard the Royal Aero Club's chartered *Homeric*, Roy Chadwick and his wife watched the sunlit spectacle of the blue and silver Supermarine

The Schneider victor Flt. Lieut. Boothman (later Air Marshal Sir John) inspects Tutor construction with Roy Chadwick.

S.6B seaplane, with 30-year-old Flt Lt Boothman at the controls, flashing past seven times on his successful attempt at an average of 340 mph — then sweep into a circling climb above Cowes and smoothly alight, having won the Trophy in perpetuity for Britain. Next day they drove on to see Sir Alliott and Lady Roe at Hamble House, afterwards inspecting the splendid buildings and hangars of the big new AST aerodrome converted from the fields adjacent to the original Avro area. It was all strangely different from those earlier days but the big Avro experimental shop still dominated the western side though now devoid of the Cierva Autogiro Co, which had transferred to Hanworth, Middlesex.

At that new base, late in November, two new types of Autogiro were displayed to invited guests. With almost fatherly interest Roy Chadwick inspected the latest solution of the rotor starting spinning problem using a mechanically driven torque tube from a gearbox on the back of the engine via interposed clutch to the rotor head. The clumsy boxtail had gone, and there was now a conventional tailplane with up-turned tips and a low central dorsal fin and rudder — but even more startling than this C.30 derivative of the C.19 was a pale blue C.24 two-seat cabin Autogiro built by de Havillands. He sampled both machines as passenger. That evening Roy's pencil was sketching possibilities for an Avro cabin rotor plane, but he soon found that John Siddeley was only interested in firm production orders.

The C.30 Autogiro was direct controlled by inverted column from universally hinged rotor head.

Chapter 9
Cautious Expansion

Reginald Joseph Mitchell, future initiator of the Spitfire.

There were congratulations from Roy Chadwick to his friend Reggie Mitchell who featured in the 1932 New Year's Honour List with a CBE in recognition of his skill in producing the successful series of Schneider racers. Nevertheless the Supermarine designer was a disappointed man because the Government, in an effort to make national economies, had cancelled completion of the great monoplane flying-boat powered with six Rolls-Royce engines which Supermarines were building to Air Ministry order.

The financial recession was biting deeply everywhere, so Chadwick, though thwarted over several of his design projects, felt relief that two of the Avro Tens cancelled by the Indian Government had been sold to the Egyptian Army Air Force, and on 11 January they left Heston for Cairo. A few days later the prototype Avro 621 Tutor K-4, now powered with a Lynx IVC, was flown by Sam Brown to Martlesham for handling trials with larger rudder and ailerons only on the lower wing.

Severe criticism during the trials led Chadwick to have the undercarriage moved a few inches forward to prevent nosing over on the rough Martlesham surface, and low pressure wheels and a brake system were fitted, and as the single pair of ailerons gave too slow a rate of roll, he reverted to four Frise ailerons of conventional arrangement. A test to destruction of the complete aeroplane in the huge Temple testing frame at the RAE showed adequate structural strength, but as a precaution the flying wires were changed from single to tandem pairs.

What with increasing overseas orders for the Type 626 multi-purpose variant and an initial production line for the Type 631 Cadets, the financial affairs of A. V. Roe & Co Ltd seemed very satisfactory to shrewd John Siddeley, though he maintained a cautious policy to ensure that his two aircraft firms did

The second 621 had a 240 hp Lynx, rounded rudder, ailerons only on lower wing, and became prototype Tutor.

260 hp Chetah V multi-role Avro 626s for Egypt for anti-hashish patrols.

The Club Cadet had minimal stagger to facilitate alignment of hinges for wing folding.

not competitively overlap. His empire was still extending. Recently he had backed tough Wallace Devereux to set up a new business after Peter Hooker Ltd, who supplied the Siddeley pistons, became bankrupt. Tom Chapman, who had joined Armstrong Siddeley Motors from Armstrong Whitworth, recalled: 'Devereux boldly came to old man Siddeley and said, "Look here, if you're going to continue with aluminium pistons give me £10,000 so that I can buy part of the Hooker business for the particular job you need me to make." Well, Devereux quickly spent that £10,000 and went back and got another £10,000, and when that went, still another; and that was the start of what became the famous High Duty Alloy Ltd.'

The technical background of designing aeroplanes and aero engines was becoming more and more involved with scientific research and government regulations. A long enquiry into the crash of a Junkers monoplane from 'buffeting' airflow led to a new edition of AP 970 defining mandatory flight tests covering a range of loadings, behaviour at speeds from stall to dive, oil and cooling suitability, and performance — but before these could be undertaken, extensive flight-handling was necessary to get controls and stability perfected. That the workmanlike Cadet was satisfactory seemed obvious when Sam Brown demonstrated its aerobatic ability with loops and rolls and spins at the opening of Skegness aerodrome on 14 May. So pleased was Roy Dobson with this new production that he himself piloted it in a subsequent handicap race and achieved fourth place.

When *The Aeroplane's* journalist-pilot, Frank Bradbrooke, flew the Cadet he said: 'The most distinctive merit is its neutral stability, enabling it to fly happily, hands and feet off, holding almost any climb or dive, and trim seems the same, engine on or off. As a result, the Cadet must be flown accurately because it is benevolently neutral and shows up clumsy pilots more distinctly than most without being nasty. Rudder and elevators seem all they should be, but the ailerons are quite brilliant and a tribute to Mr Chadwick's study of lateral control. They are of curious design, part Frise balance and part plain flap on all four wings. I tried them from 40 to 140 mph, finding no noticeable difference in their frictionless ease. Slots on the top plane help at the 40 mph stall, which can be held in a laterally level nose drop or put into a spin that recovers at the slightest opposition.'

Already Chadwick was engrossed with the next design, intended to match the increasing interest in small civil monoplanes, of which the recently introduced shoulder-wing DH Puss Moth was a noteable example. Accordingly his Avro 634 was a low-wing two-seater monoplane of 30 ft span, though much faster because of its Lynx engine.

Suspecting the market was too restricted he turned to a bigger concept of 39 ft span, powered by a Lynx IVC, and daringly featured a retractable undercarriage — but concurrently, the new firm of Airspeed Ltd had just tested a similar, but slightly larger, low-winger, so the Avro was dropped.

Everywhere there was an upsurge of private flying. Aviation meetings at weekends were almost commonplace. On the wettest and last day of May the Guild of Air Pilots held a display at Brooklands which was opened by trilby-hatted John Siddeley, Chairman of the SBAC — but it rained and rained. Despite his wide business interests, he always found time to attend major aeronautical events, such as the King's Cup Race with which he had been closely associated since 1922, and in 1928 had presented a perpetual Challenge Trophy for competing private owners.

So dynamic a man could not go unnoticed. The Birthday Honours published in June announced his appointment as a Knight Batchelor. His employees were delighted. An admirer said: 'The story of his achievements is that of a great leader who in requiring efficiency from others, himself sets an example of efficiency that will never be forgotten. Yet his is also the story of a very human man who loves pictures and the flowers in his garden; a man for whom no responsibility is too great and always shouldered the public work in the community in which he lived. He is treasurer of the Society of Motor Manufacturers, chairman of the SBAC, served Warwickshire as High Sheriff, and was Master of the Worshipful Company of Coachmakers.'

Sir John Siddeley (Lord Kenilworth).

As though indicative of the Air Ministry's approval of Siddeley's honour A. V. Roe and Co Ltd received official confirmation that the Lynx-powered Avro 621 Tutor would replace the time-honoured 504N as the official trainer, and this was immediately endorsed by a contract for 94. Armstrong Whitworth added to the occasion with the first flight of the long-rumoured 4-engined AW XV "Atalanta" monoplane built for Imperial Airways. Though designed by Major Green and John Lloyd its cantilever ply-covered Fokker-like shoulder-wing was indicative of co-operation with Roy Chadwick, and the stubby cantilever wheel axles projecting from the fuselage added to the impression that the new airliner was the epitomy of advanced aerodynamics. Handling was sufficiently satisfactory for it to be shown in the New Type Aircraft Park at the 13th RAF Display on 25 June in company with the up-dated Avro Mailplane in readiness for the innovatory 'Open Day' on Monday when all aircraft could be inspected by the SBAC's overseas visitors and special guests — the first occasion on which the British Aviation industry was permitted to do so. Though not comparable with the RAF Display it was a commercially outstanding event. C. G. Grey reported: 'We sat in the sun on the hottest day of the last two years and thoroughly enjoyed a magnificent exhibition by the various test pilots. Thirty aircraft from 13 firms were flown, beginning with the Handley Page night bomber and slotted-winged Gugnunc. Bristols followed with their new Type 120 two-seater featuring a gun cupola. Next were

The Atalanta marked the introduction of monoplanes for Imperial Airways.

the Atlas II Army Co-op two-seater, AWXVI Fighter, and AWXV "Atalanta" which floated off the ground with obvious ease, and after the demonstration came down in the most cushioned landing ever seen.' Saunders-Roe, de Havillands, Hawkers, Glosters, Vickers followed, and then it was the turn of Avro with Mailplane, Avian and 626 demonstrator in very effective demonstration, and the Tutor 621 flown 'blind' with the pilot under a hood.

The King's Cup Race a fortnight later had a field of 43 flying a zig-zag course the length and breadth of England. Siddeley had entered the Avro Mailplane flown by Sam Brown who was placed scratch, but long before he took off on the first day's lap, Wally Hope, flying a Fox Moth, was more than half-way round the circuit, and easily first when he landed at Brooklands, and though next day the Mailplane had not taken off until Hope passed the winning post, Brown won the prize for fastest time, averaging 175.9 mph for the two days. Roy Chadwick felt that was a vindication qualifying him for Siddeley's approval to design a wider range of military aircraft than his restriction to single-engined Fleet Air Arm biplanes and instructional aircraft among the 30 design studies he had made in the past four years.

Nor was the political and social background encouraging. Unemployment had soared so high that 22 per cent of the insured population were out of work, and there were consequent 'hunger marches' of companies of men plodding to London from workless areas. But there was also the ominous threat of war. Well aware that Germany was secretly re-arming, France was pressing the useless League of Nations for a pact of mutual assistance to any State which was the victim of aggression — but as a safeguard it already had the biggest Air Force in the world, with some 3,000 operational aircraft. Even the Foreign Secretary publicly stressed the horrors of a future war and Prime Minister Baldwin said: 'I think it is well for the man in the street to realise that no power on earth can prevent him from being bombed. The bomber will always get through.'

As though implementing his words the Annual Air Exercises followed on 18 July enshrouded in greater secrecy than ever before. Certainly there was a plethora of bombers and fighters when Chadwick visited Martlesham in August to discuss the A & AEE's evaluation of the modified prototype Tutor. As a result, further changes were incorporated in K-1797, which went there in September for final Service trials with a long-travel undercarriage and the engine encircled with a Townend ring. Concurrently, the Prefect navigation trainer version was flown to Martlesham for Service trials and C of A performance evaluation.

Structural and control matters were still much to the fore. The strength of monoplanes remained suspect, so Chadwick was particularly interested in recent R & Ms dealing with a new branch of aeronautical science known as 'aero-elasticity' and its affect on flutter, control reversal, and stability divergence. But however erudite the team of designers, there were always unexpected problems with every new type of aircraft. Thus on 21 October, Sir John Siddeley's consortium suffered a bad set-back when the prototype "Atalanta", piloted by Campbell-Orde and his assistant Don Green, crashed into the notorious hill on the edge of Whitley aerodrome after an airlock during take-off caused all four engines to cut. The aeroplane was badly damaged and the crew injured, but news of the accident was suppressed lest it impair the public image of the "Atalanta" as an airliner.

Concurrently to Roy Chadwick's fiery

irritation Dobson had trespassed on his design province by patenting a manually-controlled, hydraulically-operated variable-pitch propeller devised by his assistant engineer Leslie Leech in expectation of competing against the recently introduced American-built Hamilton-Standard two-pitch system, but perhaps it was fortunate that despite extensive machine shop facilities at the Armstrong Siddeley Engine factory, Sir John Siddeley considered a further £100,000 would be required to initiate rival propeller manufacturing, so the project was dropped. Nevertheless, when the Avro and Armstrong Whitworth team visited the Paris Aero Show in November they found that though British designers were not convinced that variable pitch propellers were essential, the French had already produced an effective pitch-change propeller, the Ratier — and Hamilton-Standard were exhibiting their own more substantial propellers. There were also more fighters and bombers at the Grand Palais than ever before. Once again Baldwin warned: 'In the next war civilians will find that any town within reach of an enemy aerodrome can be bombed within the first five minutes to an extent inconceivable in the last war, and the question will be "whose morale will be shattered quickest by the preliminary bombing?".'

Certainly Germany was well aware of these factors. *The Times* reported: 'The first school in Germany for training the civil population in defensive measures against the mass air attack has opened in Nuremberg.'

Britain was beginning similar action, Baldwin explained: 'I will not pretend we are not taking precautions in this country. Considering the years necessary for preparation, any government of this country in the present world circumstances would be guilty of criminal negligence had they neglected to make such preparation.' It sounded ominous.

* * *

At 3 am on 7 January 1933 Bert Hinkler left Fairey's new aerodrome at Harmondsworth in his DH Puss Moth, intent on beating the record of 9 days 4 hours to Australia set up by Charles Scott with a Gipsy Moth in April 1932. None except his wife and the night-watchman were there to see him off, his navigation lights briefly glowing in the dark sky. Then nothing more. Nearly four months later the wreckage of his machine, with his body 300 yards away, was found on the slopes of the Pratanagno Mountains above Florence. For many a day after, the thought of little Bert Hinkler was uppermost in Roy Chadwick's thoughts, for a big share in the Avro successes in the years after the war had depended on this doughty little pilot's engineering knowledge and analysis of flight quality. Ever since the earliest Hamble days his wife and Mary had been close friends — but now Mrs Hinkler was left destitute. Dobson and Chadwick clubbed together and gave immediate, but necessarily limited, financial help.

Meanwhile at the end of January, Adolph Hitler had become Chancellor of Germany, intent on re-arming. In fact the nucleus of the future German Luftwaffe had already been achieved in secret with the development of fighters and bombers such as the Dornier Do 11, Heinkel HE 51, and Arado AR 65 under the aegis of Capt Göring, the Reich Commissioner for Aviation.

Consequently development of military aircraft continued everywhere. That led Chadwick to scheme a 420 hp Jaguar-powered, 36 ft span, low-wing reconnaissance bomber Type 644, but as Siddeley's policy was for him primarily to engage on civil aircraft, he turned to a possible 54 ft span, six-seater powered by two 340 hp Double Mongoose engines, and as a side-line redesigned the successful Type 631 Cadet as Type 638 by almost eliminating stagger and fitting folding wing hinges so that Clubs and private owners could economise in hangar space.

At the instigation of the Far East Aviation Co, the Avro Agents in Hong Kong, he further revised the Type 626 Tutor, which as Type 637 became a light two-seat fighter of slightly greater span for 'frontier patrol duties' by the Kwangsi Air Force. To his envy John Lloyd at Armstrong Whitworth was not only involved in development of the "Atalanta" airliner but with military designs, including a solid-looking, low-winger twin-engined AW XXIII transport bomber. However John suffered a bad set-back when the Argosy *City of Liverpool* caught fire in the air and dived to the ground near Dixmude on 28 March, killing all aboard.

In fact these days there were crashes gallore, particularly in the RAF at home and abroad. Although civilian pilots fared rather better, there was current concern over Capt Lancaster who had left Lympne on 11 April flying the Avro Avian *Southern Cross Junior*, formerly owned by Sir Charles Kingsford-Smith, in an attempt to break Amy Mollison's recent record to the Cape. He reached Oran the same day and Goa the next, but nothing more was heard of him until many years later when his wrecked machine was found in the Algerian desert.

May brought the beginning of better things for Roy Chadwick when Woods-Humphrey, managing director of Imperial Airways, met Sir John Siddeley to discuss the possibilities of a small and fast long-range twin-engined low-winger for charter work. The requirement could almost be satisfied by the 54 ft span Avro 654 six-seater which Roy had schemed in March, but the estimated landing speed was too high and the range too low, so design studies of two smaller low-wingers of 50 ft and 46 ft span were initiated, designated Avro 647 and 648, and powered with twin Genet Majors.

Considerable discussion ensued with Major Mayo, the Imperial Airways technical adviser, and Chadwick was quick to seize on the possibilities of other aircraft such as an eight-seater powered by four Genets and a bigger tri-motor with Jaguar in the nose and Lynx engines outboard. In due course ideas crystallized into a 56 ft span revision of Type 645 redesignated 652 utilizing the standard Avro welded tube structure with cabin accommodating six, and fuselage mounted on a typical Fokker-type wooden wing carrying two Cheetah-engine nacelles into which the

Roy Chadwick and daughters picnic in the countryside.

undercarriage retracted. He was also contemplating a considerably enlarged revision of the basic Avro Ten, powered with twin 460 hp Jaguar engines, and carrying two crew and 16 passengers.

Despite the vigorous manner in which this 40-year-old designer was engrossed with ever-recurring design problems it was not all work and no play. His daughter Margaret recollects that when she was ten: 'My father took me with my mother and little sister for many a run in the countryside at weekends. On one excursion we drove to Frodsham Heights and then he led us to the steep edge of the hill where there was a magnificent view, and said in reflective manner: "Down there is where I was born," and my mother squeezed his arm and smiled at him'.

* * *

Scanning the *Financial Times* on 23 May, Sir John Siddeley must have observed with interest that his friend and rival, Tom Sopwith, had turned his long-established

The Spartan Cruiser had similar performance to the tri-motor Avro 'Five'.

The Saro Cloud amphibian with Fokker-type wing.

business of H. G. Hawker Engineering Co into a public company, re-named Hawker Aircraft Ltd. The paper stated that 'the new company has no less than nine types of aircraft in service in the RAF' — but at least Siddeley could match that with four RAF types and five for airline or private use.

There was also a change of name for that publicity-shunning aircraft pioneer so widely known as 'A.V.', for he was granted permission by the Supreme Court of Judicature to insert a hyphen between Verdon and Roe to perpetuate his mother's maiden name of Verdon, and so became Sir Alliott Verdon-Roe. Vigorous as ever, he commuted several times a week to Cowes in his high-speed Saunders-Roe motor boat. In many ways that business seemed an extension of his long cherished Avro company, because the Fokker-winged tradition was continued not only by his Cutty Sark, Cloud, and Windhover flying-boats but also the tri-motor Spartan cruiser equivalent of the Avro Five, and there was a Spartan Arrow biplane rival of the Avian, but in the spirit of earlier years he and Lady Roe maintained friendly contact with the Chadwick family.

Roy and his wife attended the annual flying display of the Household Brigade Flying Club at Heston on 7 June, for it was always an elegant social occasion, but 'this year it was too drawn out and the pilots in several events definitely overstayed their welcome,' reported *Flight.* Nevertheless among the visiting aircraft the Avro designer was interested to see the new Waco 4-seat cabin biplane which Lady Drummond Hay had imported from the USA. Either the Tutor or the Cadet, he mused, could be converted to a similar cabin aeroplane at no great expense. Next day he discussed the possibilities with Roy Dobson at Newton Heath after Harold Rogerson had sketched the modification on an existing drawing of the Cadet, and within a few days construction began of a windowed fuselage filling the mainplane gap.

The great annual RAF Display followed on 24 June as the high spot of the year, attended by the usual huge crowd — but it poured, so the flying seemed terrifyingly dangerous in the poor visibility and low cloud. This was also the last time the crazy flying Avro 504s would appear, but it seemed to add to their zeal, for they careered across the aerodrome missing each other by a hair's breadth. The crowd was no less thrilled by the polished inverted flying with an Avro Tutor from CFS in lieu of their programmed Squadron inversions. Pilots enjoyed the Tutor, for it had no tricks or vices and was ideal for aerobatics; but as Frank Tredrey recorded in *Pilots Summer:* 'There is a difficulty which even few in the Service realise. The carburettor has to function upside down, so while turning over onto one's back not only has one to turn an oil cock to keep a small engine-sump system going, but switch over the petrol to feed another jet, and that jet gives practically no throttle control, thus one has only two speeds — full-out and stop.' Of that, Roy Chadwick was of course aware, but there was no other solution and he greatly admired the dexterity with which the pilots handled this complication — yet on this occasion it had to be done within a few hundred feet of the ground!

Leading the latest experimental aircraft from the New Type Park was the new C.30 Autogiro. Gently if flip-flapped around the aerodrome, then with engine off made a perfect flare-out landing. Sir John Siddeley was visibly impressed. 'I think I'll obtain a licence to construct those machines,' he told his henchmen. 'This could mark a new era in aviation.' He was also delighted to find on the following Monday with the SBAC's 'Open Day' that exhibits of the Siddeley Group exceeded all others by showing the AWXV 4-engined airliner *Aurora,* latest AWXVI fighter, Avro Tutor, 631 Cadet, Club Cadet, and Mailplane, backed by a static display of the full range of engines.

Among other aircraft parked nearby was reminder of Alliott Roe's interests in the form of his amphibious Cutty Sark flying boat, trimotor Cruiser and newly introduced Clipper two-seater monoplane. As though emphasising his success, three Saro amphibian Clouds took off to herald the fly-past of bigger flying-boats from the Short and Supermarine stables. With concern Roy Chadwick learned that the latter's designer, Reggie Mitchell, had recently been operated upon for cancer.

For the Chadwick family the King's Cup Race on 8 July became a special occasion. The venue was Hatfield aerodrome owned by de Havillands, but also home of the London Aeroplane Club at whose splendid premises Chadwick had booked overnight accommodation. 'Off we went on Friday evening in my father's comfortable new Armstrong Siddeley' recollected Margaret. 'In those days the journey to London through the quiet countryside and towns seemed much more interesting, but it was midnight and

Pilots of the Central Flying School formate inverted with their Avro 621 Tutors.

pitch dark when we arrived at the outskirts of St. Albans and though Hatfield must have been just round the corner, no signposts were visible. So my father asked a solitary policeman on nightly vigil to tell him the way, but he was from Scotland, and having just joined the Force didn't know where Hatfield was. "But this is Denham," he said, "and those are the Film Studios. If you ask the night-watchman, perhaps he can help you." We motored into what seemed a giant yard beside a huge red building and knocked on a side door. An old night-watchman listened to our story, shook his head, told us that every hotel would be closed, and said we'd better stay in the Studios for the night. He led us up flights of steps and ushered us into one of the dressing rooms where we rested on chairs and a small couch till dawn; then in he came with steaming cups of tea and fruit cake from his own provisions. It was nearly 5 am he said, and everyone would soon be arriving, so would we mind leaving and finding our way to Hatfield? Soon we set off, and it seemed in no time that we were all fast asleep in glorious soft beds at the London Aeroplane Club.'

Eventually they awakened to the sound of engines being tested. It was a cloudy, cool morning with a fresh south-west wind. Presently, 35 of the original 42 entries were ready, but to the children, and even to many adults, it was all a confusion of gaily coloured aeroplanes arriving and departing, until in the final heat there were only eight, and to everyone's satisfaction, Geoffrey de Havilland won with his new Leopard Moth monoplane at an average speed of 139.5 mph. Said C. G. Gray: 'I have never yet known so much popular enthusiasm for the winner of a big event in aviation. Nobody handles an aeroplane better nor has anybody produced so many different types of successful aeroplanes.' In fact the Leopard Moth was his 75th since starting with Airco in 1915, though he had built his first prototype in 1909 and had a big share in designing the BE sequence.

Nevertheless, Chadwick had been primarily responsible for twice as many projects since the Avro 504, and his twin Cheetah-powered Avro 652 was still under consideration by Imperial Airways, but there was also indication that the Air Ministry might be interested in a military version. Performance estimates were made by W. R. Andrews, who had joined A. V. Roe & Co in 1928, and he recollected that: 'Mr Chadwick was very comfortable to work for. Once confidence was established you were free to do your job without hindrance. However, when I estimated the speed of the Avro 652 as 195 mph, he said: "If it does, I'll eat my hat!", but he allowed the figures to stay in the brochure, and I always felt that it was a kindness on his part to save me any possible embarrassment.' In fact it was confidence in his trained staff.

Currently there was not that same confidence at Armstrong Whitworth. To Chadwick's secret relief, Major Green, tired of difficulties with Sir John Siddeley, threw in his hand as chief engineer — a position held since January 1917. In a way it was remarkable that he had stayed so long with the Group, for his was a formidable and outspoken character; but Siddeley was equally blunt and ruthless, strong in the conviction that he was the boss and final arbiter on every proposal offered by his aircraft and engine designers.

The departure of Green was followed by that of his pioneer engine specialist S. M. Viale, who abruptly left for Italy. Harry Cantrill replaced him as chief designer, and Tom Chapman, who had joined in 1926 as a draughtsman, was placed in charge of engine development. Sir John's son, E. H. Siddeley, was appointed works manager of Armstrong Siddeley Motors.

While these changes were taking place Roy Chadwick was holidaying with his family at Anglesey, but despite the fun of inventing splendid sandcastles for young Margaret and 3-year-old Rosemary, he could not forbear ringing Harold Rogerson to discover how the special Tutor E.59 for the Greek Air Force was progressing at Martlesham, and whether work on the three-seat Avro 642 Cadet had started. Transferring to Roy Dobson, he anxiously enquired whether there was any response to the Avro 652 brochure which he

The 140 hp Hermes-powered Avro 640 Cadet had a widened metal-framed fuselage to accommodate two passengers side-by-side in the front cockpit.

had submitted to Imperial Airways.

'Eh, Roy — give them time! They are probably all on holiday like you,' came the answer.

Re-energised by the break, Chadwick returned to work intent on securing John Siddeley's permission to proceed with the Waco-like design of the Avro 641 Commodore as a four-seat cabin variant of the Avro 637 Tutor development for China which had longer wings with rounded tips. Perhaps Lady Drummond Hay's imported Waco led Siddeley to believe there was a ready market for an aeroplane with much better performance than the recently introduced DH four-seater Fox Moth; in any case, after experiencing the comfort of the enclosed cabin Avro 639 version of the Cadet, he agreed that a prototype Commodore could be built. Meanwhile de Havillands, on discovering that Avros had built the cabin Cadet, decided to emulate it with a similiar biplane designated DH 87 Hornet Moth, but inevitably powered with their 130 hp Gipsy Major instead of the 135 hp Armstrong Siddeley radial Genet.

The Air Exercises commencing on 22 September were less a reminder that aircraft were instruments of war than a programmed tussle of Navy versus RAF. There was no decisive result, for the RAF was convinced that it sank every ship in the Fleet at least twice, and the Navy's anti-aircraft gunners and fighters were adamant they had brought down every RAF machine four times. At least it indicated the certainty of continuing RAF and FAA orders — and that satisfied the British aircraft industry because it meant money without risk.

October had further encouraging moments for Avro. Hot on the heels of Sir Charles Kingsford Smith's record England to Australia flight with a Percival Gull in 7 days 4 hrs 50 mins on the 11th, C. T. P. Ulm with three crew left the Fairey aerodrome next day bound for Australia in his Avro Ten monoplane, and on 20 October landed at Derby, Western Australia, having beaten Kingsford Smith's time by 11 hours to Chadwick's great satisfaction. This offered hope that the new joint company formed by Imperial Airways and Qantas might order Avro Tens for the eastern section of their proposed England-Australia service.

But now there was crucial contention at Armstrong Whitworth. John Lloyd had defied Sir John Siddeley by tendering for a single-seater fighter to Air Ministry Specification 14/32 with a biplane powered with the latest Rolls-Royce Kestrel to ensure a fuselage of minimum resistance as

Charles Ulm with crew comprising G. V. Allen, P. G. Taylor and W. O. Edwards on visit to Woodford.

exemplified by the Hawker Fury currently in production.

Sir John irrascibly thumped the table. 'Why don't you obey my instructions? You are fully aware that my policy is to use Armstrong Siddeley engines and no others.'

'But I must insist, Sir, that if you wish to win the competition for this class of fighter the only possible engine is a Rolls-Royce.'

Altercation continued. Lloyd stood his ground and was sacked — though re-instated at the beginning of the following year on the understanding that he would revise the design to take the latest Panther of identical power to the Rolls-Royce. That resulted in the Scimitar, which proved to be 20 mph slower than the winning Fury Mk 2 of which 100 were eventually ordered. However fiery Sir John Siddeley bore no malice, having got his way; but it also dispelled any chance of Roy Chadwick using Rolls-Royce engines.

Woods-Humphery, the autocratic general manager of Imperial Airways, was still dallying over the Avro twin-engined monoplane, and now stipulated that it must be suitable for the Karachi-Bombay-Colombo mail run — necessitating re-stressing and stiffening the structure because this extended the weight to 7,650 lbs due to increased fuel and additional night-flying equipment.

Concurrently the Tutor for Greece, fitted with drag-reducing Townend ring cowling for the engine, modified exhausts, a slimmer undercarriage leg designed by Dowty, low-pressure wheels, and a strut interconnecting top and bottom ailerons, had proved so effective that a production Tutor, K1389, was similarly modified and sent to Martlesham for clearance as the future standard.

But the year ended badly. On 30 December the Imperial Airways Avro Ten, *Apollo,* piloted by Captain J. N. Gittens, en route from Cologne to Croydon, ran into thick fog on leaving Brussels, and just after mid-day hit a stay of the 900 ft wireless mast near Bruges, swung violently round, and entangled in the broken mast, dived to the ground killing all aboard. Two minutes later the tanks caught fire, badly burning nine Belgians who attempted to rescue the occupants.

As always with Avro crashes, Chadwick felt a sense of personal responsibility, and certainly it would involve him in the official Air Ministry investigation that would follow.

* * *

The big Avro 642/2m 'Ten' powered with twin 450 hp Jaguars was the fastest of the series with 156 mph and outstanding climb of almost 1000 ft/min.

During the latter part of 1933, he and his staff had been busily adapting the Avro Ten design to a twin-engined version with the wing lowered to a shoulder position on a 20 ft longer fuselage having a semi-circular nose in profile and cabin accommodating 16 passengers. The two 460 hp Townend-cowled Jaguar radials were mounted on the leading edge to give a slightly higher thrust line than before, and because of the greater power, a larger fin and rudder was fitted to overcome the asymmetrical thrust if one engine failed. Known in the factory as the 'Eighteen' but designated Avro 642/2m, it was completed in December and delivered to Martlesham for C of A trials early in January 1934. However, the A & AEE confirmed Sam Brown's report that the curved windscreen panels gave imperfect view, whereupon the nose was extended and flat Triplex glass substituted. So clean was the machine, thanks to wind tunnel tests conducted by Reggie Reynolds at Armstrong Whitworth, that top speed was 156 mph, compared with 115 mph of the original 3-engined Fokker-Avro, and climb had increased from 670 ft/min to 970 ft/min.

Good salesmanship by Dobbie ensured purchase of this prototype by Midland and Scottish Air Ferries Ltd. Even more encouraging was an order from the Indian Government for a 4-engined version as the result of Col Shermerdine's recommendation.

In February Chadwick again became involved with Autogiros when Sir John Siddeley secured a licence to produce Cierva C.30As. Because of the considerable Avro experience in constructing Cierva C.19s, Dobson had no hesitation in undertaking the complete machining sequence instead of sub-contracting the rotor system. Three pre-production aircraft, referenced Avro 671, were put in hand, of which one ordered by the Air Ministry was for Army Co-operation evaluation. A typical Chadwick modification was re-design of the rotor blade attachments to the rotor-head to permit folding the blades for tight storage.

Indicative of the times, further consolidation of the British aircraft industry now followed Siddeley's lead in aquiring Avro. On 20 February, the Gloster Aircraft Co Ltd was taken over by Hawker Aircraft Ltd. Tom Sopwith became chairman of both firms and joint managing director with Fred Sigrist. Frank Spriggs, the business genius of Hawkers, became general organising director. Siddeley noted the merger with shrewd interest.

International figureheads were also making moves. Hitler pronounced and Göring asserted that Germany required an Air Force of at least 30 to 40 per cent of the combined strength of her neighbours France, Belgium, Czechoslovakia and Poland: that meant 900 to 1,200 aeroplanes — which made the RAF seem insignificant. Consequently Britain's Air Estimates of £20,165,600 became the focus of attention, but the total available for new aeroplanes was only £2,810,000 and £1,940,000 for engines: *in toto* less than the cost of one battleship.

'Dobbie' said Chadwick when they met at lunch-time, 'I am sure that Churchill is right. We should be re-arming faster, even though the present production aircraft are obsolete.'

Dobbie grinned. 'Well, at least the factory is full of profitable work,' and he pointed to the line of production Tutors.

'I hope it will soon have a row of Commodores,' his colleague replied. 'Sam thinks the prototype is pretty good.'

Sam Brown at Woodford had just made the first flight of this very practical looking, rigidly strut-braced cabin biplane. A few weeks later, registered G-ACNT, it was flown to Martlesham for C of A trials. Concurrently Alan Marsh of the Cierva Company tested the prototype Avro 671 C.30A Autogiro, and in April flew it to Martlesham where the C of A trials largely comprised tuition for the Establishment's pilots amid great enthusiasm for the versatility of this machine, but at £1950 the prospect of sales was not very promising. Nor was that of the Commodore 641, but the prototype, silver painted and beautifully furnished, was sold to W. Westhead, a wealthy private-owner pilot who took delivery at Woodford on 24 May. Few orders subsequently materialized, but the second of the batch being built at Avro's

The Commodore spanned 37 ft 4 ins compared with 34 ft of the Tutor and similarly had a 240 hp Lynx IVc yet was 10 mph faster.

Failsworth factory was bought by the Earl of Amherst, and four more were eventually sold.

Roy Chadwick's elder daughter remembers the pleasure of flying in one of them: 'One day, just after the school term started, my father said: "I'm flying down to Southampton, would you like to come?" Would I not? It was terribly exciting. Nice Mr Tomkins was the pilot, and the cabin of his elegant aeroplane was luxuriously furnished with two seats in front and three behind just like our car. We flew at 3,000 ft, and the view was enormous. There was even the thrill of going into a cloud, then emerging into brilliant sunshine the other side! Presently we saw Southampton in the distance, and further still was the distinctive Isle of Wight. We landed on the AST aerodrome at Hamble, and my father pointed out the office building where he used to work. We went to Hamble House for discussion and lunch with Sir Alliott and Lady Verdon-Roe, and I had mine with their children Patricia and Royce whose governess told them, "We needn't speak French today as Margaret is here." Afterwards Trishy put on a Spanish dress and danced with castanets, and sang *Ma Curly-headed Baby* to the piano accompaniment of the governess. Then home again through the evening skies to end a perfect day.'

Of vital importance that April was Imperial Airways' acceptance of Chadwick's twin-engined Type 652 low-wing monoplane design, followed almost immediately by receipt of a Specification from the Air Ministry for the proposed coastal reconnaissance landplane, and since the Director of Contracts had asked for 'details of the extent to which any of your existing types can be adapted to meet the requirement', it seemed worth submitting an adaptation of the same machine, and under typical pressure from Chadwick, the design incorporating a gun turret was completed by 19 May — but acceptance was by no means certain because other firms were known to be tendering, among them de Havilland and Airspeed with derivations of existing machines. The inevitable months of waiting for a decision began, but concurrently work commenced on the two monoplanes for Imperial Airways.

Since there was a lull in the design office, Sir John Siddeley took the opportunity of sending Roy Chadwick on a combined business and holiday journey to Turkey by the luxurious *Orient Express* in an effort to sell Tutors to the Turkish Air Force — an engagement eagerly accepted because of the extensive spectrum of countries and peoples he would swiftly encompass, and to see the fabled towers, minarets and domes of the mysterious East was a great experience in itself. But there was also the quiet, majestic glory of the Acropolis high upon its hill when he returned via Athens for discussions with the Greek Air Force. Eventually orders followed from both Turkey and Greece, though he was less successful in Italy on stopping off for a few days at Rome but was delighted at visiting the great Stadium, the dominating magnificence of St. Paul's, and the beautiful frescoes of Michelangelo in the Sistine Chapel of the Vatican Palace.

'His intimate love of beauty and line, his sense of history, and his firm belief as a Christian, made the visit very memorable,' explained his daughter Margaret. 'He was not a Roman Catholic but we were all regular attenders at St. Peter's Church, some seven minutes' walk from our house at Hale. He would be the first into the pew, with me beside him, and would kneel in prayer, forehead cradled in his right hand. I used to look up at him when he stood, tall and slender in his black overcoat, singing the difficult phrases of the Psalms just as he did when a young man.'

On returning to Manchester, he had been dismayed to learn that 56-year-old Lord Londonderry, Secretary of State for Air and proud possessor of an Avro Cadet, had crashed at Heston on 7 June when he stalled on his approach; but luckily he and his lady passenger escaped with only facial injuries. 'Everybody admired Londonderry's courage in learning to fly at his age,' said a commentator, 'and he has earned the respect and liking of the inner circle of British aviation by his frankness and humour and lack of officialness.'

There were important changes in the Air Ministry and Higher Commands early that month. The Department of Supply and Research was sub-divided: Air Marshal Sir Hugh Dowding, known as 'Stuffy', was appointed Air Member for Research and Development (AMRD), and Air Marshal Sir Cyril Newall, a figure of stern discipline, became Air Member for Supply and Organisation (AMSO). Air Commodore R. H. Verney, a quiet and knowledgeable man, took office as Director of Technical Development (DTD), but Major Harry Wimperis retained his distinguished position as Director of Scientific Research (DSR). On these men the whole future of the RAF, and indeed of Great Britain, depended.

The extensive nature of RAF operations was once again illustrated by the annual Display held at Hendon in glorious sunshine on 30 June — but for the first time there was tragedy. The engine of a Hawker Hart piloted by F/O Leigh failed during a formation diving salute to the Prince of Wales by No. 600 Auxiliary Squadron, and in attempting to land, Leigh undershot and crashed outside the aerodrome, killing his passenger, the Lord Mayor's son, Sqn Ldr Stanley Collet, who was CO of the Squadron.

In typical RAF tradition the Display continued, and Tutors from CFS, with top wings painted in radial stripes of red and white, performed amazing aerobatics and inverted flying in tight formation. Frank Tredrey recollected: 'The pilots are used to hanging on their shoulder straps and floating round the sky with their eyes bulging out, but it's all very queer upside down. Stick and rudder go over to opposite sides, and you rely on your inverted senses to tell when slipping in or skidding out or doing a correct turn, while keeping level with the leader to a foot and hold him just one span away. Not as artless as it may look from your enclosure at Hendon on Display Day!'

On the following Monday the third SBAC Display attracted 1,500 guests, and more than 40 aircraft from 18 British firms were on display. Among them, Avros had a comprehensive range including the Commodore, a black and silver Cadet from AST Ltd, the 626 Trainer demonstrator, an RAF Tutor, and the twin Jaguar-powered Fokker-type 642-2m monoplane *Marchioness of Londonderry* which was fated to be wrecked a few days later in a forced landing in Merionethshire. However, the most outstanding display was that of Lloyd's AW 35 Scimitar spectacularly flown by Charles 'Toc H' Turner-Hughes, who made such fierce turns from left to right and back again that Roy Chadwick was visibly impressed, and began to dream up a two-seat fighter biplane trainer of almost identical size but half the power.

Indicative of changing outlook were the many monoplanes competing in the King's Cup Race on 13 and 14 July, which Harry Schofield won with the new ST10 Monospar. A week later the Gorell Committee issued its long-awaited report on Control of Private Flying — resulting in the Air Ministry establising an Air Registration Board (ARB) to control the network of 'approved' firms, issue and renewal of Certificates of Airworthiness, supervise modification procedure and inspection certification, and establish competency of pilots and ground engineers. The Report coincided with the Government's equally long-delayed announcement of 31 additional Home Defence Squadrons spread over five years, and eight divided between Overseas Commands and the Fleet Air Arm. In the ensuing Parliamentary debate, Baldwin made the historic statement: 'Our Air Defence frontier is no longer the white cliffs of Dover but the Rhine.'

Chadwick was already developing his initial outline of the fighter trainer inspired by the Scimitar. One of the draughtsmen was 31-year-old Jimmy Orrell, an ex-RAF flying instructor who had recently joined the company on finding there were few piloting jobs available on leaving the Service. 'I therefore decided to return to my basic trade of a draughtsman and wrote to Mr Dobson who recommended me to Roy Chadwick with the specific idea that I could help out with flying. This suited me at the time because I was gaining experience in both activities, though Sam Brown as chief pilot did most of the flying. Mr Chadwick, I found, was greatly respected by all the design staff. His design record was good, and even at that time the projects in the office were most encouraging for the future, and aircraft for the Turkish Air Force, the Irish Air Force, and the two monoplanes for Imperial Airways were well advanced in the drawing office and experimental department.

'He was the well-educated, artistic type, always smartly attired, giving an atmosphere of efficiency. Many stories emerged of his tours around the drawing boards and how he remarked on good work, giving credit where it was due, though it was not unknown for him to scribble "rubbish" across a drawing, then quietly outline his scheme and encourage the draughtsman to get on with the job. However, I finally encountered disaster on designing a fuel system with main tank in the fuselage, then went away delivering aircraft and on return found I had located the legs of a cantilever undercarriage right through the main tank. Luckily, Imperial Airways came to the rescue at that point with the offer of a piloting job, which I quickly accepted.'

That long-legged aeroplane was the eventual Avro 636 two-seat fighter trainer, for which Chadwick had the co-operation of John Lloyd in designing the wings with built-up, flange-rivetted, steel box spars and channel ribs of typical Armstrong Whitworth type, but the fuselage was standard Avro-Fokker type with conventional frame of welded steel tube. Controls and equipment were readily accessible by removing the forward panels and fabric covered curved panels aft. The eye-catching undercarriage was designed in conjunction with George Dowty, who at last had financially established his Aircraft Components Ltd with production orders for oleo legs.

But now came the Air Ministry's confirmation of a contract for the Avro 652A monoplane, specifying delivery by March, 1935. That meant only six months in which to design and build this machine, and as a stimulus, a military conversion of the twin-engined DH89 Rapide was ordered from de Havillands for comparative trials.

A few days earlier, Roy Chadwick, piloted by Sam Brown, had flown to Martlesham in the Cabin Cadet, and to their great interest found the new Boeing and Douglas airliners for the forthcoming MacRobertson Race to Australia were there. As one of the pioneers of metal monocoque Chadwick was greatly impressed by the smoothly contoured duralumin-skinned wings and fuselages of the

Bristol's trend-setting bomber was faster than the RAF's contemporary fighters.

two American machines, and carefully studied the hydraulically operated retractable undercarriages — whereas he had designed a simple mechanical hand crank system for the Avro 652 and its military version.

At dawn on 20 October, Chadwick was at Mildenhall, to see the start. One by one, at half-minute intervals, the competitors took off. Outstanding were the three specially designed two-seat, twin-engined DH Comet racers featuring variable pitch propellers and retractable undercarriage, and it was the Comet of Black and Scott which won the £10,000 race but was ineligible for the handicap prize, so it was awarded to the Dutch Airlines DC-2 flown by Parmentier and Moll in close pursuit at second place.

Certainly the American airliners, which were a long way ahead on the technical count, meditated Chadwick — for he had been considering the possibility of Sir John Siddeley permitting him to design a very large 4-engined airliner for Imperial Airways; but instead the task was allotted to John Lloyd, and in September the airline established a £70,000 contract with Armstrong Siddeley for a prototype eventually named Ensign.

At the 14th International Aero Exhibition in Paris, which opened on 16 November, Roy Chadwick found that the French had built a Breguet 46T replica of the Douglas DC-2. Nearby was Frances's fastest fighter, the Dewoitine D 511 all-metal low-winger which, despite the fixed undercarriage, was indicative of the new trend. Britain's aircraft representation was limited to the Armstrong Whitworth Scimitar, an Avro 626 Trainer and C30B Autogiro, special Hawker Fury biplane, and attracting everyone to the adjacent Bristol Stand was the glittering monocoque duralumin fuselage of a military version of the epoch-making twin-engined Type 142 'Feeder' high-speed monoplane built for Lord Rothermere.

But no aviation matters could match public interest in the wedding on 29 November of the King's youngest son, the Duke of Kent, to the beautiful Princess Marina of Greece in a colourful ceremony at Westminster Abbey. At Heston, six aeroplanes were ready to rush the first pictures to the provinces, among them Banco's Avro Commodore, which sailed away into the misty sky aided by its newly fitted Vickers-Armstrong landing lights.

Chapter 10
New Horizons

At Woodford, activities centred on the prototype twin-engined Avro 652 low-winger for Imperial Airways. For the last few weeks it had been substantially complete yet there always seemed more to do; but on 6 January 1935, named *Avalon*, it was pushed out for engine runs, and next day was ready for initial flight. Sam Brown was in South America, demonstrating the first Avro 626 ordered by Chile, so his assistant pilot, Tommy Tomkins, stepped into the breach, and under the watchful eyes of Dobson and Chadwick carried out the initial routine of fast taxying, then straights across the aerodrome, and finally that moment of tenseness to the spectators when he opened the throttles wide and took off with one of the inspectors aboard to crank the many turns required to lift the undercarriage.

His reports was enthusiastic. 'She is so directionally stable, even with feet off the rudder pedals, that if either engine is switched off she briefly swings about 15 degrees, then back and continues on a straight course.' Manoeuvrability seemed excellent and there was no hint of longitudinal instability at this light loading. 'She flies much like the old 504,' said Tomkins — and that certainly pleased Chadwick.

In view of Sam Brown's many demonstrations abroad it was decided to take on an assistant chief pilot, and S. A. 'Bill' Thorn, a former CFS instructor and Farnborough test pilot but currently chief instructor of the Brooklands Flying Club, was selected.

The initial flight of *Avatar* (soon changed to *Ava*), the second Avro 652, followed a fortnight later and the development flying urgently proceeded whenever weather permitted. Everything seemed promising, so there seemed little risk of fundamental modifications to the RAF's special 652A version which was speedily taking form under the vigorous care of Avro's production genius Ted Fielding. The massed lines of Tutors in various stages of completion were flourishing, and currently he was establishing construction of four Jaguar-powered Avro 636 two-seat fighter trainers for which Roy

'Avalon', first of the Avro 625s for Imperial Airways, initially had a horn-balanced rudder, and to retract the undercarriage took over seventy turns of a small hand-crank!

Dual control C.30 'Rota' for the RAF.

Dobson had secured a contract from his Irish Army Air Corps acquaintances at Baldonnel.

There was also an increasing line of C.30A Autogiros, of which the Service version was named 'Rota' by the Air Ministry, and K4230 was delivered early in February to Martlesham for the Army Co-operation trials. Thanks to outstanding publicity by de la Cierva and his pilots, interest in rotary-winged flight was becoming widely established, though the first fatal accident in England had just occurred when the RAF's latest Autogiro acquisition at Old Sarum disappeared in cloud at 2,000 ft, and on reappearing dived at 45 degrees into the ground. Though at first inexplicable, it presently transpired that control had been lost through torsion of the blades. Meanwhile, Cierva revealed the jump-start capability of a modified C.30 at a Hanworth demonstration where everyone was fascinated to see the machine leap 10 to 20 feet high and then proceed forward on a normal climb.

That stirred the ever imaginative Chadwick to design a twin-engined cabin Autogiro, designated Type 668, but Sir John Siddeley preferred the modest but assured profits of the C.30 production rather than venture more money on a prototype. Despite his personal generosity in public affairs, and sometimes to people, he was always anxiously concerned at the heavy drain on capital absorbed by new engine and aeroplane projects and the gamble of sufficient financial return, so it must have been with interest that he read in the *Financial Times* of an extraordinary General Meeting of Hawker Aircraft Ltd at which a resolution was passed increasing the capital to £900,000 — a vast sum in those days.

But always there are risks. At the beginning of March, the Avro 652 *Avalon* was flown to Martlesham for C of A trials, and on certification both monoplanes left Woodford for delivery to Croydon on 11 March. 'The arrival was dramatic,' recollected Chadwick's erstwhile technician, Bill Andrews: 'Sam Brown and I were in the first plane to take off and Tommy Tomkins was pilot in the second with Jimmy Kay as passenger, but we lost sight of them over the Derbyshire hills where it transpired that their machine was damaged by a violent bump which fractured the pilot's windscreen and Jimmy was knocked out by hitting the cabin roof.

'Meanwhile we recorded our time to climb to Service ceiling and then ran level speeds at various heights on the way down. Soon we located Croydon, and Sam prepared to land; but I had to remind him that we had to do a stall test, so up we went again. Satisfied that all was finished, we came in to land — but both of us entirely forgot that these machines had a retractable undercarriage and we landed with it up to the enormous delight of the Imperial Airways pilots who had been wondering what would happen in just such an event. However, Mr Chadwick, with his usual thoughtfulness, had arranged that the wheels slightly projected when the undercarriage was up, and consequently there was little damage except for two bent propellers.'

Overcoming his initial dismay, Chadwick typically tempered some of the blame. 'I should have fitted some form of hooter as a warning in addition to the red lights,' he said. Soon that became a mandatory requirement for all aircraft with the retractable undercarriage.

A newcomer on his staff was Herbert Mettam MA, late of Westland where he had been chief technician of the tail-less Pterodactyl development. Many years later he told me: 'When I joined Avros in February, Chadwick still had Jim Turner as chief draughtsman, and he was a first-class designer in his own right but had to spend most of his time doing administration. Leader of the stressing team was Harold Rogerson, a delightful chief, universally known as 'The Squire'. As assistant designer there was a sturdy Scot named Alan Cameron, and I became the second assistant designer. Later that year we were joined by Stuart Davies from Glosters, who became the third assistant designer.

'There were, of course, a number of section leaders skilled in particular aspects of design to whom appropriate work was allocated, and though some of the draughtsmen remained with the same leader, most were moved from section to section in accordance with the work-load. It was a very happy set-up. Chadwick had a special office and there were smaller ones for us, and all the rest of the staff were in a large room which had roof skylights but no windows.

'Chadwick was always heavily involved with policy and planning, so the onus for detailed design fell largely on the section leaders, but I suspect that he found it a relaxation to emerge from his office and demand to know what some draughtsman, apparently selected at random, was doing and why — particularly why? Those chosen were often terrified by such a visitation, and Turner or Rogerson had to leap to their rescue. Certainly Chadwick had an uncanny knack of being able to gaze at some large drawing for some moments then put his finger on what was likely to prove to be the only error in a mass of detail. If he altered the drawing, he might well tell the draughtsman: "Do it that way, even if Mr Cameron or Mr Mettam or the Archangel Gabriel tells you something different." However, if it was one of the seniors whom he felt was at fault, he would be called to his office where Chadwick would be very outspoken, though once described himself as "a kind-hearted fellow at bottom". Having made his point, he would be completely friendly again and on several occasions subsequently offered me a lift home, although he had to drive several miles more than his normal route.'

Mettam, with his wife and three children, lived at Bowdon in Cheshire. Though some of his colleagues had the idea that this area was a millionaire's paradise, his five-bedroomed, semi-detached house was a typical £65 per year, matching his initial £500 a year salary.

'Apart from Sundays and Bank Holidays,' he said, 'the only holiday we got was Bank Holiday week and the one before or after. Concessions were given grudgingly, even for special aeronautical occasions such as the RAF Display or the one-day SBAC Show as normally we only had Saturday afternoons free. When the pressure really began to build up we were required to work overtime until 7.30 p.m. on three evenings a week and did not get paid for that overtime although we were given a Yorkshire cold tea which included such things as egg on haddock. My day-long absence often was 13½ hours, including travel by train and by bus, but though the men on the shop floor worked equally long hours there were no strikes in the four years I was with Avros.'

Chadwick's working hours were even longer, and his current concern centred on the military Avro 652A prototype K4771 which

The RAF 652A prototype was almost identical with the civil version except for nacelles, windows and gun turret.

had its maiden flight on 24 March piloted by Bill Thorn. In the following week it was flown to Martlesham for handling and performance trials, but preliminary tests revealed longitudinal instability at the aft c.g. position when flying at a gross weight of 7,400 lbs. That shook Chadwick because not only did the tail arm and area comply with his empirical data, but a model had been wind-tunnel tested for stability. As a hopeful cure, he had the tailplane tips extended to pointed form, giving 20 per cent greater area, but as the elevators were an unnecessarily large 50 per cent of the tailplane area, their chord was slightly decreased and the area became 30 per cent of the total tail. In May the modified machine was flown by the RAF to the Coast Defence Development Unit at Gosport for competitive trials against the DH 89M No. K4772.

The speed and manoeuvrability of the Avro was regarded as extraordinary, earning the comment: 'Certainly it is an aeroplane fit for gentlemen to fight from. She has a top speed in the neighbourhood of 190 mph. In the nose there is a bomber's compartment, with a pilot's cabin, navigator's compartment and WC compartment behind. To the rear of the WC is a gun turret of the Armstrong Whitworth type, half of which protrudes above the top fuselage decking. Except in very tight turns when 'g' took a hand in the proceedings, one could just sit and shoot, or be shot at, as the case might be. At present the take-off is somewhat extended, but split flaps and c.p. airscrews should attend to that.'

Soon after the Gosport trials, a Fleet exercise off the east coast showed that the Avro had superiority in range and endurance over its rivals. On 24 May, Air Chief Marshal Sir Edward Ellington, Chief of Staff, decided to adopt it as standard equipment for the RAF's new coastal reconnaissance squadrons. Accordingly the design became the basis for a new Specification, No 18/35, which listed 38 special requirements, and a contract was signed for 174 of these low-wingers serialed K6152-K6325 and named Anson.

But there were matters of greater significance. Germany's Deutsche Luftsportverband (DLV) officially became

The Rapide 89M rival.

At A. V. Roe & Co., Woodford, Roy Chadwick, Mr. Wilmot, Roy Dobson, Thomas Sopwith, Arthur Woodburn MP and Air Ministry official.

the military Reichsluftwaffe. That stirred the British Government to vigorous action with revised schemes for expansion of the RAF whereby the strength at home, irrespective of the FAA, would be 1,500 first-line machines by 31 March, 1937. That would require an additional 22,500 personnel, including 2,500 pilots to add to the existing 2,700, together with 400 trainees and a reserve of 1,200. Seventy-one new Home Defence Squadrons would be formed instead of twenty-two under the previous programme, and the number of aerodromes would be increased from the envisaged eighteen to thirty-one.

To amateur enthusiasts it seemed that the golden age of sporting flying ended with an announcement by de Havillands at the beginning of June that the open cockpit Gipsy Moth would no longer be manufactured. It was now the day of the monoplane for keen private owners requiring the fastest means of travel, but the procession of weekend flying meetings retained a big quota of biplanes, so Chadwick was interested to find that Amy Johnson had taken on the British agency for Beachcraft biplanes that rivalled his Commodore, but he guessed correctly that sales would be unlikely.

Then came the bombshell. On 25 June, every member of Sir John Siddeley's empire was devastated to discover that arrangements had been completed to merge with Hawker Aircraft Ltd by forming a new company named Hawker-Siddeley Development Co Ltd, of which the directors were T. O. M. Sopwith, Fred Sigrist, F. S. Spriggs as managing director, and Philip D. Hill who was a well-known financier. Capital was £2 million, of which the Armstrong-Siddeley Development Co Ltd would be paid £1 million and Sir John Siddeley would retire.

Once again the whole future had become uncertain. There had been no inkling of Sir John's intentions. Would Lloyd and Chadwick now become subservient to Hawker's outstandingly successful designer

Sydney Camm whose two-seat and single-seat military biplanes seemed the acme of perfection to the RAF? Siddeley was quick to reassure his two chief designers. Separately, they were summoned to his home at Crackley in Kenilworth and told: 'Spriggs has agreed that each of you will continue as the independent chief designer of your respective company, though design policy will be dictated by Mr Sopwith and Mr Spriggs.'

John Lloyd told me: 'My reaction that weekend was of great uncertainty of the future because I had never met Frank Spriggs, who in future would be my boss — though after the meeting I was quite happy and he subsequently proved to be just the opposite to that ruthless autocrat, Sir John.'

Virtually the constituent design teams of Hawker, Armstrong Siddeley, Avro, and Gloster, continued individually, each company retaining its personality and had its own Board. The irrepressible Roy Dobson was made general manager of Avro. 'I often wonder how two such forceful characters as he and Chadwick were able to run amicably in double harness,' said Mettam. Certainly to all appearances they did, despite occasional outspoken clashes. On the workshop side Dobson was supported by a number of highly competent departmental heads and foremen whom he drove as hard as he drove himself. Ted Fielding became works manager when Dobbie was promoted, Sandy Jack was chief inspector, and Jack Green was the very able works engineer despite the handicap of deafness.

The annual RAF Display took place four days after the Hawker take-over. The Avro 652A Anson attracted much attention, but Dobson and Chadwick in the Hawker enclosure were chaffed by their colleagues when a demonstration of instructor and pupil flying a Tutor in crazily clambering attitudes ended suddenly by the plane hitting the ground and collapsing with drooping wings, though without injury to the crew. Certainly that famous editor, C. G. Grey, seemed depressed that day, for he wrote: 'Apart from the beautiful precision of flying, the Show was dull. We have seen Harts, Audaxes, Demons and Ospreys till we know them backwards, and the Hind and the Hardy look the same.' A few days later came the first sign of Hawker influence on Avro in the form of a sub-contract to build Audaxes.

* * *

By now, there was a diffused realisation among the general public that Germany was a potential enemy; nevertheless, it was a shock to every householder in July to find a circular popped through the letterbox explaining the action to be taken in the event of a long war. As though to emphasise the certainty, a great Naval Review was held on 16 July, and six days later the Annual Air Exercises of ADGB began, aimed at discovering the probability of interceptions of approaching raiders by standing patrols of fighters warned by radio of an enemy located by the newly developed ground radar system.

Chadwick's contemplation of the possibilities of this new development of aerial detection was abruptly dismissed by a telephone call from Southampton announcing the death of his 63-year-old father. He had been standing in a crowded bus when suddenly he collapsed and died within minutes from a coronary thrombosis. The crowded church at his choral funeral service showed the great affection and esteem with which he and his wife were regarded. They had always worked with united purpose and latterly were instrumental in raising what seemed the enormous sum of £10,000 for an X-ray unit at the Southampton & South Hants Hospital where their son Roy had languished after his crash.

Somewhat uneasily Roy Chadwick snatched a brief holiday with his family in August at the quiet little harbour town of Pwllheli. On his return, the first of the four Irish Avro 636 dual-purpose biplanes was cleared for flight, powered with a 460 hp Jaguar taken from one of the Vickers Vespa biplanes which the Irish Air Corps had recently scrapped. Sam Brown found that the new aeroplane handled delightfully, and though originally intended for a 650 hp Panther, it nevertheless achieved 175 mph. To those on the ground, the very long cantilever undercarriage legs made it instantly distinguishable from the Tutor of similar dimensions, and the longer top wing and outwardly raked interplane struts added to its elegance. As soon as the other three were completed, all four were flown to Baldonel without the customary visit to Martlesham for Airworthiness certification.

By then Chadwick was dreaming up the next aeroplane and the next. In October he completed preliminary design of a Tiger-powered Army Co-operation sesquiplane to Specification A30/34. That same month, he was designing a twin-engined reconnaissance monoplane to Specification G24/35, followed by a twin Gipsy-powered enclosed monoplane trainer Type 673 — and always there were those Phoenix-like sketches of ideas scribbled on any odd piece of paper while he rested in the evenings listening to radio or gramophone. Matters were further complicated by an accident that month to the Imperial Airways Avro 652 *Ava* through landing at Croydon with undercarriage accidentally retracted — but that at least made Sam Brown smile reflectively.

As President of the Lancashire and Derbyshire Gliding Club, Chadwick deemed it his duty to find time for occasional visits to the steep ridge of Eyam Edge above Great Hucklow to watch the flying. Basil Meads, who succeeded him as President had a cottage near the Club House. 'It was Roy Chadwick who started us off when he was Chairman of the Manchester Branch of the Aeronautical Society in 1930,' he said. 'I first knew him in the early days of the Lancashire Aero Club and was proud to share a deep interest in aviation with this very accomplished professional, though I was only a lowly paid insurance official, scraping pennies together in order to learn to fly!

'He used to talk to my wife and I about his schoolboy fascination with model aeroplanes and kite flying, and how all his pocket money went on bits and pieces. As a supplement he would, by sleight of hand, sometimes hold back a portion of his Sunday church money, but was greatly distressed on one occasion

Almost identical with the Scimitar in size and weight, the Avro 636 had the prevailing welded-tube fuselage, but the steel-framed wings were of Armstrong Whitworth construction.

Launching the Club glider.

when he dropped a half-crown into the offertory bag instead of the penny piece he had intended. Not surprisingly, he inspired the Avro apprentices to form a model aeroplane club and a gliding section whose members built a simple Zogling glider after Mr Chadwick obtained drawings and materials, and he organised competitions and prizes.'

The relaxation of watching sailplanes in flight was now becoming all to infrequent and so were excursions with his family to other beauty spots. The pressure of work was inexorably increasing, and the week was often foreshortened by rushed visits to London for discussion of new RAF requirements, or there might be the interruption of day-long conferences at the Works with visiting Air Ministry Officials. In the background there was growing concern over Germany and Italy. Hitler had proclaimed conscription. Baldwin agreed that the newly named Luftwaffe already equalled the RAF in men and aircraft, and was building faster. Before the year was out, Italy invaded Abyssinia. Re-armamant became the *sine qua non.* Hitler grew ever-more blatant with his resurgent Germany, and in the distance Japan was posing a threat to Anglo-American strength in the Pacific. Darkly there loomed the enigmatic figure of Stalin and the Red threat of Communism.

Nevertheless on recovering at the Christmas break from a bout of influenza, Chadwick was gratified to receive a letter from the London office signed by his late chairman, Sir John Siddeley:-

> 'In sending the enclosed cheque for £722.6s. as a bonus on the result of the Company's operations for the past year, it gives me very great pleasure to express my thanks for the good work you have done, which is appreciated by all, and to express my hope that the future operations will be even more successful.
>
> 'Please accept my good wishes to you and your wife for Christmas and for 1936.
>
> 'I remain yours sincerely,
>
> 'J. D. Siddeley'

Certainly the business prospects seemed promising, for it was indicative that on the last day of the year, thanks to the forceful Dobson and practised skill of Fielding, the first production Avro Anson, K6152, was tested by Geoffrey Tyson at Woodford, the other pilots being on demonstration visits abroad.

* * *

In the wintery air of Norfolk, 71-year-old King George V suffered a chill whilst staying at his country house of Sandringham, and

First production Anson at Woodford.

John Lord.

died peacefully on the night of 20 January 1936. Amid national mourning he was brought to Westminster Hall where he lay in state until the funeral at Windsor on the 28th. Five days later the Chadwick family was shocked to learn of the death, following a stroke, of Sir Alliott Roe's great business partner, John Lord. Ever since those early pre-war years he had been the close friend and supporter of Roy Chadwick, offering shrewd commonsense encouragement and many a funny story to lighten the way, and to Alliott Roe he had been the concomitant of success by lifting all business worries from his shoulders. As the result of Lord's financial acumen, Saunders-Roe was building a very big erection shop on the east bank of the Medina at Cowes to meet the RAF's expansion programme. Similarly the Hawker-Siddeley Development Company was extending its facilities with a new Hawker aerodrome and extensive factory at Langley, near Slough. Roy Dobson also appreciated the necessity of expansion and with Sprigg's agreement was extending the Newton Heath factory by 250,000 sq ft, and now added two more flight sheds at Woodford with another under construction. In view of the increasing complexity the invaluable Ted Fielding was made assistant general manager.

Swift progress was evident with the Ansons, and early in February the second was delivered to No. 48 Squadron at Manston, rapidly followed by nine more so that on 6 March the complete Squadron was fully commissioned, historically becoming the first post-war unit to have monoplanes and the first to experience the use of a retractable undercarriage. By now the entire aircraft industry was concentrating on new types of fighters and bombers foreseen as essential if war with Germany occurred. The Air Staff was intent on schemes of deployment for every possible wartime contingency, and although their Scheme C of the previous year for sixty-eight bomber squadrons of twin-engined machines to Specification B1/35 had resulted in acceptance of tenders from Vickers, Bristol, Armstrong Whitworth and Handley Page, it was superseded in February by Scheme F for the same number of squadrons but requiring bigger twin and 4-engined aircraft carrying double the previous bomb load, and on his next visit to the Air Ministry, Chadwick picked up early rumours of these and other forthcoming requirements.

To co-ordinate all manufacturing programmes of the expanding industry, the Air Ministry appointed Lieut-Col Disney as Director of Production in the AMSO's department, with effect from 31 March. As a further safeguard, Lord Weir, who had gained such great experience of aircraft production during the Great War, was co-opted by the Air Ministry as adviser. Concurrently the dourly restrained AV-M Sir Hugh Dowding, who as AMRD had initiated the RAF's new look in weapons, monoplane fighters, and bombers, was appointed C-in-C Fighter Command. His former task was allocated to AV-M Freeman, to whom the industry quickly responded with mutual friendliness.

That early Spring, Germany made a great show of strength with dive-bombers and fighters flying over Cologne Cathedral to secure world reportage. Because of that policy of advertising its military strength, Roy Chadwick was permitted to visit some of the German aircraft factories after he had been to

Holland early in May to discuss improvements he had made to the Fokker-type wing of the Anson by using synthetic covering instead of ply. On return to Manchester, he was immediately involved in finalising a Design Tender brochure for his twin-engined Avro 672 reconnaissance/bomber monoplane to Specifications G24/35 and M15/35 on which his technicians had been working, followed by design studies of Types 676 and 677 R-R Kestrel-powered advanced trainer monoplanes to Specification T6/36 — but to no avail because the small firm of Miles Aircraft Ltd was being brought into the expansion programme to build trainers so that the major consortiums could concentrate on more complex production.

Certainly A. V. Roe & Co Ltd had done well with the Tutor and its derivatives — nearly 1,000 having been built in the past five years, and there was still the possibility that a batch might be modified to take double-bay wings, of which a sample, K3308, was being tested by Sam Brown and would shortly go to Martlesham for performance trials.

Having set the stage at Newton Heath with such considerable production embodying welding techniques, Dobson and Fielding were confident there would be few problems in manufacturing Ansons in even greater number, and already a further 106 had been ordered including 20 for diversion to the Royal Australian Air Force. Meanwhile the Government was establishing shadow factories for increased production of engines, and a similar scheme was contemplated for airframe manufacture.

As a sign of the times, Hawker-Siddeley doubled their registered capital by issuing one million £1 cumulative preference shares and four million ordinary shares of 5s which were eagerly snapped up by the public. At that, Frank Spriggs in addition to his Hawker-Siddeley directorship was placed in charge of the entire organisation of A. V. Roe at Manchester, the Armstrong Whitworth Group at Coventry, and Air Service Training at Hamble. At Langley the associated Hawker Division directed by Sigrist was

The Prefect Type 626 was a navigational trainer development of the Tutor with large rear windscreen, drift indicator, etc., and had a tailwheel instead of skid.

completing the Henley two-seat dive-bomber and its re-design as the Hotspur fighter which Spriggs intended to produce at Avro.

He also proposed closing down Avro's London office as redundant. Reg Parrott had retired some months ago because of ill health — and now it was learned that he had died of cancer, unhonoured and unsung, his pioneering work with Alliott Roe long overlooked.

* * *

For the first time monoplanes filled the New Type Park at the 17th RAF Display on 26 June; yet no less strikingly, every event featured the RAF's cherished biplanes except for three Ansons and three Autogiros. *The Aeroplane* described the occasion as 'a vast advertisement for the Hawker-Gloster-Siddeley combine, barring the flying-boat parade.' Nevertheless, the Supermarine Spitfire fighter, painted pale blue-grey, made its awe inspiring first public appearance, followed by the twin-engined Bristol *Britain First* with RAF roundels — but though the mid-wing Blenheim bomber version had made its first flight a few days earlier, it was too secret to display.

At the SBAC Show on the following Monday, Roy Chadwick had opportunity of meeting General Milch, the Chief of the German Luftwaffe under Göring, General Linquist of the Finnish Air Force, and Captain José Cabral of the Portuguese Air Force — but though introduction to the German was little more than a formality, the other two were interested in the Anson.

On 8 July H.M. King Edward VIII as Marshal of the RAF toured four stations of the Air Force, accompanied by his brother Air Marshal the Duke of York, flying first to Northolt and its antiquated Fury and Gauntlet biplane fighter squadrons, then to No. 11 FTS and its Tutors and Ansons at Wittering, thence to the Heyford Bomber Squadrons of Mildenhall, and so the the A & AEE at Martlesham and the Spitfire, Hurricane, and Vickers Venom prototypes, the hitherto unrevealed twin-engined Bristol Blenheim, the Westland Lysander, Fairey Battle, Vickers Wellesley, and finally the new heavier twin-engined bombers comprising Vickers Wellington, Handley Page Hampden and Armstrong Whitworth Whitley. Reassured that his Air Force was receiving such splendid machines, though unaware that they were already obsolete, the King flew back to Windsor in the Royal Rapide.

Soon afterwards revolution erupted in Spain. Ten days later Mussolini dispatched twelve tri-motor aircraft to ferry the Fascist General Franco's overseas force of Moroccan soldiers to Spain and Hitler sent twenty Ju52s, followed on 1 August by six Heinkel fighters and twenty-two anti-aircraft guns to protect the Junkers. Several units of the Spanish Air Force joined the General, but the Republican government also had aircraft, and a bombing war began.

That led the British Government to speed contracts for more airframes and engines and new specifications were issued. On 28 August, A. V. Roe & Co received a copy of Air Staff Requirements relating to fighters, bombers, and flying-boats, inspiring Chadwick to prepare a scheme for a tandem airscrew fighter, Avro 678, powered by a single Rolls-Royce Merlin. A further contract for thirty-

A typical scene at Woodford with export C.30, Tutor, and Anson being re-fuelled.

The 66 ft span Bristol 138A was all-wood for lightness and the pilot wore a pressurised suit to prevent aero-embolism.

nine Ansons followed in September, specifying metal framed ailerons, steeper windscreens with direct vision panels, and hydraulically operated Schrenk drag flaps to steepen the Anson's glide if it was overshooting.

However, there were problems with the factory hands. The Avro Shop Stewards Council was claiming that the hourly rate should be increased by 2d to a minimum of 1s 4½d, and that cuts made in the depression of 1931 should be restored, but ignored the fact that the wages in 1934 had been increased by 2s weekly and as recently as June a further 3s was conceded in stages of 1s every two months until December. One of the trouble-makers was threatened with dismissal. A mass meeting followed at which he induced the men to go on strike. At that, Roy Dobson jumped onto a canteen table and addressed them in such vehemently abusive terms that they revoked their decision, but other firms were also under pressure.

The tempo everywhere was increasing, yet the general public seemed only aware of the more sporting or spectacular aviation events such as Sqn Ldr Swain breaking the world's height record on 28 September flying a special Pegasus-powered Bristol cabin monoplane with which he achieved 49,943 ft — and next day came the start of a great international race from England to Johannesburg for a prize of £4,000: but it became a fiasco of accidents except for the Vega Gull flown by tough Charles Scott and Giles Guthrie who won in just under 53 hours. The dismays of that venture had scarcely subsided when Jean Batten, the rival of Amy Mollison, took off from Lympne on 5 October and in a series of long flight stages reached New Zealand in eleven days. In somewhat less gruelling manner, Jim Mollison flew from Harbourgrace, Newfoundland, to Croydon on 29/30 October, making the fastest westward crossing of the North Atlantic to date in just over 13 hours.

That same month a special Mk II Anson registered SU-AAO, and re-stressed for a take-off weight of 8,000 lbs instead of 7,400, was flown to Egypt for their Army Air Force to assess its suitability for a bomber-transport squadron — but even its success became of secondary importance to Chadwick in November when the far reaching P13/36 Specification, dated 8 September, was at last issued, and A. V. Roe & Co was invited to tender for this big twin-engined bomber of 45,000 lbs all-up weight in competition with Handley Page and, surprisingly, with Hawkers.

The idea of matching wits against his very successful associate Sydney Camm appealed to Roy Chadwick though the problems of design, let along manufacture, were considerable because the DO would have to embark on substantially different metal techniques from that of the hitherto favoured welded steel tube fuselage and fabric-covered, open-structured wing. That was the chief designer's fundamental responsibility, but the Specification stipulated two of the still undeveloped 1,700 hp Rolls-Royce Vulture engines comprising four banks of six cylinders in 'X' formation, and required a speed of not less than 275 mph at 15,000 ft on two-thirds power, a Service ceiling of 28,000 ft and ability to fly at 10,000 ft on one engine. Take-off in 500 yards with 1,000 lb bomb load and fuel for 1,000 miles was required, or 700 yards in the over-load case with a 3,000 lb bomb load and fuel for 2,000 miles. The maximum bomb load contemplated was 8,000 lbs. with 2,000 miles range after a catapult-accelerated take-off. Stowage for a wide range of bombs was essential and alternatively two 18″ torpedoes 18 ft 3 ins long — all carried internally. A crew of four was specified, and a nose turret mounting two guns and tail turret with four guns was mandatory together with specified ammunition. Good all-round view for the pilot and adequate manoeuvrability at high speed for dive-bombing was vital. Not only must the design be suitable for easy quantity production but the central span and longest fuselage section was limited to 35 ft and other portions of wing or fuselage to 22 ft. Like the B12/36 Specification for a still bigger 4-engined bomber of 55,000 lbs. for which Shorts and Supermarine had successfully tendered, the P13/36 emphasised that 'design, construction, and satisfactory operation of all services, must proceed at greatest possible speed.'

Chadwick gathered his team of top specialists for discussion and spelt out the requirements so that preliminary investigation of size, component weights, and overall performance could be made based on the wing area and flap-aided lift coefficients that would ensure the crucial 500-yard take-off. Like all designers, he had become instantly obsessed with every creative aspect.

A metal-skinned structure was fundamental. In the past five years there had been much mathematical and experimental investigation by the RAE, resulting in a number of valuable R & Ms which had been deeply studied by Chadwick and Rogerson on such subjects as Stress Diffusion, Sheer Lag, Buckling in Box Structures, and in October they had attended a lecture on *Aerodynamic and Structural Features of Tapered Wings* by Dr Lachmann of Handley Page who declared: 'Strictly speaking the term "stressed skin" can only be applied to structures where the skin takes practically the entire bending load as well as the sheer due to torsion and anti-drag.' Such a wing could be lighter than one in which the spar took the bending load and the skin only the sheer.

'The take-off requirement,' said Rogerson, caused many a sleepless night because the engine loading could not be reduced to compensate for the higher wing loading, but a measure of compensation was provided by the variable speed propellers which were then in process of development. What appeared the best chance of success at the heaviest take-off loading was a catapult devised by Mr Salmon of the RAE, which took the form of a trolley temporarily attached to the aeroplane and propelled by a huge compound cylinder like a collapsible telescope 60 ft long and 4½ ft in diameter extended by compressed air. However applying the experimental gear to a large bomber necessitated a trolley of 8 to 10 tons, so the problem of bringing it to a stop from a speed of 110 mph proved so Herculean a task that the project was eventually dropped. Nevertheless, we had to stress for this contingency, and that gave a reserve strength factor for currently unimaginable later contingencies.'

December came while with Chadwick and his men were mightily employed in meeting the P13/36 requirements with his Type 679 design which had an 80 ft monoplane wing mounted mid-way down the fuselage depth — but on the 9th he was startled to read that Don Juan de la Cierva had been killed the previous morning when flying as passenger in a KLM Douglas DC-2 which took off from Croydon in fog and almost immediately crashed into houses, burst into flames, and killed everyone aboard. A great man had gone. Chadwick and Dobson, like many another, felt it a personal loss. Ten days later, a memorial service and High Mass was held in his honour, attended by representatives of the entire industry as well as the Air Ministry and Services.

But politically even worse had befallen. Two days after Cierva's death the King signed an 'Instrument of Abdication' irrevocably renouncing the throne for himself and his descendants. After Parliament had hurriedly passed an Abdication Act he declared his farewell through the BBC radio network: 'It is impossible to discharge my duties as King without the help and support of the woman I love.' The entire nation was stirred and deeply divided. In valediction the editor of *The Aeroplane* commented: 'Edward VIII endeared himself to aeronautical people by being the first English King to use air transport, in spite of its known dangers, as a normal means of locomotion . . . Our new King, George VI has had an even more official connection with aviation. To him is due the same loyalty as we gave to his brother.'

Chapter 11
Re-armament begins

Overtime in the Avro DO had been the rule from the moment the P13/36 project had started, and the draughtsmen deemed it wise to present a unitedly industrious front whenever 'the chief' appeared, so an early warning system was devised. Each man had an Anglepoise lamp shining on his drawing board. When the individual nearest Roy Chadwick's office heard the well-known footsteps approaching, he would take up his ruler and ting the lamp's metal shade, and the signal would be picked up by others who would repeat the warning all round the office so that when Chadwick stepped into the room, all heads were down and they were busily at work. As a stern disciplinarian he required his draughtsmen to be neatly dressed and well turned out. Smoking was banned. Although discreetly referred to as 'Chaddie', it was 'Sir' when addressing him. Every morning his first action was to walk round the DO and stop by each man to study his work and note progress. If it was not to his liking, or needed correction, he would take a thick soft pencil and draw what he required on top of the original; but though that meant starting all over again because it could not be erased, the draughtsman took it like a soldier on parade. The completed drawing was therefore always Chadwick's expression of what was required.

In a sense he was not only directly responsible to Roy Dobson and the Board of Hawker-Siddeley but also to the new AMRD, AV-M Freeman, from whom he discovered that Sidney Camm at Hawkers had already presented his rival brochure and Tender, and George Volkert at Handley Page was apparently making much the same swift progress as Chadwick. With a feeling of *deja vu* he also learned that Henry Folland had resigned from Gloster Aircraft because he found it impossible to accept subordination to the Hawker-Siddeley masters whom he believed were giving preference to Camm's designs.

There was news too of an expansion of Government plans for construction of six shadow factories for mass production of aero engines by the Bristol Aeroplane Co and the Austin, Daimler, Rootes, Rover, and Standard car manufacturers, for on 17 February, Sir Thomas Inskip ominously stated in the Commons: 'Of these firms, Messrs Austin Motor Co and Rootes Securities will undertake the manufacture of airframes as well as aero engines.' How would that affect the pioneer aircraft industry which was again embroiled in pay disputes? There were 'unofficial' strikes at A. V. Roe, Fairey, Vickers, Boulton Paul, and Rolls-Royce but when the AEU held a strike ballot of all skilled aircraft workers it was defeated by a large majority. Meanwhile such was the zeal of the Avro technical staff that by the end of February the P13/36 Design Tender with appropriate drawings was completed, and early in March both Chadwick and Volkert submitted their work to the Air Ministry pundits.

While the Avro tender was being considered, Chadwick at Dobson's insistence took the opportunity of flying by Luft Hansa to Poland for sales promotion of the Anson. To fly in a 3-engined all-metal, low-wing Junkers afforded interesting comparison with the stately old-fashioned 4-engined Handley Page biplanes which Imperial Airways used, and certainly the corrugated duralumin skinning of the German machine was of great interest to a designer. Noise was considerably greater than the quiet and luxuriously

HP42 or Junkers tri-motor.

furnished Handley Page, but the extent of upward flexure of the Junker wing at first seemed alarming whereas the Fokker-type Anson wings were remarkably stiff. The very wide chord of the Junker wing also detracted from the interest of the journey by obstructing downward view of the countryside — so in the end, despite welcome breaks at Cologne, Hannover, and Berlin, the journey across the unrelieved flat plain and marshes of the Vistula Basin to the thriving city of Warsaw was dull and uninspiring. Next day it all felt very different. Warsaw, with its distinctive architecture, palaces, fortress, Catholic cathedral, and distinctive architecture was fascinating after dull Manchester. Near the Casimir Palace, home of the University, was the headquarters of the Polish Air Ministry where Chadwick found that despite their own aircraft industry there was interest in the Avro productions, but even more in re-armament of the British Air Force! Sandwiched between Russia and what had been Prussia, they were very sensitive to risk of invasion if war broke out.

His return to springtime England coincided with the Air Estimates which were £17,500,000 greater than the previous year, and amounted to £88,600,000 gross. In the ensuing debate Sir Philip Sassoon, emphasized that the expansion programme was without parallel in the peacetime history of Great Britain.

'To expedite production,' he said, 'the Air Ministry aim at reducing the number of types. Accelerated production can only be secured by more skilled personnel, so the Shadow Factory scheme is a practical policy which gives us a war potential without interfering with the normal aviation industry.' But the general public was largely indifferent to the wrangling in Parliament over estimates of expenditure and re-armament, and regarded Churchill as a warmonger with his threats that: 'The effective fighting force of Germany must be at least 1,700 or 1,800 machines capable of going to action and being continuously maintained in action during the course of a war.' Certainly Chadwick believed that and anxiously discussed the position with Dobson.

'Don't worry, Roy. We're now producing one Anson a day,' he grinned. 'Just get that contract for your new bomber and we'll save England yet!'

George Volkert, an Anglo-Swiss, who had joined Handley Page nine months after Chadwick joined A. V. Roe.

His words were prophetic. On 30 April, the Tender for the Avro 679 twin-engined P13/16 bomber was accepted in preference to Camm's, and Volkert's HP56 was also selected. Still bigger bombers of 50,000 all-up weight had been ordered from Short Bros and Supermarine. In view of the advanced complexity of these designs, all four firms sought more draughtsmen and technicians.

The Avro DO had become noticeably depleted since completion of the Anson manufacturing drawings because at Frank Spriggs' instigation a group of draughtsmen had been sent to Hawkers at Kingston to prepare production drawings for the Hotspurs, which though intended for Newton Heath, were eventually constructed by Glosters. Several more draughtsmen had been induced by better pay to leave Avro and join other companies in the throes of expansion.

Chadwick therefore urgently advertised for replacements, and as a first step, Herbert Mettam was transferred from rotor responsibility to the bomber development. Spriggs also agreed that John Cuss of Glosters could be loaned to Avros because of his considerable experience of stressed skin construction during design of the impressively huge, twin tandem-engined, experimental Gloster TC31 bomber-transport biplane, and though he initially came for only six months, he stayed for 16 years.

One of those answering the advertisements was Charles Goldberg, seeking improvement on his position as a stressman at Boulton Paul Aircraft Ltd. On his arrival from Wolverhampton the great city of Manchester presented a drab picture with its dark buildings and wet streets. 'The Avro factory was an unpretentious, large two-storey building, constructed of brick and very dirty with years and years of soot,' he said. 'The brightest thing about this place was the well polished brass plate proclaiming to the world that this was the registered office of A. V. Roe & Co Ltd. The uniformed doorman was a burly ex-sergeant major who showed me to a room where a line of seated young applicants was waiting. Through the glass partition we could see rows of draughtsmen busy at their drawing boards. Then the door at the far end of the DO opened and in walked Roy Chadwick with Harold Rogerson. My abiding impression of Mr Chadwick was of a very tall man, the paleness of his face emphasized by a thin, dark moustache and his dark hair parted in the middle and brushed straight each side of his head. He said "Good morning," in a deep commanding voice — and there was instant silence in the room!'

When interviewing the applicants Chadwick had fired a series of questions: 'What is your name? Which firm? How long? What have you been working on?' He gave Goldberg a large sheet of paper, specified a particular fitting and told him to draw it, then have it blue-printed and take it to the shop floor to have the fitting made. Goldberg passed the test, was welcomed by Rogerson, given a desk in the technical section and told to take over the work of a young man who had decided that his conscience did not permit him to work on bombers.

'Mr Chadwick was a perfectionist,' said Charles Goldberg. 'He was the most diligent man I have ever met. I always think of the biblical injunction "Seek ye a man who is diligent in his work, he should stand before Kings." He was also very interested in the future of the young men who worked for him. He was looking for potential designers of responsibility, future chief designers, and he always encouraged enthusiastic youngsters, just as he himself had been encouraged by A. V. Roe. He always asked them if they were going to attend the meetings of the Royal Aeronautical Society's local branch, and if not would want to know why, urging them to join in for their own good.'

However in May it was the forthcoming Coronation which was attracting wide-spread attention, and even the tragic disaster of the German airship *Hindenberg* crashing in flames at Lakehurst, USA, on the 6th made only briefly horrifying intrusion on the nation's excitement. Everywhere was lively with buntings and flags, and as part of the jubilations the RAeS held its Annual Garden Party on 9 May. *Flight* reported: 'That suggests sunshades, silk hats, and strawberries. Instead it was gumboots, golloshes and gamps.' Nevertheless over 3,000 guests, among them the Dobson and Chadwick families, managed to shelter in hangar doorways or under accommodating wings while various stout-hearted pilots displayed their aeroplanes.

But nothing could match the Coronation. The sun shone brilliantly on that morning of

Ensign.

12 May 1937 when the King and Queen in the great gilded State Coach drove down the crowded Mall to Westminster Abbey and were crowned with magnificent ceremony. In the Coronation Honours' List, Sir John Davenport Siddeley was elevated to the Baronage as Lord Kenilworth — the first member of the aircraft industry to be honoured in that manner, though it also reflected his recent purchase, as a near-millionaire, of Kenilworth Castle which we had presented to the nation.

The rest of May was crowded with events. There was a Royal Review of the Fleet at Spithead on the 20th. Seven days later came the Royal Tournament at Olympia attended by the King and Queen, but coincidentally, Baldwin resigned as Prime Minister in favour of Neville Chamberlain, who took office next day. In gala fashion, Empire Day was held on the following Saturday with crowds in their hundreds of thousands visiting RAF Stations and various civil aerodromes open to the public. In the Hawker-Siddeley-owned Air Service Training hangar at Hamble the new 123 ft span Armstrong Whitworth Ensign airliner prototype designed by Lloyd was visible, the components having been transferred there because the Coventry factory was full to capacity with Whitley bomber construction.

* * *

Early in June the sportsmen pilots of Europe flew to a great international gathering hosted by British pilots at York Municipal Airport. Roy Chadwick drove there with is family at the weekend. Among the many visitors they saw a Stieglitz biplane land, piloted by Herr von Braun of possibly later fame, with a man named Kurt Tank as passenger whom nobody recognized as the technical director of Focke-Wulf where a radial engined, single-seater fighter was being designed to supplement the formidable Messerschmitt Bf 109 equivalent of the Spitfire.

Coincidentally on 11 June, Chadwick was saddened to learn that the brilliant Supermarine designer, Reggie Mitchell had died, following a sequence of cancer operations from which the last, in March, had shown the disease was incurable — but at least he had lingered long enough to see his Spitfire fly. Like the Avro designer, who was a year older, Mitchell had orchestrated his team of draughtsmen and technicians as though he was a conductor, insisting on a change of note or an emphasis here and there in his pursuit of perfection.

Chadwick was now wrestling with many problems. Decision after decision had to be made which would fundamentally control the success or failure of his bomber design. Thus having settled the aerodynamics after considerable model testing in the Armstrong Whitworth wind tunnel, he elected to use relatively low-stressed constructional materials which did not develop fatigue cracks as easily as those with higher tension fields. 'Nevertheless,' said Charles Goldberg, 'we were unsure of the stability of this thin metal fuselage and wing structure because there was no adequate theoretical knowledge available. We therefore had many specimen components and fittings made up for strength tests under load imposed by simple lifting gear or sandbags filled with lead shot, and measured deflections against angular scale, clock gauges and other simple devices. Roy Chadwick was always present at these tests — proding, poking, questioning.'

Rogerson and Goldberg, on arriving at the test department one day found the immaculate Chadwick diligently jumping up and down on a sample of the fuselage floor he intended to use. 'We have special gauges to test this specimen, Sir,' said Goldberg anxiously.

'Oh! Let him have his fun. He needs the exercise,' murmured Rogerson in a stage whisper — but Chadwick heard and grinned. 'Always use the simplest way,' he said. 'Not only does it save expense but it can give you a personal feel for the problem!'

But there were many matters of lucky design such as the 33 ft length of the bomb bay necessitated by the carriage of torpedoes, whereas those of the bigger 4-engined machines mounted their bombs in shorter space. Fortunately the spacial design of the Avro bomb bay had been basically determined by the strength required for the proposed catapult launching, and that gave potential capability of carrying still greater bomb loads than the specification stipulated.

Preliminary structural investigation of various methods of arranging the spar system and bulkheads took considerable time, eventuating in discussions wth High Duty Alloys Ltd and decision to use their form of extrusions for the spar by cutting a length of appropriate section diagonally into two tapering booms which were then machined to leave the exact amount of metal proportionate to the load as it lessened towards the wing tips. That required a large and costly tool, and as Fielding said: 'This was a big problem, for the only such machine tools at that time were Kendal & Gent Plano Millers. When Roy Dobson saw these in operation, he went through the roof, and instructed our works engineer Jack Green to contact the well-known firm of Wadkins, who specialised in wood-working machinery, and give them a specification. That eventually resulted in production of a metal-working machine which was five times faster than the old Plano-Miller.'

Wherever possible, extrusions were used for other components, and Chadwick adopted the idea of large port and starboard forgings joined on the centre line for attachment of wings to the fuselage. Everything was designed to facilitate mass production. To that end, Avro production specialists, such as Roland Taylor, and later George Oldham and Dick Wild, were detailed to advise the drawing office on manufacturing desiderata and discuss schemes before they were completed, then clear them for issue.

Blenheim production.

Meanwhile, the Air Ministry was holding discussions with Dobson on the possibility of Avro construction of the outstanding Bristol Blenheim twin-engined light bomber. 'We were given an order for 250,' said Fielding. 'That was our first production aircraft to be built with an all-metal stressed skin. Dobbie took over a factory of 40,000 sq ft at Collyhurst to make the first aircraft. We did one component at a time, using the maximum semi-skilled labour, and when this was established, we transferred the job to another of our factories. We adapted this method for the complete aircraft and finished up with Blenheim components in all our factories, using a big percentage of semi-skilled labour. We then transported the components for assembly and flight trials at Woodford.'

In August, Roy Chadwick snatched a much-needed holiday in Anglesey, staying with his young family at a hotel in Benllech Bay where there were sands for young Rosemary and the new pleasure of horse-riding for Margaret. A bare week was enough, then away, only too well aware that his presence at Manchester was essential in making the day-to-day decisions governing structural integrity of the bomber and the pursuit of light weight.

As the Anson still commanded a certain amount of his attention, he established a special section to keep tabs on Squadron reports and deal with modifications such as a top secret re-arrangement of radio and space provision for trials installation of unspecified equipment. That was radar. On 4 September this Anson was tested with dramatic results during Home Fleet exercises. Though previously used from the ground to detect aircraft up to 50 miles distant, this was the first airborne use, and though the sea was lost in mist the radar blips picked up *Courageous, Southampton*, and attendant destroyers nine miles distant. Then the Anson was safely guided by radar blips through the murk to its base. Intensive research followed to develop a radar system that could pinpoint bombing targets, and around the coast of Britain the construction of twenty radar location stations began.

A week after the Anson's radar success, Roy Chadwick's popular Martlesham acquaintance Wing Cdr Ted Hilton, and his co-pilot Wing Cdr Sherren, were killed during the King's Cup Race when they were flung from their aeroplane on encountering tremendous turbulence as they passed over the cliffs of Scarborough. Ted, a quietly friendly man, was highly regarded as commander of the multi-engine Flight at the A & AEE, and had therefore participated in the various Anson trials which had brought such financial success to Avro.

Indications of the enormous sums of money involved in aircraft production could be gleaned from the report of the 3rd Ordinary General Meeting of Hawker-Siddeley Aircraft Co, held on 21 November. The order book was described as enormous. 'The Directors feel it imperative that the Group should be adequately provided with funds to finance the actual work in progress,' stated T. O. M. Sopwith, and thereupon moved a resolution to extend the capital to £6 million by creating two million redeemable cumulative £1 preference shares. He also explained that 'the Secretary of State for Air recently announced that orders had been given, on behalf of the Government, for the erection and equipment of two factories — one at Manchester and the other at Gloucester, at a cost of over £2 million. These factories will be operated by two of your subsidiary companies, and this is the first occasion on which Government factories have been entrusted to the professional aircraft industry. It is a tribute, of which we may well be proud, to the proved productive ability of A. V. Roe & Co and the Gloster Aircraft Co that they have been selected to initiate and control these new organisations.'

The new Avro factory was to be at Chadderton, some four miles north of the Newton Heath establishment. Jack Green had the task of preparing the drawings for the new factory. On asking Roy Dobson for the dimensional requirements, he was told to see what the other shadow factories were like and then make Avro's twice the size! That resulted in a floor space of 760,000 sq ft. News of the projected factory quickly spread among the employees, bringing an undercurrent of apprehension that this portended the imminence of war. Technicians who had long cloaked their activities in belief that they were solving scientific problems, began to realize that their engineering skills were vital in making a machine of destruction — yet concern turned to jubilation in December because the Air Ministry, convinced by Chadwick's reputation as the man who could deliver the goods, took the speculative risk of placing a contract for 200 of the twin-engined bombers to modified Air Ministry Specification 19/37, with the requirement that deliveries must begin by 1940.

But now it was Christmas, with its ancient spell and feasting, and on the Saturday that preceded it, Roy Chadwick drove with Margaret in the gathering dusk to buy the ritual turkey from the market at Altrincham, a small but thriving industrial and market town south of Manchester. 'I shall never forget the scene,' said Margaret. 'My father, dressed as always in his black coat and Homberg hat, standing in the light of the stall flares, smiling and interested, listening with me to the vendor auctioning his Christmas fare. He bought a huge cock bird and I felt like the Wassailers of old when eventually we carried it into the house and told my mother of our adventures.'

* * *

The New Year of 1938 heralded many meetings chaired by Roy Dobson to discuss drawing issues and extend production arrangements for the Avro 679, now named 'Manchester' in tribute to their 1918 bomber. The schedule of work was enormous; the planning precise. More production engineers as well as draughtsmen were being engaged. There were vast schedules of parts to be assembled, sequences planned, materials ordered, allocation of sub-contractors decided, more and more tools to be bought, and the factory floor space extended because the considerable Anson production must continue in parallel and was likely to be enormously increased. So complex was the planning and ordering for the 'Manchester' that at least six months would elapse before the first metal could be cut and construction started.

Early in the year Neville Chamberlain declared: 'I am about to enter upon a fresh attempt to reach a reasonable understanding with Germany and Italy, and I am by no means unhopeful of getting results.' Even Hitler announced that he hoped for a year of peace, but that did not deter him from using the war in Spain as a battleground for training his Luftwaffe pilots. With equal purpose, the RAF was consolidating operational strategies and tactics and using every moment of good weather for pilot and crew training.

But world affairs were moving fast. That there was disagreement on British policy was indicated by the resignation of Anthony Eden, the Foreign Secretary, who strongly opposed the palliative of appeasement because it was already clear that Hitler was putting pressure on Austria despite the Treaty of Versailles forbiding union between Germany and that country. Summoning the Austrian Chancellor von Schuschnigg, the Führer presented an ultimatum demanding replacement of that government by a Nazi administration or else 200,000 troops would cross the frontier. On 12 March, the German forces marched into Austria, occupied Vienna with hundreds of infantrymen landed by troop carriers, and took control of the Brenner Pass, yet just as in the Rhineland Occupation two years earlier, Hitler escaped recriminatory action — but at last the British people realised what Nazism meant. Churchill warned: 'The time will come when Germany will turn westward.'

The Air Estimates presented to the Commons on 15 March encompassed what seemed the enormous sum of £103,500,000 gross — which was 25 per cent more than in 1937, and targeted 1,750 aircraft by March 1939. 'The problem is to keep a balance between speed of production and being up-to-date,' warned Col Muirhead, the Under-Secretary of State for Air. 'Developments and improvements have been so big and rapid and so fundamental that the machines now being turned out are only nominally new types.'

Certainly the design and production schedule for Chadwick's P13/36 'Manchester' meant that by the time the prototype was completed the design would be based on requirements envisaged nearly three years earlier. His constant endeavour was therefore to use the very latest techniques and materials, so that his bomber would be the last word in modernity and perfection. Score by score and hundred by hundred, the detailed drawings steadily evolved, and when each specialised structural component had been built, it was subjected to rigorous testing for stiffness and strength.

There were many associated activities. Specialist firms were building guns, and power-operated turrets were a notable step forward. Armament was under review. Swifter bomb-loading methods were being investigated. There was intense development of engines, and 100-octane fuel was being experimentally used to give considerably increased power compared with the standard 87-octane. These things and many more were part and parcel of the varied aspects of design that were like a game of chess in Chadwick's mind. That April, further recognition of his status was a Fellowship awarded by the Royal Aeronautical Society.

What pleased him even more was the success of his Ansons in combined exercises between RAF and Royal Navy, held in the Western Approaches to the Channel. Low cloud at 200 ft and a heavy smoke screen prevented sight of the Fleet on the first day, but at dawn on the next an Avro Anson sighted the convoy 45 miles south of the Lizard, and combined attacks followed. 'That should consolidate Anson production,' he mused, and began planning an operational trainer version.

On 29 April, the Air Ministry announced formation of a Supplies Committee, chaired by Earl Winterton, to place orders and arrange extension of existing factories or creation of new ones. 'The new plan was prepared by the Air Ministry after consultation with representatives of the aircraft industry,' reported *The Times*. 'The composers hope it will provide increased output almost immediately. Provision has been made for the formation of extra squadrons and an increase in the strength of

Ansons of the second production batch which had been ordered in 1936 and delivered the following year.

other squadrons, and for an increase in personnel of all ranks.'

Led by Sir Hugh Seely, a heavy attack on the Air Ministry followed in the Commons on 12 May. Vigorously he asserted: 'We are dealing with a Germany which has an enormous number of aeroplanes; I believe about 8,000, of which some 3,500 are front line. The Germans can produce 400 to 500 a month and within a year will have 6,000 first line aeroplanes. Under our latest scheme, we shall have 2,700 front line machines in two year's time. When MPs inspected the Hurricane in June, 1936, they were told 340 or more would be completed this year. That was two years ago. Can the Minister deny there are only 28 in service?

Earl Winterton could only say: 'Disappointment over production of aircraft is not always due to mistakes by the Air Ministry. There were those years of folly when the whole country demanded disarmament, the folly of Parliament. Today there is a closer relationship between Air Ministry and the industry. This is no sudden and panicky plan which has been prepared. It is a natural extension and acceleration of an already growing Air Force, but I do not think that if the Archangel Gabriel stood at this box and produced an expansion scheme that it would satisfy the Rt. Hon. member for Epping, Mr Churchill.'

In the Upper House Lord Weir as production adviser declared: 'I see nothing likely to prevent the realisation of the new programme, even after conservative allowances for technical delays, and obtaining and effectively absorbing the new labour required and its application to new classes of work.' Nevertheless, Lord Swinton, as Secretary of State for Air, resigned in high dudgeon, followed next day by Lord Weir and Col Muirhead the Under Secretary. Succeeding the austere Swinton came the recent Postmaster General, Sir Kingsley Wood, cherubic behind round glasses and with no knowledge of aviation — but the Under-Secretary he appointed was Capt Harold Balfour, who had all the necessary ability and aeronautical experience to support him. However, the attack on the Air Ministry continued. The Prime Minister did his best to quieten the affray, explaining that three years of expansion coincided with one of those forward leaps which periodically take place in applied science. The features were threefold: development of the all-metal monoplane, design of new engines of unprecedented efficiency, and invention of variable-pitch airscrews. The combination not only completely altered design, but necessarily altered the strategy of using the newly developed machines. Explaining their complexity, he pointed out that while a Ford V-8 engine in mass production had about 1,700 parts, a modern bomber had 11,000 in the engine alone, and the airframe additionally had 70,000 parts, for which 5,000 to 8,000 separate drawings were required.

That was the kind of enormous draughting achievement which was engrossing Chadwick. Most was straightforward structural design, but location of loan equipment and armament operational systems required numerous meetings with appropriate Air Ministry and RAF officials, and necessitated much consultation grouped around the mock-up, where the location of each fitment had to be approved. There were progress meetings in London; visits to Rolls-Royce at Derby for detailed discussion of the big Vulture engines and ancillary services; briefing from Devereux and his experts from High Duty Alloys on use of extrusions; and George Dowty came into the picture again with design of the massive retractable undercarriage. Hitherto a private business, his Aircraft Components Co Ltd, backed by A. W. Martyn, the late chairman of Gloster Aircraft, had become a public company with capital of £30,000, and was now established at Arle Court, Cheltenham, which had been bought in July 1935 together with 100 acres for £6,500. As managing director, Dowty's salary was £1,200 a year, with equity of 200,000 in 5s shares. It had been a hard struggle to get to this point, but he never forgot that his first practical experience had been through Chadwick.

Despite the pressures, there was still the

George Dowty (later Sir George) testing his Avro retractable undercarriage.

social round, heralded by the RAeS Garden Party on 8 May at Faireys' aerodrome (now a minor area of London Airport). 'All the usual pillars of the aircraft industry were there, bulked out by people from the shadow factories and sub-contractors and sub-sub-contractors,' wrote C. G. Gray, and *Flight* commented: 'The weather proved so fickle that party frocks were at a discount; escorts seemed to prefer green Tyrolean pork-pies to toppers and even the band had thrown away Sullivan in favour of Cole Porter; but the Society's curtain-raiser to the flying season has not suffered by this onslaught of informality. Everybody comes to see the newest and best of British aviation, civil and military, to meet old friends, and to enjoy himself or herself generally.' That certainly applied to Roy and Mary Chadwick.

Two days later the King, attired as Marshal of the RAF, flew to each of his four home commands: fighters at Northolt; bombers at Harwell; Training Command at Upavon; Coastal Command at Thorney Island. At the end of the day he despatched a message to the Secretary of State for Air congratulating the RAF on the determined and successful way in which it was meeting the heavy demands made by the expansion of their Service — but most of the aircraft were still outmoded.

Mass formation flights above nearly 200 towns preluded Empire Air Day on 28 May, but such was the concentration on operational training that the Air Ministry decided to cancel the annual Royal Air Force Display and substitute an invitation for the public to visit any RAF or civil aerodrome that day except for a limited few of semi-secret nature. The crowds poured in by hundreds of thousands. But those immersed in the rearmament programme wondered if there would ever be another Empire Air Day, and this was endorsed when the SBAC announced that no Trade flying display would be held this year because 'it is not in the public interest to show the latest types of military aircraft and engines, and the immense amount of work devolving upon the industry makes undesirable the diversion of time and energy to the organisation of such a display'.

Though a huge section of aviation was absorbed in the development and mass production of military aircraft, the pilots of the light aeroplane and gliding Clubs were happily disporting in ever-increasing numbers. There were also the amateur stalwarts of the Auxiliary Air Force Squadrons flying their Wallaces and Harts at weekends in happy emulation of the professional RAF. To supplement that reserve, Sir Kingsley Wood was considering the formation of a Civil Air Guard, comprising men and women who could undertake, in the event of a national emergency, to offer their services to the RAF.

June opened with an International Air Race from Hatfield to the Isle of Man, but though the sun shone brightly at the start, the clouds had dropped to 700 ft and it was raining by the time the winner crossed the finishing line. A few days later, as bleak reminder of stormier skies, the Government announced a decision to order from the United States 200 twin-engined Lockheed reconnaissance Hudsons and 200 North American Harvard trainers to augment the RAF's British equivalents. That produced outcry from politicians and aircraft manufacturers alike. 'We could easily have doubled the Anson production,' Dobson aggressively commented.

To make up for the absence of the RAF Display, the *Daily Express* held a great Air Display at Gatwick on 25 June. Notable foreign pilots gave thrilling performances. The RAF displayed formations of Hawker Furys, Hurricanes, and single examples of Lysander, Battle, Blenheim, and Whitley — described as 'secret war planes'. However, this spectacular equivalent of the RAF Display was not witnessed by the Chadwick and Dobson families. They were attending the ceremonial opening by Sir Kingsley Wood of Manchester's new airport which had been under construction at Ringway since Spring of 1936. A typical display of civil and RAF aircraft enthralled the attendant Mancunian public, and a service to Amsterdam was inaugurated by the great Dutch airline, KLM.

Though Barton aerodrome near Trafford Park was now superseded, it continued as a popular centre for private flying. Half Manchester was there, except for most of those at A. V. Roe on overtime, to watch the competing aeroplanes of the King's Cup Race on 2 July rounding in as northern turning point of the 20-lap triangular course from Hatfield. Wealthy young Alex Henshaw, with his racing Mew Gull, became the winner and was presented with the cup by Sir Kingsley Wood — and that was the end of the King's Cup Race for more than a decade.

* * *

Holidays for the Chadwicks that busy year were at Filey, Yorkshire, where Roy took an apartment for his family at Gristhorpe Hall for a month with intention of visiting them each weekend — but it started sadly enough, for on 2 August, his old acquaintance the

Capt. Frank Barnwell, RAF Reservist and famous designer.

Bristol chief designer, Frank Sowter Barnwell, was killed when flying a light aeroplane of his own construction, following a stall from 70 ft. He had joined the Bristol & Colonial Aeroplane Co as a draughtsman in the same year that Chadwick joined Avro, and the Great War established his fame as designer of the renowned Bristol Fighter, and latterly of the Blenheims which were now so familiar in the Avro factory.

Over-shadowing everything was the growing threat of Germany. On 15 September Neville Chamberlain took the initiative and decided to meet Hitler in person, for he was convinced that what appeared a simple dispute between the Czechoslovak Government and its internal German minority could be resolved by wise concessions. Accompanied by his entourage of advisers, he flew by British Airways to Munich, met the German Foreign Secretary von Ribbentrop, and with the British and German Ambassadors continued by train to Hitler's mountain retreat at Berchtesgaden where amicable discussion ensued with the Führer. Next day Chamberlain returned to England. Consultation with the French Prime Minister and his Foreign Minister on the 18th resulted in proposals for extensive cession of

Sudatenland territory. Four days later Chamberlain again flew to Germany and met Hitler at Bad Godesberg, only to find that he dismissed the proposed partition boundaries and demanded immediate military occupation of a still greater area. A dispirited Prime Ministry returned to London 24 September. The King signed a State of Emergency. The Navy was mobilised. Slit trenches were dug in London parks. Buildings were protected with sandbags. Trainloads of children with gas masks were evacuated to the country. London hospitals were ready for casualties. The secret radar system was on a 24-hour watch.

Despairingly, Chamberlain wrote a last appeal to Hitler, who then invited him to a conference at Munich attended by Deladier and Mussolini. On 29 September, Chamberlain made his third flight to Germany. Anxiously the British nation awaited the result. Next day he notified the world Press that an Anglo-German Agreement had been signed. That afternoon at Heston, he stepped from the cabin doorway of the British Airways Lockheed and triumphantly waved a piece of paper. 'We have plucked this nettle danger,' he said, and after reporting to the King, declared from the steps of 10 Downing Street, 'I believe it is peace for our time . . . '

For Roy Chadwick there was a rather different glow of achievement because on 10 October, at the Autumn meeting of the Royal Society of Arts, he was awarded the rare distinction of election as Fellow with categorization of Royal Designer for Industry — an honour extended to few in the sphere of aviation, the first of whom had been Sir Hiram Maxim at the turn of the century, followed by J. W. Dunne of tail-less aircraft fame in 1911, and latterly R. J. Mitchel because of his spectacular Schneider racers.

Congratulations poured in, adding zest to the task of what he was certain must be preparation for war. Sir Samuel Hoare was urgently calling for a million volunteers for air-raid precautions, The Home Office warned on 26 October that an attack might come with appalling suddenness. The appointment of Sir John Anderson as Lord Privy Seal and Minister of Defence followed on 1 November. Concurrently the Labour Party's new Manifesto described the defence of the country as 'criminally neglected'.

To rectify that, money must now be expended out by the million. Thus assets of the profitable Hawker-Siddeley Group were valued at £10 million, but liabilities approached 3½ million largely because of losses by Armstrong Whitworth in building Ensigns for Imperial Airways. At the Group A. G. M. Tom Sopwith said: 'In view of the unsettled world political situation it is unwise to attempt any forecast of the future, but it seems reasonable to anticipate a fair commercial return for the work and responsibility we are undertaking. The extensive work in progress will therefore be funded by creation of £5 million in short term first debenture stock.' Of those proceeds Avro would certainly require a considerable share to cover the cost of 'Manchester' production.

In that interest, Dobson, Fielding and Chadwick attended a crowded meeting of the RAeS at the Institution of Mechanical Engineers on 9 November to hear Theodore P. Wright, the director of engineering of the Curtis-Wright Corporation, lecture on *American Methods of Aircraft Production* — from which it was clear that the aircraft industry of the USA had developed a high state of efficiency with lofting full-scale layouts, use of forgings, castings and extrusions, and programming the flow of materials, tools, and finished parts in precalculated time sequence. A. V. Roe & Co was well advanced in those respects, for Ted Fielding had perfected a masterpiece of comprehensive planning. As his motto, he would quote from Benjamin Franklin: 'Drive thy business, let not thy business drive thee'.

Though there had been problems with strikes in Britain, the situation in France was so bad that the opening of the Annual Paris Aeronautical Salon had to be delayed until 25 November. Nevertheless, there was an impressive display by 28 French firms, but the British exhibits of a Blenheim, Hurricane, and Spitfire seemed superior fighting weapons to their rivals though with Gallic discrimination were tucked away in the south-east corner of the great domed building. Equally discreetly a Dornier Do 17 slim-fuselage bomber was featured inconspicuously, and the latest German fighters were ominously missing.

Chadwick took opportunity to cut short his visit and fly by Swedish Airlines to Stockholm, thence across the Baltic by ship to snow-bound Helsinki to discuss the Finnish Air Force Command's interest in the Anson — but subsequently the British Air Ministry proved unwilling to permit sales to a country so close to Russia, although two years earlier there had been no bar to accepting orders from adjacent Estonia and Lithuania for the military version of the Tutor.

With Christmas, all thought of war was temporarily dismissed. There was the customary Dinner Dance for the Avro staff at a large restaurant in Manchester. After speeches from the two Roys, the tables were cleared 'to make a dance floor which appeared vast and exciting to me,' said Margaret. 'One of the staff, symbolically wearing white gloves, was Master of Ceremonies, and the dance band rang the changes without flagging as we waltzed, did the quickstep and joined in the Paul Jones — and there was much laughter and lots of energetic movement as we whirled into the new dances, such as the *Lambeth Walk, Hokey-Cokey,* and the *Palais Glide.* With Christmas over we always stayed up to see the New Year in, and about two minutes to midnight my father would be asked to "bring in the New Year" because it was a tradition in the north that a dark haired man should knock at the front door, bringing with him a piece of coal and some bread, and he did this, holding out the tokens of food and warmth for the coming year, and we delightedly welcomed him in.'

Chapter 12
The Trials of War

To co-ordinate construction of the Manchester prototype, Dobson and Chadwick promoted 32-year-old Stuart Davies BSc early in 1939 as manager of the experimental department. Major components of the two contractual prototypes had already been completed and were being transported to a big new hangar at Ringway for assembly, but Chadwick's big worry was that the Rolls-Royce Vulture had encountered development problems at Derby yet was being rushed into production. The design had seemed straightforward because it comprised four banks of cylinders derived from the well-tried Kestrel arranged in X formation with a mutual highly stressed crank-shaft, and in every way followed standard Rolls-Royce practice. One of the prototype engines was being installed in a Hawker Henley two-seater for flight trials.

Chadwick now knew that the rival Handley Page HP56 to the same P13/36 Specification as the Manchester had been revised as the HP57 with four Rolls-Royce Merlin Xs substituted for the twin Vultures, and that a production order for 100 had been awarded. Lest the Handley Page proved a failure he intended to step in with a 4-engined heavy bomber he was designing to Specification V.1/39 with Air Marshal Freeman's agreement and designated Avro 680 — but it was never built.

The Avro empire now employed some 5,000 men, and when the new £1,000,000 factory at Chadderton was ready, Dobson expected to double the employees within twelve months. Ansons these days were being poured out in their hundreds. What with these, the Blenheims, and the incipient Manchester bomber production, Dobson's problems had become legion, but this blunt and forceful Yorkshireman was in no way over-awed. There was swift decision on every snag and he would authorise immediate action, even to the extent of short-circuiting official procedures — but some things were beyond control, so he and Chadwick were disconcerted when the experimental Vulture in the Hawker Henley revealed coolant problems on its first flight, and shortly afterwards developed a big-end failure due to a defect in the oil circulation system. That meant more arduous bench testing, and therefore delay in the production programme.

Perhaps there was a slight sense of relief when they discovered that the new Handley Page, now named Halifax, was well behind schedule and unlikely to fly until Autumn.

Typical problem with a new type aeroplane – pile up of the Stirling prototype.

Nevertheless, Chadwick was sympathetic on learning early in March that the still bigger Short Stirling 4-engined bomber had crashed at the end of a brief first flight through collapse of its stalky landing gear, tipping the machine violently onto wing-tip and nose and so badly damaging the structure that the prototype was a write-off. Yet the cause was simple — a seized brake which in a matter of seconds had eliminated two years' work.

Lancashire these days was more preoccupied with aircraft than cotton, so it was not surprising that a large crowd attending the Empire Air Day Display at Ringway on 20 March, during which the recently formed No. 613 Auxiliary (City of Manchester) Squadron performed with their Hawker Hinds to the pride and delight of all. One of the few available Spitfires was dashingly demonstrated by an RAF pilot, and a squadron of Armstrong Whitley bombers thundered across the skies. A trio of Tiger Moths performed aerobatics, and as representatives of the RAF's still persisting biplane era made dignified circuits, followed by a Mancunian Anson and a Fairey Battle built at nearby Heaton Chapel and assembled at Ringway.

On the far side of the aerodrome, away from the crowds, the first assembled Manchester with its 80 ft wing and huge fuselage was dominating the erecting shop. There was still a great deal to do, and the Vulture engines had not yet been delivered. Three months of testing and modification by Rolls-Royce at Derby ensued. Not only Chadwick but Freeman and the Air Staff became increasingly concerned until at last bench-running showed acceptable behaviour. Early in July, the engines arrived at Ringway, together with their three-bladed, variable pitch de Havilland propellers. Installation urgently proceeded, during which there was check upon check of the functioning of every system from instrument accuracy to hydraulic operation of fuel pumps, flaps, and repeated retractions of the undercarriage with the machine jacked up. In mid-July the big monoplane was towed on to the aerodrome tarmac to test and adjust the engines. That took several days, during which Roy Chadwick danced anxious attendance though outwardly calm. Eventually final inspection and flight clearance began, supervised by the AID. On 25 July, the Manchester was ready for its momentous first flight. The nose, dorsal, and tail turrets had not arrived from contractors, so their locations had been faired to give a smooth shape, resulting in a remarkably clean over-all appearance. With dangling parachute packs, Sam Brown and Bill Thorn climbed through the entrance door in the port side followed by two volunteer engineers. By then numerous workmen were discreetly lurking by the hangars. Close to the scene of activity were Roy Chadwick, Roy Dobson, and Ted Fielding, backed discreetly by a group comprising the chief inspector Roland Taylor, his AID colleague, and the Resident Technical Officer with several Air

L7247 with full armament – also an experimental trial of a 'Park bench' balance for the elevators.

Ministry officials. There was strained silence as they watched the engine-starting procedures begin. Sam Brown ran up the engines to an engulfing roar, throttled back, waved for removal of chocks, released his brakes and taxied to the far end of the aerodrome. The roar of the engines could be distantly heard as he turned into wind, opened up, and began the long run to get airborne. With mingled relief they saw the wheels leave the ground and the huge machine slant steadily away.

'Seems all right,' Dobson laconically said to relieve his colleagues' tension.

'So far, so good,' replied Chadwick, and beckoned Harold Rogerson to get his impression of the take-off distance.

After what seemed a long, long wait, the big monoplane was seen returning. There was no radio contact in those early days, and the airfield controller relied on light signals. The ponderous Manchester curved distantly round, nosed into a steady approach, and with impeccable judgement Sam Brown touched gently down and the machine ran and ran while the crowd intently watched.

On taxying back he gave thumbs up on arriving at the tarmac. The two Roys hurried to the entrance door and climbed inside to congratulate the crew and discuss the flight. They were told that in general the machine handled reasonably well, but there was the inevitable miscellany of problems, including indications of insufficient fin area, though that might change when the dorsal turret was fitted. In the following week performance and directional behaviour were more fully explored, but though a top speed of 265 mph was recorded, the climb to Chadwick's dismay was below estimate, and Sam Brown confirmed that more fin was essential.

Harold Rogerson was deputed to make urgent investigation of extending the wing to 90 ft span for better climb, and increasing the area of the fins and rudders on the tailplane tips. As an immediate expedient Chadwick put in hand a shark-like dorsal fin which could readily be mounted just forward of the tail, but while it was being constructed, engine problems became evident, badly slowing the test programme, so he seized the opportunity of renting a house at Filey for his family's annual holiday with intention of visiting them each week-end.

* * *

There was a general air of carefree optimism among the British people that summer, largely engendered by the fact that holidays with pay had been made mandatory by Parliament the previous year, giving some eleven million families the opportunity of a fortnight by the sea. But events were marching towards a crisis. On 8 August 1,300 RAF aircraft began a great exercise to test air and ground defence of SE England, in which 500 bombers under the direction of Air Chief Marshal Sir Edgar Ludlow-Hewitt made the attack. Air Marshal Sir Hugh Dowding defended with 500 fighters, 50 general reconnaissance aircraft and 250 bombers, as well as anti-aircraft divisions and a great balloon barrage surrounding London. The crux was to discover whether the score or so of highly secret radar stations, backed by fifteen groups of the newly organised Observer Corps, could spot the approaching bombers, Low cloud, wind, rain, and ground fog, hampered bombers and defenders alike — yet nearly every attack was intercepted. Speaking from the BBC, Dowding admitted that various new methods had been tried, and declared: 'I confidently believe that serious attack on these islands would be brought to a standstill within a short space of time.'

In the following weeks, seven Wings of bombers, fighters, and reconnaissance aircraft of the French Army of the Air flew over England for a foray in which Fighter Command participated. An official communiqué stated: 'The exercise gave opportunity for intervention by the British and French detector services working in co-operation, and these manoeuvres form a contribution to air co-operation between France and Britain which each day becomes closer and more efficacious.'

On 22 August the British Cabinet met to discuss reports of menacing movement of German troops towards the Polish border.

Two days later an Emergency Powers (Defence) Bill was enacted and reserves of the Army, Navy, and Air Force were called up. Chamberlain warned Hitler that no greater mistake could be made than thinking that British intervention on behalf of Poland could be ignored.

The Führer promptly summoned our Ambassador Sir Neville Henderson, but though placatory, made no concessions over Poland. Thereupon Chamberlain signed an Anglo-Polish Treaty of Alliance, and Daladier immediately re-stated France's pledge of aid to Poland. Crucial instructions were sent to Henderson in hope of opening the way 'for a wider and more complete understanding' between Britain and Germany. At midnight on 30 August he was summoned by von Ribbentrop, who tersely defined Germany's offer to Poland; but Hitler had already confirmed instructions for invasion at dawn on 1 September. On the afternoon of that assault the British Cabinet sent instructions to Henderson declaring that Britain would stand by her obligations unless the German forces were withdrawn. Complete mobilisation was ordered. France followed suit. A blackout of lights throughout Britain from sunset became mandatory. The full ARP organisation was put into effect. Evacuation from London of small children and their mothers immediately began.

Next day, ten Fairey Battle Squadrons of the Advanced Air Striking Force flew to France, and at 9 am on 3 September our Ambassador presented an ultimatum to the German Government that if no satisfactory reply to the note of 1 September was received by 11 am BST, a state of war would exist from that hour.

There was no reply. At 11.15 am the Prime Minister broadcast to the nation that no undertaking to withdraw troops from Poland had been received, consequently Britain was at war with Germany. Five hours later, France declared war on Germany. That night, Whitley bombers flew without opposition to Hamburg, Bremen, and the Rhur, to drop bundles of propaganda leaflets telling of the iniquities of Hitler — but in England a jeering radio voice, soon to be known as Lord Haw-haw, announced that the Cunarder *Athenia,* bound for Canada, had been sunk by an U-boat. That brought home the reality of war. There was quick retaliation with ten Blenheims and fourteen Wellingtons attacking the German Fleet off Brünsbuttel — but before this crucial month ended, the aircraft carrier *Courageous* was also sunk by German U-boats.

In the stress of the moment, Roy Chadwick planned to send his wife and two daughters to Canada to avoid what he believed would be the inevitable bombing of Manchester — but on discovering that the maximum quota age was 15, he decided to follow official ARP advice and had the cellars of his house reinforced with props holding up the ceiling, and sandbags piled around the walls and basement windows. There were a number of compartments in these cellars, so each member had a 'bedroom' if the sirens began their warning wail.

Long planned production orders were now put into effect throughout the British aircraft industry and its associated shadow factories. Among them was Roy Chadwick's former *alma mater* British Westinghouse, reconstituted as Metropolitan-Vickers Ltd at Trafford Park, which received a contract for

The alternative 4-engined bomber rival – the Halifax.

100 Manchesters for assembly and testing at Ringway. That added to the load on the Avro Works staff, for it was necessary to teach Metro-Vick's general engineering employees the more delicate art of aeronautical structures, jigging for interchangeability, and to adopt specialised inspection standards even though well versed in precision methods. In all this, Chadwick felt he had again become a participator in the familiar scene of his youth, and there was pleasure in renewing acquaintance with George Bayley who was now managing director.

Stretching Avro facilities to the full came an order for a further 1,000 Ansons. Although earlier regarded as virtually obsolescent, Ansons had gone into immediate action on declaration of war, and on the second day, one had successfully bombed a German U-boat. Later that month another shot down a Dornier Do 18 flyingboat.

Towards the end of October, news filtered through the 'bush telegraph' that the Handley Page Halifax prototype had been assembled at No.13 OTU at Bicester where there was a long runway, and had made its first flight on the 25th but the fact that no attempt was made to retract the undercarriage indicated problems. That caused Chadwick to reflect that his Manchester's lead was only marginal, for it had achieved a mere half dozen flights because of engine adjustments and small aerodynamic changes. However, its ninth flight on 28 November was delivery to Boscombe Down in Wiltshire, which had just replaced the former Martlesham home of the A & AEE. A team of service engineers from Avro and Rolls-Royce was there to receive it. Chadwick and Rogerson attended by car.

After a few days testing the Bomber Flight decided that directional characteristics must be improved. The precautionary central fin was duly fitted and gave the requisite improvement. But there were still engine problems. One of the Vultures failed in flight on 12 December, resulting in a forced landing in a large cabbage field and consequent superficial damage to the Manchester that necessitated dismantling and transporting to Newton Heath for repair. Somewhat offsetting Dobson's irritation at this setback was a government agreement signed six days later, launching a vast Commonwealth Air Training Plan, aiming at 20,000 aircrew a year from a hundred overseas bases — and the Anson was selected as one of the standard training aircraft. Concurrently, Chadwick learned that the replacement 4-engined Short Stirling bomber had its first flight at Rochester Airport on 3 December, and was airborne for half-an-hour but also left the undercarriage extended. On Christmas Eve the second flight was made, including full retraction. Both Stirling and Halifax would still take months to complete manufacturers' trials, so at least the Manchester had a head start if repairs could be hurried forward.

* * *

To help speed production drawings of the Manchester, a group of draughtsmen from the Gloster subsidiary of Hawker-Siddeley had been loaned to Roy Chadwick, whose aim was to ensure that every item of equipment was self-contained in its specific section of the five portions of the fuselage. These were built as easily linked entities with appropriate junctions for electrical wiring, hydraulics, and control rods. Similarly the wings were built in self-contained units for multiple assembly, and already had been revised to give 90 ft 1 ins span by pitching the existing wing ribs slightly further apart and extending the outboard spar by 6 ft. Not only was Chadwick complying with the original specified transport lengths of sub-assemblies but effectively putting into practice the time-honoured adage of his early master, Alliott Roe, that Avro aeroplanes must be made in easily assembled, self-contained units to save factory floor space.

To obtain sufficient area for the envisaged Anson and Manchester production, a new shadow factory with floor space of 1½ million sq ft was being constructed at Yeadon, near Leeds. Meanwhile , comprehensive planning for Manchester production already resulted in an assembly line which had progressed to fuselages complete with wing integration for the first few machines.

These early months of war in 1940 seemed uncannily quiet, but more and more British troops were pouring into France to join the French in holding the much vaunted Maginot Line of forts deemed adequate defence against the still invisible Germans whose army was still largely engaged in Poland. In England the only obvious signs of war were the encirclement of balloons above London and each great manufacturing city, but armament factories everywhere were working to capacity, and there was intensive concentration on ship building to replace inevitable losses from U-boats. Nevertheless, the British people began to feel that this was a 'phoney war', despite the nation-wide emphasis on more munitions, guns and aircraft. Concurrently, 1,770 Anson Mk Is were ordered and 223 Mk IVs were allocated for shipment to Canada, where they would be fitted with 300 hp Wright Whirlwind radials. Plans were being considered for extensive sub-contracting in Canada. As token of Dominion co-operation, the first units of the Royal Canadian Air Force arrived in Britain on 25 February. This was quickly followed by announcement of Australian plans for implementing the Empire Air Training Scheme, for which Britain would provide over 1,700 aircraft.

In February, the repaired prototype Manchester, still without equipment, had been returned to Boscombe Down, but the A & AEE pilots remained chary of the Vulture engine, yet Rolls-Royce had commenced full production in January. The take-off rating had now been increased to 1,800 hp at 3,200 rpm, but it was soon found that take-off was no better than at 3,000 rpm because of better propeller efficiency at those revs. It was therefore decided to transfer the machine to Farnborough for engine/propeller experimentation and further investigation of directional characteristics.

As there was a brief lull in proceedings, Roy Chadwick and Mary accepted an invitation from Bill Devereaux, that hospitable but forceful supplier of alloy extrusions, to spend a long weekend at his house at Whitehaven in Cumberland so that they could experience the glories of the Lake District.

While they were away, a Peace Treaty had been signed between Russia and Finland, ending three months of bitter fighting. but the war was accelerating. On 9 April, German forces over-ran Denmark, and landed at key places in Norway. On the 10th, German and British naval forces clashed off Narvik and next day Coastal Command Wellingtons attacked Stavanger airfield. On 13 April there was a further battle off Narvik and eight German destroyers were sunk. That same day, fifteen Hampden bombers began laying mines around the Danish coast, and British landed unopposed for operations against Narvik, but barely a fortnight later the C-in-C of the Expeditionary Force in Norway advised that operations should be abandoned.

More ominously on 10 May, Germany invaded Holland, Belgium, and Luxembourg. Neville Chamberlain resigned as Prime Minister and a Coalition Government was formed with Winston Churchill in dual role as Prime Minister and Minister of Defence. Four days later a Ministry of Aircraft Production was formed, headed by Lord Beaverbrook. That same day the Germans bombed Rotterdam, killing nearly 1,000 during negotiations for surrender of the city. On the following morning the Dutch capitulated. That night the first large-scale raids on German industrial targets in the Ruhr were made by 90 RAF aircraft. Five days later, German armoured divisions and troop transports had taken Arras, Abbeville, and Amiens, and next day occupied Boulogne. On 25 May they claimed to have surrounded the Belgian and French Armies and most of the British Expeditionary Force.

The Sunday paper that week-end provided a more personal shock for the Chadwicks. It so happened that on 23 May, Sir Oswald Mosley, founder of the British Union of Fascists had been arrested and taken to Brixton Prison, but Chadwick was now devastated to read a banner headline THESE MEN ARE DANGEROUS captioning a dozen or more small photographs of prominent industrialists commencing with Lords Northcliffe, Inchape, and Nuffield, and the fourth was Sir Alliott Verdon-Roe as he looked in 1910 with cap reversed prior to flying his triplane. All were described as Mosley-Nazi supporters who ought to be locked up, but though Roe had made a donation to the BUF in 1935 because Mosley's ideas on Currency Reform coincided with his, he certainly was not interested in Fascist politics. That this scandalous attack on Sir Alliott and others was a vicious piece of propaganda, is emphasized by the fact that AV was not subjected to interrogation by Home Office officials, and continued as a Saunders-Roe director, eventually becoming President.

Not long after this damaging affair Dobson received a letter from Sir Alliott promoting the advantage of tail-less wings: 'I have long been of the opinion that a tailplane is unnecessary and its elimination should save a worthwhile percentage of structure weight and cost. The tailplane is generally negatively loaded, so the force of the air in addition to the tail has to be carried . . . With present conventional design the control surfaces on the tail unit operate in disturbed air; obviously it must be beneficial to have them clear of the turbulent region.'

Dobson showed Chadwick the letter and sketches. 'Tell him,' said the designer, 'we are too busy with the Manchester, otherwise we might give it a trial.'

* * *

Amid deepening wartime gloom, the second Manchester prototype, L7247, had been completed with full Service equipment and armed with a hydraulically operated Fraser-Nash FN5 nose turret, FN20 tail turret, and FN21A ventral turret (soon to be replaced by an FN7 dorsal turret), each with two .303 Browning guns. On 26 May, after considerable engine testing and adjustment, it was flown by Sam Brown and Bill Thorn at Ringway while anxiously watched by Chadwick, who only with difficulty had been persuaded by Dobson not to join them. In the following days there were more flights to adjust the new type of servo-tab balance and conduct brief performance trials before flying the machine to Boscombe Down for full Service trials in lieu of the first prototype which Farnborough was retaining for catapult tests.

The Manchester's performance and efficiency, and particularly the single-engine ability, was deeply concerning Chadwick. He was therefore envisaging a far-reaching alternative. As with all designers, he worked in close conjunction with Air Ministry technicians. AV-M Wilfred Freeman was well aware of the problems, and accordingly sent his assertively efficient Director of Technical Development, William Farren, to Manchester, accompanied by the Deputy DTD, Norbert E. Rowe, for discussions with Chadwick. All three were old acquaintances, and Rowe until recently has been Chief Technical Officer at Martlesham, where he was always known as 'Nero' because of his initials.

Years later he wrote: 'Chadwick told us that the prototype would come out overweight; moreover, the engines were not giving the power he had been led to expect. Characteristically he explained that the Manchester was his first attempt at an all-metal aircraft of that size and stiffness, resulting in a skin of too great a thickness. Hence the ratio of bomb load to range performance was quite inadequate. What was to be done?

'To help visualise matters, a model of the Manchester had been made with a twin-engined centre section which was instantly detachable so that a 4-engined version of 12 ft greater span could be substituted and fitted with the same outer wings, giving a scale span of 102 ft. He then went through his proposals for stretching the wing-span in a manner entailing minimum re-design of major components and details, retaining the basic aerodynamic wing profile. On this increased span he would instal four Rolls-Royce Merlin engines — again involving no drastic structural or aerodynamic modifications. He showed us on the drawing board how he would plan the work, and answered our many queries in a satisfactory way. We accepted this as the best way out of the Manchester impasse. Indeed Roy Chadwick showed himself to be a most resourceful and courageous designer, ultimately snatching success from failure in the most ingenious way with a superlatively successful operational aircraft.'

Luckily the load factors remained adequate because the airframe had been designed to take the high inertia loads of catapult launching, but accelerated take-off was no longer a vital requirement because aerodromes were being made much bigger and would have longer runways, so there were strength reserves in hand. Dobbie therefore proposed to modify a machine as a private venture after discussing the project with Ernest Hives, the ebulliently thrusting managing director of Rolls-Royce at Derby — but Lord Beaverbrook, the newly appointed Minister of Aircraft Production, immediately banned any allocation of Merlin engines for the 4-engined Manchester, insisting that all were required for Hurricane and Spitfire fighters as first priority. Hives grinned and privately declared to Dobson and Chadwick that he himself would provide four engines in the form of power plant units devised for the Bristol Beaufighter which could be fitted virtually unchanged to new nacelles. That could lead to big political trouble, so Roy Chadwick counselled the wisdom of securing AV-M Freeman's reversal of Beaverbrook's dictum.

By now the pressures everywhere were mounting. The Belgian Army capitulated on 29 May and next day the Germans occupied Ostend. Complete annihilation of the French Army and most of the British Army seemed probable. Already a huge fleet of shallow draught pleasure cruisers, life-boats, tugs and fishing vessels had been assembled in the hope of rescuing the soldiers trapped at Ostend. On 30 May, Operation *Dynamo* began, and by 3 June, four-fifths of the British Expeditionary Force had been brought to England, despite dive bomber attacks, many casualties and the loss of destroyers and transports, and destruction of numerous British aircraft. Concurrently, evacuation of Narvik began — but the Battle of France dragged on.

On 14 June the Germans entered Paris. Three days later the evacuation of the British Expeditionary Force was completed and Marshal Pétain requested terms for France's surrender. RAF aircraft attacked Bremen and Hamburg and 100 German aircraft raided Britain, but everyone at Avro found special encouragement on learning that during an attack by three Me 109s on three Ansons patrolling the Channel, the British pilots had used the slow flying ability of their mounts by suddenly throttling back and as the overtaking Messerschmitts raced past they shot down two and damaged the third.

On 22 June, the French accepted the German Armistice terms and those of the latter's new ally, Italy. Britain was alone.

With stirring oration, Churchill declared: 'What General Weygand called the Battle of France is over. I expect that the Battle of Britain is about to begin . . . Let us therefore brace ourselves to our duties, and so bear ourselves that if the British Empire and its Commonwealth lasts for a thousand years, men will still say "This was their finest hour".'

For months on end, every night would now be disturbed by wailing air-raid sirens and thunder of exploding bombs — and by day the summer skies were streaked with vapour trails where a handful of Hurricanes and Spitfires battled against armadas of bombers and their fighter escorts. Even the Coastal Command Ansons, despite their very different role, added to their laurels in July by shooting down another Me 110 fighter, an He 111 bomber, and an He 115 seaplane.

In July, not only was there the continuous flow of Ansons but the first production Manchester I was flown and handed over to the RAF. Concurrently, assembly of the first of 100 sub-contracted Manchesters began at the Metropolitan-Vickers Works at Trafford Park. Such was the expanded and interlocking factory system devised by Ted

Production Avro 679 Manchester of first operational Squadron, No. 207 at Waddington.

Fielding that all was now set for a 'run of the mill' Manchester production, but far more important to Roy Chadwick was the 4-engined Manchester which was still the prime subject of discussion at the Air Ministry; but official decision to proceed was delayed until the A & AEE at Boscombe Down could report on the fully armed and equipped second prototype Handley Page Halifax which at last arrived there in late August. If handling and performance were good, was there any point in proceeding with a 4-engined Manchester?

That able and perceptive man, AV-M Wilfred Freeman, had fully backed the Avro project. His engine specialist, Major Bulman, recorded: 'Freeman and Tedder visited Avros just after the prototype Manchester had unfortunately spun in, and had a short flight in the second aircraft. In the firm's office afterwards, Dobbie, the irrepressible, with a model Manchester in his hand, said none of them were happy with the results to date and that Rolls-Royce seemed luke-warm about the Vultures. Whereupon he slipped off the model's wing and replaced it with another mounting four Merlins. Hence the Lancaster, which was destined to become the best British bomber of the war, and the great decision made on the spot was Wilfred Freeman's.'

Soon afterwards, Freeman was elevated from the Ministry of Aircraft Production to become Air Marshal and Vice-Chief of Air Staff, and his former Deputy Director of Research and Development, the cynically witty AV-M Tedder, also reverted to operational duties. Replacing them came the bespectacled, sandy-haired, brilliant Sir Henry Tizard as Technical Adviser to the Minister, but he wanted to scrap the Manchester and divert A. V. Roe and Armstrong Whitworth to construction of Stirling or Halifax. J. V. Connolly recollected: 'When this was conveyed to Roy Dobson there was a furious reaction. The following day he and Roy Chadwick were in Mr Hennessy's office at the Ministry with a model of a four-Merlin-engined version — the future Lancaster. Forthwith they went to Capt R. N. Liprot, the Specification authority, who with his usual flair, intuition, speed of decision, and in this case considerable courage, wrote the masterly understatement of the war: "There is no reason why this aircraft with its four Merlins should not have the same performance as the twin-engined Manchester". A new programme was immediately written and A. V. Roe & Co promised to deliver two Lancasters in July, 1941.'

Concurrently, a secret device with which Tizard had been closely associated was the electronic Ultra, capable of making interception of German troop instructions and thus revealed Göring's instructions to the Luftwaffe to mount a final mighty onslaught on Britain on 15 September. If successful, Hitler would invade immedately. By one o'clock that day the heights were webbed with vapour trails of 25 squadrons of Hurricanes and Spitfires battling against the massed Luftwaffe — ending in crushing defeat of Göring's bomber forces. Two days later a decrypted signal revealed that Hitler had abandoned plans for invasion. Dowding's men had saved England, and he was made a Knight Grand Commander of the Bath.

Not until mid-November was the official Contract received for the 4-engined 'stretched' Manchester (Mk III). Dobson had already allocated a Manchester I in a suitable stage of construction, and top priority was now given to building the new middle wing portion and completing the assembly. Production Manchester deliveries had been proceeding since early August, and now in November the first squadron, No. 207, was formed at Waddington, Lincs., commanded by Air Commodore John Boothman, winner of the last Schneider Trophy Contest. The Squadron pilots, most of whom were experienced with Hampdens, Whitleys, or Wellingtons — though several had only flown Ansons — were pleased with the pleasant handing of the more massive and initially intimidating Manchester. But problems with the Vulture soon became apparent. Though the machine would cruise readily enough on a single engine, a crash was inevitable if one cut during initial climb before 150 mph had been attained — as I discovered under simulated conditions at a safe height — and that could also happen when approaching to land. All twin-engined aircraft have this danger, and with two engines cut on a 4-engined aircraft, there can be similar problems, but such odds were negligible compared with the ordeal on encountering flak during bombing raids. However, there was little thought for the similiar anxieties of German bomber pilots when Manchester was attacked on the night of 23 December and the Metropolitan-Vickers factory was hit, destroying their first production Manchester, together with twelve others in advanced stages of construction.

Roy Chadwick was gravely concerned, yet he joked with his family: 'I think they were looking for me! Dobbie says I'm on the Nazi black-list of people who will be dealt with by the SS when they conquer England!'

* * *

The new look of the 4-engined Manchester III (Lancaster).

At the beginning of January 1941 the 4-engined prototype Avro 683 Manchester III was towed onto the aerodrome at Woodford for comprehensive engine testing and adjustment. On the 9th this hugely impressive machine, BT308, was cleared for initial flight, and like the original Manchester I, was bereft of its dorsal turret for the occasion but had a similar tail to the production Manchesters comprising dorsal tail-fin as well as slightly increased fins and rudders at the tips of the 20 ft span tailplane.

'Would you like to drive to Woodford with me?' said Roy Chadwick to 18-year-old Margaret that morning. 'With luck, it's going to be a special day because Sam is likely to fly the new big bomber.'

She remembers: 'It was a lovely day, with blue sky and a few scattered white clouds, but very cold, so we were well wrapped up. All the way there we chatted happily in his car — a black Armstrong-Siddeley, for he had laid up the big Buick because of petrol rationing. He much preferred the Buick because he adored the speed, but at least the Armstrong had a sun-shine roof and was neatly finished in walnut décor with little tables at the back of the front seat, and had pre-selector gears. We always turned down the small lane at the side of Woodford Church that led directly to the Club House and the Avro hangars and tarmac apron where my father parked the car. A few hundred yards away stood the huge new Avro, its four engines already ticking over. Sam Brown and Bill Thorn, distinctive in white overalls, could be seen sitting side-by-side in the cockpit high above the ground.

'We strolled across to a crowd intently watching the proceedings and were greeted by Roy Dobson and Mr Fielding with whom my father talked for a while as we stood together at the left-hand side of the group. Presently the engines began to roar, and as the plane moved forward my father turned and walked away with me for quite a distance. Though he seemed calm and expressionless, I'm sure he was very tense. Then the plane began its run and soared upward, climbing into the blue between the occasional large white clouds, and sailed away into the distance. Presently it returned and circled the aerodrome; then with impressive din flew low in front of us, climbed up again and made smoothly banked turns to left and right before magnificently rumbling in and landing. We all began to move across the field to where it rested. As we approached, the fuselage door opened, and Capt Brown, his white overalls brilliant in the sun, appeared in the doorway. There was an eager cry of "How did it go, Sam?", and smilingly he said, "It was marvellous — easy to handle and light on the controls". Then he descended the steps and everyone was talking to him.

'When we were in the car going home, I turned to my father and said: "Well, Daddy, you must be very pleased that this new aeroplane is such a success." He replied, "Yes I am — but in this business one cannot rest on one's laurels. There is always another and another aeroplane, and at the moment we are considering a possible bomber which will fly higher than any other in the world — but that is a top secret, my dear." '

He was aware that Vickers had fitted a tank-like pressure cabin to one of their twin-engined Wellington light bombers, but the air density had to be constantly adjusted by a crew member. Chadwick's scheme was much more ambitious. Sequenced as Type 684, his aeroplane was based on a Lancaster of still greater span, powered by four R-R Merlin XX supercharged engines, and had a large operational cabin for which the atmosphere was compressed by a special small engine and the pressure appropriate to any given height was controlled by an ingenious leak valve designed by Westland for the revolutionary stratospheric Welkin fighter they were constructing.

For the moment all effort was concentrated on the re-named new Lancaster. With 1,000 hp more than the Manchester, the performance was only slightly greater than with twin-engined Vultures, but safety was enormously enhanced, climb and ceiling improved, and handling was pleasant, though longitudinal stability proved marginal for a machine of that size. On 27 January it was flown to the A & EE at Boscombe Down for Service trials.

Meanwhile the Manchester had been receiving tremendous attention at Waddington, where 207 Squadron was working up to operational efficiency. Though lacking various Air Ministry Supply items because of bottlenecks, much intensive flying was carried out and inevitable minor defects were discovered, requiring rectification action — that bugbear of every aircraft manufacturer which necessitates a big modification section in the Drawing Office.

However, sufficent progress was made for six Manchesters to be available for the Squadron's first operational sortie on the night of 24 — 25 February, with Brest as target in an attempt to bomb their German pocket battleship *Scharnhorst*. The logbook of air gunner Bob Storey DFM records: 'Crash-landed in L7284. Undercart failure.' Ten days later they raided Brest again, and a week later participated in the first 1,000 bomber raid on Hamburg and Cologne, but 'the Vultures gave trouble and on return a blind approach had to be made to Finningley, Doncaster,' noted Storey. Though hydraulic problems were readily solved, the unreliability of the engines led to many modifications.

Farnborough and Boscombe Down investigations of the Manchester's slight deficiency in longitudinal stability at aftmost loading resulted in all machines from the 21st onward being fitted with a 33 ft span tailplane which had larger area tip fins and rudders to compensate for elimination of the central fin, and in this guise they were designated Mk 1A. Metropolitan-Vickers were contributing their quota, and the number of Squadrons was steadily increasing. But for doubts of engine reliability, causing every Manchester to be grounded on several occasions, all pilots, whatever their experience, felt confident in handling this easily controllable machine despite low speed, single-engine problems.

As a viable alternative to the Vultures, Chadwick revised this design as a Mk II version, either with two 2,100 hp Napier Sabre engines or the well-developed 2,520 hp Bristol Centaurus radials, and two Manchester airframes were set aside for this

Roy Chadwick takes a flight in the Lancaster piloted by Bill Thorn.

purpose; but though both engine types were experimentally installed, neither aircraft was flown, and the Napier-powered version with wings removed became a Sabre engine test-stand at Luton.

Currently, the prototype Manchester III (Lancaster) had the central fin removed and was fitted with the newly standardised Manchester IA 33 ft tailplane. Reports from the A & AEE indicated that pilots much preferred this embryo Lancaster to the equivalent 4-engined Handley Page Halifax because of superior handling characteristics, though both had much the same top speed.

Sir George Edwards, as later chairman of the British Aircraft Corporation, recollected Roy Chadwick saying to him at this juncture: 'George — the biggest bit of luck was the change of tailplane and fin. I never expected it to improve the handling characteristics the way it did, but it absolutely revolutionised them, and now I am getting the credit for it!'

'That,' added Sir George, 'was an example of the modesty which I always found inherently part of his personality but was also a factor that has delayed recognition of his remarkable abilities.'

George Edwards had first visited the Avro Works when he was experimental manager at Vickers, Weybridge, and was given the job of

George Edwards who became the post-war chief designer of Vickers Ltd

converting the American 'Lease-lend' Havoc bombers into night fighters, for which Avros would be the 'mother company at Burtonwood. 'My first call on Roy was, as always, very much to the point,' he said. 'He knew I had been responsible for the prototypes and therefore had first-hand knowledge of the armament side of the job. His awareness of the importance of the programme produced a brisk instruction to all involved at Avros that I was to be helped as though part of his outfit. Half the week was spent at Weybridge and the other half in the north. One new aeroplane I was building was the Vickers Windsor, which involved difficult manufacturing problems on the leading edge of the wing "geodedic". Our hydraulic press had not sufficient size and pressure to do the job, so I asked Roy if I might use the Shaw Press at Avro. When he saw what I had arrived with, he said with a grin: "They'd never left me design a thing like that!" But once again he gave me great assistance.'

The second prototype Lancaster was now ready to fly, but at this stage an MAP official gratuitously invited the chief designers of each of the bomber-producing companies to inspect the Boeing Flying Fortress and other American types 'to see what modern bombers should look like'. Chadwick was furious, cancelled the test flight, and took twenty or more draughtsmen, headed by S. D. Davies, to Woodford, intent on refining his bomber to prove the superiority of British design. Ted Fielding recollected: 'He ranged his men around the aircraft with their drawing-boards and personally went over the aircraft to examine and consider every detail. He threw out every item not worth its weight, re-arranged equipment to make it more accessible and more easily fitted and serviced, thus contributing immensely to reducing constructional man-hours.' The work of 'productionising' this prototype, DG585, rapidly proceeded, and on 13 May it was flown to Boscombe Down for acceptance trials.

Fielding recorded that: 'S. D. Davies was in charge of the experimental department at that time and must be credited with the conversion of the Manchester to the Lancaster prototype in record time. His department carried out all the work and I kept in close touch with progress so that manufacturing plans could be modified as quickly as possible to prepare the way for full production.'

Though the Air Ministry remained critical of the manner in which Dobson and Chadwick had cut corners and taken independent action in establishing the Lancaster, nobody could dismiss the fact that it was now the most efficient heavy bomber so far produced and undoubtedly had big potential. Contract B69274/40 was therefore amended to change over from Manchester to Lancaster production, commencing with the 159th airframe at A. V. Roe & Co and the 44th at Metropolitan-Vickers. On discussing the Lancaster production programme at the Air Ministry's Harrogate headquarters, Fielding and Dobson proposed a peak programme of 80 aircraft per month, but were audaciously told that they did not appreciate the problems because they had never built a run of big aircraft. Nevertheless in June an order was placed for 450, and in the ensuing months Fielding soon proved he could produce them fast despite the half million manufacturing operations to make and marry up the 55,000 parts.

* * *

Meanwhile the night bombing of British cities continued. Wrecked and burned buildings had become commonplace, but people remained cheerfully confident that Churchill would see them through to victory, despite set-backs in North Africa, Greece and Crete, and the sinking of H.M.S. *Hood*. In the East, Germany was beginning an attack on Russia.

Ansons were still flowing in great numbers from the Avro factories. To ensure maximum serviceability a special design section at Chadderton was busy with modifications and design revisions applicable alike to RAF aircraft and those built in Canada by Federal Aircraft Ltd, the first of which flew on 21 August and had hydraulically operated flaps and undercarriage.

Design of the stratospheric Avro 684 bomber was now temporarily shelved until more experience had been obtained with the pressurised Vickers Wellington prototype and Merlin-powered successor. Consequently Roy Chadwick's thoughts turned to other possible variants of the Lancaster theme, including a troop or passenger-carrier to meet the requirements of RAF Transport Command which had been formed on 18 July to take over the MAP Atlantic Ferry Organisation. Pilots who had ferried 'lease-lend' aircraft to England were flown back to the USA in Liberator bombers which were cold and cramped and noisy, and certainly unsuitable for transport of civilian VIPs unaccustomed to such conditions. Chadwick therefore contemplated a comfortable 12-seater using the same mainplane, tail, power-units and undercarriage as the Lancaster but with a flat-sided, metal-skinned fuselage of

Genesis of the Avro 685 York with Roy Chadwick describing design features to Roy Dobson (centre).

twice the volume to give comfortable headroom and seating. The Lancaster mid-wing position was unsuitable for a transport as the spar would restrict the cabin, so Chadwick mounted it at shoulder position, thus lowering the fuselage bottom relative to the ground but keeping the distance between wheels and thrust line unchanged. Designed as the simplest possible conversion, it could be swiftly produced, and with a range of 2,700 miles was suitable for non-stop trans-Atlantic transport.

But there was an immediate snag. The British Government, as a placatory gesture to the USA, had agreed that Britain would concentrate on fighters and bombers and the Americans produce all war-time transport aircraft. Officially, the Air Ministry could not therefore sanction construction of the machine and supply of engines. 'Leave it to me,' growled Roy Dobson. 'We got away with the Lancaster, so we'll do the same with this transport. Press on with the design.'

Amid the pressure of war there was no time for holidays this year. Everyone was working full-out, and in the Avro factories the average working week was 60 hours. Indicative of the times, clothes rationing had commenced because the Lancashire mills were too busy

Lancaster BII.

with uniforms, rucksacks, webbing, and tarpaulins. At the Avro factories production was steadily increasing, and the first production Lancaster, L7527, was rolled out from the Woodford flight sheds on 31 October for its maiden flight by Sam Brown. That was less than 10 months since the first flight of the experimental prototype, and in the intervening time Rolls-Royce had developed the Merlin from the 1,145 hp of Type X to the XX of 1,280 hp, thus affording enhanced performance which was augmented by constant-speed propellers, and these could be feathered individually to reduce drag if an engine failed. As always on these occasions, Roy Chadwick was an anxious watcher — but Sam had no adverse comments, other than minor details.

During the following weeks, whenever the harsh northern weather gave opportunity, speed runs and climbs were made at full load, handling and stability checked with the c.g. in the crucial aft position, and dives made to limiting speed; then the machine was flown to Boscombe Down for further trials and received high commendation from the pilots for its outstanding performance. A contract for 2050 followed the existing 1070, and on Christmas Eve, with great jubilation, the next three machines, L7537, L7538, and L7541 were delivered to No. 44 (Rhodesian) Squadron at Waddington — the first overseas unit to become operational with Lancasters.

Chapter 13
Riding the Storm

Because of the ever-increasing complexity of sub-contracting, a 'Lancaster Group' was formed comprising A. V. Roe, Metropolitan-Vickers, Armstrong Whitworth, Vickers (West Bromwich and Chester), and Austin Motors. Each firm was not only provided with every design detail, drawings of special tools and jigs, and data on requisite floor space and height of buildings, but also with a complete Lancaster, five structural sets of fuselage, wings, and other major components, together with assembly equipment. Under Fielding's chairmanship the Group organised sub-committees to deal with materials, bought-out items, spares and sub-contracting, and a representative of each daughter firm was stationed at Avro Works so that advice on problems could be immediately secured.

During January 1942 ten more Lancasters were delivered to No. 44 Squadron, and No. 97 Squadron at Coningsby also began re-equipping with them. To ensure minimum hold-ups and assist in every way, a team of Avro service engineers was established at each base, and the Avro pilots made frequent liaison visits so that the RAF personnel could discuss any problems. Troubles were minimal. Pilots and ground-crews alike regarded the Lancaster as the perfect bomber. Lest there was failure of Merlin engine supply through bombing the Derby and shadow factories, Chadwick redesigned the Lancaster engine nacelles to take the 1,650 hp Bristol Hercules VI as an alternative. For the 430 machines being built by Victory Aircraft Ltd at Malton, Canada, a further revision became the Lancaster III with the American-built 1,300 hp Packard Merlin 28 engines.

Early in February, he issued to the experimental shop the drawings of the new cabin fuselage for his Lancaster Transport

The Lancaster was made in sections transported from various factories and assembled at Woodford.

Royal occasion: The King with Roy Dobson, Capt. Sam Brown, and Sir Hartley Shawross; talking to the Queen, Roy Dobson (right) and Ted Fielding.

derivative Type 685, and day and night shifts proceeded with its fabrication. Every aspect of design had simplicity, and therefore ease of construction, as its target. Meanwhile bombers continued to have top priority. Air Marshal Arthur Harris was appointed C-in-C Bomber Command on 20 February with forty-four Squadrons, though only fourteen had received the latest 'heavies', including the two Lancaster Squadrons from whom a few snags were now being reported to which Chadwick gave personal attention, followed by immediate rectification.

Typically there was an early instance of wing-tip failure. 'In 1941, I had been posted to Bomber Command Operational Training Unit (OTU) at Finningley, where I wondered if I would ever manage to fly the Wellington successfully,' wrote the pilot involved in this incident. 'However, the course was switched to Manchesters, which were an absolute pleasure to fly. Posting followed to No. 97 Squadron at the bleak station of Coningsby. I completed several operational flights with never a complaint about the aircraft. Presently pilots reported seeing a 4-engined Manchester speeding around the countryside. This was the Lancaster, and soon the Squadron was re-equipped with these aeroplanes. On 3 March, four of our Lancasters were sent on a mine-laying trip in the Heligoland Bight. My return ended in ditching the machine in the Wash because the wingtips had failed in flight. Next day the whole crew were interrogated by Air Vice-Marshal Alex Corrington, the AOC of our No. 5 Group. He listened courteously, but it quickly became apparent that his Group Engineer did not believe us, and I felt very angry. However the AOC calmed matters down and was quite charming.

'A day or so later, I was called to Woodhall Spa and instructed to introduce myself to a civilian at the Watch Office. "My name is Chadwick," he quietly said. "I'm from Avros and I would like you to tell me about the wingtip trouble. You will realise that it is terribly important to get the Lancaster right without delay, but to examine them all would be a terrific task, so I want you to tell me in complete confidence the whole story and I can assure you that nothing will get back to the Air Force. I don't care what you were up to when the tips failed — but I must know!"

'His demeanour was so straightforward and man-to-man that if I had been looping the Lanc, I would have confessed. So I repeated my story in detail and was impressed by the way he accepted that my speed was moderate when the tips went. He asked a few searching questions and then we walked back to his car, and thanking me very politely, he drove away, leaving me with the impression of his gentlemanly nature, completely devoid of airs, despite his outstanding achievements. I was even fanciful enough to think that his character was reflected in his aeroplanes!'

Action swiftly followed. All mainplane tips were stiffened, and there were no more failures. Soon afterwards one of the Lancasters forced landed with two engines out of action due to failure of the fuel pumps. Though quickly solved by the Avro team, it prompted Rolls-Royce to obtain a Lancaster for direct flight experience of engine installation modifications, and the prototype BT308 was flown to their Hucknall Aerodrome for extended engine development trials. However 26 March proved an encouraging occasion for the Avro workers because their Majesties, King George VI and Queen Elizabeth visited the Yeadon factory and walked through the shops amid cheering employees, afterwards christening the next two Lancasters that were about to be tested 'George' and 'Elizabeth' — then the King was conducted to the door of his machine and made his way to the cockpit where Roy Chadwick sat by his side, and they talked of their early flying experiences with Avro 504s.

Meanwhile Her Majesty was listening with gracious dignity to Roy Dobson's bubbling enthusiasm on such subjects as welfare of employees, and how aeroplanes are made. When the King re-joined her, she turned from Dobson to the Avro designer and said: 'Tell me, Mr Chadwick, how do you manage to design such huge and complex aeroplanes as these?'

He gave it a moment's thought, then smilingly replied: 'Well, Mam . . . You don't *have* to be crazy but it's a help!' At which royal protocol collapsed in laughter.

That Spring, Jimmy Orrell re-joined the Avro test team. Since 1935 he had been flying for Imperial Airways and its reincarnation at British Overseas Airways, and thus had extensive experience of piloting 4-engined airliners. His contract having expired, he therefore re-turned to test flying. 'The Manchester and the Lancaster production aircraft were my main responsibility,' he said, 'but a certain amount of development flying crept into the programme as time went on and the all-up weight and power increased. Chadwick was always on the spot to know and witness, if possible, the success or otherwise of each development. Always he explained his reasons for doing these things and what he expected to obtain by way of results. This constant contact between design, project engineers, and aircrews made for a happy and keen team.

'Dobbie was an entirely different character — a forceful, tough Yorkshireman who worked extremely hard and influenced others to do the same. He kept contact with the shop floor by regular walks throughout the factories and talked to workers in a personal way. He and Chadwick made a remarkable partnership. There might be considerable argument on occasions, but they had great respect for each other. Having decided on a project, Chadwick set the scene and Dobbie provided the hardware and manpower. As a result the Lancaster became the most important bomber in the world.'

Inevitably there were tragedies and Chadwick sighed for the brave when seven of the twelve Lancasters from No. 44 and 97 Squadrons were shot down on 17 April during an attack on a diesel engine factory at Augsburg, but he was proud to learn later that Sqn Ldr J. D. Nettleton, the South African who led the Lancasters, was awarded the Victoria Cross.

The day after that raid there was shattering news from Boscombe Down. A Lancaster engaged on terminal dive trials to 375 mph had crashed and the entire crew killed. Roy

Chadwick and his chief stressman, together with the Avro chief inspector, drove through the night to town of Amesbury so that they could be at the aerodrome first thing next day to help determine the cause. The sense of accountability weighs heavily upon a designer because a crash relates directly to his own conception of a machine for which every aspect was his responsibility. Had there been structural failure? And so it proved.

Twenty satisfactory dives had been made, and then a different pilot took over and on his first dive some of the top skinning of the port wing came adrift at the rivetting line attachment to the front spar flange. The machine had stalled into the ground at low altitude and burned out. To Chadwick's partial relief, sufficient evidence remained to show that the failure was due to the manufacturing method of making the lap joint, and a relatively simple variation of technique ensured that such failure could not occur again. But only with time was his sense of tragedy subdued by the mounting tragedies of many another aircrew loss in the mounting bombing assault against Germany.

The Manchesters were still valiantly playing their part, but though the use of 100 octane fuel instead of 87 octane had increased take-off power from 1,800 hp to 2,010 hp, performance remained inferior to the Lancaster and the engines still gave trouble Nevertheless on 30 — 31 May, the Manchesters, Lancasters, Halifaxes and

Chadwick always supported the Air Training Corps activities.

Stirlings participated in the first massed raid by bombers against Cologne. The crews of nearly 900 aircraft claimed they had reached their target, and 1,455 tons of bombs were dropped. In the terrible massacre, buildings covering 600 acres were destroyed, and the fires were visible from the Dutch coast. Forty bombers did not return, among them a Manchester piloted by young F/O L. T. Manser who was awarded a posthumous Victoria Cross.

The Flying Classroom – an Anson with astrodome for the Fleet Air Arm.

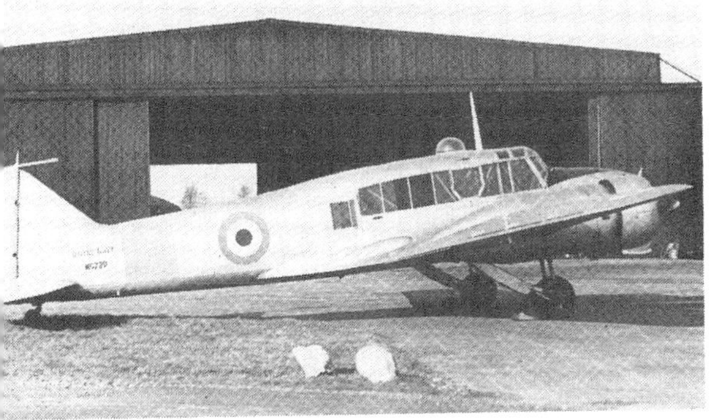

Behind the scenes in modest guise there was still the Anson — 'Faithful Annie' to every pilot — and production at Yeadon was heading towards 130 a week. Though now replaced by the Hudson in Coastal Command, the Anson was making an outstanding contribution to the war effort not only as a communication machine but as a trainer for hundreds upon hundreds of bomber pilots and crews. To meet that requirement Chadwick's modification section had been busy. On some Ansons the turret was converted for use as an astrodome, on others it was removed, and those of the Air Gunnery Schools were fitted with hydraulically operated Bristol VI turrets. Cabins were modified as schoolrooms for W/T Operators, and ASV radar was fitted for

Air-Sea Rescue Squadrons. By now, there were ten marks of Anson, and three more were Canadian variants, of which the Anson Mk V with 450 hp Pratt & Whitney Wasp engines and constant-speed propellers was adopted by the Royal Canadian Air Force and Royal Canadian Navy. Meanwhile, the all-up weight had increased step by step from 7,400 lbs of the prototype to the current 9,960 lbs in order to accommodate more crew, equipment and bombs, yet top speed was the same and the rate of climb had doubled.

* * *

In addition to his manifold duties embracing design, construction, flight testing, Air Ministry liaison, and many meetings with Dobson to discuss policies, Chadwick was also a member of the Advisory Technical Committee which the Royal Aeronautical Society had etablished at Lord Brabazon's invitation to draw on the experience of the industry's technicians. Major Barlow of Fairey, Sidney Camm of Hawker, Roy Fedden of Bristol, Arthur Gouge of Shorts, Rex Pierson of Vickers, C. C. Walker of de Havillands, and Eric Hives of Rolls-Royce were the initial members, but Hives and Barlow soon withdrew and were replaced by Halford of Napiers and Roy Chadwick. Leslie Aitchison was co-opted as metalurgical expert, and J. Laurence Pritchard as Secretary of the RAeS was Secretary to the Committee. In this form, the Advisory Committee functioned throughout the rest of the war, and its reports and crucial recommendations were submitted directly to the Minister. On his part no information, however secret, was with-held from the members. Thus in January 1942, AV-M Sorley, the Deputy Chief of Air Staff, gave detailed information on envisaged future requirements for fighters and bombers and described latest enemy developments. That same day, the Committee submitted a Memorandum stressing that bomb design had not altered for twenty years, and showed that by redesign nearly double the current weight of bombs could be carried. In May, the Committee sent a Memorandum on 'Technical versus Production Policy', advising production of high-performance aircraft in comparatively small quantities rather than aircraft of lesser performance in large quantities. In July, a further Memorandum re-expressed in strong terms the importance of quality over quantity, and emphasised that 'the war situation is so critical that words cannot and must not be spared with regard to the whole question of development. Some of the troubles are because Air Staff members are apt to change their minds and have not always the engineering background to know what can be done.'

However, the Air Staff maintained that ever-increasing numbers of aircraft would be essential to win the war, so contracts for experimental machines were often slow to materialise. Chadwick's Avro 685, tentatively named the York, was a case in point. Though Dobson's men had started building it in February, a contract for four was not issued until June, when the prototype was already being assembled at Ringway.

June also closed another chapter. On the night of the 25th the Manchesters made their last operational sortie by participating in a 1,000 bomber raid on Bremen, during which the Focke-Wulf Aircraft Works was seriously damaged. They were now relegated to pilot training conversion, but continued to be of concern because of the engines.

Though the Manchesters had only been a partial success the Lancasters were going from strength to strength, and on 5 July, Chadwick was further encouraged by the first flight of the prototype York a mere six months after issue of drawings. Sam Brown was quietly pleased with the handling, though there was a slight tendency for the nose to lift in side-slip due to the increased forward side area. On the second flight, with Chadwick sitting alongside, he demonstrated this slight directional fault, but they decided to make no change and leave the A & AEE to assess the handling qualities. Accordingly, the prototype LV626, bearing the new type of RAF roundels on wings and fuselage and the letter 'P' signifying prototype, was delivered

The Avro 685 York after addition of central fin.

to Boscombe Down in mid-August as an unfurnished freighter. In contrast, the second machine, LV629, was being fitted with cabin accommodation for twelve. An air of great mystery surrounded the third because it was specially modified to have square windows instead of round, and drawings marked 'Secret', showing a different cabin disposition, had just been issued and were closely guarded. The appropriate DO section was also revising the structure of the fourth machine with doors in the floor for paratroop deployment.

Concurrently even the tremendous production rate of Merlins by Rolls-Royce was proving insufficient. Consequently production Lancasters were being ferried to maintenance units for storage and their engines removed for transport to Woodford and re-installation in the next Lancaster awaiting tests. To overcome the hold-up the MAP decided to implement Chadwick's earlier scheme for installation of Hercules engines, and the third protoype, DT810, was allocated for this purpose, re-designated Lancaster II, fitted with an easily jigged, welded steel engine mounting, and the engines encircled with NACA annular cowls as used on Short Stirlings.

There was also a modified Lancaster being fitted with four Packard-built Merlin 28 engines imported from the USA, and after flight testing at Woodford, it was flown to Canada during August as a reference machine for the Lancaster III production undertaking by Victory Aircraft, a subsidiary of the National Steel Corporation of Canada.

Another Lancaster was being modified as a 'Pathfinder' bomber, which would precede bombing attacks in order to drop flares lighting the precise target so that the bomb aimers could hit accurately instead of an indiscrimate pattern characterising earlier raids. On 15 August an initial Pathfinder Force of four Squadrons of Stirlings, Halifaxes, Lancasters, and Wellingtons was established under the command of Grp Capt Don Bennett, the former Imperial Airways pilot who until recently had been Flight Superintendent of the Atlantic Ferry Service.

News of the progress of war remained obscure, but optimistic propaganda was made of the extensive air-raids on Germany and of American successes in the Far East. Soothingly the Minister of Information stated: 'Japanese successes in the Pacific can only be a flash in the pan. Mr Churchill and Mr Roosevelt have been together in Washington to decide how the combined strengths of the British Empire and the United States can be brought to bear on this enemy.' But they also decided there could be no second front in Europe before 1943, and plans were discussed for invasion of French North

Africa in October as Operation *Torch,* with General Eisenhower as C-in-C. On 4 August, Churchill landed in Moscow, having flown via Cairo and Tehran to inform Stalin of these decisions, returning to England via Gibraltar after a week's further stay in Cairo.

At this juncture, Roy Chadwick, utterly over-worked and nervously exhausted, fell victim to that painful skin-nerve disease of shingles; but to rest was impossible. The Canadian Lancaster III sample with nose and tail turrets faired and dorsal turret removed was about to be flown to England for A. V. Roe & Co to fit a properly engineered nose and tail for which drawings were being rushed through, and there was confirmation from Boscombe Down that the production Yorks required additional fin area, so the third prototype was being fitted with a central fin, similar to the Manchester arrangement. Of deeper concern was a potential new design to Specification B3/42 for a 350 mph heavy bomber which might ultimately replace the Lancaster. Spurring Chadwick on was the knowledge that Roy Pierson at Vickers was also tendering for this specification. In any case, the sheer management complexity of handling the greatly enlarged design staff in their splendid drawing office at Chadderton was formidable task, for he had some 200 draughtsmen, 100 technicians, and 40 tracers drawing the negatives for the blue-print department.

Towards the end of September news filtered through from Avro teams at RAF Stations that preparations were in hand for a secret bombing offensive, for which more than 100 Lancasters from nine squadrons participated in a full-scale rehearsal on 1 October. Such was the secrecy that the target in Germany was not revealed until 17 October, when crews were briefed to make a dusk attack on the Schnieder munition works at Le Creusot, France, and 94 Lancasters from No. 5 Group flew in loose formation westward from Upper Heyford and swept over the Bay of Biscay before turning across Occupied France to their target, where 100 tons of explosives and 40 tons of incendiaries were dropped. Typically, little damage was done to the factory, despite extensive surrounding damage. A more accurate means of target location was essential, but though the Telecommunications Research Establishment had evolved an electronic navigation aid known as 'Gee' it was not yet in use lest the Germans discovered its nature before the bomber force was equipped in adequate number.

October also saw delivery from Armstrong Whitworth at Baginton of the first production Lancaster II with Hercules engines, but it was disappointing to find that the crucial service ceiling was lower than that of the Lancaster I, and had higher fuel consumption when the cooling gills were open. Since these were standard cowlings, little could be done except ensure precise use in relation to the cylinder

The Hercules-powered Lancaster II of which 300 were built by Armstrong Whitworth.

Stafford Cripps investigates the Lancaster flight deck.

temperature gauges, so not unexpectedly several Lancaster IIs were lost through running out of fuel during operations.

In November came a Cabinet re-shuffle in which Churchill created a sensation by appointing Sir Stafford Cripps as Minister of Aircraft Production in place of Col J. J. Llewellyn, who had endeared himself to his colleagues by his calm understanding and charming personality but now became Minister of Food. By contrast, Cripps was a man of austere personality and notorious as a Labour left-wing barrister of great brilliance. The aircraft industry awaited his activities with trepidation, but soon discovered that he had an unexpected depth of humanity coupled with absolute objectivity in his approach to every problem. His monthly meetings with the special RAeS Technical Committee did much to create a sense of mutual regard and trust, and it so happened that the first matter for his consideration was one on which Chadwick had been engaged for the past month and was submitted on 14 December as 'A Memorandum on the Large Bomber'. That was followed by a 'Memorandum on Jet Propulsion' recommending urgent development work on units exceeding 3,000 lbs thrust as those of lower power would not do justice to the jet in competition with the reciprocating engine.

However, to more practical purpose, Chadwick and Dobson just before Christmas were gratified to receive Contract 2429/C4A for 200 Avro Yorks to Specification C1/42.

* * *

As always, Roy Chadwick made little of his disability and continued his unremitting pressure of work, but internationally the storm of war continued unabated. New dispositions of German forces necessitated another meeting between Churchill and Roosevelt in January 1943, and on the 12th, accompanied by Air Chief Marshal Sir Charles Portal as Chief of Air Staff, the Prime Minister flew in his personal Liberator to Casablanca, North Africa, to confer with the President. Vital decisions were reached on operations against submarines, invasion of Europe, intensive bombing of Germany, a major offensive against Japan after Germany was beaten, unified air control over the North African areas, and an effort to persuade Turkey to join the Allies.

February proved to be a vital month for other decisions. A fortnight after Churchill's return, Roy Chadwick was summoned to a

Barnes Nevil Wallis BSc (later Sir Barnes Wallis CBE, DSc).

meeting with the DTD, 'Nero' Rowe, and was told that as a matter of utmost secrecy, Vickers Ltd had modified a Wellington to carry a special type of rotating bomb, devised by that company's Mr Barnes Wallis. There had been good results in special tests when dropped in the calm waters of the Fleet on the landward side of Chesil Beach, near Weymouth. As the bomb was intended as the prototype of a still bigger bomb which might be carried by a Lancaster, Rowe requested Chadwick's attendance at a high-level meeting to be chaired by Air Marshal Linnell, the CRD, at the Ministry of Aircraft Production on 26 February. 'The bomb skips along the surface just like a skimming stone,' explained Rowe. 'Approval to go ahead has only just been given. You will learn details at the meeting.'

Mystified, Chadwick returned to Manchester. Everyone knew Barnes Wallis as a very imaginative, if temperamental, creative engineer, notable for the part he played in the design of the R100 airship, and the similar geodetic instruction which he had applied to the Vickers Wellesley and Wellington. Typical of his ingenuity was the idea of destroying German magnetic mines by an aeroplane carrying its own magnetic field in the form of a 48 ft diameter coil of 90 kilowatts fitted to the under-side of a Wellington.

He had long been studying German industrial economics, and in a monograph entitled *A Note on a Method of Attacking the Axis Powers*, gave a closely reasoned argument for the destruction of energy power sources by dropping a 10-ton penetration bomb which he regarded as a priority development. For a civilian to tell the Military how war should be conducted was certainly a novel step, but in fact as far back as 1938 there had been a Bomber Command Paper on the possibility of air attacks on German reservoirs and dams, and in July 1940 Air Marshal Portal had recommended an attack on the Möhne dam. Extensive investigation showed that 20,000 lbs of explosives detonated 40 ft below the top of the dam would be required. An 'Aerial attack on dams (AAD) Advisory Committee' was therefore instituted, but Wallis felt that it discounted his views on the big bomb, so he pondered over other methods of destruction.

'Early in 1942,' he recorded, 'I had the idea of a missile which if dropped on the water at a considerable distance upstream of the dam would reach the dam in a series of ricochets, and after impact against the crest of the dam would sink in close contact with the upstream face of the masonry before exploding.' That led to trials with a model 'spherical bomb-surface torpedo' extensive testing at the National Physical Laboratory, and ultimately to full-scale trials using the Wellington.

At the meeting on 26 February, Wallis was certain that the huge rotating bomb he had devised for the Lancaster was about to be turned down and so great was his resentment that he barely assimilated the chairman's opening remarks until he heard him say that the Chief of Air Staff required every effort to be made to prepare aircraft and weapons for an attack on the dams by 26 May at the latest, and delivery by the beginning of that month to give time for training and experiments. Even Chadwick was taken aback when told that three Lancasters would be allocated for earliest possible trials and another 27 to be similiarly modified.

'The crux is, can Avros do this in time?' demanded Air Marshal Linnel.

Anxiously Wallis pointed out that no detailed scheme for modifying the Lancasters had been discussed with Chadwick. But though only sparsely briefed by Rowe, the Avro designer had already deduced the necessities and time required. Taking the plunge, he said: 'Yes — we will do it if Vickers will take the responsibility for the attachment arms and driving mechanism of the mines. I will send draughtsmen to Weybridge at once to finalise details.'

Wallis gave a sigh of relief. Nevertheless, it was a great gamble. The design work, let along modification of the Lancasters, was tremendous. Chadwick set the first week in April as completion date. The problems of the Vickers' Armament Works at Newcastle were even worse, for Wallis had not yet made detailed drawings of the great bomb, nor the self-destructive mechanism, and in any case it would take three weeks to load the proposed 100 mines with the special explosive. Over everything a great security curtain was drawn.

But Chadwick also had other preoccupations. With great interest he studied the report of the Government-sponsored Brabazon Committee which on 10 February had recommended five classes of British commercial aircraft likely to be required after the war. They were very much the types he had in mind, and as an initial transitional step a Lancaster with commodious circular section fuselage seemed an easy possibility, but he had already envisaged a jet airliner, and had discussed with the National Gas Turbine Establishment proposals for a Metro-Vick jet in the tail of a Lancaster.

Meanwhile, there was the Avro York, the third of which, LV633, had been completed with a luxuriously appointed cabin-conference room and was revealed as the personal transport of Winston Churchill, who gave it the classic name *Ascalon* in token of the Crusaders who defended Jerusalem against a superior Egyptian army. This princely York was flown shortly after the Battle of the Ruhr opened on 5 March when more than 400 bombers, led by eight Mosquitoes equipped with the newly introduced bombing and navigation aid 'Oboe', attacked the Krupps' works at Essen and over 160 acres of the city were devastated. Fourteen Bomber Command aircraft failed to return. On the night of 12 March, over 380 bombers again attacked Essen. For the first time 8,000 lb bombs were deployed, but could only be accommodated in the huge bomb bay of the Lancasters.

Through those early days of March, the Avro teams were working at top pressure on modifications of the Lancaster III specials to enable the secret Wallis 'Type 464 Provisioning' to be transversly pivotted from external 'Vee' supports provided by Vickers. Spinning the bomb was effected by V-belt drive from a cockpit-mounted hydraulic motor. Though weight had been saved by eliminating the 33 ft bomb doors and upper gun turret, the additional fitments amounted to more than half a ton. Meanwhile Vickers-Armstrong at Barrow completed the first five bomb cases from sketches, but they were found too long to fit the bomb bay and had to be reduced by 1 $^{1}/_{8}$ ins. Scores of other matters necessitated close co-ordination between Vickers, Vickers-Armstrong, Avro, the Royal Ordnance Factory, the Director of Armament and representatives of MAP.

On 15 March, the AOC-in-C, Air Marshal Harris, allocated AV-M Cochrane the responsibility for the dam operation and established a special squadron, No. 617, based at Scampton where 24-year-old Sqn Ldr Guy Penrose-Gibson, veteran of 157 night fighter and bombing operations, was assigned the task of selecting personnel comprising 'volunteer tour-expired crews for a special mission.' On 27 March, Gibson was issued with 'most secret' written orders outlining a general plan of attack on unnamed German dams, and a week later was

Flt. Lt. 'Mutt' Summers of Vickers was a former A&EE pilot.

promoted to Wing Commander. Low-level flying practice then began with standard Lancasters fitted with two-stage amber screening to give the impression of dusk.

Towards the end of the first week in April, the first of the three modified Lancasters (ED765G), looking somewhat odd with gaping bomb bay and excresence of V-struts each side, was ready for test by Sam Brown, and after minor adjustments he flew it to Farnborough on 8 April for Vickers-Armstrong to fit the necessary equipment. Concurrently, the second machine, ED865/G was tested and delivered to Gibson at Scampton.

On the following day Wallis and Chadwick were anxiously concentrating on installation of the bomb in the Vickers-Armstrong hangar at Farnborough, followed by flying trials in the hands of the chief Vickers test pilot Mutt Summers, and next evening, with Wallis as passenger, he flew the Lancaster to Manston as the base for live trials at the Reculver range in the Thames Estuary.

Chadwick kept in close touch with the ensuing sequence of trials of the Wallis bomb, but his computer-like mind was also dealing with new complexities of design progress and policy for which he had the fullest support from Roy Dobson despite occasional intense arguments on pros and cons. While the bomb trials were in progress, his modified Lancaster Mk VI, known as the 'Universal Test Bed', arrived at the RAE for flight tests with a 2,600 lb static thrust Armstrong Siddeley ASX jet turbine mounted in the bomb bay, though still powered with four Merlin 20s. Within a few days he called at Ringway to check progress with a Lancaster II to which Metropolitan Vickers, in conjunction with Avro, was fitting their experimental F2/1 gas turbine in the tail.

But there was also a more ominous development. On 15 April the Prime Minister was informed by the Chiefs of Staff that the Germans were experimenting with long-range rockets.

Three days later Mutt Summers dropped the first three spherically cased mock-up bombs, two of which sank and the third broke from the wooden sheathing, leaving the cylindrical steel cylinder skipping along the surface. Consequently it was decided to use only the cylinders for the operational bomb. To confirm the behaviour Sam Brown, with Bob Handasyde of Vickers-Armstrong as second pilot, tried dropping a cylinder from low level and found that it shattered and sank. This seemed disaster because the attack on the dam was scheduled for a mere three weeks ahead when the reservoir of water would be at highest level. Wallis re-cast his calculations and found that if the bomb was released precisely at 60 ft height and some 30 mph slower then everything would work perfectly. A week later a fourth series of trials at Reculver proved he was right.

Meanwhile No 617 Squadron had been training hard, thundering around the Lake District at low level to the dismay of the inhabitants. None of them except Gibson yet knew the object, nor were they much enlightened when the first fully modified Lancaster, ED864/G, was delivered to the Squadron on 18 April. At the beginning of May, training transferred to the Eyebrook Reservoir just south of Uppingham, Rutland, and also by night at Colchester Reservoir. By then the 20 crews were working as highly skilled teams. Gibson confirmed to Wallis, who in turn told Chadwick, that he was entirely confident that the Squadron could carry out the bombing project. To ensure flying exactly at the requisite height, two lights were fitted so that their beams would converge on the water at exactly 60 ft.

* * *

On 12 May General von Arnim, Commander of the Axis forces in Tunis, was captured and the Italian First Army had surrendered. That same day, the final live drop of Wallis' bomb proved 'entirely satisfactory technically and tactically'. This was so near zero hour that two days later the Chiefs of Staff approved 'Operation Chastise', as it was now called, for an attack on the dams at the earliest opportunity. AV-M Cochrane immediately drove to Scampton and informed Gibson that the operation must

Practice Flight of Lancasters

take place next day, Sunday 16 May. Only then did the crews learn the objective of all their training. There was frenzied activity. All that afternoon the Lancasters were being made ready and armed with the cylindrical mines, using a lifting drill devised by Roy Chadwick with which the tail of the big bomber was raised by a 10 ton crane to a slight nose-down position so that the great bomb on a modified low-loader trailer could be pushed under the machine, winched into position, and the spinning drive connected.

Wallis had been warned of the forthcoming operation and shortly before 4 pm arrived at Scampton in a Red Cross Wellington, piloted by Mutt Summers, just in time for a quick word with Cochrane before he left with Gibson to discuss the draft operation. Two hours later Gibson returned and, with Wallis present, briefed all the aircraft captains. Next morning Roy Chadwick arrived, and he and Wallis spent an arduous afternoon checking the aircraft, their bombs, and bomb spinning installation. At 6 pm, amidst such tight security that nobody was allowed to leave the Station, there was a final briefing at which Wallis described techniques of the bomb, then Cochrane assured the crew that the raid would create tremendous damage and the operation become historic, and Gibson re-emphasised the operational details in which wave one of nine Lancasters would take off in formations of three at ten minute intervals to attack the Möhne, Eder, and Sorpe dams; wave two of five Lancasters would go to the Sorpe independently; and the third wave of five would take off 2½ hours later as airborne reserves. At 11 pm a red Very light signal was fired for the first two waves to start engines and taxi into position. Fifteen minutes later came the green light for take-off. Darkly illuminated by a misty full moon, Gibson and his Flight thundered into the distance and vanished.

An hour and more slowly dragged by. In the Group Operations Room at Scampton, Air Marshal Harris and AV-M Cochrane and their staffs, with Wallis and Chadwick in the background, were tensely awaiting the coded Morse signals spelling success or failure. At last came the code word 'Gonner', signifying a bomb dropped without result. Three more followed at long intervals. Clearly the whole thing was a failure. Wallis was deeply concerned. Suddenly the Morse began again, and with a yell of excitement the Signals Officer spelled 'Nigger', the code word for success. There was a stunned moment of silence — then jubilation!

But in the skies above Germany, Gibson

The fractured Möhne Dam.

was curbing the R/T chatter, for there were still three other dams to attack. Below him the waters of the Möhne were surging down the valley from the great breach that had been made. He called in the reserve Lancasters and headed for the Eder, and there at the third attempt chunks of masonry were hurled into the air and the water gushed out in a tidal wave. Concurrently, the second wave of Lancasters was attacking the earth dam at Sorpe but failed to breach it. In the meantime, the third wave had taken off from Scampton and, finding that the Möhne and Eder Dams had been breached, attacked the subsidiary targets of the Lister and Diemel Dams.

In ones and twos, eleven of the nineteen Lancasters returned. The others had crashed with loss of all crews except one man who parachuted from the only Lancaster destroyed over the Möhne. The damage inflicted on the Ruhr was apparent in all its ghastly nature next morning when reconnaissance Mosquitos took photographs. Huge floods inundated 50 miles of countryside. Power stations, factories, railway lines, bridges, and a thousand or so houses and farms were destroyed or damaged. German casualties amounted to some 1,300; thousands more were made homeless, arable land rendered useless, and more than 6,000 animals were drowned. The crucial question was whether the war potential had been vitally damaged — but at least Wallis's theory had been vindicated.

The daily Press on 18 May dramatically flaunted the story of 'The Dam Busters'. Their exploits were lauded all over the world and particularly in the USA. On 23 May, Wing Cdr Gibson was awarded the VC for bravery in circling low over the Möhne Dam for 30 minutes under heavy flak, following his own opening attack, in order to supervise the rest of the Lancasters and draw enemy fire from them. The thirty-four other participators variously received the DSO, DFC, DFM, and Conspicuous Gallantry Medal. Wallis refused a Knighthood but accepted a CBE, and Roy Chadwick, who had regarded his key participation in modifying the Lancasters as merely part and parcel of his vigorous war effort, was gratified to be similarly awarded a CBE but typically stressed that the honour was not his alone, but that each of his large staff had an equal share because it was their work which had made the great 'Operation Chastise' so successful.

That night, Wallis wrote to him: 'I deeply appreciate all the work which you and your assistants have done, and to you personally in special degree was given the making or breaking of this enterprise, for if at that fateful meeting in CRD's office on 26 February, you had declared the task impossible to fulfil in the given time, the powers of opposition were so great that I should never have got instructions to go ahead. Possibly you did not realise how much hung on your instantaneous reaction, but I can assure you that I nearly had heart failure until you decided to join in the great adventure. You yourself said it would be a miracle if we completed the work in time, and I think the whole thing is one of the most amazing examples of team-work and co-operation in the whole of the history of the war. May I offer you my very deep thanks for the existence of your wonderful Lancaster, for it was the only aircraft in the world capable of doing the job, and I should like to pay my tribute of congratulations and admiration to you, the designer.'

* * *

That epic was a fleeting interlude for both designers. They were immensely busy with other projects — Wallis with bigger blockbusting bombs; Chadwick with the 120 ft span Lancaster replacement he had schemed which now had to accord with the currently issued B14/43 specification, and was designated Avro 694 — later known as the Lincoln. Though larger and more powerful than its predecessor, it incorporated many Lancaster parts including the tail unit with enlarged rudders, and to speed production, mushroom-headed rivets would replace flush rivetting despite the increased drag, though with four R-R 1750 hp Merlin 85 engines the same speed as the Lancaster was expected and the vital ceiling would be 3,000 ft higher. Soon there was an exciting break of routine for Roy's investiture at Buckingham Palace on 22 June, with Mary Chadwick and daughter Margaret attending the ceremony. It so happened that the King was inspecting his troops in North West Africa and Malta, having left England on 10 June aboard *Ascalon,* piloted by Grp Capt Fielden, Captain of the King's Flight. The Queen therefore took his place to award the honours and decorations. The *Daily Mail* reported: 'She stood for two hours smiling and shaking hands with a procession of nearly 300 men and women. But it was the day of the "Dam Busters". Wing Commander Gibson was the first to step up to get the VC and a bar to his DSO. The Queen told him that the King had asked her to say he was sorry he could not be there. Then, hatless and with a spray of roses pinned on her beige frock, the Queen decorated the 33 other RAF men as they followed Gibson. With them at the Palace was Mr Roy Chadwick, head of the team of designers who created the Lancaster. He received the CBE for his services to British aviation. The first to congratulate him was Wing Commander Gibson and a number of his pilots who had flown in the raid.'

That evening, A. V. Roe & Co, with Tom Sopwith, Chairman of the Group as host, gave a celebratory dinner for No. 617 Squadron at London's Hungaria Restaurant. With typical Chadwick humour, the menu

Wing Cdr. Guy Penrose Gibson VC with Roy Chadwick CBE.

card was headed 'Damn Busters'. The *Daily Mail* reported: 'Conversation inevitably turned to the RAF's latest exploit of the Lancaster raid on Friedrichshaven on Sunday night, and so to the part Mr Chadwick played in the first raid on that German town far back on 21 November, 1914.' In very different circumstance on the current occasion, fifty-four Lancasters of No 5 Group, led by four Pathfinders equipped with the newly developed H_2S position indicators, had attacked the former Zeppelin Works where vital radar scanning equipment was being produced, and because it was impossible to travel that distance and return in the short hours of darkness, they had flown on to North Africa, and on the night of 23 June bombed the Italian Naval Base at Spezia before flying back to Britain next day

Among those looking after the guests at the Avro party was Sam Brown. Tragedy followed. His son Alan was expected home on leave. Instead came the ever-dreaded telegram saying 'missing, believed killed.' In fact he had finished his tour of operations, but one pilot had reported ill for the next night's raid so he volunteered to take his place and was shot down over Germany and all the crew were killed.

Lancaster with Metro-Vick gas turbine in tail.

With quiet resolution Sam carried on with testing more and more Lancasters, but without sense of revenge, for he knew only too well what German parents would feel when they lost their own sons in this havoc of war. On 29 June he flew the Lancaster II which Chadwick had revised for tests of the latest version of the Metropolitan Vickers F2/1 gas turbine which had been mounted in the tail in similar fashion to that of the Lancaster prototype BT308 with which the RAE at Farnborough were still experimenting. Development of such jets could not be rushed, so for the moment there was time for reflection, and Chadwick took brief opportunity of consolidating his health with a week's holiday in July, accompanied by Mary and their daughters.

Shortly before leaving for Anglesey, Chadwick had been visited by Wallis to discuss the possibility of carrying a still bigger load than the 9,000 lb dam-busting bomb, and after much consideration of graphs and calculations, they decided that 20,000 lbs was feasible. Wallis explained that Bomber Command had agreed he should design a shock-wave deep penetration bomb of that size to destroy the rocket base which reconnaissance had discovered at Peenemunde on the Baltic coast. A few days after returning Chadwick received clearance to design an adaptation of the Lancaster to carry this bomb, but not until early September was a contract issued for A. V. Roe & Co to apply these modifications to 14 Lancasters of 617 Squadron. Soon afterwards Wallis was told that his bomb no longer had priority because an attack on Peenemunde by 600 bombers in mid-August had shattered the establishment and the Germans were now preparing dispersal sites for mobile rocket-launching equipment. He was therefore instructed to design a scaled down penetration bomb of 12,000 lb which was 22½ ft long and code-named 'Tallboy', and the eventual 22,000 lb bomb was designated 'Grand Slam'.

Of even greater importance was the airborne H_2S radar system developed by the Telecommunications Research Establishment directed by the astronomer-scientist Bernard Lovell for it enabled accurate pin-pointing of targets beyond the range of ground-based electronic navigational aids of Gee and Oboe, and crucially implemented the lethal nature of Air Marshal Harris' widespread bombing campaign to destroy the industrial resources of Germany. But the success of H_2S also depended on the technical ability of Britain's aircraft designers to install it effectively.

Sir Bernard told me: 'When I first met Chadwick in the Spring of 1942 at the Avro Works in north Manchester, I did not expect a pleasant encounter since I had to persuade him to design a large cupola to protrude underneath the belly of his beautiful

Lancaster bomber. I had already faced Mr Handley Page with the same problem. He had raged and said it would spoil the performance of his bomber, and was reluctant to do anything until informed from high level that it was better to drop a few bombs in the right place rather than waste the entire load — which had so far been the case. Chadwick's reaction was entirely different. He was anxious to help so that his Lancasters could operate with maximum efficiency, and he had the wisdom to realise that maximum altitude and speed were only part of the equation of getting the bombs on to the assigned target, so the meeting which I had expected to be a stormy one turned out to be calm and helpful. I gave him the details and had no doubt that before long he would have a Lancaster modified as we desired.

'In late October 1942 we met again — not in his office, but at Ringway where this Lancaster was waiting for our test installation of the H_2S scanner mounted in his perspex cupola just forward of the bomb bay. Meanwhile development of our equipment had received many setbacks, of which the worst was the crash of our experimental Halifax bomber on 7 June 1942 with tragic loss of several members of my small group and of the team from EMI who had the job of manufacturing the equipment. Notwithstanding this disaster and loss of all our flight testing installation, Churchill demanded that we equip two Squadrons by that Autumn — though this did not affect Chadwick because it had been decided in midsummer that the H_2S should have priority for the Halifax and Stirling squadrons of the Pathfinder Force, and eventually the first use was on the night of 30-31 January 1943 in the attack on Hamburg.

'Already the Stirling bombers were being phased out in favour of the Lancaster, which became our dominant interest and soon a considerable number were equipped with our early H_2S, but that worked on a wavelength of 9 cms. When in August, Bomber Command mounted somewhat unsuccessful attacks on Berlin and suffered heavy losses, it became an urgent requirement that the Pathfinder Force should be able to mark the target from an altitude well above the operational ceiling of the Halifax and Stirling aircraft. Our reply was to ask for six Lancasters which we equipped with a high definition H_2S working on 3 cm that we then had under development. The decision was made in mid-September. We equipped and tested the aircraft from our aerodrome at Defford in Worcestershire. Before the end of November these H_2S aircraft were marking precise targets in Berlin from an altitude of 28,000 ft and in this way the Lancasters using our special equipment played an unique role in guiding the main bomber force to these distant targets.

'Chadwick had accommodated our ungainly device skilfully and without fuss or complaint, and it soon became production line equipment. Thirty years later I visited an aerodrome where a Lancaster equipped with H_2S was still in flying condition. The slender aircraft looked elegant with a particular beauty which Chadwick had created, and I remembered with pleasure and gratitude my contacts with him in those perilous years of 1942 and 1943.'

Relentlessly Bomber Command continued its attacks on industrial Germany. To meet the ever-changing requirements, Chadwick had to keep track of a host of modifications and experimental trials to increase armament, range, or bomb load — though the Lancaster needed no basic changes throughout its life. In every bomber Squadron, pilots and aircrews sang its praises, and maintenance crews were delighted by its serviceability and lack of problems.

However the intense Lancaster production had its effect on the York. Only three had been completed because of the enormous priority demand on Rolls-Royce for Merlin engines. Consequently a trial installation of the 1,650 hp radial Bristol Hercules IV was tested on the original prototype LV626. Flown in October by Sam Brown, it was soon apparent that the changed nacelle shape had reduced the directional stability, necessitating fitment of a central fin in the manner of the Manchester, and this was retained for the Merlin-powered production aircraft, but no

Ultimate Lancaster production at Chadderton was 150 per month.

further Hercules York C.Mk 2s were built.

The possibility of building Yorks in Canada, powered with Packard Merlin engines had potential, so in October it was decided to fly in one of the production machines across the Atlantic to visit Victory Aircraft Ltd at Malton, Ontario where the Packard-powered Lancaster B Mk.X was in full production.

A *Daily Mail* reporter was present when the York returned on 12 November, and next day his paper announced: 'Britain's giant 56-seater passenger plane, the Avro York, crossed the Atlantic on her return flight at an average airspeed of 213 mph in 10 hrs 25 mins for the west-east trip from Montreal. Mr R. H. Dobson, managing director of A. V. Roe, told me: "We originally set out from the North of England. Our party included Mr Frank Spriggs (our chairman), Mr Roy Chadwick, high ranking officials and the only woman in the party — young Mrs Alfred Steward, whose husband had gone to Canada as technical adviser on our production plant there.

' "The York was one of the earliest of her type to come off our assembly lines, and had been flown only about 3½ hours, and that included testing. She took off as smoothly as a feather and we all sat back and congratulated ourselves on the comfort. Although the temperature was 20 degrees below freezing, the atmosphere inside the York was cosy. As this was my first trans-Atlantic crossing, I kept a log of the two-way journey. On the way over she was adapted to 12 seats and 8 beds. I sat at the controls for a few minutes, just to get the feel of her. She impressed me by her lightness of touch and was very easy to handle. On the return journey we saw little because we took off at midnight and flew most of the time in darkness. Two high ranking officers were with us. One turned in as soon as we left, and when he woke up said it was the most comfortable sleep he had ever had in 21 trans-Atlantic flights." '

In fact, Dobson and Chadwick had been away for a month, and after arriving in Canada on 10 October had immediately flown on to Washington for high level discussion. Next morning Roy Chadwick had written to his 13-year-old daughter, Rosemary, affectionately nicknamed 'Osie': 'I arrived here last night and have spent a very entertaining day — perhaps after the war I will be able to bring you to see this delightful city. This picture shows our hotel at the Connecticut Avenue entrance to the Rock Creek and Potomac Parks. Much love to you and Mummy and Margaret.' Six days later, she received another postcard: "I am writing this to you whilst in the aeroplane flying from Los Angeles to San Fransisco. The countryside is a wonderful sight in the sunset. I am very well, and enjoying my tour very much.'

Of the import of all the discussions, nothing has been recorded; but Chadwick and Dobson certainly enlarged their experience by going to every major aircraft manufacturer in the USA and studying the latest developments of aircraft techniques and research, as well as methods of production. Their visit to the Consolidated-Vultee Aircraft Corporation in San Diego was particularly enlightening, for Chadwick was privileged to see a civil version of the Liberator being constructed with a capacious airline fuselage which had a central fin and rudder instead of the previous tailplane tip fins that were similar to the Lancaster's. Perhaps the American design influenced Chadwick's thoughts, for on return to England he continued his earlier investigation of a large civil aircraft designated Avro 688, based on the far from complete Lincoln bomber, and drew it with capacious circular section fuselage and a large central fin and rudder instead of the twins of his recent designs. Passenger comfort would be paramount, so he proposed to instal the Normalair pressure system which he had schemed for the now abandoned stratospheric Avro 684 bomber project. Discussions with the Brabazon Committee and the relevant Air Ministry technicans soon followed, with a view to securing an MAP contract. That in itself would take many weeks and must depend upon a favourable trend in hostilities.

Preparations were being mounted for a final great offensive against the Germans. Churchill arrived at Alexandria in HMS *Renown* on 21 November for a Cairo Conference with Roosevelt and the combined Chiefs of Staff. Six days later they flew by different routes to meet Marshal Stalin at Teheran, and on 1 December, the three national leaders initiated a document stating that Operation *Overlord*, the liberation of France, would begin in May, 1944.

That of course was kept secret, nor did civilians know that air photographs at Peenemunde revealed small pilotless aircraft on a launching ramp, or that the many missile sites on the French north coast were evidence that Britain soon would be attacked by flying bombs. Meanwhile, production of Lancasters remained paramount; but Anson construction also continued unabated at five Canadian firms as well as A. V. Roe & Co where Chadwick was revising this machine as Mk 11 with high cabin and hydraulic operation of landing flaps and undercarriage. A Mk 12 was already visualised with still more powerful A-S Cheetah engines and variable pitch propellers to cope with an all-up weight now 50 per cent greater than original.

Chapter 14
War and Aftermath

January 1944 opened with lethal bombing attacks on Berlin and Hamburg but also provided a hint of more peaceful purpose, for in the experimental shop at Woodford a Lancaster still in war-paint was having the gun turrets and war-like equipment removed, and the nose and tail were being elegantly streamlined. Re-named Lancastrian and referenced Avro 691, it was registered as G-AGJI, and delivered on 20 January to the Development Flight of the British Overseas' Airways Corporation (BOAC) based at Hurn so that equipment and guidance systems for post-war airliners could be tested under operating conditions. BOAC was also negotiating for release of five Yorks though production was only three per month, and now urged the Air Ministry to put the Lancastrian into production as a civil airliner or freighter. Concurrently TCA of Canada were using the similar derivative of the Lancaster X built by Victory Aircraft as trans-Atlantic 10-seaters with an extended range of 4,000 miles. On 3 March, one of these machines set up a west-bound record from Prestwick to Montreal of 12 hrs 59 mins,

Interior of Lancastrian. (Quick).

carrying nearly two tons of mail and freight and four passengers.

Later that month Chadwick received Air Ministry Specification 29/43, consolidating the many discussions he had had with their technicians to establish a 4-engined airliner of similar all-up weight and disposable load as

The Avro 691 Lancastrian I had a still air range of 4000 miles and carried nine passengers.

the Lancaster VII, but with a range of 4,000 miles — which was even greater than that of the prototype Lincoln now taking form at Ringway. He was sure that his original idea of a Lancaster conversion could be much improved, so he departed from the well-proven mid-wing of the bomber and shoulder-wing arrangement of the York and made his machine a low-winger like the Douglas airliner series so that the spar could run under the cabin floor and thus avoid obstructing the accommodation. However so great was the pressure to complete the Lincoln design that only a small group could be spared to proceed with the design study of this new Avro 668, later known as the Tudor. As he discovered in April, George Volkert of Handley Page Ltd was designing an almost identical civil version of the Halifax, but was similarly short of draughtsmen and had sub-contracted the single fin empennage to the DO of Avro's old Yorkshire rival, Blackburn Aircraft Ltd.

Certainly A. V. Roe & Co was leading the way with BOAC, for the Corporation had soon been successful in securing the five 12-seater Avro Yorks, and on 22 April Dobson and Chadwick experienced the reflected glory when the first of these machines inaugurated the official route to Morocco via Cairo. From there, great loads of accumulated stores were being uplifted to Calcutta by Armstrong Whitworth Ensigns for onward transmission to Burma where the Japanese had opened a new offensive, and it was for this theatre of war that the new Lincolns were primarily intended.

Throughout these recent months there were many schemes for development of the Lancaster to meet the ever-changing necessities of war. To back up the American strategic bombing of Japan, Chadwick envisaged fitting saddle tanks of 1,200 gallon capacity on top of the fuselage, and two Lancasters were put through their paces with mock-ups fitted: but the scheme was eventually dropped in favour of refuelling from tanker aircraft — and that required close co-operation with Sir Alan Cobham's Flight Refuelling Ltd in designing appropriate modification of the Lancaster fuel system.

Bigger and better armament and bomb load capacity had taken much of Chadwick's attention throughout the war, and currently a Lancaster III was fitted with a special Bristol turret mounting two 20mm cannon, and was flown early in May. Successful handling and gun-firing trials resulting in orders for 250 designated Lancaster IV, which would be built by Vickers Armstrong. In turn that led to further trials with remotely controlled 20mm cannon in dorsal and ventral barbettes. The swift development of offensive and

The Lincoln became the RAF's post-war bomber, equipping 20 Squadrons.

defensive radar and associated radio had become a study in itself yet was only a small part of the many facets which Chadwick had to understand in order to supervise a comprehensive design section on electronics responsible for the installation of such curiously named devices as Gee, Oboe G-H, IFF, H_2S ASV, ECM, as well as the constantly improving inter-com and radio sets. One of the remarkable things about Chadwick was the way he kept track of everything that was going on, yet could dream up new types of aeroplanes by way of recreation!

But everything was overwhelmed on 6 June by D-Day, preceded by 5,000 tons of bombs dropped on enemy coastal batteries while 4,000 transport ships and small craft set out for the Normandy beaches, and Allied aircraft flew nearly 15,000 sorties to keep the Luftwaffe at bay. Soon the beach-head was firmly established.

By then the impressive 120 ft span Avro 694 Lincoln prototype had been completed at Ringway, and piloted by Sam Brown with Bill Thorn alongside, made its initial flight on 9 June. The handling, said Sam, was every bit as good as the Lancaster. Chadwick gave a sigh of relief. However, subsequent flights showed that good could be bettered by fitting larger trim tabs to the rudder in order to reduce the footload when two engines on one side were cut. After performance tests and dives had been completed, a special Glenn Martin mid-upper turret from the USA was fitted, and this splendid machine, numbered PW925, was flown to Boscombe Down for Service trials. Meanwhile, a preliminary contract for 162 aircraft was established with A. V. Roe & Co, soon followed by an order for 200 from Armstrong Whitworth.

To keep England well aware that Germany still had aggressive teeth, the first V-1 flying bombs were launched on 11 June — but three exploded in mid air, four fell back near the launching site, and the other three went off-course, but next day at dawn the first flying bomb fell in Britain at Swanscombe near Gravesend, and a few minutes later another dropped at Cuckfield, Essex, and a third killed six people and injured nine at London's Bethnal Green. From now on the distinctive sound of the rocket, and its ominous cut into silence preceding an explosion, became increasingly familiar. Thus between the nights of the 15th and 16th, 144 V-1s dropped over a wide area between Kent and Suffolk, and though 21 were shot down by fighters or anti-aircraft guns, 73 reached London. By the 17th they were arriving at nearly 100 every 24 hours.

That same day, Margaret Chadwick married John Dove of the Merchant Navy at St. Ann's Church in the ancient square of Deansgate in Manchester — and in their honour the bells were rung for the first time since war was declared, for they had long been silent because the earlier intention was to use them as a signal if the country became invaded; but that threat was over at last. Within a few days it was back to their tasks for the young couple: John to the menace of submarine and aircraft attack; Margaret to the Avro canteen at Wythenshaw where she had worked since 1940.

Shortly before the wedding Roy Chadwick had received notification from the University of Manchester that a special Honorary Degree day would be held on Saturday, 1 July, to celebrate his work and award him an Honorary Master of Science Degree. In the University's great Assembly Hall that day, the Principal of the University, proclaimed: 'Mr Vice-Chancellor: I present to you the

The Manchester College of Technology where young Chadwick first studied is now part of the present University.

composer of one of our more vehement protests against Nazi aggression — the designer of the Lancaster bomber. He has helped to make sure of two things. First that the authors of the most savage and abominable tyranny in human history should experience within their own borders the kind of havoc they chose to let loose on us. Second, that the gallant men who are given the hard task of destroying that tyranny should have in their hands an instrument worthy of their courage and skill.

'The whole story of the conception, creation, and full operation of the Lancaster bomber has still to be told. We hope that by the time it is told, the inventive genius of the Lancaster's designer will be directed to the task of peace, and that there he will have the greatest success, as in tackling the grim problems of war. Mr Vice-Chancellor: On behalf of the University, I present to you Roy Chadwick for the degree of Master of Science, *Honoris Causa.*'

By now Roy knew that the Air Ministry proposed to back the Tudor airliner, so a special design section had been set up and a few detailed drawings were already being issued to the shops. More immediateley urgent was adaptation of a Lancaster I, No. PD328, for investigatory long-range navigation flights — and in in working days of 24 hours, the Avro repair depot at Waddington excelled itself by stripping paint from fuselage and wings and polishing them to a silvery brightness, fitting streamlined Lancastrian nose and tail sections, installing supplementary tanks in nose and bomb bay, and substituting a Lincoln undercarriage. Named *Aries,* it was then delivered to the Empire Air Navigation School at Shawbury after brief tests by the Avro pilots. Concurrently, several Anson Mk 11s were being completed as ambulances with port wing root fillet ingeniously hinged so that stretchers could be pushed into the cabin, and the first of these machines was flown on 30 July. By then, plans had been completed for production of a more refined version of the Canadian Lancastrians, revised by Chadwick as the Avro 691 C Mk 2, for which an order for 33 supplemented the earlier contract of 23 Mk 1s.

* * *

Overwhelming everything was the progress of war. From the consolidated beachheads of Normandy the British and American forces had steadily advanced. On 13 August Hitler authorised retreat of his troops across the Seine between Paris and Le Havre. Two days later, Allied landings in southern France began in which some 9,000 airborne troops participated. Winston Churchill, who had flown out to Naples in his Avro York, watched the landings in St. Tropez Bay from the British destroyer *Kimberley*, and subsequently it was announced that General Dwight Eisenhower had taken over personal command of the Allied Expeditionary Force and was directing operations in France. On the 23rd, Paris was liberated.

'Except possibly for a few last shots, the Battle of London in over,' Duncan Sandys declared to the Press on 7 September. During the past 80 days the enemy had launched over 8,000 flying bombs, of which 2,300 fell in the London region, but so able was the defence that 70 per cent were being brought down and only 9 per cent reached London. But Sandys had been wrong. Next day at dusk, the first German V-2 rockets exploded in Chiswick, killing two and injuring ten. A few seconds later another dropped at Epping.

For those at A. V. Roe & Co there was different tragedy. In the late afternoon of Monday, 11 September, came a telephone call to Woodford Airfield Control, reporting that a 4-engined aircraft, believed to be a Lancaster, had crashed near Siddington, some eight miles away. The only machine on test at that time was a Lancaster III piloted by Sam Brown's third assistant, Sid Gleave. Sam and Sandy Jack rushed to a car and raced to the scene. 'On arrival,' recollected Sandy Jack,' we found on top of a broad hillock in open ground a large crater which had four holes in which were embedded the engines, and small fragments of wreckage were scattered over a wide area. Without doubt it was our Lanc.' The impact had been too tremendous even to leave trace of the two-man crew, for the Lancaster had been making the customary dive to 375 mph as a check on every 10th machine. Judging by the trail of wreckage, the pilot had been unable to pull out throught malfunctioning of the controls or structural failure. It seemed a repetition of the tragic crash in the Spring of 1942 at Boscombe Down. Everyone was devastated because of their close personal link with Gleave and his engineer Barnes.

Chadwick was deeply concerned that other Lancasters might be at risk. Harold Rogerson was put in charge of an enquiry. The ground was searched for clues, and presently revealed an indication that the elevators might have lost their fabric covering. That the pilot may have pulled out too hard could be dismissed because at high speed the elevators were fairly heavy and required a touch of trimmer to effect recovery. A week later two small doors were found by two children and immediately identified as jettison valve compartment covers from the wing, and must have been torn off under high 'g'. Immediate action followed to modify the doors of every Lancaster in service and fit intermediate wooden ribs in every elevator.

Meanwhile the events of war had been crowding fast. The Allied forces were fighting on Reich territory. A huge airborne attempt to capture the bridges at Arnhem in Holland using more than 4,000 aircraft, including 500 gliders, failed with heavy casualties; but there was encouraging news that a Flight of specially modified Lancasters carrying Wallis's latest Tallboy 12,000 lb bombs was operating from Russia and had managed to partially damage the German battleship *Tirpitz* moored in Norway's Altenfjord. Everywhere Bomber Command and the U.S. Army AirForce were raining bombs down on German oil refineries, factories and airfields, but during a Lancaster attack on Munchen-Gladbach on the night 19 September, Wing Commander Gibson VC was killed. Sad though that was to Chadwick and many another, September ended on an encouraging note for A. V. Roe & Co with a confirmed Air Ministry order for two prototype Avro 688 Tudors powered with four 1750 hp R-R Merlin 102 engines.

The arrival of Winston Churchill in Moscow by air on 9 October for discussion with Marshal Stalin was also a hopeful sign that victory might be sight, reaffirmed two days later when King George flew in a Dakota to Holland to visit the Western Front. A great daylight attack on Duisburg with over 1,000 bombers escorted by 300 fighters followed on the 14th. Hamburg, Essen, Cologne, Bremen, Dortmund, Berlin — nowhere was safe. To those in England, it all seemed a blur of events. Of more personal interest to the Avro team was news that the Lancaster *Aries* equipped with a ton of the latest navigational aids, had taken off from Shawbury on the first stage of an attempt to circumnavigate the world. The results of this arduous testing would have considerable impact on the type of navigational equipment to be fitted to the Tudor.

Following a sequence of discussions between BOAC and Chadwick during the past two months an MOS order for fourteen more of these airliners was placed in November. That at least was encouraging, particularly as it gave A. V. Roe & Co a considerable lead over the similiar Handley Page Hermes which was only at the mock-up stage at Cricklewood, whereas in the Avro Experimental Shop some of the circular fuselage formers for the Tudor were already being assembled.

Further success also came to the Lancasters of Nos 9 and 617 Squadrons after returning from Russia to Lossiemouth, Scotland, for a renewed attack by 21 machines on the battleship *Tirpitz* which had transferred to Tromso Fjord, this time three of their huge 12,000 lb Tallboy bombs made direct hits, and the great battleship capsized with loss of more than half her 1,900 crew.

Everywhere the German cities were now a scene of devastation — but nor had rocket attacks on Britain diminished despite hundreds of sorties flown between 15 October and 25 November by the USA Second Tactical AirForce and 600 by Fighter

Command in an attempt to detect and destroy suspected rocket sites. However, December introduced a sense of relaxation among the British population when Herbert Morrison, the Home Secretary, announced that because most of the attacks on Britain were now being made by pilotless aircraft or missiles, the 'black-out' of lights could forthwith be reduced to a 'dim-out'.

Mid-December also marked the triumphant return of the Lancaster *Aries* on completing its global circumnavigation via San Fransisco to New Zealand and return via Ceylon, Cairo and Malta to Scampton. But that was not the end of its navigational career. More flights were planned for the following year.

At Manchester, Roy Chadwick and his wife were preparing Christmas with the happier feeling that the New Year might well bring the end of hostilities, but on the morning of Christmas Eve there was harsh reminder of the dangers when several squadrons of Heinkel He 111 bombers escaped British fighter vigilance and flew low across the North Sea to the vicinity of Hull and then released 40 or more V-1 flying bombs targeted on Manchester, creating considerable tension because of the unmistakeable noise of their approach and the silence preceding explosion. Damage was extensive and there were numerous casualites, leaving the Mancunians with the presentiment that another attack might occur at any moment — but in fact it was the last.

The Anson 652A had civil and RAF application.

* * *

The New Years Honours of 1945 rewarded Roy Dobson's 'outstanding services to aviation' with a knighthood. Lancaster production was currently an amazing 150 a month. By now he was controlling a floor area of over 6,000,000 sq ft in 22 factories, employing 40,000 men and women. Full Lincoln production had also been established at Armstrong Whitworth and Metropolitan-Vickers in addition to the 162 aircraft being built at Manchester. Initial deliveries were targeted for mid-summer.

By late January, General Eisenhower had pushed the Germans from the bulge in the Allied line and the Russians had moved deep into Eastern Germany. In the Far East, the Burma Road to China had re-opened. In this more hopeful atmosphere, the British aircraft industry felt freer to concentrate on the post-war world of the Brabazon design proposals, though that in no way disturbed the great flow of military aircraft from every factory. Chadwick's Anson team had been revising one of the Mk 12s, MG159, to meet the Brabazon XIX feeder-line specification as a 9-seater with the cabin fenestrated by five Perspex ovals each side. Flown early in January, it was handed over to the Associated Airways Joint Committee as G-AGNI on the 23rd for evaluation on BOAC's proposed internal air routes. Because of its Brabazon reference number, this machine and its production version somewhat misleadingly became known as the Avro 'Nineteen'.

But more significant things were happening. On 29 January, Winston Churchill left Northolt for Malta in the special Douglas DC-4 Skymaster which was presented to him by General Arnold, Chief of the US Army Air Force. President Roosevelt arrived at the island by sea on 2 February, and that night he and Churchill flew in separate aircraft to Saki airfield in the Crimea to confer with Marshal Stalin at Yalta. The arrangements were far more complex than contemporary accounts suggest. British and American delegations alone numbered some 700 people, and the organisation involved not only a ship to convey the advance party of the British contingent but also extensive air transport services by the RAF from 21 January to 17 February.

The pilot of one of the several Avro Yorks recollected: 'On 31 January we set course in the early evening for Malta where we anxiously awaited another York carrying high-ranking officer passengers which had left after us. Several hours passed, then a signal came saying it had crashed into the sea off the island of Lampedusa to the west of Malta. Only five passengers survived. Aircraft connected with the operation were constantly arriving and were parked either side of the tarmac, the British with a medley of Yorks, Liberators, and smaller aircraft, all looking like war-scarred battle-wagons in their camouflage paint, but the Americans were spick and span with Skymasters in gleaming silver.

'Next day, loaded with delegates, we all left for Saki, flying through cloud and rain above mountainous terrain, but as darkness gave way to dawn we reached the Crimea corridor and let down to our snow-covered destination. Sometime later the VIP aircraft arrived overhead, making an impressive sight with the President's fighter escort of Lockheed Lightnings in close formation around his special Skymaster. After disembarking the VIPs, their aircraft were marshalled away from the others and segregated by strict Russian security, and we watched the Russian top brass in their fur Cossack hats welcoming visitors, with Stalin himself there to meet the President and Mr Churchill. When at last the Conference at Yalta ended we flew to Hassani airfield at Athens to re-fuel and were parked near to Churchill's Skymaster and Eden's York.'

In fact Churchill had flown there from Saki on the 14th and next day flew to Alexandria for lunch with President Roosevelt, who was returning from the Yalta Conference in an American cruiser. This was their last meeting. That same night, the Americans gave the *coup de grace* to Dresden, following a raid by Bomber Command the previous night. A holocaust of fires ensued, devastating 1,600 acres and killing or disabling some 30,000 people, allegedly to help the Russians because Dresden was the centre for communications with German forces on the southern sectors of the Eastern Front.

Bomb power had enormously increased. The capacious bomb bay of the Lancaster had been adapted time and again to take a variety of bombs, such as a 4,000 lb 'cookie', three 1,000 pounders, twelve 250 pounders plus six incendiaries, and easily carried the 12,000 lb Tallboy which had proved so effective in penetrating railway tunnels, submarine pens, and the flying bomb concrete launching sites. Chadwick had also been engineering a further adaptation in which the bomb doors were removed and the fuselage floor lifted and arched so that a 22,000 lb Grand Slam torpedo-like Wallis penetration bomb could be slung externally underneath, and several of No 617's Lancasters were being modified for that purpose. While this was underweigh the first of the production Lancastrians, G-AGLF, intended as an interim type for BOAC's Australian routes, achieved its C of A on 7 February and was handed over to the Corporation Development Flight at Hurn, and the next, named *Nelson*, was delivered on 9 March.

Five days later the first two of the 25 ft long, 10 ton Grand Slam bombs were delivered to 617 Squadron and fitted to their specially strengthened, more powerful Lancaster B1 bombers. On the night on the 14th, in a very long run, they took off in company with the rest of the Squadron, which had Tallboys, and droned through the night to Germany where Sq Ldr Calder hit their target, the Beilefeld railway viaduct, with his Grand Slam which penetrated the ground for some 100 ft and in a tremendous explosion wrecked two of the arches. Next day more bombs were delivered to the Squadron and used on 19 March to destroy the viaduct at Arnsberg. In the following week the remaining three bridges over the Rhine were similarly destroyed — coinciding with the last bombs dropped on England by a piloted German aircraft, and on the 28th the last flying bomb to arrive over Britain was destroyed near Sittingbourne.

Events were moving fast. On 12 April, Roosevelt died and Harry Truman became President. Meanwhile, bombs were hurtling onto the principal cities of Japan. It seemed significant that despite the intense atmosphere of war, the Ministry of Supply in April increased BOAC's allocation of Tudors from 14 to 20. By then, the prototype was in the final stages of assembly, with the beautifully streamlined fuselage mounted on the wings and the engines in process of being installed.

On the 25th, the Russians completed their encirclement of Berlin. Three days later, Mussolini and his mistress were captured while trying to escape to the Swiss Frontier and were shot dead. On 29 April, Hitler and his Eva Braun committed suicide in the air-raid shelter under the Chancellory in Berlin. The German news communiqué stated that the Berlin garrison 'herded in a very narrow space, is defending itself heroically against the enemy's mass onslaught'. In occupied Italy, German envoys signed unconditional terms of surrender, and the war in that country ended with capture of a million Germans. In the Far East, the United States Air Force continued heavily attacking the airfields of Japan.

Germany's powers of defence were virtually at an end, and Admiral Donitz, who had succeeded Hitler, sought surrender terms from Field Marshal Montgomery. On 7 May the agreement for total and unconditional surrender was signed at General Eisenhower's

The Tudor I at Woodford ready for first flight. (Signed by Sam Brown, Bill Thorn, Roy Dobson, Ted Fielden, Roy Chadwick).

headquarters near Rheims. Next day in the House of Commons Winston Churchill announced the German surrender — but it engendered more a sense of relief than wild jubilation.

* * *

For any designer, the special successes of his aeroplane gives a personal sense of gratification, so for Roy Chadwick there was certainly satisfaction when BOAC, operating jointly with Qantas, inaugurated the east-bound service to Australia with their Lancastrian G-AGLV, which left Hurn, near

After the flight: A. Stewart, Bill Thorn, Ted Fielding, J. Orrell and Jack Dobson.

Bournemouth, on 31 May, and on 2 June the first west-bound machine, G-AGLS, left Sydney for England. But overwhelming all other matters was the maiden flight of the silver bright Avro Tudor prototype G-AGPF on 14 June. To Sam Brown's intense disappointment, he was prevented from Captaining because he had failed his last medical through anomalous blood pressure, so the task fell to that experienced pair, Bill Thorn and Jimmy Orrell. To emphasise his confidence in this attractive-looking new airliner, and as a mark of respect to the two test pilots and their flight engineer, Roy Chadwick joined in as observer, keen as ever to discover how every one of his new designs flew. As it had standard Lincoln wings and the centrally finned tail was conventional, there was no reason to doubt that the Tudor would fly as perfectly as his twin-finned bombers.

There were the usual preliminaries. Sam Brown watched the proceedings, and Teddy Fielding with Alf Stewart, his manager at Chaddington, were there accompanied by Roy Dobson's eldest son Jack to witness this special occasion marking the new era of civil aviation. In front of the hangar doors the usual keen crowd of employees had assembled. There was a cheer as the machine left the ground and climbed away. That there were problems was immediately obvious to Thorn, for he had to use considerable rudder to prevent swinging at take-off, and there was also a tendency to rudder oscillation. Deliberate application of rudder and then releasing indicated that despite the big fin area the machine was directionally unstable, and a faster level run revealed slight longitudinal instability. They tried a stall. Slowly the machine lost speed. Suddenly buffeting began, causing the control to shake backwards and forwards and then the nose abruptly dropped.

In the weeks that followed, not only were these defects confirmed in extent but performance was also down on the estimates, reducing the still-air range from 4,000 miles to 3,600, and unless that could be improved the Tudor was a problematical starter for Atlantic flying. Yet she looked the epitome of aeronautical perfection. First cause for suspicion was the wing juncture fillet based on the concave curves which had proved entirely satisfactory on the Anson — but in this case the lower periphery of the Tudor fuselage was an outwardly inclined circular segment whereas the Anson's was substantially flat. To overcome the stability defects, Chadwick added more area to the top of the fin, and fitted a shielded rudder which had set-back hinges, and the tailplane was extended with new tips giving a span of 40 ft compared with 30 ft of the well proved Lincoln.

Orrell told me: 'During these trials, Chadwick constantly visited us at Woodford to discuss the tests, and if possible to witness the testing of these modifications. He always explained his reasons for doing the alterations and what he expected to get. This continuous contact between design, project engineers, and aircrew made for a happy team working all hours of the clock.'

Comparisons of fuel consumption with that of the famous *Aries*, which on 7 June had flown some 4,000 miles non-stop from Prestwick to Manitoba, indicated that the Lancaster with unfilleted wing attached midway up the fuselage had noticeably lower drag than the Tudor. Neither the Lancaster nor the shoulder-wing York had shown marked sign of buffeting at the stall. But there were also aspects of other aircraft to attend to, such as the experimental Lancaster flying with a Metro-Vick Beryl gas-turbine mounted in the tail from which a long jet pipe extended like a sting, and there was a hump-like dorsal air intake forward of the tailplane. Of lesser matters the C of A for the latest Anson 19 Commuter G-AGPG was about to be issued — yet who could have guessed that she was destined to remain in the service of the company for the next 16 years!

Nor was there any indication that the most devastating event in history was about to take place — but on 6 August the world was changed for all time by an atomic bomb dropped by the Americans on Japan's city of Hiroshima, destroying half the buildings and causing 80,000 deaths. Vast vistas of global destruction had opened. Three days later an identical bomb was dropped on the Naval Base at Nagasaki and again the results were appalling. On 10 August the Tokyo Radio broadcast that the Japanese Government would accept peace terms, providing the Emperor's prerogatives were not prejudiced. Four days later the Japanese agreed to unconditional surrender, and on 2 September the terms were signed aboard the American battleship *Missouri* in Tokyo Bay.

Everywhere, cutbacks on contracts began. Work was slowed down on the Lincolns because they had been specifically designed for Far East operations, so initial deliveries were made to maintenance units; but in September a Flight was attached to 57 Squadron at East Kirkby, Lincs, for Service trials, and subsequently a Flight was added to 44 Squadron, Mildenhall, Suffolk. In due course this led to adoption of the Lincoln as the basic peacetime bomber of the RAF, but orders had been cut from 800 to 168 in all.

Crews were proud to have 'the mightiest bomber in the world'. Flt Lt Jones DFC, of 57 Squadron at an open Press day, said: 'I first flew the Lincoln of 9 September and carried out circuits, landings, overshoots, stalls and landings with first one and then two engines cut. Pilots had no difficulty in converting to the Lincoln because it had no vices and was a pleasure to handle, but understandably some with extensive experience of the Lancaster were unwilling to concede its pride of place even to a bigger and better Avro which was rather more stable and held its trim with remarkable accuracy. The stall with flaps and undercarriage down occurred at about 65 knots and was very gentle, with no tendency to drop a wing, and recovery was immediate.'

Thirty years later Jones reminisced: 'Today I have 10,000 hours flying aircraft of all types, but can say without doubt that the Lancaster was my favourite wartime aircraft — but given longer with the Lincoln, I would have become just as attached to it. Certainly if granted a wish with my crew (all alive and in touch), I would chose to fly a Lincoln, or her little sister the Lancaster, for a few minutes once again. In the Latin words of 57 Squadron's motto, "I change my body, not my spirit".'

Lancaster as peace-time bomber with lifeboat.

RAF Lancastrian at England's famous Research Establishment – Farnborough.

The Lancaster in fact long remained the standard equipment of surviving bomber squadrons, and even found a new outlet for use of Coastal Command as substitutes for the American Lend-Lease aircraft for which all supplies had been cancelled as soon as the second atomic bomb was dropped. The new task entailed yet another revision of the capaciously famous bomb-bay, but to more peaceful purpose by accommodating a 30 ft moulded mahogany air-sea lifeboat designed by the famous yacht-builder Uffa Fox, and Chadwick devised a single point bomb-slip which enabled the boats to be dropped safely with the aid of four automatic parachutes. A number of BIII Lancasters were therefore dispatched to Eastleigh, Southampton, for Cunliffe-Owen Aircraft Ltd to convert, redesignated ASR Mk 3.

The Lancastrian was also in high favour, though several had crashed. Six were still flying twice weekly between Canada's Dorval and Prestwick. At the beginning of October the last of the twenty-one earmarked for BOAC was delivered for their Kangeroo service to Australia. On the 5th Captain O. P. Jones began an outstanding flight with their Lancastrian G-AGMG to test the machine's South Atlantic capability by flying non-stop from Hurn, near Bournemouth, to Buenos Aires; thence over the Andes to Santiago and Lima, and back to England.

A White Paper had defined the Government's policy of setting up three national airlines of which BOAC, in association with shipping interests, would operate the North Atlantic and Commonwealth routes; BOAC-backed British European Airways would be established for Home and Continental routes; and the South American route would be assigned to British Shipping Lines associated as British Latin-American Air Lines Ltd in which BOAC would participate in capital and management. The Corporation therefore proposed to use six Lancastrian 30-seaters for their South American service next year. The RAF Transport Command also favoured the Lancastrian to meet its commitments in India, the Far East, and Australia. Thirty-

Air Marshal Sir Norman Bottomley (AOC-in-C Bomber Command) with Roy Chadwick and Roy Dobson at the Lancaster Group Party.

three to Specification C16/44 had therefore been ordered as nine-seaters, the first of which was delivered on 16 October, and an order for twenty 13-seaters soon followed. Lancastrian prospects seemed good. They were further enhanced by a 34,000 mile flight round the world in 36 days, made by AV-M Fiddament in Lancastrian VM701 which left Blackbushe on 12 November.

The Ansons also were doing well. Railway Air Services had been the first internal airline to resume activities after the collapse of Germany, and as replacement for their ancient 4-engined DH 86 biplanes had ordered four Anson 19s, the first of which was delivered in November. The Ministry of Civil Aviation already had six civil Ansons at Gatwick used for airport radio calibration and instrument rating tests for the new input of commercial-licensed pilots. However, the major output of Ansons proved to be for world-wide export. Since their pre-war introduction, thousand upon thousand had been built, and had become one of the most famous aircraft in the world. Eventually, they would total over 11,000 — but that was still seven years ahead.

Meanwhile it was the Tudor which was deeply troubling Chadwick, but such was his reputation and achievement that BOAC placed a contract for a stretched version, Type 689, carrying 60 passengers, and Qantas and South African Airways followed suit — so the original order for 30 was increased to 79. Roy Chadwick was therefore vigorously supervising design of a fuselage almost 106 ft long compared with the 80 ft of the Tudor I. That was accomplished by inserting tapered cabin sections in front and behind the standard low-wing central structure, the added length between wing and tail greatly enhancing the leverage arm and so should improve the stability and reduce interference from the wing wake.

Perhaps he even made grim comparison when news came through that on Sunday, 2 December, the rival Handley Page Hermes had crashed on its first flight through severe longitudinal instability causing the machine to porpoise with increasing violence after take-off, ending in a stall and the machine plunging upside down into a field a few miles from its base at Radlett; but as a man of humanity, he was saddened that the two test pilots were killed.

However it was an air of *bonhomie* that characterized a great dinner party given by Dobson and Chadwick three days later at Claridges, when the key 'Lancaster Group' was formally wound up with glowing tributes to the representatives of the five great British companies which had produced the 7,000 war-time Lancasters, of which A. V. Roe & Co Ltd had contributed more than half.

'The Board has agreed to appoint you technical director,' Roy Dobson told Chadwick later that month. 'There'll be the usual perks,' he said with a grin, 'but you'll have to delegate some of that design work.'

'I'll promote Stuart Davies to chief designer — he did outstandingly well with the Lancaster development work.'

'Good,' said Dobbie. 'Let's have a celebratory drink.'

Chapter 15
Last Curtain

On New Year's Day 1946 the war-time ban on civilian flying was lifted — but how different it was from the carefree days of the 1930s. There were now extensive navigational facilities with 21 radio stations available, and 35 airfields had the war-time Beam-approach system, lights and beacons. A great new airport for London was being constructed at Heathrow, which would embrace 2,800 acres, including the Fairey Aviation Company's aerodrome. New York was going one better by building a huge airport on the outskirts of Idlewild which would handle 360 aircraft an hour. The re-establishment of airlines in both countries had become of paramount importance, and on 15 January a Civil Aviation Conference of British and USA representatives opened in Bermuda which duly resulted in a bilateral agreement for the operation of trans-Atlantic services between the two countries. As though emphasising the advanced state of USA airliners, a Pan-American Constellation flew the 3,425 miles from New York to Lisbon in what seemed the astounding time of 9 hrs 58 mins, but the famous Lancaster *Aries* maintained British prestige with an England to the Cape record of 32 hrs 21 mins, during which the Cairo-Capetown sector was flown non-stop.

However, Pan-American Airways played a trump card on 4 February with a Constellation which made the first scheduled trans-Atlantic flight from La Guardia, New York, via Newfoundland and Eire, and landed its 29 passengers at Hurn after a flight of 12 hrs 9 mins. Not to be outdone, British Overseas Airways placed an order for five of these American airliners for delivery by the end of April and into service in July. That was the beginning of distrust between A. V. Roe & Co Ltd and the airline because everything had been gambled on the new Tudor 2. In fact BOAC, well aware of the Tudor I problems, regarded the Constellations as an insurance because they had been flying since 1943, the Americans having had a free hand to continue airliner development during the war.

Tudor II ready to be towed out at Woodford.

The greatly enlarged Tudor 2, Avro 689, powered with Merlin 102s, was now ready for its initial flight — a remarkable achievement as it had been built in bare six months. Sam Brown had given up hope of flying it, for his blood-pressure problems had become worse so he was appointed flight-test manager, and

Thorn and Orrell report to Chadwick.

Bill Thorn was made chief pilot.

'Sam was not a great talker,' Jimmy Orrell told me, 'but he was an outstanding test pilot. All the aircraft he tested became favourites of the pilots of those days, thus adding to the reputation of their designer Roy Chadwick.'

Like the Tudor 1 prototype, the Tudor 2 had full pressurisation using the Westland automatic system. Registered G-AGSU, the revised airliner was flown by Thorn and Orrell after the usual many preliminaries on 10 March. Everyone tensely waited for their verdict, though Chadwick seemed impassive. As soon as they landed he hurried the two pilots to his office, where Thorn told him that the machine was quite pleasant to fly but that there were signs of similar defects to those of the Tudor 1. Further flights were therefore programmed to explore the aerodynamics more thoroughly and gain early indication of performance and effectiveness of the cabin air-pressure system.

Chadwick was always punctilious in thanking those who co-operated with him, and on the 23rd wrote to Westland's chief designer, Arthur Davenport:-

'I am sure you will be very glad to know that we had a very successful flight with the Tudor yesterday with cabin pressure operating. Everything worked perfectly except the cabin heater, which only functioned intermittently, but I expect the trouble will be quickly overcome. We shall now be able to carry out all our future tests under pressure and build up some experience in this area.

'May I congratulate you and your associates who have been of such great assistance to us in this matter.'

The Avro team was concurrently still tackling the problems of the Tudor 1. The weeks of testing were becoming months because only one change could be made at a time in order to have direct evidence of its effect, otherwise there would be confusion. Thus a modified wing fillet might improve the stall, yet the changed airflow could alter rudder behaviour. Chadwick was the detective interpreting the clues given by his pilots.

During these months, the six Lancasters acquired by what was now the British South American Airways Corporation, had been converted by A. V. Roe & Co into Lancastrians, four of which were freighters and the other two had 14-seat cabins. The new Corporation, managed by 'Pathfinder' AV-M Don Bennett, also ordered four Tudors designated Type 4 which were revisions of the Tudor 1 with front fuselage lengthened 6 ft and seating increased to thirty-two.

On 15 March, *Star Trail,* one of the modified Lancaster 14-seaters, inaugurated the airline's twice-weekly service between London and Buenos Aires. Only a week earlier a Lancastrian of the Air Navigation School at Shawbury had demonstrated its sterling quality with a four-day, 12,500 mile trouble-free flight to New Zealand and return in less than a week. However it was BOAC's Lancastrian G-AGLX, which brought great grief to the Dobson family, for it was lost at sea on 24 March, and their son Jack was aboard *en route* to Australian to organise production of the Avro Lincoln by the Australian Government aircraft factory at Melbourne, following selection as the RAAF's standard big bomber. No trace of the Lancastrian and crew was ever found.

* * *

The world spun on regardless and Springtime brought an invitation from the Air Ministry to tender for a competitive three-seat, all metal trainer to a much delayed Specification T7/45. Because of engrossment with the Tudor 1 and its bigger sister, Chadwick could only give the design a speculative start, but it presented a new line of thought and he began sketching possible outlines which were presently developed by Stuart Davies as a low-wing monoplane of 40 ft span, powered with an A-S Mamba turbo-prop, and designated Type 701 was ultimately known as the Athena.

In April, modifications to the Tudor 1 appeared to have made it reasonably viable, but runway limitations at Woodford restricted flight trials to an all-up weight of 65,000 lbs, so it was decided to complete them at Boscombe Down where there was ample length for maximum take-off weight at 80,000 lbs. Tests then revealed sudden stalling at touch-down and dropping hard enough to bounce. Chadwick decided that the static ground attitude set by main wheels and tail wheel was too steep. The machine was therefore laid up for the undercarriage to be shortened, and opportunity was taken to replace the Merlin 600s with Merlin 621s which had greater power and were suitable for fitment of reversible pitch propellers acting as brakes.

Already the first production Tudor 2, G-AGRX, redesignated Tudor 7, had been completed as an experiment with four 1,750 hp Bristol Hercules radial engines instead of the Merlins, using the mountings and nacelles of the wartime Lancaster II. When flown on 17 April the handling appeared unchanged, but top speed was much slower — yet specific consumption was less and extended the range by 420 miles.

In May the second Tudor 1 prototype G-AGST was flown, and then continued with development trials while the prototype was being modified. 'During this period,' recollected test pilot Ken Cook, who had been seconded to Avro from the A & AEE, 'there were many long meetings with the design staff, chaired by the chief designer, Roy Chadwick. Many modifications and gimmicks were tried, and after each flight Mr Chadwick would be waiting on the tarmac. "Any luck, boys?" he would say, and for many flights the answer was "Afraid not." My impression was of a gentleman dedicated

BOAC, led by Deputy Chairman Whitney-Straight (centre) visits Woodford to discuss and try an early production Tudor I. Chadwick third from left. Orrell extreme right.

to his job. I do not ever remember him flying off the handle. Having got all the relevant facts from the test pilots, he would express his gratitude and motor quietly back to his office at Chadderton.'

But there were other complexities. BOAC was proving difficult. Their inspectors had followed every stage of construction and flight trials, and latterly seemed needlessly critical of the Tudor as an airliner. At a two-day Conference preliminary to handing over the Tudor 1, the management of the BOAC Engineering Division demanded 343 modifications, many of them of niggling nature concerned with décor. 'Why the hell couldn't you specify what you wanted in the first place?' angrily demanded Dobson.

There was no recourse but to comply because BOAC, backed by the Air Ministry, was so important a customer. That meant further delays affecting the entire production line. Meanwhile the RAF was so satisfied with the Lincoln bomber that Chadwick was invited to tender for a Coastal Command long-range version to Specification R5/46. After preliminary perusal there was a full conference of his senior technical staff at which he outlined the requirements and associated changes, and in the course of the next few weeks this resulted in drawings and mock-up of a wider and deeper, stressed-skin fuselage, but used the standard Lincoln wing re-powered with the newly designed R-R 2,450 hp Griffin engines driving contra-rotating propellers. To ensure no repetition of the Tudor difficulties with airflow, a model was made for wind-tunnel testing, ultimately resulting in a tailplane of greater chord, mounted twice as high and carrying tip fins and rudders of proportionately increased size. A contract followed from MAP in March for 29 of these Avro 696s.

Happy at the prospect, Chadwick told his wife: 'They are a kind of maritime exploring aeroplane, so I hope to have them named 'Shackleton' in memory of your family's relationship with Sir Ernest Shackleton and that happy pre-war day we spent with him aboard the *Quest.*'

That month the high regard for Roy Chadwick as an aircraft designer was emphasized by a ceremony in the Courtroom of London's historic Guildhall when the Lord Mayor read in his presence and that of his sponsors from the Worshipful Company of Coachmakers a declaration appointing him a Freeman of the City of London.

In his extended role as technical director there were many time-consuming business discussions with Dobson and the Board, let alone conferences with RAE scientists, or with Air Marshal Sir Alex Coryton's staff at the new Ministry of Supply (MOS) which on 1 April replaced the MAP. Significantly, Sir Alex informed the Press that the Ministry was now only interested in fighters and bombers powered with jet engines.

However piston-engines still held the field so it was gratifying to the two Roys that a Lancastrian inaugurated BOAC's opening regular services from London Airport on 22 May, setting off with six passengers for Sydney, Australia. Nine days later the airport was officially opened to international traffic, though it had only one runway, and tents had to serve for passenger waiting rooms and Customs' clearance. The first aircraft to land were two Constellations from Pan-American and American Overseas Airlines respectively, followed next day by a BOAC Lancastrian which arrived two hours ahead of schedule, having flown from Sydney in 63 hours flying time. At the end of that month the Lancastrians of British South American Airways began a weekly return service between London and Santiago.

To the fury of Roy Dobson and a grim look from Chadwick, BOAC's attitude towards trans-Atlantic flying with Tudors had been publicly expressed by the airline's chairman Lord Knollys, who said: 'We shall require a subsidy on every flight. The bigger the share of the North Atlantic business we win, the bigger the bill the British taxpayer must pay. If it were a straight commercial undertaking, the Tudor would not be a good proposition.'

That was underlined on 1 July, when BOAC opened a service between London and New York with Lockheed Constellations. But revenge was sweet. Almost immediately all

Constellations were grounded for 30 days by the US Civil Aeronautics Board while investigating a fatal crash of one owned by Trans-World Airlines.

Meanwhile in a further effort to overcome the Tudor 1 problems, the second production machine, G-AGRD, was despatched to Farnborough that month with numerous little masts of wool tufts for airflow investigation of the top surface of the wing, both surfaces of the tailplane, and one side of the fuselage. Tests by Lt Cdr 'Winkle' Brown revealed that stalling speed was much less than Boscombe Down had reported, and the tufts showed that the intense buffeting was due to violent breakaway of airflow at the wing root and the disturbed wake passing over the tail. Though the directional stability was satisfactory with the enlarged fin and rudder there was still rudder oscillation at the considerable angle required for directional trim when one engine was cut, but that was eventually traced to the projecting flat faces of the balance cut-outs at the hinges when the rudder was angled. While the tests were proceeding, Chadwick used the second Tudor 1 prototype, G-AGST, to try out the modifications of fairing the rudder cut-outs and fitting a larger concave fillet at the wing root.

Duly altered to suit BOAC's multitudinous requirements, the Tudor 2, which now had Merlin 600A engines, was flown to Boscombe Down for C of A tests, but the increased tareweight due to structural changes and modifications, resulted in lower performance which made it inadequate for operations in extreme temperatures. However Chadwick was not alone in his troubles, for the Handley Page Hermes replacement prototype was suffering similar problems and to improve stability had been fitted with a bigger span tailplane, increased fin area, and different balance-tab mechanism.

When the big fillet and rudder hinge modification of Tudor G-AGST was completed, the machine was flown to Farnborough for further experiments during which Winkle Brown found that though buffeting had been reduced to a vestige, the stalling speed had increased by 10 mph. To elucidate this required much experimental work, but was traced to the dual sources of an air leak around the wing-root leading edge and the wing leading-edge de-icers spoiling the aerofoil contour. Alterations were made, and behaviour proved satisfactory. The rudder was now more effective, enabling the engine-cut safety speed to be established at 100 knots, and similarly afforded greater power to overcome the tendency to swing during initial take-off.

On 8 August Chadwick had the satisfaction of knowing that he was well on the way to designing airliners and bombers with jet engines because Sqn Ldr 'Shep' Shepherd, who like Bill Thorn had been a pre-war Flying Club instructor, made the maiden flight of Lancastrian VH742 which had been fitted with a Rolls-Royce Nene turbo-jet replacing the Merlin of each outboard nacelle, but retaining the piston engines as the inboard pair. With 10,000 lbs static thrust available from the Nenes, the Lancastrian once airborne had ample jet power to complete the entire flight with the Merlins stopped and their propellers feathered.

The expanding horizons of aeroplane performance were ever beckoning to Chadwick. There had been many discussions with Sir Alan Cobham and his technicians on refuelling civil aircraft in the air to save time and thus bring distant destinations closer. That August four Lancaster IIIs were released to Flight Refuelling Ltd for conversion to a pair of fuel tankers and a pair of receiver aircraft using Cobham's latest drogue system with automatic coupling. That conventional re-fuelling en route required a day's added time to the 60 hours airborne time to fly the Lancaster *Aries* from Blackbushe airport, England, to New Plymouth, New Zealand, emphasised the great saving that could have been made using Cobham's system.

* * *

BOAC's lack of confidence in the Tudor gained credence at the end of the month when the Boeing Airplane Co of Seattle, Washington, disclosed that six Stratocruiser airliners, developed from their wartime B-29 Super Fortress, had been ordered by the Corporation with permission of Lord Winster, the Minister of Civil Aviation. Nevertheless, on 5 September BOAC at last received the first of the 20 Tudor 1s; but two days later came disaster for British South American Airways when its Lancaster-derived transport, the York *Star Leader,* crashed soon after take-off from Bathhurst, Gambia killing 19 passengers and four crew. Chadwick was still worrying about it when he visited the Central Bomber Establishment Development Flight at Marham on the 9th to see the Avro Lincoln *Excalibur* take-off for an ambitious flight to the Far East, Australia and New Zealand.

Of combined social and technical interest, was the revival on 12 September of the SBAC Air Show, held at the Handley Page aerodrome at Radlett. Like the last in 1938, one day was allocated for inspection of aircraft on the ground, and next day a flying display was held. One of the hangars was arranged as an exhibition hall where the engine and component manufacturers displayed their products. For many, this was a great reunion, though the intention was strictly commercial and to that end widely ranging representatives from every country had been invited. Few people had ever seen an aeroplane breathtakingly flash past at 600 mph in the manner of the Gloster Meteor, but the Nene-powered Lancastrian flying on its two turbo jets with inboard engines stopped seemed almost as spectacular. Parked a little disdainfully some distance from each other were the Tudor 7 version of the Tudor 2 and the Hastings derivative of the Hermes, both powered with Hercules engines. As I walked past, I discerned Roy Chadwick and the Handley Page designer, George Volkert, in earnest discussion beneath the long nose of the Tudor.

The Tudor G-AGST was still at Farnborough. Extended wool tufting had revealed turbulence at the tail of the inboard engine's nacelles. They were shorter than those of the Lancaster to avoid mechanical interference with the landing flap, so better faired cowling extending to a pointed end projecting some 18 ins astern the trailing edge was being fitted. Re-test showed vast improvement, with no sign of flow breakdown at any speed.

All beneficial modifications arising from the RAE trials were being applied to the design of the Shackleton as it was still in the early stages of draughting, with first flight not expected until 1949. More expeditiously the production Tudors were being modified to match G-AGST, which returned to Woodford on 24 October.

Concurrently there was publicity for three Lincolns which flew 20,000 miles from Scampton to Santiago, Chile, and back as a long-distance navigational exercise. Another, named *Crusader* left Marham for South Africa on 26 October in emulation of *Excalibur's* navigational exercise to the Far East, Australia, and New Zealand. From the Empire Air Armament School at Manby, *Thor II* flew to Canada on 2 November and then continued to the USA. To become an aerial globe-trotter was regarded as a high honour by the pilots of the RAF, and to Chadwick these long flights seemed a vindication of the hard work in designing this redoubtable type of aeroplane.

But it was the Lancastrian which came to

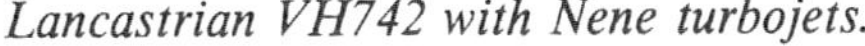

Lancastrian VH742 with Nene turbojets.

Roy Chadwick congratulates Capt. R. T. Shepherd, the Rolls-Royce test-pilot, after their record flight.

the fore again on 18 November when the composite Nene-powered machine, piloted by Shepherd with Roy Chadwick sitting alongside, made a record flight from London to Le Bourget in 50 minutes at 263 mph, using only the turbo jets. That gave opportunity of visiting the first post-war Paris Aero Show before Shepherd flew him back to England on the 22nd, breaking their new record by one minute! Not to be outdone, the de Havilland Engine Co obtained a Lancastrian with intention of modifying it to take two DH Ghost turbo-jets of similiar thrust to the Nene.

A week later, on 30 November, Chadwick received renewed approbation as an aircraft designer, which he described next day in a letter to his devoted schoolgirl daughter Rosemary:-

'I had an interesting experience yesterday, when in company with Professor Cockcroft and Sir Harold Hartley I had the Honorary Associateship of the Manchester College of Technology conferred on me. Mummy and Margaret attended the ceremony but unfortunately could not be present at the dinner which followed as ladies were not invited. I wore my MSc robes with evening dress and CBE, and that delighted Mummy.'

Sir James Myers, Principal of the

The Chancellor of Manchester University, Sir John Stopford and his honoured guests.

University, made the citation: 'I present to you an eminent designer of wings which have most appropriately borne him to the highest altitudes in the field of research to which he had devoted himself. That he has been so much more successful than his remote predecessor Icarus, may perhaps be attributed to the fact that as a former student of this College he got away to flying start, though incidentally had at his disposal superior materials.

'A pioneer in aircraft design, he has been the guiding genius for the firm of A. V. Roe from the time it expanded from its cellar home in Ancoats, some 35 years ago, to the vast factories of today. In the fierce competition for mastery of the air during the last war, he showed that when necessity demanded a machine worthy of the phenomenal endurance of the men who manned it, Britain made it. His clear vision and foresight, combined with great tenacity of purpose and technical skill of the highest order, enabled him to bring his genius to full fruition at the most critical time in the nation's history. Under his inspiration, great monsters flew from his drawing-board carrying the names of Lancaster and York once more into historic battle — a source of pride and strength to the Allies, and of fear and destruction to the Axis powers. Except in the field of Old Trafford, Headingley, and Bramall Lane, the Battle of the Roses are now happily past, but his inventive genius is still at work, and we look forward with confidence to the Tudor monarch of the skies to bring to this country in the realm of Civil Aviation, glory comparable to those of its wartime predecessors and of the great Tudor period from which it takes its name.'

Adding to his quiet pleasure, Chadwick learned on returning to Chadderton that the Ministry of Civil Aviation had publicly announced the grant of a Certificate of Airworthiness for the Avro Tudor 1 on the recommendation of the Air Registration Board, and the statement added: 'The aircraft is intended to be used by BOAC on the North Atlantic.'

* * *

During the latter part of 1946, Roy Chadwick, grossly overworked, had been somewhat under the weather but Rosemary's return from school for the family Christmas festivities had certainly cheered him. After her Christmas break he wrote to her on 16 January:-

'It was so nice having you home, and we all enjoyed the holiday together, didn't we? I am feeling much better, so you need not be disturbed about me. Margaret came to lunch today and she sends her love. Mummy has been busy as usual. She is a darling and always doing everything she can for all of us.'

In the following week he wrote to tell her that the fourth production Tudor, G-AGRF, had been chosen as the flagship of the future Tudor fleet, and at a colourful ceremony at the embryo London Airport on 21 January 1947 had been named *Elizabeth of England* by Princess Elizabeth:-

'I enjoyed the occasion very much. The Princess was most charming when I talked with her after being presented as the designer. Mummy and I were glad to receive your letter

Margaret, Mary and Roy Chadwick.

and to know that you have the photos that were taken of you. Which will you have enlarged? I hope it will be No 28, because you look like your beautiful mother. She asks me to tell you that I have almost entirely recovered from the shingles and think that another couple of days should see me clear.'

In fact he was busily at work. On 7 January the Air Ministry had despatched Specification B35/46 to Armstrong Whitworth, A. V. Roe, Bristol, English Electric, Handley Page, Short Bros, and Vickers, inviting tenders for a medium bomber capable of carrying an atomic weapon. The operational requirement was the result of plans formulated during the previous year by the Air Staff, finalised as OR229 requiring a 4-jet aeroplane with pressure cabin and a gross weight not exceeding 100,000 lbs so that it could operate from existing airfields.

The requisite performance was impossible with conventional straight wing because at about 570 mph the airflow would begin to develop turbulence at a quarter chord, and was so critical that any slight increase in speed would cause the flow to break down entirely, resulting in loss of all lift. Germany had found the key to greater speed as far back as 1936 when Professor A. Busemann discovered the mitigating effect of sweep-back, and during the war extending research led to the design of the Messerschmitt Me 262 with slightly swept wings, and a successor with 45 degrees sweep back in expectation of flying at the speed of sound (Mach 1) — though that had not yet been achieved. By now some of the German aerodynamic data had become available, and it was clear that a similiar major sweep-back would be essential to meet the requirements of the new RAF Specification. To win this contract was vital for Avro prestige because the resultant bomber was envisaged as a replacement of the Lincoln within ten years.

As the Athena trainer design was ready for issue to the shops, Chadwick was able to allocate most of his technical team to the bomber project, which he initially schemed as a conventionally tailed monoplane with swept and tapered wings — but calculations soon showed that it would be almost twice the target weight. This led to deletion of the tail but introduced possible problems of wing flexure, and again proved overweight. The next step, Roy Chadwick decided, must be reduction of aspect ratio, and he began doodling new ideas which presently resulted in a stubbier Delta shape by joining the swept tips with a straight trailing edge. His sketches with draft calculations are still extant.

As always, there were many other matters requiring his attention. Thus a Lincoln was being flown at Luton which had required his design co-operation to mount a Bristol Phoebus turbojet in the bomb bay. At Filton another had been revised with a Bristol Theseus engine in each outer nacelle and was currently flown on 17 February.

A Lincoln of the Empire Air Navigation School had been modified by the Avro team into a handsome looking machine with Lancastrian type nose and tail. Margaret Dove recollected visiting her parents on the

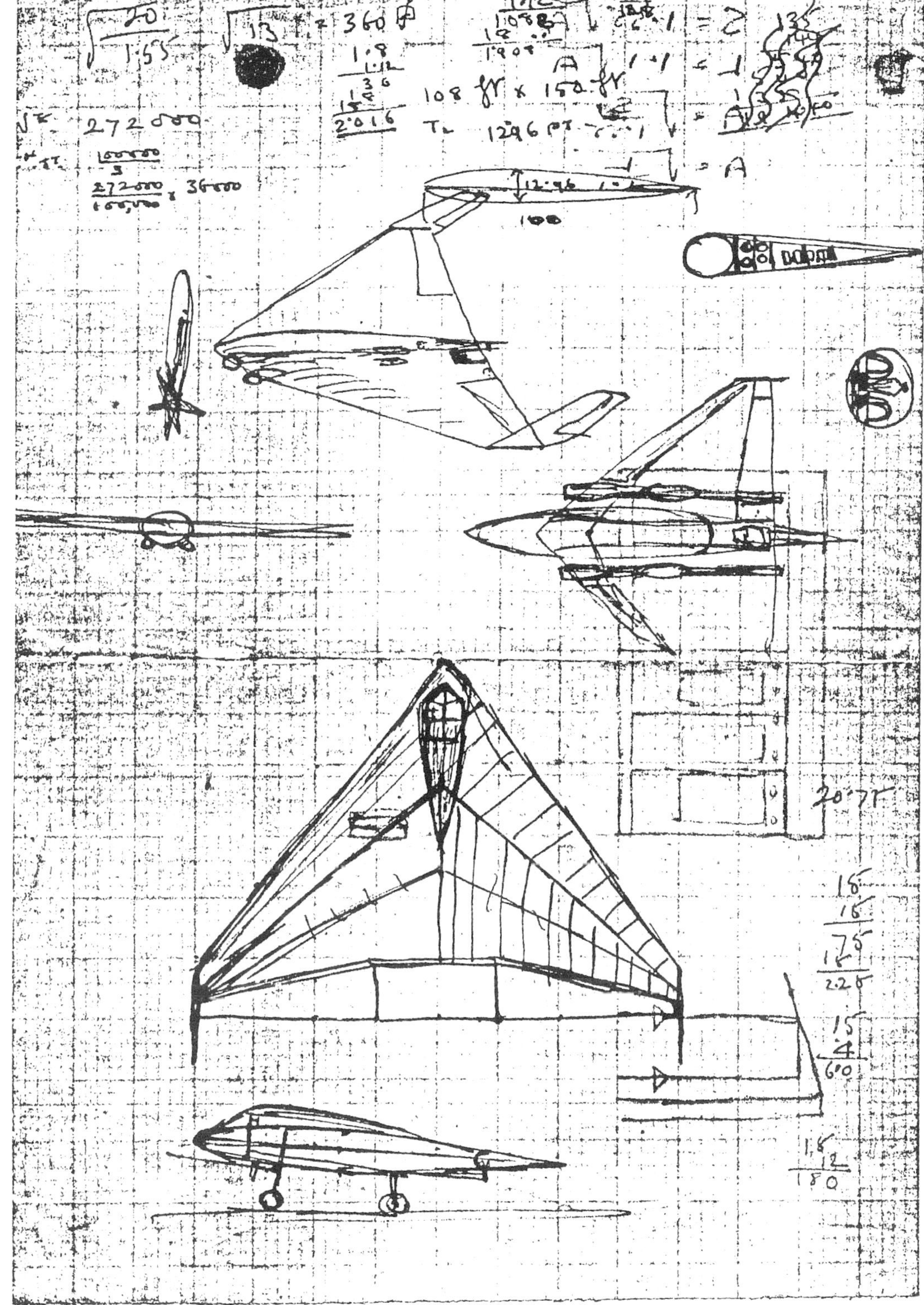

Chadwick's initial sketches of the future Vulcan.

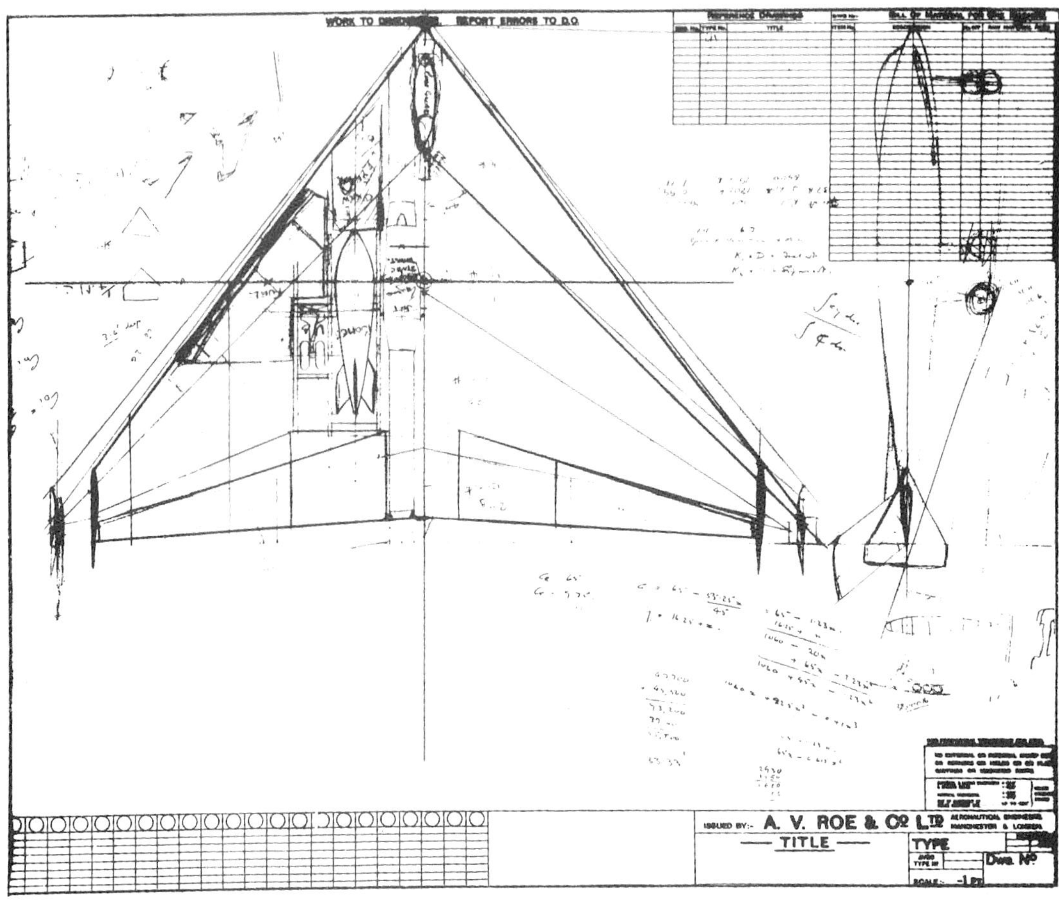

Chadwick's drawing of developed Delta annotated by Eric Priestley, chief aerodynamicist.

morning of 24 February and Roy asking if she would like to go with him to Shawbury for a ceremony of christening this machine as *Aries II,* replacing the now obsolete Lancaster of that name. 'I was very pleased and set off that frosty morning in my father's Armstrong-Siddeley Typhoon. The Commandant, Air Commodore D'Aeth gave a private lunch in honour of the C-in-C of Flying Training Command, Sir Arthur Coningham and his lady, and I sat next to an old friend of my father's who begged me to get Roy to go for a holiday — but that proved impossible, and when my mother subsequently suggested Switzerland, he said there was too much work to do.

'After lunch we had the christening in a hangar. Lady Coningham was very charming and performed the ceremony delightfully in the course of a short church service, and as so often in these later years, my father was very moved. Afterwards we drove to the Officers' Mess and had afternoon tea — then Sir Arthur and Lady Coningham flew away in their very smart Anson 19.'

Next day Roy Chadwick wrote to Rosemary describing it all as 'a most enjoyable day, but very sorry that Mummy

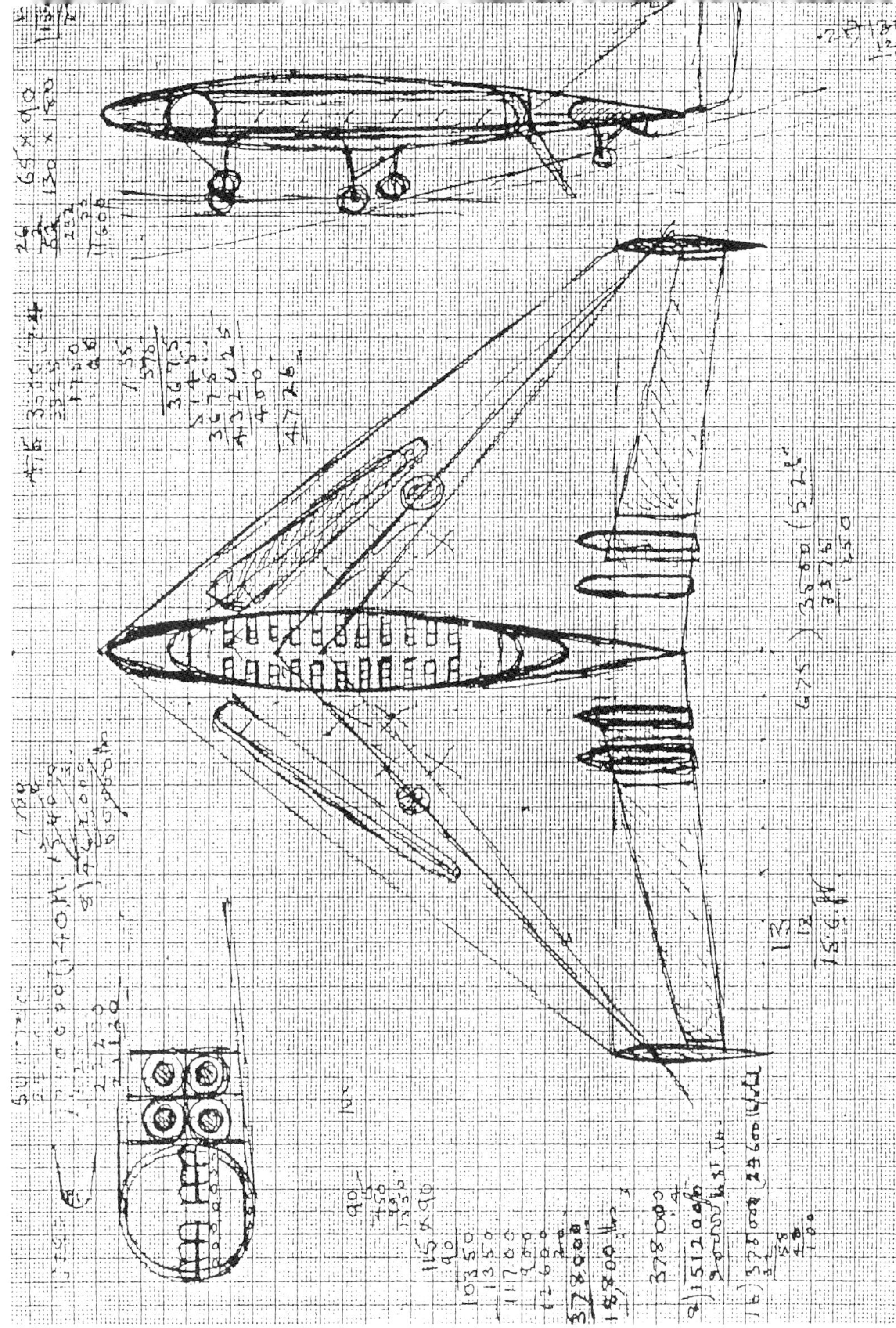

Delta airliner scheme of Roy Chadwick's.

and you were not with us.' That was the ever-conscious family side of his life; but at his Chadderton office it was concentration on the new Delta bomber arrangement which now took the form of a 100 ft span triangle of sufficient wing depth to accommodate the crew's canopied pressure cabin in the apex. Each side of the centre line, upper and lower turbojet engines were mounted in the plane of the c.g., with the bomb bay compartment alongside, and adjacent outboard was the main undercarriage well. Fixed fins with rudders were mounted at the wing-tips, and a triple form of elevon formed the trailing edge, later adjusted to inner and outer elevons.

Stuart Davies recorded: 'From an engineering point of view the whole design was ideal for its purpose as specified, and yet capable of development in any or all the directions of increased load, range or altitude without having to make fundamental alterations in the layout or structural design. It was now March. More than two months had been absorbed by preliminary studies, and at this stage Roy Chadwick decided to back this proposal as a Company submission to meet the requirements of the B/46 specification. For a designer to risk his reputation on such a venture was an act of high courage that has not been sufficiently recognised.'

Much further technical consideration and drawing office work lay ahead, including investigation of an airliner with four turbine-jets in the leading edge and a wide pressurized cabin with 56 seats arranged in pairs and triples each side of a central gangway. Chadwick's intentions had been to submit it with the bomber brochure to show the adaptability of the design, but eventually it was put aside through lack of time. Designing an aeroplane had become a most complex matter. Consequently there were many discussions with Grp Capt Silyn-Roberts the DOR; conferences with Rolls-Royce on power-plant development; briefing on radar equipment and scanners; consultations with the RAE on aerodynamics; discussions with Chadwick's old friend George Dowty on the special undercarriage; even scares such as DOR's proposal that the entire pressure cabin should be jettisonable. Gradually the design consolidated.

J. D. Towers, who was a junior draughtsman at that time said: 'Roy Chadwick's very presence in the office used to spur his team to greater effort. He was always deeply respected. Though a genuine humanist, his thinking and actions were tightly disciplined within the constraints of the Official Secrets Act. That made him somewhat distant and aloof.'

But there were always other complexities and worries and although it was encouraging the *Star Panther*, first of the Tudor 4s for British South American Airways, was flown at Woodford by Bill Thorn on 9 April, the Tudor I was finally rejected by BOAC two days later.

Interested parties were well aware that the airline had a big financial deficit and was the subject of an Enquiry by a Select Committee. The chairman, Lord Knollys wrote to the Minister:-

'The Corporation has concluded that, irrespective of whether the flying qualities of the Tudor 1 can be rectified and whether its deficiency in performance can be fully recovered, there is no longer any justification for including Tudor 1 in the Corporation's operating programme. Our main handicap today is having to use obsolete and uncommercial aircraft resulting in restriction to the development of our Empire routes forced on us by circumstance — so if we aquiesce in further attempts to rectify the Tudor 1 the continuance of this restriction would be regarded as our own choice.'

The much modified Tudor II prototype with revised tail and deeper wing fillets.

That opened the door to Government decision and permission for BOAC to purchase more American airliners at a cost of $12,000,000, yet the Tudor 2 was still in the running and having the inner nacelles lengthened in accordance with the Farnborough recommendations; but Qantas and South African Airways had backed out, and the contract was now reduced to fifty.

In no way did AV-M Bennett of BSAA agree with BOAC's dismaying reflection on the Tudor, and had earlier reported to the Ministry of Civil Aviation that his Corporation considered it to be a normal 4-engined aircraft suitable for its use. That was based on his personal piloting experience, and he now proceeded to test *Star Panther* under widely ranging conditions and found it entirely satisfactory, with ample range for the longest BSAA route of 2,250 miles from Santa Maria to Bermuda.

Despite the disappointments there were also celebrations. The 30th of April was Chadwick's 54th birthday. Everywhere he was highly regarded for his far-sightedness combined with practicality. That BOAC was critical of the Tudor, he regarded as largely political because the Corporation was hell-bent on American machines for the trans-Atlantic services, whereas if given the opportunity of starting from scratch he could beat the Americans at their own game. That led him to further ideas of supersonic flight. Meanwhile the new bomber design had achieved a presentable form with the pressure cabin now projecting beyond the wing apex and embraced each side by a large circular air intake.

On perusing the design brochure, Roy Dobson said with a chuckle: 'You know, our good old friend A. V. would claim that he inspired you! Do you remember him writing to me early in the war to say that the tail unit was an unnecessary appendage and if eliminated would save weight and so save cost? Our late master was a shrewd old bird.'

On 7 May, Dobson had the satisfaction of submitting the Tender to the Ministry, together with Chadwick's descriptive brochure, performance calculations, drawings, and model of the Delta bomber now designated Avro Type 698, which in the course of time would eventuate as the Vulcan.

Though Chadwick had six other design projects in hand he zealously found time to attend the departure of AV-M Bennett on 28 May when he flew the BSAA *Star Panther* in the inaugural service from London to Bermuda, during which the tanks were re-filled in the air by a Flight Refuelling Lancaster based at the Azores, enabling the 3,600 mile journey to be made non-stop. A twice-weekly experimental service continued for the next three months, during which 22 South Atlantic crossings were made. As soon as his other Tudors became available, Bennett intended to establish a more viable service with stages to Lisbon, Azores, Bermuda, and Nassau to Cuba, as well as a more southward route from Dakar to Natal, thence to Rio de Janeiro, Buenos Aires and Santiago.

With summer, Chadwick had largely regained his health, aided by an occasional weekend break with Mary at such places as West Kirby Hydro. But he was still over-working. One of his weekly letters to Rosemary mentioned: 'I'm a bit fagged because I did not leave the Air Ministry until 6 this evening and drove all the way home at speed, arriving at 10.50. I've just had supper and will be off to bed soon. London was terribly hot and I was busy all day. However, I had a most interesting time during the few days I was away, visiting several aircraft works and meeting lots of my old friends. With much love from us both, and a good night, bless you.'

But 28 July proved a day of rejuvenation, for he and Dobson were instructed by long-distance call from their chairman, Sir Thomas Sopwith, to go to his house in Scotland without delay as he had secret information to impart. There they were told in confidence that he had been rung by Stuart Scott-Hall, the Director-General of Technical Development, to say that both the crescent-winged Handley Page HP80 and the Avro Delta 698 bomber had been selected and prototypes would be ordered, provided that aerodynamic models in the super high-speed wind tunnel at Farnborough proved that the theoretical basis of their design was satisfactory. Those investigations by the RAE presently led to revision of both machines which included substitution of central tail-fin and rudder instead of wing-tip vertical surfaces, and presently to a thinner wing thickness for the Avro, though that was beyond Chadwick's immediate visualisation.

The day of Scott-Hall's pronouncement also marked the successful arrival at Andrews Field, Maryland, of sixteen RAF Lincoln bombers from No. 617 Squadron, having flown the North Atlantic to Newfoundland, thence to New York to take part in the 40th Anniversary celebrations of the United States Air Forces. But high spirits over the expected bomber contract gave place to deep concern when Roy Chadwick learned on 2 August that the BSAA's Lancastrian airliner, *Star Dust* had disappeared during a flight from Buenos Aires to Santiago. What had happened? Was it due to some fault in design or manufacture — or was it a navigational error causing the machine to crash into the Andes? Chadwick would never know.

* * *

In his weekly letter dated 11 August to Rosemary, who with other girls from her school was enjoying a three-week holiday camp at Bournemouth, her father wrote: 'To wish you an enjoyable time, and to say that we are all well; but it is very quiet here and we shall be glad to have you home again. Take great care of yourself.'

A week later she had a horrifying dream that while standing with her father 'a huge machine appeared and crashed into the ground in front of us'. On awakening, she was so upset that she was permitted to go home next day instead of staying a further fortnight. There was a delighted reunion with her father and mother, and she remembers Roy's amusement on the third day at finding wife and daughter busily engaged that evening in re-papering the landing ceiling in what he described as 'an abortive pasting operation' when the strips dropped down on him and they all collapsed in laughter.

With vivid recollection, many years later, she recorded: 'Next morning, Saturday the 23rd August, dawned as a beautiful day. At breakfast-time, my father asked what I would like for my birthday next week and I told him "A little watch with lovely sparkling little diamonds all round it".'

' "Well, I think we can manage the watch, but I am not sure about the diamonds," he said, and asked if I would like to go with him to Woodford to see the Tudor 2 fly — but though I very much wanted to, I had promised Mother to help her, and he agreed that I must. However, later there was time to cycle the mile to the shopping centre of Altrincham to look at the watches at Parkers, the jewellers. On my return we had lunch, but in the middle of the meal the telephone suddenly rang and Mother left the room to answer it. A few minutes later there was an agonising scream and I rushed into the hall. Struggling to control herself, she said: "They told me that Roy is in Stockport mortuary." I thought she had made a mistake and he must be in hospital because of a car accident.

'I phoned the doctor to come to Mother and rode on her bicycle to the Vicarage to ask the Revd Eric Jones to come, then rang Margaret's mother-in-law, Mrs Dove, to ask her to contact John and my sister so that they could drive here from Sale, where they had their new home. All our world seemed to have crumbled in ruins.'

Already reporters had gleaned the story. The *Manchester Evening News* blazoned the tragedy:-

A. V. Roe Designer in Tudor Disaster

ROY CHADWICK ONE OF FOUR IN WOODFORD CRASH.
Crashed airliner ends in a pond.

The *Sunday Despatch* gave a full account under the banner headlines: TUDOR 2 KILLS DESIGNER:-

'The flashing new Tudor had just taken off in brilliant sunshine when it suddenly faltered, skimmed over the Shirfold Farm and struck the ground. It ploughed across two fields, ripping its silver wings through a high fence of trees, and plunged nose first into a pond. Wreckage flew for 400 yards in all directions. Rescuers who plunged at once into the pond had to swim through fuming petrol and thick oil, but not until the pond was pumped dry was the last of the bodies recovered. Killed with Mr Chadwick were Mr Sidney A. Thorn the chief test pilot, Sqn Ldr D. J. B. Wilson, assistant pilot, and Mr John Webster, the senior radio operator. Flight engineer E. Talbot was pulled out of the plane with multiple injuries, and Mr S. D. Davies, 40-year-old chief designer of A. V. Roe, climbed through a torn hole in the fuselage, his face streaming with blood.'

On Monday, every paper in the land and many abroad told the story, paying tribute to Chadwick as one of the world's greatest designers. Jimmy Orrell, the successor chief pilot, told me: 'The Tudor was scheduled to fly on Friday afternoon or evening and was duly cleared with the normal double check on flying controls, but the weather proved unsuitable, so it was decided to make the test flight on Saturday. Bill Thorn and I tossed a coin to decide who should do the task, and it fell in him.

'During Friday night a job had to be done in the fuselage and unknown to us the aileron controls were disconnected to do so, then re-attached, but inadvertently were secured to the wrong side of the cross-shaft, which meant that movement of the pilot's control wheel would give bank in the wrong direction — but nobody was aware of this.

The wrecked Tudor II.

'On Saturday morning the aircraft history sheet was checked for work done by the nightshift and there was no mention of the controls having been dismantled. Final inspection for flight therefore proceeded, but the only check on all three controls was to ensure that they moved freely.

'Dobbie, Chadwick, and Davies decided to fly that morning and they followed the crew aboard, but before the engines could be started a messenger told Dobbie that he was wanted on the phone so he got out, saying he would be back in a few minutes. In fact we waited for quite a time, and then Chadwick said: "Shut the door and let's get on with the flight."

'There was a cross wind on the runway, and Bill began to feel its yawing effect, necessitating slight aileron to compensate, but when the wing responded in the wrong direction he would naturally continue to apply more and more aileron in the brief time available. As a result the starboard wing tip touched the runway and the big aeroplane swung off course — at which he abruptly throttled and the machine continued to career uncontrollably across the ground towards a tree surrounded pond. The fuselage split behind the centre section, and Chadwick was catapulted 60 yards and hit a tree, fatally fracturing his skull. The nose of the fuselage went into the pond; the radio officer died from a fractured skull, and Bill Thorn and co-pilot Wilson were injured and drowned. Thus came the end of a great designer whose genius was exemplified by the drawing in his office of the future Vulcan bomber.'

Among the hundreds of tributes, Marshal of the Royal Air Force Sir Arthur Harris, that famous wartime Chief of Bomber Command, wrote to Chadwick's daughter Margaret: 'Your father never received a tithe of the

Beneath the Lancaster at the RAF Museum in October 1976, Air Marshal Sir Arthur Harris unveils a plaque in memory of Roy Chadwick.

recognition and honours due from the nation for his services. The Lancaster took the major part in winning the war with its attacks on Germany. On *land* it forced the Germans to retrieve from their armies half their sorely needed anti-tank guns for use as anti-aircraft guns by over a million soldiers who would otherwise have been serving in the field. The Lancaster won the *naval* war by destroying over one-third of the German submarines in their ports, together with hundreds of small naval craft and six of their largest warships. Above all, the Lancaster won the *air* war by taking the major part in forcing Germany to concentrate on building and using fighters to defend the Fatherland, thereby depriving their armies of essential air and particularly bomber support. But the Lancaster was Roy Chadwick, and it was he who did all that for his country.'

His inspiration lived on. The designs of the Athena Trainer, Coastal Command Shackleton, Tudor development into the jet-powered Ashton, and the thunderous long-serving Vulcan bomber were completed in due course by Stuart Davies, and to this day the surviving pilots who flew the wartime Lancasters speak of their machines with nostalgic admiration, and regard Roy Chadwick as the greatest aircaft designer of all. *Ave Atque Vale.*

Index